A CITY ON A LAKE

A book in the series

RADICAL PERSPECTIVES:

A RADICAL HISTORY REVIEW BOOK SERIES

———

SERIES EDITORS:

Daniel J. Walkowitz, New York University

Barbara Weinstein, New York University

A CITY ON A LAKE

Urban Political Ecology and the
Growth of Mexico City

MATTHEW VITZ

Duke University Press / *Durham and London* / *2018*

© 2018 Duke University Press
All rights reserved
Printed in the United States of America on
acid-free paper ∞
Designed by Matthew Tauch
Typeset in Minion Pro and Univers LT Std by Westchester
Publishing Services

Library of Congress Cataloging-in-Publication Data
Names: Vitz, Matthew, [date] author.
Title: A city on a lake : urban political ecology and the
    growth of Mexico City / Matthew Vitz.
Description: Durham : Duke University Press, 2018. |
    Series: Radical perspectives
Identifiers: LCCN 2017043538 (print)
LCCN 2017047390 (ebook)
ISBN 9780822372097 (ebook)
ISBN 9780822370291 (hardcover : alk. paper)
ISBN 9780822370406 (pbk. : alk. paper)
Subjects: LCSH: Political ecology—Mexico—Mexico
    City—History. | Urban ecology (Sociology)—Mexico—
    Mexico City. | Mexico City (Mexico)—Environmental
    conditions—History. | Mexico City (Mexico)—Social
    conditions—History. | Urban policy—Mexico—Mexico
    City—History.
Classification: LCC GE160.M6 (ebook) | LCC GE160.M6 V58
    2018 (print) | DDC 304.20972/53—dc23
LC record available at https://lccn.loc.gov/2017043538

Cover art: Montage of flooded Madero Street that simu-
lates the presence of *trajineras*, canoe-like boats from
Xochimilco, 1945 (Casasola). Courtesy of INAH, Fototeca
Nacional.

CONTENTS

ABBREVIATIONS

AGA	Archivo General Agrario
AGN	Archivo General de la Nación
AHA	Archivo Histórico del Agua
AHDF	Archivo Histórico del Distrito Federal
ALR	Abelardo L. Rodríguez
AN	Aguas Nacionales
AS	Aguas Superficiales
CGT	General Workers Confederation
CROM	Regional Confederation of Mexican Workers
DDF	Departamento del Distrito Federal
LCR	Lázaro Cárdenas del Río
MAC	Manuel Ávila Camacho
O/C	Obregón/Calles
OP	Obras Públicas
PCM	Mexican Communist Party
PRI	Institutional Revolutionary Party
PRM	Party of the Mexican Revolution
SAF	Ministry of Agriculture and Fomento
SARH	Ministry of Agriculture and Hydraulic Resources
SCOP	Ministry of Public Works and Communications
UIEF	Industrial Units for Forest Development

ACKNOWLEDGMENTS

This book would have been impossible to write without the help of numerous fellowships and grants, institutional support in Mexico and the United States, and astute advice, sharp criticism, and useful tips from dozens of individuals both in and outside of academia. New York University's McCracken fellowship, a Fulbright–García Robles grant, and an ACLS-Mellon Dissertation Completion Fellowship provided me with the resources to research and write the dissertation on which this book is based. Since I completed the dissertation, the Center for U.S.-Mexican Studies, the Instituto de Investigaciones Históricas at the Universidad Nacional Autónoma de México, and a Hellman award provided by the University of California, San Diego, have been essential to the publication of this book.

Long before I arrived at New York University, I took a keen interest in history and questions on the environment. Andrew Vitz, my older brother (now an ornithologist in Massachusetts), imbued in me an early ecological awareness, or as much of one as a young kid is able to have. Bob Turansky, my high school European history teacher, was electric in the classroom, taught me to think critically about class and social power, and encouraged my first dabbling in radical social theory. As an undergraduate student at the University of Wisconsin–Madison and the Complutense in Madrid, I owe gratitude to Florencia Mallon, Francisco Scarano, and Pedro Pérez Herrero for introducing me to Latin American studies, and to Bill Cronon for introducing me to the vibrant field of environmental history. At New York University, Greg Grandin and Sinclair Thomson encouraged me to develop my initial ideas about the environmental history of modern Mexico City and find my voice as a Latin Americanist. I thank Karl Appuhn for his generosity in training me in environmental historiography as well as Gil Joseph, at Yale University, for his willingness to serve on my dissertation committee and share his deep knowledge of Mexico. Greg, Sinclair, Karl, and Gil, in addition to Ada Ferrer and Barbara Weinstein, offered incisive and valuable criticism of my dissertation from which this book has benefited greatly. Moreover, the collegiality and intellectual rigor of the graduate student community at New York University were tremendous. I would especially like to thank Joaquín Chávez, Michelle Chase, Aldo Marchesi, Franny Sullivan, Paul Kershaw, and Tracy Neumann.

In Mexico City, where I researched and wrote most of this book, I am indebted to countless individuals for the varied kinds of support they so kindly offered. Luis Aboites, Chris Boyer, Emily Wakild, and Ariel Rodríguez Kuri offered helpful archival tips and pointed me in new research directions. Sarah Osten, Germán Vergara, Sergio Miranda Pacheco, Georg Leidenberger, Alejandro Tortolero Villaseñor, Angus Wright, Lance Ingwersen, Claudia Agostoni, Sandra Rozental, and Chris Boyer read and provided insightful comments on one or more chapter drafts. Juan Humberto Urquiza, Elisa Speckman, Daniela Spenser, Louise Walker, Elías Cattan, Paulina Suárez, Marat Ocampo, Bill Beezley, Tracy Goode, Robero Gómez Mostajo, and Manuel Perló Cohen provided encouragement as well as stimulating conversations about Mexico City and its history.

Since I arrived at the History Department at the University of California, San Diego, I have received perspicacious feedback on chapter drafts from several smart colleagues, including Wendy Matsumura, Claire Edington, Jessica Graham, Nancy Kwak, Eric Van Young, Dana Murillo, and Christine Hunefeldt. Many other people beyond New York, Mexico City, and San Diego have helped me in one capacity or another along the winding journey from dissertation idea to published book. Vera Candiani and Chris Boyer read the entire manuscript, and this book is better by leaps and bounds because of their hard work. Isabella Furth offered brilliant editorial assistance on each chapter. My editor at Duke, Gisela Fosado, encouraged me to write a stronger introduction and has been incredibly patient with me. The following individuals also merit a special thank you: Emilio de Antuñano, Ulises Piña, Pablo Piccato, Myrna Santiago, Drew Konove, Mark Healey, Brodie Fischer, Dain Borges, Mauricio Tenorio-Trillo, Michèle Dagenais, Sterling Evans, Mikael Wolfe, Zephyr Frank, John Soluri, and James Garza.

I have presented chapter drafts at numerous colloquiums, seminars, and writing groups in Mexico City, San Diego, New York, and Chicago. It would be impossible to recount, much less remember, all the individuals who generously offered their time to read and comment on my work at these events, but I am equally grateful for your close readings and your words.

Most of all, I would like to thank my mother and father and my partner, Lorena. My parents, Bob and Margaret, have been my biggest champions since I began at New York University. Their love, encouragement, and unwavering support have, over many years, kept me afloat through rough and calm waters. Lorena, your compassion and love have sustained me and enriched my life for over a decade. This book is as much yours as it is mine. You shared your city, your delightful friends, and your beautiful family with me. You accompanied (and sometimes took) me on trips to many of the places that fill this book. You have always known when to encourage me, when to challenge me, and when to tell me to slow down. I hope you enjoy this history of Mexico City, the enticing and enigmatic urban behemoth that you know so well.

FIGURE I.1 — Juan O'Gorman, *Paisaje de la Ciudad de México*, 1949.

INTRODUCTION

In 1949 the daily *Excélsior* organized the artistic competition "Mexico City as Interpreted by Its Painters," with the backing of the city government and the Banco de México. The exhibition, held in December 1949, displayed 257 paintings submitted by national and international artists, attracting some thirty thousand visitors over its nine-day tenure. The modernist architect-turned-painter Juan O'Gorman won first prize for his now-famous *Paisaje de la Ciudad de México* (*Landscape of Mexico City*). (See figure I.1.) Most critics have interpreted O'Gorman's painting as an acclamation of Mexico City's mid-twentieth-century development under the Institutional Revolutionary Party (PRI). The painting features a vibrant city with clean skies, green space, and modernist architecture. However, O'Gorman, a prominent socialist critical of the capitalist modernization Mexico was undergoing after 1940, also subtly depicted the erosion of national culture and the abandonment of the working class that PRI rule had wrought. The early colonial map in the foreground shows the formerly aquatic Basin of Mexico where the capital city was situated—a reminder to Mexican viewers of their lost indigenous

FIGURE I.2 — Guillermo Meza, *La Tolvanera*, 1949.

civilization—juxtaposed with the mostly barren lands beyond the cityscape where Lake Texcoco once stood. The indigenous-featured mason, representative of Mexican workmanship, is seen being pushed aside by the reinforced concrete, steel, and glass of buildings designed using foreign architectural styles.[1]

The winner of the second prize, Guillermo Meza, displayed not O'Gorman's metaphorical ambivalence about the city's growth but rather dread of environmental catastrophe. Meza's *La Tolvanera* (*The Dust Storm*) takes us to those barren lands of the old Texcoco lakebed, where briny soil swirled and tormented Mexico City's inhabitants, primarily the working-class settlers driven to live on hazardous lands. Children mingle inside one of two drainage-pipe fragments, an allusion to the hydraulic infrastructure that helped desiccate the basin's vast lake system (see figure I.2). Meza was not alone in his apocalyptic midcentury vision of Mexico City. He drew on other artistic work such as Carlos Tejeda's dystopian painting *La Ciudad de México por allí de 1970* (*Mexico City around 1970*), from 1947, which depicted a dried, deforested, earthquake-ravaged city, and lithographer Alfredo Zalce's portrayals of urban corruption and chaos.[2]

The apocalyptic imaginary intensified in the following decades. Urban chronicler Arturo Sotomayor imagined space aliens visiting the ruins of the basin to determine what had caused the decline of a once-magnificent civilization. The lesson: Mexicans had not learned to live within the limits of nature, having converted a forested, water-rich environment into a smog-infested desert of concrete sprawl that subsumed the Federal District and spilled into the adjacent State of Mexico.[3] A few years later, in "Return to the Labyrinth of Solitude," Octavio Paz fulminated against government technocrats for turning Mexico City "into a monstrous inflated head crushing the frail body that holds it up."[4] The witty essayist Jorge Ibargüengoitia continued the corporal analogy, likening Mexico City to a fast-growing boy who made his parents proud. When the boy reached a height of ten feet at the age of eighteen months, people said nothing. But then the boy ate the maid, "and someone mustered up the courage to ask his mother: 'Look here, has he seen a doctor?'"[5] Seeing the city devastated by the earthquake of 1985, daily smog attacks, and a bleak economy, distinguished cultural critic Carlos Monsiváis reflected whether Mexico City might be "post-apocalyptic": "Here is the first megalopolis to fall victim to its own excess. . . . The main topic of conversation at gatherings is whether we are actually living the disaster to come or among its ruins."[6]

All of this lies in stark contrast to the many florid descriptions of the city and its surroundings during much of the nineteenth century. Mexico City, located seventy-two hundred feet above sea level in a giant basin improperly named the Valley of Mexico, is surrounded by mammoth volcanic peaks and towering mountains to the south and west, lower ridges to the east, and a high mesa to the north. It was a place that lent itself to admiration.[7] Visitors to the basin lauded "the beautiful city . . . surrounded by various shaded promenades and brilliant country fields."[8] They relished the "thick forests" of the Ajusco mountain range to the south, the Sierra de las Cruces to the west, and the sinuous slopes of the Iztaccíhuatl and Popocatépetl volcanoes, commonly known as the Sierra Nevada, as well as the immense basin below, "praised in all parts of the world . . . with its large lakes and fertile plains encircling Moctezuma's favorite city."[9] Australian diplomat Charles La Trobe named Mexico City "the city of palaces," and Prussian geographer Alexander von Humboldt at the tail end of his journey through Spanish America remarked on the clarity of the valley's air. Perhaps the most lavish admiration came from the American writer Brantz Mayer, for whom the valley was an incomparable sight, a place that surpassed all the natural wonders of Europe combined. Mayer observed, "No other panorama of valleys and mountains offers a similar set of elements [as this one], because in no other part are the mountains so high and at the same time the valley so spacious and so full of a variety of lands and waters."[10] Mayer, like the travelers preceding him, viewed peaks of fourteen thousand feet or more, rising well above the tree line. Below the tree line grew pine, conifer, and oak forests, where heavy summer rains fed seasonal rivers that flowed through the piedmont—a medley of fertile fields in the south and sterile land made of the hardened rocky soil known as *tepetate* in the north—down into the lakes below: Chalco and Xochimilco to the south, Texcoco to the east, and several more to the north.

Mexicans proffered their own decorative descriptions. The Basin of Mexico inspired the liberal poet and military officer Ramón I. Alcázar, whose poem "A la vista del valle de México" ("In Sight of the Valley of Mexico," 1860) exalted its "green hills" and "crystalline lake water."[11] The renowned late nineteenth-century landscape painter José María Velasco contrasted with his brush the modernity of Mexico City with the pastoral, lacustrine beauty of the hinterland. Echoing Humboldt's words and María Velasco's imagery, the geographer Antonio García Cubas referred to the "picturesque Valley of Mexico" and boasted of its abundant natural elements (see map I.1).[12]

Yet as Humboldt, María Velasco, and Fanny Calderón de la Barca, the flowery travel writer and wife of the first Spanish ambassador to Mexico, made clear, the Basin of Mexico was hardly in a state of environmental equilibrium during the nineteenth century.[13] Owing to the needs of the capital city nestled near its center, the basin had undergone gradual environmental changes since the apex of Mexica civilization. Land clearing for Old World ungulates diminished forest cover, as did demand for firewood, charcoal, and construction material; unsustainable land use accelerated soil erosion and aggravated sediment buildup in lakebeds. And the Spanish colonial elite, whose property holdings were jeopardized by floodwaters settling in the lowest parts of the basin, built massive drainage infrastructure that reduced the lake system by nearly 80 percent, from a thousand square kilometers in 1519 to two hundred square kilometers by 1850.[14] These early changes, however dramatic they may have been, were dwarfed by the rapid environmental and social transformations of the late nineteenth and early twentieth centuries, a period in which Mexico City became the national hub of capitalist urbanization and state-directed environmental planning. The turning point was the 1870s, which city chronicler Jesús Galindo y Villa denoted as the beginning of the Mexico City "of our times."[15]

Writing in the 1920s, Galindo y Villa claimed that it was the "luck" of his generation "to witness Mexico City's surge toward modern life, to feel its

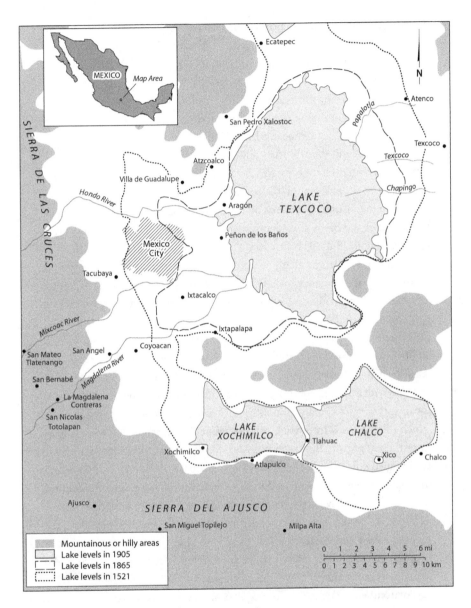

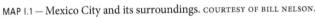

MAP I.1 — Mexico City and its surroundings. COURTESY OF BILL NELSON.

extraordinary evolution, its prodigious expansion, the transformation of its municipal services, in short its progress."[16] This zeal for progress was shared by a host of urban boosters, planners, and developers and hinged on a series of key environmental projects and policies. It is this city's environmental, political, and social transformation from a small and rather stagnant national capital at the beginning of the nineteenth century to a major metropolis by the mid-twentieth century that is the subject of this book.

The post–World War II artists and intellectuals of an ecocritical bent captured an essential truth: Mexico City is, indeed, a city facing extraordinary social and environmental predicaments. This book helps explain the origins and evolution of these problems by tracking the rapid environmental transformation of the basin and identifying the assorted variables driving those transformations. But this is just scratching the surface of a deeper history.

From Sotomayor and Ibargüengoitia to environmentalists and the public at large, there is a tendency to depict the recent history of the Americas' largest city as one of inevitable and inexorable decline. It is a unidirectional history that conceives of the environment and people as mere victims of sociostructural forces. As the city grew, the story goes, communities were disempowered and nature bulldozed, never to rise again (even if nature has of late reasserted itself in such undesirable forms as flooding). Such a narrative offers uncanny parallels with Mexico's political narrative. The monolithic, monstrous city was the offspring of an equally monolithic and monstrous political party, the PRI, which ruled Mexico from 1929 to 2000, propelling the capital down a path of unrestrained growth. In this telling, Mexico City encapsulated the ruling party's bungled governance, emerging as a microcosm of national ruination and disempowerment. However accurate a depiction of late twentieth-century Mexico City this may be, the narrative—if one accepts its coherence as such—occludes an earlier, more open-ended urban history. This book employs the tools of social and environmental history to challenge assumptions about the city's growth and its relation to the surrounding Basin of Mexico from the late nineteenth to the mid-twentieth century.

Environmental decline is an unequivocal reality in the basin. Mexico City is not the place to upend declensionism within environmental historiography. But the destruction of nature is not the only, or the most important, story to tell; indeed, this story omits a great deal. In this book I underscore the ways in which nonhuman nature, rather than being torn asunder, was inextricably joined to the built environment in the process of urbanization. I uncover largely forgotten histories of popular groups, government officials, and planners disputing urban growth and, at certain moments, promoting more just and environmentally sound visions of the city and its hinterland. Mexico City's enormous twentieth-century growth was embedded in and forged out of an overlapping set of contingent, if structurally conditioned, social conflicts and scientific disputes over its dynamic metropolitan environment—the lands, waters, forests, networked infrastructure, and new subdivisions, all of which were tightly bound to urbanization.[17]

Mexico City, like other booming Latin American metropolises of the twentieth century, was the product of much struggle and negotiation over its metropolitan environment. To borrow from Marxist philosopher-geographer Henri Lefebvre, the capitalist city undergoes an urban revolution that consumes space through market expansion and the creation of industrial zones, infrastructural networks, population flows, and settlements—the warp and woof of what he deemed an urban fabric extending well beyond the confines of the city itself.[18] Lefebvre, however, for all his understanding of urbanization as a spatial process, retreated to the conventional opposition of city and nature. In this he was not alone. His contemporary from across the Atlantic, the urban theorist Lewis Mumford, declared, "As the pavement spreads, nature is pushed away," conflating an idyllic countryside with nature itself and setting up a false dichotomy between the urban as the realm of pure artifice and the rural as spaces of nature.[19] Yet the dynamic interaction between people and their changing environments holds a key to unlocking the social and political character of modern metropolitan development.

The world's largest cities, like Mexico City, provide insight into the historical, spatial, and environmental process of urbanization. Water, energy, construction material, and other resources must be obtained, controlled, and circulated, an effort that necessitates much state power, technical expertise, and capital investment. These efforts transform environments, shape political structures, and engender myriad social struggles over the spaces impacted by urbanization. I contend that the development of Latin American (indeed all) metropolises needs to be understood within wider sociospatial scales, which are ever more global in scope. Cities are not discrete entities but rather are dynamically interconnected to larger metropolitan environments created through infrastructural works; through the harnessing of resources and the disposal of wastes; through commodity flows, population growth, and capitalist strategies; through ecological changes across disparate spaces; and through state-making practices and popular politics. The metropolitan environment, in turn, has molded what is politically possible for a range of actors—popular groups, planners, industrialists, developers, and state officials—operating on an uneven field of play who have had competing claims to a resource, space, or city service.

A *City on a Lake* explains the why, how, and for whom of urban growth and draws on the scholarship of urban political ecology to zoom in on the interplay among power, planners, environmental change, and popular politics in Mexico City. It places nonhuman nature—reworked, regulated, and contested—squarely within the urban fabric. By following water, waste, dust, and forest products and other commodities, as well as urban experts and developers, in and out of cities, we can gain a more sophisticated understanding of how urban power has been exercised, reproduced, and challenged. Such a framework is vital to the urban historiographical endeavor as well as to the politics of urban justice and sustainability.

Mexico City is a palimpsest of infrastructures, urban design, physical transformation, and settlement patterns. Scraping away several layers of this palimpsest takes us back to the mid-nineteenth century when Mexico City, with a population of 150,000, was portrayed as a quaint, bucolic "city of palaces." Even then the Basin of Mexico was a highly engineered environment; the capital depended on the salubrious flow of water. Mexican sanitarians, however, many of whom served key planning roles by 1900, depicted not a city of splendor but a city of stagnant water, of disease and disorder, of failed and outdated engineering. Like those found in other cities, Mexico City's waste disposal system was a hodgepodge of septic pits, open gutters, and, in some central sections, underground pipes. Downtown streets featured open canals, which were designed to flush wastewater to the Texcoco lakebed, the lowest-lying and closest lake. Design rarely met function. The renowned geographer Manuel Orozco y Berra noted the "noxious miasmas" that rose from "fecal matter and animal and plant remains" in open sewers lacking declivity.[20] The budding engineer Roberto Gayol found that many of the canals had sunk so far that they drained away from the lake and that some overflowed upon heavy rainfall.[21] Most residents deposited their wastes into the open gutters or directly onto the street. The Mexican slang phrase "¡Aguas!" (Watch out!) derives from the historical practice of tossing waste from upper-story windows. Outdoor defecation was commonplace since lower-class homes and tenements lacked toilets, and public restrooms were scarce and poorly kept.

If pollution from within the city had been the only trouble facing public health officials, Mexico City would have resembled most metropolises. But most other cities enjoyed more auspicious geographic locations than at the bottom of an endorheic basin. The much-reduced Lake Texcoco, which received the city's wastewater via the San Lázaro Canal, constituted a public health menace like no other. A shell of its former grandeur, Texcoco exhaled a foul odor approximating "rotten shellfish," spewing what were believed to be illness-laced miasmas across Mexico City. Colonial-era drainage infrastructure had taken its toll, but so had soil sedimentation, and the extension of the lake varied drastically depending on the rainfall.[22] On his visit to the lakebed in March 1883, the late-century savant Antonio Peñafiel described not waters one or two meters deep, a common sight two centuries before, but rather "a moribund lake" of "putrefied organic waste" with "cadavers in decomposition." He wryly remarked that the city was "threatened with asphyxiation."[23]

Residents feared more than deadly vapors. During the dry season, the prevailing northerly winds lifted up briny dust from the dried Texcoco bed and the denuded hillsides, which mixed with the city's animal and human waste to form a pernicious cocktail. Invading floodwaters replaced swirling dust during the rainy season, and Texcoco overflowed onto city streets in 1856, 1865, and 1886. The flood in 1886 provoked one major city paper to ask facetiously, "Is this city a seaport?"[24]

Urban experts also derided the potable-water system. Open-air aqueducts carried waters from Desierto de los Leones and Santa Fe in the southwestern mountains, and the closer Chapultepec Forest, to the capital. After traversing villages, ranches, farms, and mills, the water arrived laden with soil, detritus, and other contaminants.[25] Engineer José Lorenzo Cossio recalled bathing on Vergara Street: "upon drying off with a towel, it turned completely muddy."[26] Lorenzo Cossio was fortunate to have a connection to the municipal supply; in the mid-1880s, only 1,600 of 7,150 residences (about 20 percent) boasted one—mainly homes of the wealthy and convents—making a water hookup a marker of social status.[27] Chronic leaking debilitated an already feeble supply, leading many wealthier residents, businesses, and convents to dig private artesian wells, while the vast majority of the population obtained water from the approximately eighty public fountains and, illicitly, the many fire hydrants that dotted the city.[28] The urban ideal of a clean and ordered water system broke down in the face of spatial inequalities and planning deficiencies.

Although urban experts' denunciations of existing infrastructure brought the atrocious health conditions of Mexico City into relief, their narrow purview missed important, often symbiotic ties between city and hinterland inhabitants. Lake Texcoco was a health threat, but it was also the ecological basis, in combination with Lakes Chalco and Xochimilco, of a vigorous economy connected to the city. As the urban market ballooned, the productive indigenous agricultural practice of *chinampería* expanded in pueblos such as San Gregorio Atlapulco, Santa María Nativitas, Tláhuac, and San Andres Mixquic around Lakes Chalco and Xochimilco. Campesinos erected soil beds (*chinampas*) in lakes, marshes, and canals, using the nutrient-rich plant life to grow corn, vegetables, and flowers. The *chinamperos* would transfer seedlings from nurseries to the chinampa plots, which were demarcated first by wooden poles and later by the ubiquitous willow and cypress trees. Irrigation was by osmosis or by the careful application of canal water into the raised bed.[29] By the end of the century as much as 75 percent of the area surrounding the city was under cultivation, and chinampa plots prevailed on lands around the southern lakes.[30]

Chinampería is what Mexicans likely recall the most about the old economy of the basin, but there were other important uses of hinterland ecosystems. Many villagers around Lake Texcoco consumed or traded in city markets the sodium carbonate and sodium chloride (*el tequesquite*) that crystallized during dry-season evaporation, and all three major lakes sustained abundant wildlife that villagers exploited. The *armada*, the lakeshore duck-hunting technique dating back to the early colonial period, was widely practiced by villagers. Using horses to corral ducks to the "site of ambush," hunters shot two rounds, one to frighten the birds into flight and a second to kill them. A well-organized armada could net thousands of ducks.[31] Water also served as a means of transport. At midcentury, around two hundred long canoes traversed the basin's lakes and canals daily, supplying various foods, charcoal, firewood, and other goods from the surrounding hinterland to the bustling urban markets such as Jamaica.[32]

Some pueblos also enjoyed access to municipal infrastructure. The western town of Santa Fe in exchange for use of its property to construct the aqueduct, had reached an agreement to open a connecting pipe to quench townspeople's thirst. In Cuajimalpa, to the southwest of the city, the city's water guard reported that villagers were stealing water to irrigate their fields, "under the pretext that it is their right."[33]

Nineteenth-century urban environmental planners—engineers, architects, and other urban experts—ignored or outright eschewed these kinds of uses of hinterland nature. Their objective was to promote capitalist urbanization by sanitizing the Valley of Mexico, regardless of the effects on outlying inhabitants. Sophisticated engineering and state regulations, they hoped, would refashion an untamed, ungoverned environment and conform its inhabitants within a decidedly urban and elite framework of resource use.[34]

A growing number of planners seized the opportunity to realize this objective when decades of civil strife slackened and foreign invasion ended in 1867. More stable governance, institution building, and economic growth commenced under Benito Juárez, but it was during the reign of the politically astute and heavy-handed Porfirio Díaz, president between 1876–1880 and 1884–1911 (the Porfiriato), that urban environmental planning took off. The Porfirian elite, steeped in Hispanic notions of *civitas* that placed cities at the epicenter of civilization, focused on Mexico City's modernization, often to the neglect of other urban areas. The late nineteenth century marked a period of urban recovery in which Mexico City could once again "speak for the nation"; most Mexican rulers wanted little to do with Jeffersonian-infused U.S. American beliefs in the pastoral ideal.[35] The rejuvenation of the Mexican polity and the nation's newfound economic vigor hastened changes to the physical landscape.

Starting at the end of the nineteenth century, Mexico City's ecology was revolutionized in two intersecting ways. The first revolution was a sanitary one. Urban experts embraced the goal of the sanitary city to efface the noxious and vitiating components of modern life, meet the requirements of capitalist growth, and project the city's urban modernity beyond national borders.[36] Selectively borrowing and adapting planning ideas shared by urban elites the world over, Mexico City's environmental planners carried out drainage, sewerage, and water-supply projects and implemented urban sanitary codes and forest-conservation policies. Together, these forged a new metropolitan environment and tended to reproduce—even enhance—inequalities around the uses and appropriations of this environment. Directed by the centralizing state, however, planning initiatives began to shift the pendulum of power in and around Mexico City from the private realm of haciendas and developers to the public realm of state bureaucracy and its regulatory codes.

The second transformation began in 1910, this time as a set of political and social changes regarding how the material environment would be regulated, rearranged, and used. The Mexican Revolution, a series of heterogeneous conflicts over political power, social relations, and regional cultural values that unfolded between 1910 and 1920, widened opportunities for popular groups to challenge Porfirian-era urbanization. Postrevolutionary rulers aimed simultaneously to continue elite urban dominance and to more equitably distribute access to and uses of the metropolitan environment. Two competing political frameworks enwrapped key spaces in the basin: one reformist and fastened to the political culture of the revolution of 1910, and the other elite and urban, with origins in the Porfirian development model guided by a centralized technocratic state. The tensions between the two frameworks molded environmental disputes between 1912 and 1940—from the forests of the Ajusco and the Texcoco lakebed, both located in the surrounding hinterland, to the newly sprouted subdivisions of the expanding capital. Cultural and political structures of power, in conjunction with the morphed ecologies wrought by planners and developers, defined the parameters of social struggle. But the struggles themselves, with their diverse actors, helped forge the urban landscape and direct urbanization through the 1930s and beyond. More equitable visions of the city succumbed to the engine of a pro-business industrial policy during the 1940s, but not without leaving cultural and physical imprints that have shaped (and continue to shape) the contemporary city.

The modern urban history of Latin America is a vast, rich, and fast-growing field dominated by two distinct lines of study. In the first, an array of historians have shed new light on urban social and political change, the politics of culture, and the popular experience of urbanity.[37] In the second, a smaller group of urban historians have explored the power and institutionalization of the state; their work has focused in particular on the role of a leading technical elite in transforming the built and natural environment during periods of urban expansion, when rule was reinforced by massive hydraulic projects that served as "monuments of progress" or "paradigms" of power politics and capitalist development.[38]

My work builds on the recent recognition that these two research lines need to be fused.[39] This broader perspective on the environmental history of Mexico City weaves together the immaterial and the material, the "built" and the "natural" environment, and resource flows and political change. It situates matter within the power relations that have molded Mexico City's growth without unduly emphasizing burgeoning bureaucracies or fetishizing elite policy-making spheres.[40] Mexico City's growth must be understood through an analysis of environmental change as well as everyday politics. The heterogeneous popular classes within the basin made claims on the metropolitan environment that a slew of environmental planners regulated and reworked under the rubric of health and hygiene and with an intricate knowledge of emerging ecological problems.

Urban political ecology lies at the crux of this narrative. This emerging field, which sprang from Marxist geography and the multidisciplinary scholarship on urban metabolisms, operates from the premise that nonhuman nature—plants, animals, soil, water, and biophysical processes—are inseparable from cities: their growth, their infrastructures, their food supplies, and their service networks.[41] The nature in cities is not merely found in public parks, the "rehabilitated spaces of cities," or rivers and harbors and their urbanized banks.[42] Rather, flora, fauna, water, industrial materials and contaminants, soil mechanics, and diseases meld with all aspects of the urban formation. As recent work in urban environmental history has implicitly alluded, and political ecology has explicitly argued, every city is a type of socionatural hybrid, a kind of urban ecology. Different people appropriate nonhuman nature and bring it within urban circuits fraught with specific constellations of power and riddled with inequalities of access and distribution.[43] Urban formations are fundamentally material, but they are also cultural and political insofar as certain classes and groups of people face different environmental conditions and envision distinct—and often contradictory—uses and practices for metropolitanized environments. In Mexico City the élan of urbanization and the quest for urban hygiene interlaced city and hinterland into a vast metropolitan environment, over which campesinos, urban residents, environmental planners, and government officials wrangled. It is crucial that scholars study the historical formation of metropolitan environments; it is out of these hybrid landscapes that solutions for a democratic urban sustainability must emerge.

Mexico City's environmental history is also the history of the Basin of Mexico. Urbanization has operated on multiple spatial scales, spanning the city and its hinterlands.[44] One main objective here is to explain how urban and hinterland populations became entangled in and joined to a material and discursive framework that rotated around urban sanitation—physical infrastructure, new settlements, commodity flows, federal property markers, and legal codes—and the social rights forged in revolutionary convulsion. This is not to say the city core and its hinterland, what Lefebvre would call the "larger urban fabric," were one and the same. There were also important disjunctures across the metropolitan space: different modes of survival, diverse popular political aims, varied responses by elite groups, and divergent ecological changes. Nor is it to say that city and hinterland were static entities; population growth and real estate speculation swallowed whole towns and villages, and the quest for additional resources integrated new hinterland spaces into metropolitan development, processes that quickened in the 1940s.

This environmental history of the Porfiriato and the revolution politicizes the history of urban sanitation, moving beyond conventional stories of technical achievement or environmental destruction to address the interaction between state formation and popular environmental politics.[45] Environmental planners, eager to sanitize Mexico City, united with the government, which gained immense authority over landscapes and the people inhabiting them. Porfirian urban sanitation constituted an essential ingredient in the territorialization of state power, a process fundamentally about the government's capacity to use technocratic agencies and commissions to include or exclude "people within particular geographic boundaries, and . . . [control] what people do and their access to natural resources within those boundaries."[46] Modern states have delineated the parameters of environmental politics, and the Basin of Mexico, where the Mexican state invested in soil, water, and trees to facilitate capitalist urbanization, was a prime example.[47] State agencies, by reworking and regulating nonhuman nature, did more than arbitrate capitalist struggles over space, à la Marxist critical geography. They directly caused environmental change and conflict in their own right.

Lest this discussion devolve into overwrought state reification, it is important to keep in mind that the governing bodies that territorialized power were born of and beholden to historical conjuncture and social contention. They were part of society, not ontologically separate from it. These diverse agencies served a legitimizing role, providing leaders with the authority to sanction and affirm uses of nonhuman nature and urban infrastructure through ideology and regulation. Relatedly, they served a redistributive function after 1910, when the burgeoning and multifaceted politics of rights (access to fertile soil, water, and forests) and healthy living spaces (access to hygienic housing) became the linchpin of state formation in the urbanizing basin.[48] Between 1912 and 1940, the interplay among state officials, environmental planners, and diverse popular groups led to more environmentally just visions of metropolitan growth, manifested not just in words but in government programs, public works projects, and specific policies. Yet these visions were also ephemeral, incomplete, and ridden with contradictions. Postrevolutionary administrations followed in familiar Porfirian footsteps; they continued to support capitalist urbanization and technocratic solutions to environmental problems, squelching alternatives advanced from above and below alike.

The book is divided into two parts. The first part, "The Making of a Metropolitan Environment," consists of two chapters. Chapter 1 explains the rise of a new and influential cadre of environmental planners who implemented urbanization codes, promoted conservationist forestry policies, and executed massive hydraulic projects to sanitize Mexico's capital, spread health and hygiene, and support urban capitalism. These interventions tied together the city and the greater hinterland of the basin more tightly than ever before. While the making of the sanitary city under Porfirian rule accentuated environmental inequalities by enclosing common lands and limiting sanitary-service extensions, planners strengthened state authority over the metropolitan environment and enwrapped the inhabitants of the Basin of Mexico within an urban-sanitary framework that molded later environmental disputes. Chapter 2 places this new metropolitan environment in the context of the revolution of 1910, when emerging political and discursive practices about environmental rights challenged elite rule over landscapes. State authority, in short, adapted to the popular revolution.

The second part, "Spaces of a Metropolitan Environment," tracks the social and scientific disputes over the nature and direction of urban growth in different—yet interconnected—landscapes around the urbanizing basin from 1917 to about 1940. Chapter 3 is organized around the tenant strike of 1922 and the water riot in downtown Mexico City later that year, which was provoked by a breakdown in the system that brought fresh hinterland spring water to urban taps. I show how the quest for hygienic, affordable homes in postrevolutionary Mexico City was enmeshed with the growth economy of urban real estate and the climate of social reform. The protests of 1922 failed to democratize sanitary services; instead, they led authorities to experiment with urban politics and revive technocratic governance.

Chapter 4 follows many of the same environmental planners involved in sanitary-service provision into the forests surrounding the city. There, they sought a balance between forest conservation, which they linked to urban hygiene, and the customary forest rights of communities recently empowered by the revolution. From 1916 to 1940, foresters, agrarian officials, and the campesinos of numerous pueblos negotiated use of and access to the woodlands along the rim of the Basin of Mexico, spaces that environmental planners believed were essential for safeguarding Mexico City's development.

As planners sought to protect dwindling forests, they also confronted the consequences of their draft-and-drain paradigm: especially the desiccation of Lakes Xochimilco and Texcoco, which diminished agricultural production and aggravated dangerous dust storms. This is the subject of chapter 5, which examines the agroecological changes around Lake Texcoco and zeroes in on the brief convergence between the state's interest in transforming Lake Texcoco's saline soils for urban hygiene and campesinos' farming interests during the *sexenios* (six-year terms) of Lázaro Cárdenas (1934–1940) and Manuel Ávila Camacho (1940–1946).

The city began to encroach on the flood- and dust-prone Texcoco lakebed during the 1930s, and in chapter 6 I explore the revolutionary politics of urban housing and sanitation in impoverished settlements. Urban environmental inequalities, particularly around housing and services, combined with rising expectations of government intervention to foster the emergence of radical architects and popular organizations that fought for hygienic and comfortable living spaces free from the yoke of landlords and speculators.

This period of vibrant popular politics and disparate movements for environmental equality did not last. Chapter 7 examines the emergence in the 1940s of a techno-bureaucratic alliance of planners and state authorities that suffocated calls for more equal urban growth, further eroding environmental rights.

I

THE MAKING OF A

METROPOLITAN ENVIRONMENT

1

The Porfirian

Metropolitan Environment

In 1862 scientists under the liberal government of Benito Juárez drafted the Hydrographic Map of the Valley of Mexico. It is no coincidence that the project was authorized the same year French forces marched toward Mexico City in Napoleon III's bid to reestablish an American empire. Mexican cartography arose out of elites' desire to imagine a coherent nation and assert national sovereignty in the wake of multiple wars and foreign interventions, most notably the U.S. invasion in 1846 and the subsequent Treaty of Guadalupe Hidalgo, which handed half of Mexico's territory to the United States.[1] Yet the map and its 1864 report (*Memoria*), both supervised by Manuel Orozco y Berra, was an urban as well as a national project. Orozco y Berra and other leading scientists meticulously described the lands, waters, and biota surrounding the city, observations that future environmental planners drew on in their quest for a prosperous and sanitary capital.

Following the execution of Emperor Maximilian of Austria, who ruled Mexico from 1864 to 1867, succeeding liberal governments, culminating with that of Porfirio Díaz, ushered in a revival of Mexican science and engineering.

Knowledge of biophysical systems was fundamental to the Porfirian scientific endeavor. Nearby forests, agricultural practices, water and its conduction to the city, defunct drainage systems, lakes, soils, and urban space were all placed under the microscope of a punctilious group of urban experts. This professional elite articulated an *urban environmental imaginary* of the basin, a set of suppositions about the city's environment and its relationship with the hinterland that had germinated during Spanish rule when experts grappled with the recurrent flooding of the colonial capital. This imaginary posited the city and hinterland nature as interdependent, but this codependency did not mean that the city ceded to the whims of the natural world. Water needed to be controlled, channeled, and harnessed; trees needed to be regulated and nurtured. Good Spencerians all, the planning elite envisioned the city sometimes as a sick organism that sanitary planning would cure, sometimes as a woman in need of caring and cultivation.[2] This imaginary laid the groundwork for the transformation and regulation of the basin.[3] Urban experts aimed to turn Mexico City into "the most beautiful and healthy city of the republic" by reworking and regulating water, lands, and forests.[4] Their aims were not so easily attained. Social and environmental forces in and around Mexico City challenged their sanitary project.

Environmental planners carried out three interconnected hydraulic projects and wrote sanitary policies that forged a new metropolitan environment.[5] Supported by a rich tradition of hydraulic engineering, combined with the negotiating prowess that finance minister José Yves Limantour wielded with British banking interests, Díaz pushed forward the Desagüe General del Valle de México (General Drainage of the Valley of Mexico). Luis Espinosa directed the drainage, a major excavation and construction project executed by the British contractors Read and Campbell and Sir Weetman Pearson. The mammoth drainage works featured the Gran Canal de Desagüe (Great Drainage Canal), which stretched from the eastern edge of the Texcoco lakebed at San Lázaro to the northern reaches of the basin, and an impressive tunnel that sliced through the basin's walls to drain Texcoco floodwaters and the city's wastewater.[6] Roberto Gayol designed the city's first comprehensive sewer system, a vast underground network of collectors, lateral pipes, street sewers made of vitrified clay, and household piping laid to evacuate wastewater and storm water into Espinosa's Gran Canal by means of gravity, augmented by the occasional burst of water from the Canal Nacional, which connected the southern lakes to the city, during dry spells (see map 1.1). It was the first sewer system to offer the possibility of daily cleaning with quick bursts of water.[7]

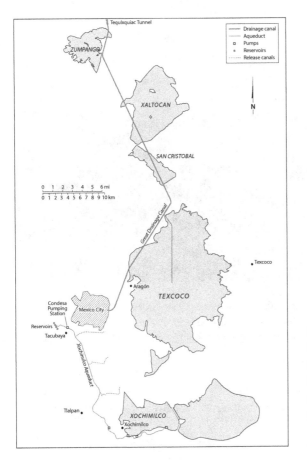

Drainage canal
Aqueduct
Pumps
Reservoirs
Release canals

Tequixquiac Tunnel

ZUMPANGO

XALTOCAN

SAN CRISTOBAL

N

0 1 2 3 4 5 6 mi
0 1 2 3 4 5 6 7 8 9 10 km

Great Drainage Canal

• Texcoco

• Aragón

TEXCOCO

Condesa
Pumping
Station

Mexico City

Reservoirs
Tacubaya

Xochimilco Aqueduct

Tlalpan •

XOCHIMILCO
• Xochimilco

MAP 1.1 — Mexico
City's hydraulic
infrastructure under
Porfirio Díaz.
COURTESY OF BILL
NELSON.

Manuel Marroquín y Rivera was the author of the city's updated water system, which tapped the fresh spring waters of Lake Xochimilco. And Miguel Ángel de Quevedo sought to ensure sanitary services in new subdivisions and protect the forests surrounding the city (see figure 1.1).

Taken together, the efforts of these men (and they were all men) exemplified the turn-of-the-century impulse to build the networked city, from transport to sewerage. Mexico City's sanitary planning integrated the water, forests, and land of the basin into the urban fabric through entwined hydraulic infrastructures and environmental policies. The result was a new metropolitan environment.[8] Conducted and catalyzed by the centralizing state, sanitary planning reinforced existing environmental inequalities across the basin. It also partially shifted the terrain of power from the private realm

FIGURE 1.1 — Texcoco secondary canal meets the Gran Canal. From Luis González Obregón, *Memoria histórica, técnica y administrativa de las obras del desagüe del valle de México, 1449–1900* (Mexico City: Oficina Impresora de Estampillas, 1902).

of haciendas and developers to the public realm of state bureaucracy, infrastructures, and regulatory codes.

THE PORFIRIAN WATERSHED

The commitment to reengineer the Basin of Mexico predated Porfirian Mexico. The Huehuetoca drainage works were begun in the early seventeenth century, though more as a way of protecting rentier capital from ruinous floodwaters than as a public health measure.[9] It was not until Bourbon rule that reformers branded the city insalubrious owing to the prevalence of unhealthy waters, toxic miasmas belching out of Lake Texcoco, and a filthy, barbarous population.[10] The postcolonial elite retained this vision. The prominent liberal José María Luis Mora, for example, urged the drainage of Lake Texcoco to prevent constant flooding, and the conservative politician Lucas Alamán proposed a commission to direct the *desagüe* and freed up funds to execute it.[11] Little was accomplished. Persistent instability—driven in part by perpetual clashes between Alamán-style conservatism and Mora's liberalism—precluded the organizational capacity and financing necessary to address sanitary short-comings. Public health languished as a result, and some officials complained that Mexico City resembled impoverished African cities more than the "modern" European metropolises to which the ruling class aspired. Not until the late 1860s did political centralization and economic growth coincide with transnational currents in health science and urban planning to enable Mexico City's rapid transformation.

Porfirio Díaz, the heroic liberal general from Oaxaca who had been instrumental in the triumph over French forces, centralized authority under the positivist banner of "Order and Progress," which became the shibboleth of a new generation of liberal elites. Much ink has been spilled over the application of Auguste Comte's positivism, or scientific politics, in Mexico, particularly with regard to economic growth.[12] However, its influence extended far beyond the economic. Scientific politics also encouraged the empirical study of nonhuman nature to promote its transformation and management and thus propel Mexico forward. Highly trained experts were tasked with administering the Basin of Mexico using the latest technologies and scientific principles. The boards (juntas) founded by Díaz to carry out the three major hydraulic projects exemplified this positivist and technocratic philosophy. Staffed by a small but blossoming group of engineers, architects, and scientists chagrined by the outdated and insalubrious colonial infrastructure, the juntas conformed to the governing imperative well. Sanitary planning also reinforced Mexican nationalism, fitting into a European-inspired, if Mexican-inflected, view of national progress and singularity. The Mexican government paraded its major sanitary public works at several world's fairs, which further encouraged the sanitization of Mexico City as a means of enhancing its national prestige on the global stage.[13]

In this context numerous professional associations arose, joining the Humboldtian Mexican Society for Geography and Statistics, founded in 1833. The Antonio Alzate Scientific Society, the National Medical Institute, the Society of Natural History, and the Society of Architects and Engineers (all created following the expulsion of the French in the 1860s) supported the close scrutiny of the basin: its people, its climate, and its waterscapes, soil, and forests—the type of knowledge crucial to environmental engineering.[14] In 1867 positivist educational philosopher Gabino Barreda opened the National Preparatory School as well as the National Engineering School, the successor to the Bourbon reformist Mining School that trained a new crop of urban engineers, including Espinosa, Gayol, and Marroquín y Rivera. This holy trinity of hydraulic engineering—the architects of desagüe, sewerage, and the water supply—had their hands in an array of other key projects around the basin. Espinosa sat on several environmental planning committees; Gayol constructed the General Hospital on the city's outskirts and the famed Italian-drafted Monument to Independence, and designed the partial drainage of Lake Chalco for the Spanish landowner Iñigo Noriega; and Marroquín y Rivera (the cofounder of the Antonio Alzate Scientific Society) served on the valley's Hydrographic Commission, which advised the government on water management. Technical education in Porfirian Mexico rarely extended to productive activities such as industrial or chemical engineering, as one economic historian has recently pointed out, and even the training of hydraulic or sanitary engineers was rather modest.[15] Yet while the capital and technology necessary for the basin's reengineering were imported from Europe and the United States, for all the dramatic ridicule of Porfirian *malinchismo* (preference for foreign over national culture) after the revolution, the study of the basin's physical environment and the supervision of its transformation were largely done by Mexicans.

The urban capitalist locomotive of real estate, industry, and the services they required also accounted for the spike in the building professions during the Porfiriato. Mexico City, as one engineer put it, entered "a construction phase," and new developments demanded new infrastructure.[16] By the first decade of the twentieth century, Mexico City had evolved from Alexander von Humboldt's "the city of palaces" into "the city of suburbs" (*la ciudad de las colonias*), a title bestowed on the city in 1908 by Guillermo Beltrán y Puga, head of the Federal District's Public Works Department.[17] The city's demographic and spatial expansion had been explosive. In 1858 the city covered a mere 8.5 square kilometers and had 200,000 residents. Fifty years later the city's surface area had increased nearly fivefold, to 40.5 square kilometers, beginning to conjoin with neighboring municipalities within the larger Federal District, and its population had more than doubled to almost 500,000.[18] This was a sign of "modern progress" for Beltrán y Puga, who imagined a colonial resident brought back to life in this completely "unfamiliar city."[19]

Construction, of course, required designers and builders. Engineers coordinated with U.S. oil magnate Edward Doheny's Mexican Eagle Petroleum Company to pave city streets utilizing oil-derived asphalt from the Huasteca of Veracruz.[20] Gayol and Beltrán y Puga signed contracts with developers to install the sewer and water systems in the new Roma and Condesa subdivisions, and Quevedo constructed the home of the London Bank of Mexico and South America and the impressive housing complex for the Buen Tono cigarette company workers.[21]

Urban real estate powered Porfirian capitalism, and the new subdivisions aggravated inequalities. Developers reaped huge profits through speculative pricing and put in public services only where steep lot prices covered the investment. Nouveaux-riche subdivisions like Juárez, Cuauhtémoc, Condesa, and Roma played on the affluent classes' fear of disease and "the 'dirty and nauseating people' of this 'mongrel city,'" with its scant and dirty drinking water, open sewage canals and flooded streets, and densely populated housing teeming with poor people.[22] These subdivisions, whose developers promised plentiful open space as well as exclusive water and drainage systems, sprouted up west of downtown around the elegant Haussmann-inspired Paseo de la Reforma, within easy reach of Chapultepec Park, and on higher ground, safe from the sewage-laden waters of Lake Texcoco. Developers located working-class subdivisions to the east, on the swampy, dust-prone lands nearest Lake Texcoco or south and north of the city center. These included La Bolsa, Morelos, Nuevo Rastro, Valle Gómez, Indianilla, and El Cuartelito, among others. Landowners in these areas erected *vecindades*, tenement buildings of one-room apartments around a small patio, or sold plots on the cheap to poor workers, who constructed shacks without public services. La Bolsa was infamous as a particularly horrendous place "with dirty and microbic streets, repulsive sights and evil smells," and the Rastro, home of the new slaughterhouse from which the well-to-do's packaged meat originated, became a foul cesspit of animal and human waste—a foretaste of the environmental injustice that prevailed in postwar industrial Mexico.[23] Lampoons of unhygienic neighborhoods abounded in the satirical newspapers *El Hijo del Ahuizote* and *El Imparcial*; the latter impugned the form urbanization had taken and described a typical suburb of up to a thousand residents as a "hospital ward" that "does not have a single sewer, a single drainage pipe, or a single toilet."[24] (See map 1.2.)

In the area surrounding the city, the capitalist engine was fueled by manufacturing and medium-sized hacienda production. The advent of the railroad in the 1870s quickened transport time, lowered costs, and opened up new markets.[25] A line that stretched to the prosperous southern town of San Ángel connected the city to the textile- and paper-manufacturing zone along the Magdalena River, one of the basin's few perennial rivers. By 1890 another line connected Mexico City to Iñigo Noriega's wheat-producing haciendas in Chalco, the forested volcanoes of Iztaccíhuatl and Popocatépetl, and the manufacturing center of Puebla. The developing rail network put considerable pressure

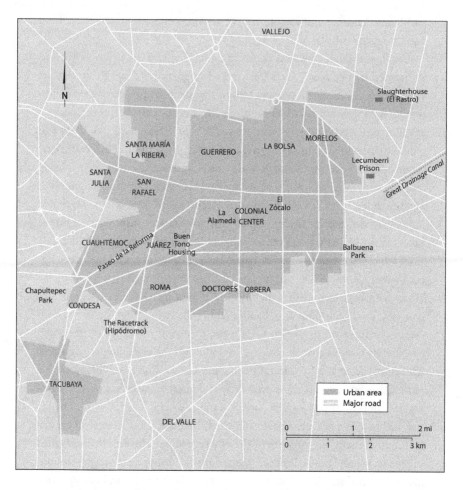

The map contains the following labels:

VALLEJO

N

Slaughterhouse (El Rastro)

MORELOS

SANTA MARÍA LA RIBERA

GUERRERO

LA BOLSA

Lecumberri Prison

SANTA JULIA

SAN RAFAEL

Great Drainage Canal

La Alameda

COLONIAL CENTER

El Zócalo

CUAUHTÉMOC

Paseo de la Reforma

JUÁREZ

Buen Tono Housing

Balbuena Park

Chapultepec Park

CONDESA

ROMA

DOCTORES OBRERA

The Racetrack (Hipódromo)

TACUBAYA

Urban area
Major road

DEL VALLE

0   1   2 mi
0   1   2   3 km

MAP 1.2 — Mexico City around 1910. COURTESY OF BILL NELSON.

on wood resources. The railroad itself required wood for fuel, ties, and station construction.[26] As freight transport became more efficient, haciendas such as Eslava, Coapa, and Xico, as well as textile and paper mills, moved to control the resources south of the city, intensifying forest extraction. Peasant communities, meanwhile, carved a limited but important niche in the growing urban charcoal and firewood markets.[27] In 1870 Manuel Payno, author of the famous novel *Los Bandidos del Río Frío* (*The Bandits from Río Frío*), whose plot unfolded in the diverse landscapes of the basin, estimated that the city housed some 600 charcoal dispensaries, 125 woodworks, 30 coachmakers, and a host of other wood-dependent manufacturers.[28] Such intensified use of woodlands alarmed urban experts, who discerned links between deforestation and urban sanitation.

Trends in international science and the culture of urban expertise also encouraged sanitary planning in Mexico City. Through trips abroad, international conferences, and the circulation of texts, the Mexican elite were attuned to both scientific and urban planning innovations in North Atlantic nations. Engineers and doctors such as Gayol, Quevedo, Antonio Peñafiel, and Eduardo Liceaga (the president of the government's Superior Health Council) borrowed ideas on city beautification, park creation, sanitary infrastructure, public health codes, and hygiene from abroad. These same Mexican experts shared with like-minded Progressive Era planners a zeal for moral reform and the notion that the city was an interdependent, collective entity that demanded public solutions to solve urban problems and uplift the poor from degeneracy and depravity.[29]

As they wrestled with questions of public health, urban experts closely followed Louis Pasteur's science of bacteriology, which dueled with the theory of miasmatic etiology throughout the last quarter of the nineteenth century. It was common for urbanists to blend, with no sense of contradiction, miasmatic and bacteriological understandings of disease, and Peñafiel illustrated this tendency in his treatise on the waters of the Valley of Mexico, published in 1884. He believed miasmas from Texcoco's putrefying matter contaminated the city's open-air aqueducts while also alluding to sickness caused by microorganisms. Miasmas coexisted with germs in Mexican science—and popular culture—into the twentieth century.[30] The gradual acceptance of germ theory, however, strengthened sanitarians' resolve by pinpointing the cause of illness. It was still believed that filth summoned disease, but the mechanism was no longer that of a diffuse miasma. Instead, germs were the true culprit, and only proper sewage, water-supply, and garbage-disposal systems would contain them.

Bacteriology tightened the connection between drinking water and sewerage. Bad water was no longer merely foul looking or tasting but intrinsically pernicious to public health. Marroquín y Rivera calculated that bacteria-ridden water was killing more than three thousand capital residents each year.[31] A separate study discovered dangerous levels of bacteria in Chapultepec water. Marroquín y Rivera associated deadly gastrointestinal diseases with tainted water and observed that the areas with the highest mortality rates tended to use poorly designed wells or stream water.[32] While this evidence affirmed the need to confront the unequal distribution of clean water in Mexico City, germ theory may have paradoxically helped deter the democratization of sanitary services. Whereas a miasma might have traveled from one neighborhood to infect the next, germs could remain segregated as long as wealthier areas possessed a full range of independent services.[33]

Mexico's sanitary ideal never diverged sharply from turn-of-the-century European developments, but neither was it derivative. Mexican sanitarians participated in a global planning and public health nexus, imbibing European and North American practices while immersed in their own intellectual heritage as well as Mexico's unique geography and supposed cultural traits.[34] Mexican forest conservation, for instance, drew on a tradition exploring the links among hydrology, soil, and deforestation. In the seventeenth century, the Franciscan friar Juan de Torquemada and drainage engineer Enrico Martínez had cautioned that deforestation risked erosion and the increasing sedimentation of the basin's lakebeds.[35] When the Crown established the Council on Forests to monitor the rational economic use of forests, the Creole priest and scientist José Antonio de Alzate y Ramírez warned authorities of the environmental consequences of deforestation. Over in Europe, the Comte de Buffon and other Enlightenment thinkers were elaborating the links between deforestation and desiccation, the kind of scientific expertise—labeled "climatic environmentalism" by one historian—that both motivated and constituted the colonization of North Africa and Asia.[36] In 1803 Alexander von Humboldt, wrapping up his scientific expedition to the Americas, saw Mexico City for the first time. A voracious reader of Old and New World scholarship, he remarked, in his usual derision of Spanish rule, "It would appear that the first conquerors wished the beautiful valley of Tenochtitlan to resemble the Castilian soil, which is dry and destitute of vegetation."[37]

The correlation between deforestation and declining rainfall, erosion, and increased flooding (also known as desiccation theory) was more tenuous than most presumed. Nineteenth-century Mexico saw a few perceptive challenges to desiccation theory, in particular questioning the causal relation between forest cover and rainfall.[38] But these voices of dissent were marginalized by the rising tide of a forest science with a colonial provenance. Mexico's geography of steep mountains surrounding wide valleys (or basins) with large urban settlements and countless lakes also helped consolidate such expertise. Without action by experts, catastrophe awaited.

Forest science as practiced in Europe also overlapped with Mexican elites' postcolonial position vis-à-vis indigenous peoples. Payno and the chemist

Leopoldo Río de la Loza pinned the blame for deforestation on Indians, a perspective with its own late-colonial roots dating back at least to the thought of the influential sculptor and architect of New Spain, Manuel Tolsá.[39] Quevedo's European training, including a degree in hydraulic engineering from France's prestigious École Polytechnique, emphasized similar themes; he studied forestry in North Africa at the time when French colonizers indicted local "nomads" for forest destruction and, with it, the desertification of an area that was once "the granary of Rome."[40] Deep-seated racism among the Mexican elite surely reinforced Quevedo's mind-set. And it was Quevedo who tirelessly championed Mexico's forests.

Hydraulic engineering, too, assumed a Mexican flavor. Espinosa mined a tradition of water conservation dating back to Dutch engineer Adrian Boot's iconoclastic proposition to the Crown in 1614 that the Mexican colony should manage the lakes rather than drain them. While Espinosa supported large-scale drainage, he heeded the warnings of dozens of experts on the environmental benefits of Lake Texcoco—as a reservoir for excess water and a buffer against dust storms—and did not intend for total desiccation.[41] In Francophile Mexico, Gayol denounced those who toured Paris's famous sewer system and concluded that "Mexico City's sewers should be exactly like the ones they visited."[42] According to Gayol, a city's sewer system functioned properly only if it was built according to solid engineering principles that conformed to a given urban environment. He made exhaustive studies of major metropolitan sewer systems, traveling throughout North America in 1886, yet these always led him back to Mexico City: its geography and its settlement patterns.

Porfirian rule revived the conception of Mexico City as the emblem of national progress. Sanitary planners advertised Mexico City abroad as the symbol of a distinctly Mexican modernity, and to the rest of the nation as a blueprint of urban development.[43] National progress depended on environmental transformation and regulation, which themselves hinged on the unique political, economic, and cultural conditions of the Porfiriato.

THE URBAN ENVIRONMENTAL IMAGINARY

If national and international trends provided the language, knowledge, and organizational groundwork for environmental planning, it fell to the Mexican scientific elite to articulate a vision of change specific to the basin that could translate into concrete action. And articulate they did, elaborating what I call an *urban environmental imaginary*: a shared set of assumptions about the relationship between the city and its environment. This shared imaginary did not mean that experts identified exactly the same problems or shared the same solutions; rather, it provided the common framework for debates over how to realize the sanitary city.

The urban environmental imaginary's first shared assumption was geographic, holding that the Basin of Mexico—although sliced into different administrative entities, principally the Federal District government, municipal governments within the district, and a portion of the State of Mexico—was an object of study in its own right. As a geologically enclosed region with its own catchment area, the basin was a biophysical entity independent of other Mexican spaces. The second assumption was the belief that Mexico City's insalubrity was rooted in the failure of past urban experts to control dangerous nature and to order urbanization along hygienic lines. The key to sanitizing Mexico City's growth, experts believed, lay in the methodical identification, measurement, and quantification of the basin's natural elements and the processes connecting them with each other and with human health. Mexican sanitary planners held a surprisingly integrated view of the basin's diverse environments, a view influenced by earlier naturalists such as Humboldt and Alzate.[44] Water, soil, and trees impacted each other, which in turn impacted human health.[45] These interdependencies and interactions, urban experts maintained, could be controlled through specific interventions in the environment that would enrich urban life. Some experts saw these interventions in terms of conquest, holding that human ingenuity would vanquish natural obstacles to urban progress. Others, particularly those planners attracted to forest conservation, argued that natural and cultural elements were so tightly interwoven that only by nurturing and cultivating nonhuman nature would urban life prosper. However, while these two visions—one of conquest and the other of cultivation—might seem to be logically opposed, Porfirian planners often upheld aspects of each, in theory and in practice. In addition, both orientations relied on public authority and skillful technical application to control people and their use of resources. This urban environmental imaginary undergirded important discussions about Porfirian planning proposals.

A striking example of this process at work occurred in 1902, when a committee that included Gayol and Espinosa considered two proposals for the design of the city's new water system. The first proposal, by the American engineer William Mackenzie, proposed to pump water from the Lerma River near Toluca and form a private firm to operate the system.[46] However, Mackenzie erroneously assumed the city wanted the cheapest water possible. The commission called out this gaffe, stating that "what the city needs and wants is to have the purest water possible, and this cannot be obtained by bringing the liquid through an open canal fifteen kilometers long."[47]

Mackenzie's proposal also clashed with experts' enduring commitment to public ownership. Nearly twenty years earlier, the city council had rejected a proposal to privatize the city's water, criticizing the attempt to "convert into a speculative business a public service that has such great influence over the health and prosperity of any population."[48] The committee in 1902 reiterated the city council's earlier position and observed that municipal authorities in Europe and the United States had been reincorporating water service because of extortionate and unequal private service. They singled out London, one of the last major cities to municipalize service, where water was "so scarce and bad in certain neighborhoods . . . that authorities have to loan [it in] vessels to thousands of poor." Water had been a wellspring of urban public authority since the Spanish Crown had established the parameters of municipal power, and events from across the Atlantic irrevocably proved that Mexico City's water needed to remain public.[49]

The second plan for city water, offered by Marroquín y Rivera, proposed to capture the Xochimilco springs. Marroquín y Rivera had thoroughly studied the quality of Xochimilco spring water and outlined a design featuring a covered aqueduct and an underground network of pipes. The commission favored this scheme, which coincided with sanitary officials' bid to defeat disease and provide clean water to the greatest number of people.

Late nineteenth-century debates over how to solve the intractable Lake Texcoco problem were more highly charged than the dilemma of the water supply. Experts agreed that the lake posed a menace; they did not, however, agree on how to address it or on the extent to which the lake should be drained or conserved. The conservationists' vision was shaped by a robust intellectual heritage that saw the lake as offering aesthetic value, economic advantage, and environmental benefits. Alzate had claimed that the desiccated basin floor would ruin building foundations, eliminate vital water-based transport, and leave behind lands unsuitable for agriculture and susceptible to alkaline dust storms that would compromise health.[50] He argued that the lake system could be properly controlled with minor drainage projects.[51] Later, Humboldt had chastised the Spanish authorities for seeing water as "a destructive element," "an enemy against which it was necessary to be defended."[52] He proposed that water not be expelled during the rainy season and instead be stored for agriculture and transport during the dry season. Although Humboldt also proposed drainage to curb flooding, the balance tilted in favor of water conservation.[53]

Much scholarship suggests that desiccation was the prevailing paradigm during the modern period, but this was not the case.[54] Postindependence Mexico was peppered with paladins of a healthy lacustrine environment, from an American lieutenant occupying Mexico City in 1848 to doctors and scientists such as José Lobato and Río de la Loza. Two of the most prominent champions of lake restoration were the engineer Manuel Balbontín and the doctor Ladislao de Belina. Balbontín supported a rehabilitated lake to prevent desiccation, which "would soon turn a place that should be gorgeous and productive . . . into a type of Pontine marsh that would eternally sustain sickness."[55] A vigorous lake would provide transport, would be ringed by green spaces with the planting of putatively health-giving eucalyptus trees, and would spruce up destitute neighborhoods and pueblos.[56] Campaigns to conserve the basin's lakes fed into a developing nationalist narrative in which iconic landscapes allegorized the nation.[57] Regenerating the basin's lost lacustrine environment through modern engineering would sanitize the city while simultaneously creating a bond with Mexico's precolonial past in an emblematic memorialization of a natural landscape.[58]

Large-scale drainage infrastructure had nonetheless prevailed. There were many reasons for this. Lake rehabilitation was an uncertain, uncharted path, considerably hindered by sedimentation and the continuous stream of human waste into the lakebed. Drainage was widely accepted as a more incontrovertible flood- and disease-prevention strategy, and it was common practice, from the Oderbruch marshlands of Prussia under Frederick the Great to California's Central Valley.[59] The desagüe consolidated state power over a fickle environment and boosted Mexico's claim to modernity. Monumental engineering was also wedded to capitalism, further eroding lake-based community subsistence, opening up new lands for investment, and better protecting existing ones.

Drainage also prevailed in the Lake Chalco basin some thirty kilometers southeast of the city. As the desagüe project moved ahead at full steam in the 1890s, the Spanish Noriega brothers, Iñigo and Remigio, were amassing their fortune in Mexico. Together they owned two tobacco factories, three haciendas in the Basin of Mexico, a cotton mill, and a budding urban real estate business.[60] Iñigo Noriega was also in the drainage business. He had acquired thousands of acres of marshland in Michoacán and desiccated it for agriculture.[61]

Captivated by his own success, he then devised a plan to expand the wheat and cornfields of his Chalco hacienda by draining the spring water that nourished the adjacent lake and uncovering over four thousand hectares of fertile fields composed of alluvial-rich topsoil deposited over millennia.[62] However, in 1888 a law federalized all navigable waterways, so Noriega had to obtain permission to undertake his project, which necessarily involved negotiating with experts' precepts for the sanitary city. The landowner painted the plan as a win-win scenario for Mexico City. His crops would feed the growing urban population, and the drainage could be used to facilitate Gayol's design of cleansing the city's sewers by sending lake water into the Canal Nacional.

Few people in the capital opined on Noriega's scheme, but environmental planners scrutinized the project. Espinosa, Gayol, Liceaga, and other sanitary leaders formed the advisory board to judge the petition. This was no rubber-stamp organization; its members dissected the project's advantages and disadvantages. As in the Texcoco debate only a few decades earlier, one major issue prevailed: would the drainage of Chalco harm Mexico City? The advisory board debated whether the water body was a lake or a stagnant swamp, a pertinent question to those espousing environmental theories of disease; they discussed the effects of the lake on rainfall and humidity and, in turn, humidity's effects on disease; and they analyzed whether a dried lakebed would expose injurious organic material and cause dust storms, as dried areas of Texcoco were prone to do.[63] Also at issue was Noriega's profit seeking at the potential expense of the public good. "As a partisan of lake drainage," Espinosa declared, "I see a danger in the way the Noriega brothers wish to carry it out. They undoubtedly submit everything to their own interests: they want above all else lands to exploit and for that [goal] sacrifice the idea of utilizing all the water of Mexico."[64] These doubts, in the end, did not kill the project. The commission concluded that the drainage of Chalco would be a boon as long as the desiccated fields were covered with crops or other vegetation to curtail dust storms and the water was correctly canalized toward Mexico City for the flushing of the city's new sewer system.[65]

The committee's findings that neither rainfall nor humidity nor health would be negatively affected by Chalco's drainage were transferred to Lake Texcoco, where construction of the Gran Canal neared completion. Scientists meticulously collected data, including soil analyses and minute calculations of rainfall and evaporation rates, that provided support for the gradual desiccation of the Basin of Mexico.[66] Yet nowhere in the troves of data was there even an inkling that scientists recognized communal uses of the lakebed.

Indeed, the entire sanitary endeavor was inextricable from Porfirian capitalism, if not reducible to it. Noriega, for example, proceeded to hire Gayol to engineer Chalco's drainage, and Gayol tailored the drainage canal so that the spring water that once sustained a dynamic lakeshore communal economy could be employed sporadically to rinse urban wastewater down collectors and out of the basin.

Late nineteenth-century sanitary planners discerned the connection between water and human health (the health of urban populations particularly), and they saw that this connection extended beyond water to include vegetation and soil. In 1884 Peñafiel proposed reforesting the basin, since "as the forests of the Valley of Mexico diminish, torrential rains rush down the mountain slopes, leaving destroyed and pulverized rocks in the lake."[67] Gayol, Marroquín y Rivera, Beltrán y Puga, and others embraced this vision of forests as well, precisely because deforestation could threaten their hydraulic projects. These urban experts accepted a series of strict, supposedly infallible, relationships among forests, water, rainfall, soil, and proper land use. Forests protected the important springs of the basin, which supplied water to the capital; they reduced flooding by fixing soil and absorbing the water from torrential downpours; and they tempered the harsh climate by bringing rainfall and lowering the dust counts. Mexican forest conservation arose from planners' desire to preserve water and harmonize the hydrological system.[68]

Quevedo made conservation his signature issue and brought deforestation into the spotlight. Following his European training, Quevedo worked on the desagüe and constructed a series of hydroelectric dams, both of which cemented his conservationist beliefs. He argued that the great civilizations of the Middle East, Rome, and Greece foundered amid the desertification of their lands, while the North Atlantic states currently flourished under a conservation ethic and a damper climate. Mexico—"salubrious, beautiful, comfortable, and immensely rich in natural resources" (a deeply rooted cultural assumption upheld by Mexicans since the Bourbon era)—would be converted, Quevedo feared, "into an insalubrious, sad, and unpleasant country impoverished of its natural elements."[69] He referred to deforestation as a "cataclysm" to which "there can be no comparable evil."[70] For Quevedo, forests governed a greater natural system, which in turn laid the foundation for civilization; in Mexico that civilization was centered in the basin. He faced a near-Sisyphean struggle to insert forest conservation within Mexico's policy-making spheres, but by the end of Díaz's rule in 1910, Quevedo headed the nation's first Forestry Department, ran an expansive tree nursery in the town of Coyoacán, and had set up the nation's first forestry school, impressing the chief of the U.S. Forest Service, Gifford Pinchot, upon his visit in 1909 and earning him the nickname "the apostle of the tree."[71]

Debates over the transformation of the Basin of Mexico were anchored in the shared urban environmental imaginary. Urban experts agreed that Mexico City was sick, that the study of the Basin of Mexico held the keys to rehabilitating the city, and that nature was interdependent and interactive with the city. Gayol tended to espouse the conquest face of the sanitarian coin, asserting that the application of science would "resolve the material difficulties with which humanity has to struggle" by conquering "physical obstacles."[72] The sick and untamed city, if not subjected to technological fixes and sound sanitary policy, "would not only not progress, it would deteriorate."[73] Once nature was controlled and harnessed, the cultivator's side of the coin could come into play, and experts like Quevedo could guide and cultivate nature to protect the city. Through a combination of subjugation, control, channeling (both literal and figurative), and cultivation of nonhuman nature, Mexico's capital would prosper under expert guidance. At the heart of the environmental imaginary was a belief that modernity would make humans the protagonists of history. Despite urbanists' proto-ecological understanding of interconnections and the reactive character of their interventions in the metropolitan environment, they adhered to an overriding conviction that nonhuman nature could be, if not rendered passive, at the very least muffled and directed. This perception proved to be severely flawed.

LIVELY NATURE

The first hints that modern engineering in the Basin of Mexico might not "conquer all physical obstacles" appeared during the construction of the hydraulic works, as abstract blueprints came up against the force of material nature. Nature is not a blank slate on which humans write their own story; it is "vibrant" or lively in unexpected ways.[74] Unable to subdue environments to human dictates, sanitary engineers had to modify their plans and wrangle with an active nature entwined with their own designs.

The drainage of the basin posed the most treacherous environmental obstacles. Díaz established a Desagüe Commission in February 1886, on the heels of a major flood that destroyed dozens of buildings in downtown Mexico City; two years later, the municipal government secured a British loan to fund the project. At this point, the project's major hurdles turned environmental in character. The seasoned Francisco de Garay, who had directed the desagüe, lost favor among Mexico's technical elite because his plan, unlike Espinosa's, was prohibitively expensive and was incompatible with designs for the city's sewer system. Espinosa's plan for a smaller canal still demanded massive excavation, and the workers and machinery, operating at the lowest elevations of the Basin of Mexico, were constantly hindered by water and soil. As the Read and Campbell firm, assisted by the junta, completed the tunnel at Tequixquiac, Weetman Pearson commenced his lucrative business foray in Mexico, accepting the contract to dig one of the longest drainage canals the world had seen. The Gran Canal de Desagüe stretched forty-eight kilometers from the gates of San Lázaro at the city's eastern edge to the tunnel's mouth at the northern fringe of the basin and also featured a shorter canal that connected the center of the Texcoco lakebed to the larger canal. Along the canal route, twelve million cubic meters of earth were moved, 60 percent using dredges from the United States and Britain, and the rest by the strength of thousands of workers.[75] Espinosa foresaw roadblocks, but the initial two-year contract signed between Pearson and the junta in 1889 suggests that engineers underestimated them; eight years later Pearson handed the canal over to the government. During those years, workers toiled through a thicket of ecological imbroglios. At the beginning they had to dig down several meters so that water from the underground aquifer would fill the bottom of the ditch, allowing for the operation of the company's dredges. This underground water facilitated excavation, but surface water caused headaches. The canal passed through some of the lowest-lying areas of the basin, and heavy summer rainfall regularly halted excavation. Water seeped through cracks in the walls of the ditch, and streams flooded the excavation site. Removing the water that had been essential for the dredges also proved dangerous, often leading to land subsidence that cracked the ditches or collapsed them altogether.[76] On September 18, 1898, high winds sent Lake Texcoco spilling over the dike engineers had constructed to contain it, and water flowing at over twenty cubic meters per second burst into the canal south toward San Lázaro and north toward the tunnel, carrying along mud that later had to be removed as well.[77] Engineers also fretted that the alkaline water was damaging workers' skin.[78] Even with the advantage of several relatively dry years, water, soil sediment, and subsidence delayed the works as much as, if not more than, technology transfers and contract disputes, premonitions of the larger environmental predicaments to follow.

The multifaceted Xochimilco water system, comprising catchment, carriage, and distribution, was the final major engineering project in the basin and the most expensive. The young architect-engineer Alberto Pani designed three pump houses, adorned with ornate Renaissance motifs, that used the power from Puebla's Necaxa hydroelectric plant to tap Xochimilco's springs. From the pumps the spring water was diverted into a twenty-seven-kilometer-long aqueduct, fully enclosed and made of reinforced concrete—the lionized construction material of the early twentieth century.[79] At the termination of the aqueduct, Marroquín y Rivera devised a large pump house to lift the waters up to the Dolores hill in Chapultepec Park, where the water was stored in four holding tanks and delivered to the city through a web of iron pipes. Marroquín y Rivera and his cadre of engineers—many of whom were students from the National Engineering School—grappled with the drying terrain of the old lakebed that the aqueduct traversed. Land subsidence in the former marshlands caused the concrete aqueduct to crack and stressed its joints. In fact, Marroquín y Rivera was the first to assert that the drainage of the basin triggered subsidence, which caused structures to sink and settle unevenly.[80] He defended the drainage paradigm, but future engineers would later build on this piece of evidence to inveigh against it. Within several months the engineer had resolved the problem, at least temporarily, by placing pilings under the aqueduct.

In the short run, engineers were able to surmount the physical obstacles Gayol had warned about, and this was enough for the city's leading boosters to commemorate Mexico City's new networked infrastructure. Díaz felt a special affinity for the desagüe, and he personally inaugurated the system on March 17, 1900. In the presence of engineers, ministers, and foreign dignitaries, Díaz proclaimed the end of inundations and called the project "the maximum achievement of his government" and one of the "greatest that modern man has been able to carry out."[81] Jesús Galindo y Villa stated that "as long as the grand work was not executed, the city could not prosper, more still its very existence was seriously threatened," and Luis González Obregón predicted the works would place Mexico City among the most pleasant capitals in the American republics for its beauty, health, and climate.[82] Federal District governor Pablo Escandón lauded the civilizing accomplishments of the Díaz regime, telling the Englishwoman Rosa King, "You cannot understand what barbarians we used to be . . . with Lake Texcoco lapping at our ankles in the rainy season."[83] Galindo y Villa extolled Gayol's new sewer system, remarking that the hygiene and health of the population depended on it, while Liceaga panegyrically declared that it would elevate Mexico City "almost to the level of the most healthful cities in the world."[84] Modern sanitary infrastructure lent itself to triumphalist narratives, for it strengthened the nation's claim to an urban capitalist modernity of linear progress.[85]

All grandiloquence aside, sanitary projects such as the desagüe, sewerage, and water supply were mere temporary fixes that brought on long-term problems owing to the interactions of this infrastructure with lively nature. Subsiding land multiplied the strength of the periodic earthquakes. Together with the sinking soil—also caused by increased use of artesian wells—these tremors ruptured pipes and eventually the main aqueduct. The sewer system expelled the microbe-laden waste that lurked above and below ground but over time land subsidence reduced the incline of gravity-reliant pipes and collectors, renewing the problem Gayol had set out to rectify. Moreover, maintenance of the system required using the Canal Nacional's waters to cleanse the pipes of sediment and waste during the dry season, but lake drainage meant less water flowed through the canal, upending this important function. The desagüe was hardly more efficient than its colonial forebear. Rainwater found new ways to inundate streets, homes, and shops. Water spilled over streambeds and overburdened collectors. Parts of the city flooded in 1900, just months after the inauguration of the canal, and again in 1901.[86] While not reaching the scale of some of the mammoth floods of the previous century, the continued flooding and persistent high mortality rates belied the rhetorical flourishes of public officials, who were mocked by *El Hijo del Ahuizote* and *El Diario del Hogar*, newspapers critical of Díaz.[87] In 1910 supporters of Díaz's political opponent, Francisco Madero, used the city's enduring insalubrity as fodder for their rebuke of the regime.[88]

After just a few decades, a series of unforeseen circumstances encumbered the desagüe. First, engineers had not accounted for the magnitude of urban growth during the first half of the twentieth century. Espinosa's canal design allowed for 17.5 cubic meters of wastewater flow, but new subdivisions with paved streets and sewer connections stressed the system by augmenting the surface area in need of drainage. This became an object of contention decades after the desagüe's completion. Francisco de Garay had put forward a canal design that would have allowed for twice the potential current that Espinosa's design did, a point Adrián de Garay, the son of the eminent engineer, belabored to defend his father's legacy.[89] Second, the sedimentation of the Gran Canal required constant dredging, but succeeding governments disregarded this task. Third, and most important, the underground collectors sent rainwater into the desagüe, which expelled it out of the basin, hastening Texcoco's desiccation. Between 1878 and 1906, according to one study, the lake lost two-thirds of its surface area.[90] Cracked, alkaline soil prone to being swept up by strong spring winds lay in its place, worsening the dust storms first observed in the sixteenth century.[91]

Sanitary engineers induced a series of ecological changes that plagued the city. Attempts to command, or temper the effects of, an unruly environment failed. Rather, the networked infrastructure implicated the water, trees, and soil in a set of interactions, interdependencies, and unforeseen consequences. And environmental consequences were at once social consequences.

HIERARCHIES OF THE SANITARY CITY

The use of nature—water, trees, soil, and even animals—was subjected to the mandates of the sanitary elite. Environmental planners, employed and emboldened by government committees and departments, enhanced inequalities throughout the urban fabric, in hinterland spaces transformed by engineering and regulation and within the city where urban infrastructure was deployed.

As noted earlier, the science of forestry as practiced by Quevedo and others was undergirded by deep-seated racism, as were other aspects of the urban environmental imaginary. From Peñafiel to Marroquín y Rivera, sanitary engineers derided indigenous means of subsistence, particularly those that revolved around nonagricultural uses of waterscapes. They labeled bathing and laundering in springs and canals antihygienic. Fishing, hunting, and tequesquite extraction were seen as primitive vestiges of the Mexican past.[92] Mexico's premier biologist, Alfonso Herrera, counted as a rare exception to those who underappreciated or simply ignored lake-centered economies, but even he sought to modernize indigenous practices. Herrera urged that the ducks and geese of Lake Texcoco be commodified by "enterprising peoples" and sold not only in Mexico but abroad as well.[93] Although he admitted the value of hunting to the basin's economy, he deplored the "men and women seen plucking the ducks, leaving behind a trail of abandoned feathers," as they brought poultry to market.[94] In a similar vein, Porfirian booster Rafael de Zayas Enríquez described indigenous agricultural practices as "brutish" and promoted, as was fashionable for the day, colonization by white Europeans.[95] The Porfirian scientific elite embraced rational and capitalistic uses of nature and condemned indigenous practices that in their view squandered resources.

FIGURE 1.2 — Chinampa farming on the edge of a Xochimilco canal. COURTESY OF
INSTITUTO NACIONAL DE ANTROPOLOGÍA Y HISTORIA FOTOTECA NACIONAL.

The fates of Lake Xochimilco and the mostly drained Lakes Chalco and
Texcoco underscored the nuanced ethnic and class politics of urban sanitation.
Hydraulic engineers, representing both capitalist agriculture and the interests
of urban health and property, moved to control and transform lacustrine environments, but Lake Xochimilco was a unique space. Its many freshwater
springs held promise as a source of city water, as well as sustaining the indigenous agricultural practice of chinampería (see figure 1.2).[96] The advent of
indigenismo, the celebration of past indigeneity in the building of the modern
Mexican nation, bolstered the positive meaning of this lake at the turn of the
century. The lake environment was a metonym of indigeneity; the unique-
ness of the chinampa represented the commendable traits of Mexico's past,
even if it was not a practice to be emulated in the present. Sanitary planning both constituted and was constituted by intersecting ethnic and class
relationships.[97]

The urban poor did not escape the racial gaze. In spite of common perceptions that urbanization wrought *mestizaje*, Porfirian criminologists saw the
skulking, iniquitous urban Indian as a menace to virtuous city life.[98] However,

environmental hierarchies within the city were articulated more through class than race. The health inspectors of Liceaga's Superior Health Council conducted yearly inspections of each district, and these visits both revealed the sanitary conditions of streets and neighborhoods and betrayed elites' own preconceptions of the lower classes' filth. Doctor and sanitary inspector J. R. de Arellano noted the scarcity of both water and drainage, "the two highest ideals of hygiene," in a working-class neighborhood.[99] But Arellano, unaware of any contradiction, bewailed residents' lack of cleanliness, "the true domestic virtue," and blamed them for their wretched condition.[100] Marroquín y Rivera was equally oblivious to the contradictions within his depictions of the urban lower class. He claimed that the poor "employ water only in the smallest quantity" yet in the same breath argued that they wasted it and needed to be inculcated with a conservation ethic that nations such as France already possessed.[101] In most instances, the affluent of the growing west side were the profligate water users, sending dirty wastewater toward lower-lying working-class neighborhoods.

Culture and class were imbricated in one another. Quevedo, the perspicacious planner who so often captured the dilemmas facing the expanding city, remarked, "We are very capable of forming model regulations yet very deficient or neglectful at carrying them out."[102] Regulations were not the problem; enforcement was. What caused lax implementation of existing laws in the city's booming suburbs? Without question, much of the difficulty stemmed from the political economy of urbanization: government regulators could not act independently of developers such as Pablo Macedo, Oscar Braniff, and Remigio Noriega—a close-knit group that held the reins of national power.[103] But also inscribed on this canvas of political power were experts' presuppositions that the poor were innately dirty and unhealthy, a belief that permitted the governing elite to emphasize lack of private hygiene over public hygiene and frame the problem as one of personal cleanliness rather than infrastructure and regulations.

The hierarchy of the sanitary city was established by specific state interventions as well. The Gran Canal endangered lakeshore communities' means of subsistence by separating villagers from lands used for farming, grazing, hunting, fishing, and salt extraction. The canal severed the residents of Santiago Atzacoalco from the lands where they extracted tequesquite.[104] The villagers of San Juan de Aragón felt "besieged" by the canal when their poorly constructed bridge collapsed, and other pueblos yearned for bridges to connect their homes to lands of economic value.[105] The lake's saline waters had given the separated lands much of their value. Villagers hunted ducks and geese on the expansive rainy-season waterscape, and dry-season evaporation brought tequesquite to the surface. Following Espinosa's drainage, these uses waned. Governing elites were largely unconcerned: while they rarely applauded desiccation, they feared excessive water much more; to them, water constituted a threat to the city rather than a resource that underpinned a rich ecology of community subsistence.

The Xochimilco waterworks marked a definitive moment of change for area residents. Urban experts saw in Xochimilco's abundant springs a rich source of tap water, but the springs sustained a larger aquatic environment that in turn sustained Xochimilcans' livelihoods. Thousands of chinamperos cultivated vegetables, maize, peppers, and flowers amid a labyrinthine network of canals, nourished by the springs, that both gave life to their crops and served as a means of transport to markets. It was a place of affective ties, where waterscapes and the economy reinforced each other.

As the lake diminished over the years, land-based hacienda agriculture moved in. In 1910 Díaz's doctor, Aureliano Urrutia, whose properties extended throughout Xochimilco and included a castle with its own boat dock, seized San Gregorio Atlapulco's marsh—once part of the lake—when finance minister José Limantour used federal powers over the wetland to favor the landowner.[106] Nonetheless, as long as the lake and the vast network of canals persisted, chinampería would prevail, as would the social relations that accompanied it. Chinampas tended to be small, and land tenure not grossly concentrated.[107] This is not to say that community land conflicts did not exist, but the smallholding pattern unified rural people around the unique farming practice.[108]

The Xochimilco water project was roughly equivalent to the contemporaneous Owens Valley appropriations made by William Mulholland and the muscular Los Angeles Department of Water and Power. Construction of the system altered the densely populated lacustrine space. To be sure, Mexico City did require a new water supply, but other ideas to improve the service, such as capturing and storing rainwater, were not given serious consideration. Federal expropriations dispossessed pueblos and ranchos of hundreds of hectares of land around the new catchment system. Marroquín y Rivera and his water board forbade access to the springs and their surroundings, even though communities such as San Gregorio Atlapulco, Xochimilco, and Santa María Nativitas used the springs for drinking water and laundry. Cattle grazing and manure storage galled hydraulic engineers, and the water board erected fences to keep out animals and nearby villagers.[109] Like the Gran Canal, the aqueduct cut off locals from their chinampas and grazing lands, directing villagers toward a new way of interacting with hinterland nature under the grip of urbanization.[110]

Marroquín y Rivera explained that the system's intake would not threaten "third-party" uses, but he also recognized that any quantity above 2,100 liters per second would reduce canal levels.[111] This extraction rate would not be reached until the 1930s; nonetheless, for many Xochimilcans, the mere existence of the waterworks constituted dispossession of land and water.

Efforts to control water—expelling the bad and extracting the good—fostered forest conservation around Mexico's largest city, as woodlands were viewed as essential safeguards for this new infrastructure. Conservationists enmeshed villages from Cuajimalpa, near the Santa Fe springs, to Milpa Alta and Amecameca, on the foothills of the Popocatépetl and Iztaccíhuatl volcanoes, in a different instantiation of the sanitary city: forestry regulations. The Federal District Forestry Bureau, founded by Quevedo in 1901 with the help of Beltrán y Puga, was converted in December 1909 into Mexico's first Forestry Department, under the Ministry of Fomento.[112] The department held jurisdiction over all of the valuable woodlands located in the southern half of the Federal District, except for those in Santa Fe and Desierto de los Leones, and immediately began to exercise authority over its forests.[113] Satisfactory regulation depended on detailed knowledge, and the department labored to assemble the country's first forest inventory. The confined scope of the new department largely limited the survey to the Federal District, where foresters estimated that 37,984 hectares were wooded out of a total formerly "forested area" of 106,392 hectares. Since the study was not diachronic, however, officials did not specify in what period this area had been forested, nor did it track depletion over the course of the Porfiriato.[114] Nonetheless, the mere suggestion of widespread deforestation was the kind of knowledge that provided the department's raison d'être. By the end of 1910, the Forestry Department oversaw concessions for forest exploitation on public and private lands in the Federal District, and was responsible for assessing the potential damage to woodlands as well as adjudicating requests. In order to surveil extraction in the southern portions of the basin, the department hired several guards for each of seven designated forest zones.

As Quevedo and others gave force to state-backed conservationism, industry and landowners put pressure on community woods. Paper mills such as Loreto and Peña Pobre and textile factories such as La Magdalena and

Santa Teresa exploited community woodlands illicitly. Haciendas, moreover, charged steep fees for access to their forested land.[115] Campesinos dealt with exploitative middlemen who monopolized transportation to market. On the vertiginous slopes of the Ajusco, broom root (*la raíz de zacatón*), used to feed cattle and to make the brooms and brushes coveted during this age of hygiene, reigned. The root of the thick zacatón grass was extracted with a lever and shovel, then prepared and sold at rock-bottom prices to landowner Casto de la Fuente y Parres, who used his monopoly to sell it in the capital and export it to the United States or Europe.[116]

Villagers along the southern rim of the basin stood between the Scylla of official forestry and the Charybdis of hinterland capitalism. And these two creatures of the urban sea were in cahoots. According to forestry experts, only the economic elite could carry out "scientific exploitation" with "a conservationist ethic." Indigenous peasants, they assumed, were less amenable to such an ethic and consequently could not be entrusted with Mexico's forests. Quevedo condemned some industries, but he saved much of his derision for peasants, bemoaning indigenous villagers who "wish to extend their cultivated land to the steepest peaks of our mountain ranges, an important cause of the great ruin of our forests and hydrological poverty."[117] He also attacked overzealous firewood extraction and charcoal and turpentine production, in which villagers supposedly cut wood wantonly.[118]

While Quevedo and other foresters much preferred rationalized capitalist uses of woodlands, the woodlands south of Mexico City were so cherished that even foreign capitalists were denied concessions. In 1904 Americans Henry and Harry Hampson intended to carry out the "scientific" and "methodical" exploitation of the communal lands of Milpa Alta. Their employment of locals (all Nahaua speakers), combined with the construction of a branch rail connecting the lands to Mexico City, would eradicate the "isolation and poverty in which today they [the villagers] live."[119] Even so, Beltrán y Puga's assessment, which denounced the plan as "extraordinarily dangerous to the springs of Xochimilco," carried more weight.[120]

Above all, the Forestry Department focused its attention on squelching community uses of woodland resources. Starting in 1909, campesinos, who until then had freely exploited their woodlands, needed permission. Guards fined and sometimes imprisoned villagers who toppled trees without a permit.[121] The most striking example of restricting peasant livelihoods was the ban on zacatón root extraction along the southern slopes, issued in 1910. The department saw in this thick grass a crucial stabilizing element of the basin's forests; "without this vegetation," they said, "[the lands] are degraded and washed out by waters, becoming improper . . . for the regeneration of wood-lands."[122] Many disobeyed official orders, and illegal exploitation proliferated given the dearth of guards. The Forestry Department asked to have the infamous Rurales (Díaz's mounted police force) assist the department, and officials boasted that the ban had allowed zacatón to regenerate.[123] Local ecology crashed against local economy in early forestry policies.

Over the span of several decades, Mexican conservation had gone from a heterogeneous set of principles espoused by a core of scientists and planners to official policy. Quevedo's urban vision entangled forestlands with the urban fabric at the same time that industry strove to meet urban demands. Elites like Quevedo maintained that the forests of the basin had more value to the inhabitants of Mexico City and its growth engine than to the campesinos who lived off them.

If the production of the sanitary city enmeshed hinterland communities in a series of transformative projects and regulations, the same forces entangled urban communities in the politics of consuming services. On the surface, the Xochimilco system was a great engineering accomplishment in the public good.[124] Marroquín y Rivera boasted in 1914 that almost twelve thousand of the nearly fourteen thousand residences of the city had obtained connections, and claimed the only areas lacking service were La Bolsa and a few streets in Indianilla (later called Doctores).[125] His claim of near-universal coverage was misleading, however, as he had used fallacious census data from the Municipal Tax Office in his calculations. The tax office excluded large swaths of unauthorized urban settlements like La Bolsa and El Cuartelito (also known as Obrera), as residents in these *colonias* (subdivisions) were neither taxed nor eligible for municipal services. According to census data from 1900, the city numbered 369,000 people and contained 14,577 shacks and homes.[126] By 1914, the year Marroquín y Rivera wrote his report, the city's population had swelled to over 500,000. Some of these new arrivals were refugees of revolution who crammed into existing rooms, but the overall number of residences had undoubtedly increased since 1900, meaning that the Xochimilco system likely supplied no more than 75 percent of residential buildings. Further, the spatial inequalities of urbanization ensured that less than 75 percent of the city's residents enjoyed access to Xochimilco water. The first three districts, located primarily in the eastern part of Mexico City where the system's coverage was limited, abounded with tenement buildings (vecindades), where as many as twenty people would squeeze into a room and split the rent. As a result, the population density of these districts was nearly double that of the Seventh and Eighth Districts, two of the wealthier areas located to the west, and water access was far more limited.

The connection process itself was beset with problems as authorities confronted the landlords' private domain. Lenient government regulations prevented many tenants from receiving safe and ample drinking water. Marroquín y Rivera's water board, charged with overseeing the process, employed permissive language such as "when it is convenient," "if desired," or "can be done" when referring to important works not mandated by authorities.[127] Most of these voluntary works involved updating or removing the ubiquitous open-air water tanks (*tinacos*), which engineers and the Superior Health Council deemed unhygienic. Yet officials gave in so that "landlords would not have to allocate important expenses."[128] Nor were tenement owners responsible for installing taps in each apartment or for building bathrooms. Some tenement owners resisted supplying residents with even the barest essentials; for instance, Manuel Campuzano would shut off the water to his tenement, opening it once every thirty days, despite "pleas and threats" from residents.[129] Hobbled by municipal leniency and landed property interests, the new system fell short of providing public hygiene to every resident.

Urban property owners also stymied efforts to order the rapid expansion of the capital, which was swept up in what one municipal publication described as "a fever of subdivision construction."[130] The proliferation of codes and urban regulations beginning in 1875—including the first sanitary code of 1891—had little influence on urban growth and sanitary conditions in new developments. Subdivision construction continued apace regardless of whether they had official approval or public services. Starting in 1899, Quevedo began promoting restraint. During a short stint on the municipal Public Works Commission, he issued a warning to the developers of the unauthorized colonia Obrera that they must install services to comply with the sanitary code. Realizing the improbability that they would take heed, Quevedo proceeded to post broadsides in the unauthorized subdivision, disavowing the city's obligation to provide residents with sewerage and drinking water.[131] This action was of doubtful advantage. It denounced irregular growth propelled by profit-hungry developers but gutted public responsibility for forlorn neighborhoods. The effect was to delimit two urban zones: one legal and hygienic, the other illegal with few prospects for improvement.

After 1903, the year Díaz demoted the municipal governments (Ayuntamientos) within the Federal District to a mere advisory board for the Federal

District government, officials continued to rubber-stamp capitalist urbanization: land speculation, the predominance of middle-class housing tracts, and the sanitation of subdivisions only when it was convenient to developers. The year 1906 saw a series of challenges to unequal urbanization, most of which were ultimately foiled. A proposal for what would have been Mexico's first state-sponsored affordable housing initiative was eventually dismantled.[132] The omnipresent Quevedo enjoyed some success beautifying the city with lustrous new park space after attending conferences in Paris and Berlin that emphasized urban greenery, but his efforts to rein in speculation faltered.[133] Quevedo despaired over plans for another subdivision called Campestre del Valle and poignantly revealed the irrationality of growth:

> It is unfortunate that some intend to devote such considerable tracts of land when one observes that, whether in rich colonias, like those of Roma, Condesa, Cuauhtemoc and others . . . , or in more modest or poor colonias like Hidalgo, Santa Julia, La Bolsa, Morelos, El Peñon, Viga . . . etc., there is extensive unpopulated space, often with residences at great distances from each other. Most of these areas lack sanitary works. . . . In spite of all this, it is not understood why it is the goal of businessmen and capitalists to speculate in the creation of new colonias that population growth does not require instead of employing capital in the urbanization or construction of already existing colonias.[134]

Mexico City's surface area expanded at a rate greater than its population, fostering overcrowding in the center and irregular, dispersed settlement on the edges. Much as they had with the del Valle subdivision, in 1913 the government approved the colonia Aragón, raised on the hacienda of the same name by Remigio Noriega, who was deemed a "strong and capable capitalist."[135] Urbanization, led by "capable capitalists," hampered later efforts to bring sanitary services and housing to the growing population.

The Porfirian sanitary planners implicated the diverse inhabitants and spaces of the Basin of Mexico within the metropolitan environment. They imposed new power relations, established new restrictive property lines and resource regulations, and aggravated inequalities. They prioritized uses of the environment that advantaged the perceived needs of a city in the thick of a real estate boom and marginalized hinterland communities in the path of urban sanitation. However, because of elite cultural norms and the capitalist logic of urbanization, urban residents did not share equally in the eulogized projects and policies of the Porfirian elite.

Up to now I have foregrounded the domination apparent in the Porfirian quest for the sanitary city. But it also constructed a "common material and meaningful framework"—federal property markers, physical infrastructures, and a set of representations and laws governing hygiene—within which people in the basin could contest, negotiate, and act within relations of domination.[136] The technical and regulatory solutions of positivist elites could neither dominate nature nor enclose expertise in some depoliticized realm.

Residents of Mexico City witnessed, on a daily basis, the sanitary revolution in the making, and most were uneasily positioned between pitiful living conditions and the hope of improvement. Between 1875 and 1912, the city government created a set of ideals, regulations, and codes on which urban residents would subsequently draw to demand the fulfillment of the sanitary city on their streets and in their homes. Integral to this framework was the notion that the government bore the responsibility to intervene in private matters for the public interest. It was this governing principle shared by municipal officials and urban experts that so many denizens appropriated as their own.

As new sewage and water-supply systems raised expectations of what constituted a decent standard of living in turn-of-the-century Mexico City, the seemingly mundane task of sewer construction morphed into a highly fraught practice. Residents were active participants in making the sewer system serve them. A chorus of voices rose against the malfeasance or neglect of the French contractors Letlier and Vezin. Residents complained of breaches in the contract: flooded streets and homes due to poorly placed or obstructed sewers and the absence of requisite domestic connections.[137] Many of these cases (especially those involving little cost) were resolved by the company, resulting in improved service. By demanding that infrastructure serve their needs, city inhabitants participated in engineers' purportedly exclusive domain of environmental transformation.

Not everyone who raised their voice saw their demands met. A major collector ran straight through La Bolsa, but without connecting lines or street sewers. In response to neighbors' bewildered petitions, Gayol vaguely responded that they should derive hope from the mere fact a collector had been constructed so close. This must have sounded like supercilious rhetoric to residents who witnessed waters "invading the interiors of many rooms" and who feared illness would be "quick to take hold" and spread across the city from a colonia they called "the poorest and thus the most worthy of connection [to the system]."[138] Other working-class inhabitants also hoped to hold sanitary officials accountable. On the eve of the revolution, residents of Santa Julia protested a recently opened mill that spilled fecal matter and other waste into an open canal adjacent to their homes.[139] They clamored for various other urban improvements as well, arguing that these were justified by their "good morals." In these arguments, residents invoked the trope of lurking disease, the specter of the miasma, and the moral force of humble and decent citizens in need of public assistance to force officials to obey the government's own public health discourses and codes.[140] They challenged the reproduction of sanitary inequalities, although their raised expectations were quickly tempered by inaction.

In hinterland communities the new discursive and material framework appeared more as imposition than opportunity. Villagers were on the outside looking in at urban sanitation, but they too negotiated environmental change before 1910. Several communities successfully petitioned for the construction of bridges over the Gran Canal to link their homes to productive land; others demanded the better channeling of rivers to curtail flooding; and the water board found it expedient to provision Xochimilcan communities with washbasins and public fountains supplied by the area's springs. These negotiations foreshadowed a revolutionary future in which the definition of public interest evolved to include not only elite urban interests but also those of poor villagers, forest users, and peasant farmers.

CONCLUSION

A bevy of scientists and engineers were involved in the transformation of Mexico City and the establishment of a new set of ecological and social relationships between urban and hinterland space. Their vision of the sanitary city required the cooperation of nature, an understanding partially reflected in Quevedo's forestry. Yet nature rarely cooperated. Erosion led to the sedimentation of lakebeds and riverbeds, worsening flooding; salts accumulated in the drying Texcoco lakebed, stifling plant growth and causing dust storms; land subsidence cracked infrastructure and buildings; and torrential rainfall led to frequent flash floods. In other words, through its canals, sewers, aqueducts, and collectors, the city became ever more deeply dependent on and interconnected with the soil, the trees and plants, the rain, and the flow of water.[141] Rather than receding, nonhuman nature became ever more integral to the city as it grew. Urban experts created a new metropolitan environment of networked infrastructures extending into the lacustrine hinterland and of regulations on health, woodlands, and urbanizing spaces.

This new environment was profoundly politicized. Into history's waste bin went much of the mid-nineteenth-century symbiosis between city and hinterland, replaced by a series of sanitary planning initiatives that simultaneously reaffirmed urban hierarchies and provided new opportunities for environmental struggle. State authority was a double-edged sword that cut across urban and rural spaces. The network of sanitary infrastructure and policies created during the Porfiriato placed Mexico City on a track of urbanization in which government-directed water and forests would serve elite urban interests and powerful economic actors first and foremost. But after 1910, when state interest shifted toward revolutionary justice, government authority over the metropolitan environment became a vehicle for a new kind of social and environmental transformation.

2

Revolution and the

Metropolitan Environment

The economic and political system that revolved around the Weetman Pearsons, the Noriegas, and the Braniffs of the world fractured the nation. Working conditions deteriorated, land and resource dispossession accelerated, and cliquish, nepotistic politics and boss rule (*caciquismo*) excluded wide swaths of the population from local, state, and federal decision making. Brutal strike repression, drought on the central Mexican plateau, and an economic downturn led to mounting dissatisfaction with the regime of Porfirio Díaz. Discontent coalesced around Francisco Madero, the scion of a Coahuilan landowning family (and a spiritualist who believed he was a medium). The liberal Madero rejected Díaz's repeated fraudulent reelections and helped establish the Antireelectionist Party to challenge the old dictator on the ballot in 1910. Díaz squashed Madero's vigorous presidential bid and had the candidate arrested just weeks before the election. Madero skipped bail and slipped across the border at Laredo on October 7, 1910, where he drafted his call to revolution: the Plan of San Luis Potosí.

Less than a year later, on June 7, 1911, urban denizens restlessly awaited the arrival of the triumphant Madero, who had knit together a loose alliance of the disaffected middle class, disgruntled peasants, and rural and urban workers. These forces defeated the federal army in several key battles in northern Mexico, prompting Díaz to renounce the presidency and flee to France on the ss *Ypiranga*. When a strong earthquake shook Mexico City in the early morning on June 11, the jubilation over Madero's imminent arrival turned to dread of collapsing buildings, crumbling walls, and shattered windows. For most of the city's population, danger dissipated and effervescence returned once the shaking subsided; some 200,000 people lined the streets to catch a glimpse of "the apostle of democracy" that afternoon. But the day was tragic for others. Several poorly constructed homes and buildings failed to withstand the quake. Over a dozen people died in the wreckage, and an untold number lost their homes and possessions.[1] Unequal urban development had placed the city's poor at greatest risk not only from floods and disease but also from the tremors that regularly shook the basin. Madero's supporters claimed the quake was a sign of God's favor and a symbol of the momentous day— hence the saying "El día que Madero llegó hasta la tierra tembló" (the day Madero arrived, even the earth trembled)—while his opponents saw it as an omen of darker times ahead.[2] The earthquake marked one of many instances in which revolution and nature intertwined in the Basin of Mexico.

Most elite Maderistas were modest political reformers, pushing for the enforcement of the liberal Constitution of 1857 but recoiling from the kind of substantive labor and land reform that energized the Maderista rank and file. Díaz purportedly remarked upon his departure, "Madero has unleashed a tiger; let's see if he can tame it." The answer was a definite "no," and revolutionary upheaval dragged on for most of the decade. The revolution crippled Porfirian growth, partially disempowered urban elites, and released a centrifugal force in which rural peoples questioned the hegemony of the capital. As state power over material environments waxed and waned, new political and discursive practices about social rights challenged state rule over the metropolitan environment. Urban environmental governance—the development and maintenance of physical infrastructure and regulations concerning food, forests, and other resources—molded how people lived through and participated in the revolution.

The Mexican Revolution created a social and political conjuncture in which succeeding federal governments—whether revolutionary or reactionary— sought to assert their authority through the control of the metropolitan environment and chaotic urban spaces. Power over the material environment translated into power over the people who sought to use those environments and, in the minds of officials, legitimized the otherwise-flagging government authority. This is what authorities tend to do in times of crisis, and the impulse is stronger in more ardently utopian revolutionary projects. Mao Tse-tung's remaking of Beijing's city center to erase tradition and conform the city to a new revolutionary design is but one instance.[3]

State power in Mexico, however, also had to adapt to the popular rebellion. Diverse rural peoples of the basin demanded a set of rights to establish common access to resources such as woods, water, and arable land, rights that would later be inscribed in the Constitution of 1917. Urban popular classes insisted on the right to food, fuel, and clean streets, and their fragmented, diffuse, and ephemeral protests would mold future struggles over sanitary services and affordable housing. The intersection of government authority and this popular groundswell for environmental rights defined postrevolutionary disputes over the metropolitan environment and the direction of urban growth. The revolution forged a new frame of governance over the metropolitan environment, albeit within a reestablished elite urban hegemony. Popular groups came to expect certain environmental rights within the urbanizing basin at the same time that postrevolutionary officials, emboldened by new constitutional authority over land and waters, made a commitment to govern in more democratic and egalitarian ways. Historian Ted Steinberg's contention that "the transformation of the natural world . . . is yet another venue for exploring the history of power" does not apply solely to a history of oppression.[4] This history of power contains a more open and bottom-up dimension in which environmental rights are created, challenged, and redefined according to the ebbs and flows of social contention.

THE MADERO YEARS

Madero's entry into Mexico City, welcomed by throngs of cheering people, marked the apex of his political career. The earthquake of the same day indeed portended tumultuous times ahead, a future that not even Madero's sweeping election victory of October 1911 could avoid. Madero had risen to power on the back of a popular rebellion that, while loosely allied with him, ultimately diverged from his staunch liberalism. Madero soon reneged on his promise in the Plan of San Luis Potosí to carry out agrarian reform, and his alliance unraveled. Peasant leader Emiliano Zapata turned his Liberation Army of the South, based in the state of Morelos, against Madero and issued the Plan of Ayala, which called for the immediate redistribution of lands, waters, and woods to communities. In the fall of 1911, Zapata's forces pushed into the Ajusco mountains of the Federal District. The Porfirian press in Mexico City derided Madero's inability to establish territorial control, impugning him as a weak and illegitimate head of state.[5] The triple threat of the Zapatista rebellion, Pascual Orozco's protean rural uprising in the north, and challenges from the old guard forced Madero to address the agrarian question and expand his capacity to control territory. His administration's efforts to repair damaged roads and railroads, add new rail lines, and dredge a port at the mouth of the sediment-clogged Grijalva River were intended, in part, to demonstrate such control.[6] But the Basin of Mexico, the nest of Madero's fledgling administration, became the crucial site for his experiments with a new revolutionary governance of land, water, and woodlands.

Díaz's lionized desagüe had altered the Lake Texcoco problem but did not resolve it. Madero embraced a new generation of hydraulic engineers, enjoining them to turn a wasteland that threatened the city into a boon to urban prosperity, an example of government authority, and a precedent for a new landholding regime. Manuel Urquidi, a longtime ally of Madero, teamed up with the young hydraulic engineer Mariano Barragán, who hatched a plan to reclaim Texcoco lands for agriculture. Barragán asserted that the desagüe had been a halfway measure. Desiccation brought on more frequent dust storms, and deforestation of the surrounding hills tended to increase erosion and thus the sedimentation of the lakebed, which Barragán declared would soon be on a level with Mexico City's downtown streets. Since, at that point, the lakebed would no longer serve as the container for the basin's water, the city's nemesis flooding would return with renewed vengeance. Barragán harnessed the knowledge of lakebed sedimentation dating back to at least Juan de Torquemada to argue that what remained of the meager lake should be channeled into a reservoir and that the desiccated land should be fertilized. This, he maintained, would safeguard the city from flooding and dust storms.[7] His plan garnered support from the Maderista leadership and a host of engineers, for it fused scientific claims, modern engineering's transformative potential to spur agricultural productivity, and the imperative to build the new state.

Díaz had laid the legal and political foundation for this audacious fertilization project. In 1888 he had federalized major bodies of water; in 1902 he had declared all desiccated lands federal property; and he gained incalculable prestige from the construction of the desagüe. This is precisely what Madero and Urquidi, following the observations of Barragán, hoped to replicate. Even if it could not quell discontent from both sides of the political spectrum, at the very least the project would offer a disquieted public something to admire about the besieged government.

While Madero would have preferred that Congress deal with the agrarian problem, Zapatista activity forced him to address the unequal distribution of land. In December 1911, a few weeks after the Plan of Ayala was declared, Madero rededicated the Bank for Irrigation Works and Agriculture, created three years earlier by José Yves Limantour to promote large-scale farming, toward the acquisition of private or national properties for division into parcels of less than three hundred hectares.[8] The president also created the National Agrarian Commission, which included Manuel Marroquín y Rivera and Roberto Gayol, who had advocated state-funded irrigation projects to boost rural production.[9] Gayol and Marroquín y Rivera left their mark on the commission, which emphasized the need for more stringent forest conservation and the rational exploitation of hydraulic resources.[10] Its conclusions on land reform, however, were moderate. The commission licensed the bank to purchase hacienda land and resell it to smallholders.[11] Madero concurred, but since the program relied on the voluntary cooperation of landowners, little land was sold.

All this amounted mainly to political finessing rather than substantive reform.[12] The Texcoco land reclamation, however, was a major undertaking. It embodied the goals of both the bank and the commission and would enable the government, Maderistas hoped, to counter the Zapatista threat. The project promoted the rational use of hydraulic resources to create a class of small farmers in a liminal zone between the capital and Zapatista strongholds—and to do so without undercutting entrenched interests.[13]

Like their Porfirian predecessors, Madero and his engineers imagined the lakebed as a place devoid of ecological obstacles or social importance, a prime laboratory for experimentation. In their vision, a productive, ordered agricultural economy of small landholdings would replace the moribund lake-based economy. Lakeshore villagers were absent from this vision; the Madero administration had no intention of giving away fertilized land. Rather, authorities hoped to sell that land and thereby turn a profit that could help replenish the government coffers. The new agricultural economy would not only rid the city of dust but also liberate it from its dependency on international food markets. Imports of most basic foods had risen steadily during the old regime as the prevailing hacienda system increasingly produced cash crops for the world economy.[14] In 1911 Mexico imported almost 230,000 tons of corn, but in 1912, because of civil strife, that plummeted to 39,000 tons. Beans and wheat followed a similar trajectory. A new era began in which the "Texcoco problem" became an opportunity to transform the swampy, saline lakebed to benefit the city and create a fertile hinterland run by small landowners. In May 1912 Madero and Urquidi toured the lakebed and attended a party in the town of Texcoco to publicize the government's designs.[15] And in a report to Congress, Madero brandished the works as evidence "that the Executive is profoundly preoccupied with the agrarian problem, upon which the economic future of the Republic depends."[16] The future, most Maderistas agreed, rested on minifundias and larger private operations when deemed appropriate, not communal agriculture.

The project was approved by the bank in July 1912, with a budget of nearly 4 million pesos.[17] Madero authorized the Board for Lake Texcoco Improvement Works (Junta de las Obras de Bonificación del Lago de Texcoco), with Barragán as its lead engineer and Urquidi as its president, to perform three tasks: drainage, "washing" to remove salts from the soil, and fertilization. He also instructed Quevedo's Forestry Department to cover parts of the saline bed with vegetation to curtail the dust storms; the Nezahualcóyotl Tree Nursery was inaugurated as part of this effort, and Madero and his vice president, Pino Suárez, attended the opening.[18] The lakebed, measured at 27,000 hectares, was to be totally reengineered so that all river and runoff water flowing into it would be channeled into a reservoir of 4,920 hectares. Barragán planned for much of the remaining salt-caked land, divided into three zones, to be washed using water from artesian wells, streams arriving from the west, and the central reservoir. Engineers would then proceed to fertilize the lands with the sediment-rich waters of the Churubusco River and other streams. At a cost of 300 pesos per hectare, engineers imagined that an agricultural oasis would replace an emerging saline desert.[19] (See map 2.1.)

Workers immediately began constructing the central dike that would separate the reservoir from surrounding fields and prepared much of Zone 1 for washing and irrigation. By early 1913 a small portion of Zone 1 had been divided into five agricultural experimentation plots and two afforestation areas.[20] Halophytes like willows, tamarixes, and eucalyptus, then populating the Americas at an extravagant pace, were planted in the afforestation areas, and the agricultural plots supported radishes, brussels sprouts, lettuce, oats, alfalfa, and barley.[21] Engineers such as Ángel García Lascuraín proclaimed rather hubristically that the project was "based on scientific principles" and

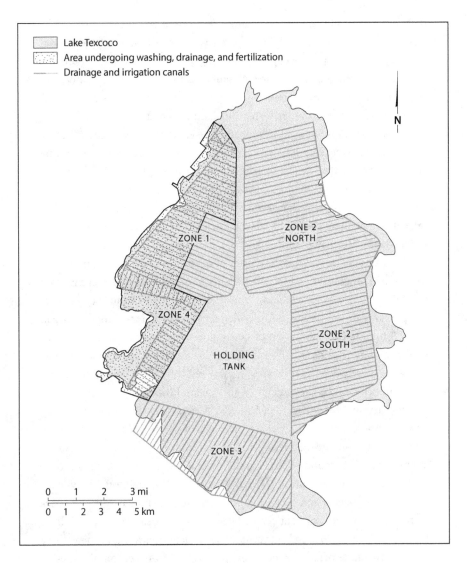

N

ZONE 1

ZONE 2
NORTH

ZONE 4

ZONE 2
SOUTH

HOLDING
TANK

ZONE 3

0   1   2   3 mi

0 1 2 3 4 5 km

MAP 2.1 — Lake Texcoco reclamation. COURTESY OF BILL NELSON.

that "only some element hitherto unknown would make the works fail."[22] García Lascuraín, however, did not specify which scientific principles he was referring to. In fact, project engineers invested little energy in seeking broader knowledge about the reclamation of saline lands. Motivated by rumors of Mormon successes draining and farming the fringes of the Great Salt Lake, one engineer requested reports on saline land reclamation from agricultural experiment stations in Logan, Utah, and Mesilla Park, New Mexico. The archival trail turns up one response, a pamphlet sent by the Utah Agricultural School in Logan that dealt exclusively with cleansing lands of salts deposited by irrigation, not by a geophysical process occurring over millennia.[23] Contemporaneous plans (later successful) to reclaim for farming the shallow saltwater inlet along the Dutch coast known as the Zuiderzee may have gone unnoticed by Mexican officials.

The issue at hand was not simply one of science and technics. To transform the lakebed, engineers had to take ownership of the land and prevent other uses of it. By law, lands resulting from the desiccation of the lakebed were the property of the nation, and the demarcation of federal property began in 1908 to "impede usurpation of newly uncovered lands," an act of enclosure of common lands, which had already been diminished by the desagüe. However, there were few surveyors to carry out the task of demarcation, and communities resisted the attempt to enclose land they had once used freely. In February 1911 the villagers of Santiago Atzacoalco were accused of lying about its borders so that they could make use of desiccated lands.[24] Even the government issued mixed messages about enclosure: despite a decree in 1902 authorizing confiscation of lands under federal jurisdiction, Madero sought to purchase tracts within the lakebed, tacitly acknowledging the previously held titles of pueblos and private landowners. In early 1912, before purchases commenced, the government claimed nearly nine thousand hectares of dried land; a year later, Madero's government had acquired an additional three thousand hectares of swampy fields and pastureland from communities, small landowners, and large haciendas.[25] In the end, the state took control of almost twelve thousand hectares of the lakebed, an area in which locals had once freely fished, hunted, farmed, and herded. Subsequently, communities were compelled to negotiate with the state for access to these lands.

While many lakeshore residents resented federal enclosures, some engineers saw it as an opportunity to further Madero's aim of addressing the agrarian problem around Mexico City. Barragán was keen on justifying the massive public work by recuperating its high cost. Estimating that each reclaimed hectare would have a market value of at least 350 pesos, Barragán calculated that each one sold would yield a profit of some 67 pesos.[26] In addition to the environmental and political benefits of the project, Barragán believed it would create a new class of smallholders on the edge of Mexico's capital. Others had different ideas. The agrarian engineer Santiago González Cordero (who in the years before the oil expropriation of 1938 would proclaim the right of the Mexican nation to conserve its petroleum resources) offered a strikingly different analysis of the necessity of Texcoco reclamation. "In this historical moment," he explained, "in which there is an inexhaustible thirst for land and multitudes of men join the Zapatista ranks each day, the need to complete these interesting works at a rapid pace becomes clear, using the least amount of machinery and the largest number of workers."[27] There was a genuine fear that lakeshore villagers would join the Zapatistas—as indeed some villagers on the eastern and southern shores of the lake had. Many hoped that the project could serve to douse the flames of peasant rebellion, and that this could be done without expropriating influential hacendados such as the Noriega brothers or the heirs of ex-president Manuel González, owners of the revered Chapingo estate. The engineer Luis C. Campoamor agreed with González Cordero and confirmed the government's interest in "possessing a large quantity of lands distributable to the indigenes."[28] As they considered the Zapatista threat to Mexico City, government employees and engineers envisioned different outcomes for the reclaimed lands. Some evoked reformist elements springing from the revolution, arguing that those lands could be used to relieve land pressures in central Mexico that seemed to incite rebellion, or that they could be converted into an improved commons fit for agricultural uses. Others, toeing Madero's line, contended that the land was best suited for small-scale farming under a private-property regime.

Meletino Nava, a forestry expert for the project, combined both perspectives, convinced that Texcoco reclamation heralded social change. In 1916, three years after Madero's death, Nava contended that the works

> would bring public benefits not only for Mexico City . . . but also for the Texcoco district, whose inhabitants, mainly indigenous, . . . have vegetated with the ruinous fishing of the unhealthy animals that the lake produces, an industry that kept them in a state of misery and ignorance. . . . Mr. Madero knew that it was humanitarian work to transform these swampy lands of Lake Texcoco into agricultural lands, converting these hapless fishermen into farmers, and, more important, into landowners, because he was aware

that the fundamental base of civilization is agriculture and forestry, and for a nation to have freedom its children/sons must be owners at least of their homes and the plots they work.[29]

Nava envisioned the project as more than just an affirmation of urban goals. He portrayed Madero as a classic nineteenth-century Mexican liberal, even a kind of Mexican Jefferson: a civilizing leader who hoped to uplift these "hapless fishermen" and lead them to liberty through small-scale production—disregarding the prohibitive land price that Barragán had proposed.

As Zapatistas made advances near Lake Chalco, Lake Xochimilco, and the forests of the Ajusco, Maderista officials scrutinized the land question in these places through a decidedly environmental lens. The young lawyer Luis Cabrera, a fierce critic of Díaz's *científicos* (positivist powerholders) before the outbreak of the revolution in 1910, had befriended the reformer Andrés Molina Enriquez. The two men shared a firm belief in community rights to water and irrigation works as well as land, but while Molina Enriquez insisted on the need for an authoritarian government, Cabrera ran for Congress under the banner of the Renovators, a group of Maderistas with a more reformist agenda.[30] During his campaign to represent the eleventh congressional district, encompassing the southern hinterlands of Mexico City, including Milpa Alta, Coyoacán, San Angel, and Tlalpan, Cabrera propounded his national vision of agrarian reform: redistribution of lands to pueblos. He compared the president's handling of the revolution to the malpractice of a surgeon who refuses to cleanse a wound before closing it. In less metaphorical language, he belittled Madero for straggling during the first, destructive stages of the revolution and for being reluctant to embark on the reconstructive stage where reform would suture the nation back together.[31]

Cabrera's ideas crystallized during his campaign and his term as a member of the Chamber of Deputies. His speech to the legislature titled "The Revolution Is the Revolution" established him as a leading voice within the Maderista camp—even if Madero himself branded his ideas as "very dangerous."[32] Cabrera nonetheless upheld small private landownership: ultimately, he believed communal property to be a bulwark against land concentration and a transitory step toward full private ownership. Thus, he backed the doctor Aureliano Urrutia, decrying "the agitation of some individuals . . . who provoke the people with claims that [Urrutia's] 'enormous estate' of 300 hectares is a threat to the sacred promises proclaimed by the 1910 revolution."[33] According to Cabrera's rather loose definition, Urrutia's property was "small," and Xochimilcans had no right to oppose him even if they had tended their chinampas and fished in the lands and waters he claimed a mere two decades before. Cabrera did not extend the same tolerance to Iñigo Noriega and his larger holdings. Cabrera called for the restoration of community lands usurped by large hacendados, arguing that this was necessary to bring about rural peace and support democracy. Noriega's relentless pursuit of village lands inspired Cabrera's critique, as did Noriega's overt support of the conservative Bernardo Reyes's presidential campaign in 1911.[34] Noriega embodied the caciquismo Cabrera derided. Cabrera groused, "Never to even the most cretinous of Spanish monarchs . . . would it have occurred that a community could live [without lands]; and yet, it was necessary that a Spanish adventurer [Noriega] convince us that the pueblos of Mexico do not need more than the land where their shacks are located."[35] With words like these, Cabrera confronted the Noriega brothers and, obliquely, the urban experts who had approved Chalco's drainage.

Cabrera was equally unwavering in his denunciation of the Forestry Department. In a salvo against exclusive forestry around Mexico City, he wrote, "I know of cases in process against hundreds of individuals for the misdemeanor of cutting firewood in their own forests, and a high employee of Fomento [likely Quevedo] believes that the towns of Milpa Alta, Tlalpan, and San Angel . . . should cease cutting of wood on their own land and behave themselves . . . because the conservation of the forests is necessary for the conservation of the springs that supply Mexico City with water."[36] As an elected official, Cabrera blamed the growth of Zapatista forces on "official injustice" and specifically rebuked the Secretaría de Fomento: "it is easier for [Ajusco peasants] to survive on the other side of the Ajusco [in the state of Morelos] with the rifle than on this side [closer to Mexico City] with the hoe."[37] Cabrera was a rare voice in defense of campesino forest and land use, but other voices would follow in his footsteps over the next several decades.

Cabrera's forceful critique of urban forestry and large landowners was made possible by a nationwide peasant rebellion, particularly the adamant protests and violent actions of the residents in and around the district he represented. Much of the contention revolved around popular efforts to restore "ecological autonomy" by repossessing lost land and resources.[38] With Madero's victory, the inhabitants of San Gregorio Atlapulco began to clamor for the return of the San Gregorio marsh that Díaz had bestowed on Urrutia in 1909. Similarly, the villagers around the old Chalco lakebed, some aligned with the Zapatistas, began to protest against Díaz's close friend Noriega.

The biggest popular threat to Madero's power in the southern part of the basin came from the Ajusco range, which separated Zapatista hotbeds in Morelos from the capital. Two months after Madero's triumph, a band of Zapatistas from San Pablo Oxtotepec, led by Joaquín Miranda, descended on the town of Milpa Alta, declaring that all the forests of the area belonged to the pueblo. Miranda, who would become a leading Zapatista commander, informed an assembly of townsfolk that they could "enjoy at their discretion [árbitro] all the products [of the forests] such as construction wood, firewood, and zacatón root without giving prior notice." He declared that forest agents "no longer had any authority" and recommended that villagers impede them by whatever means necessary.[39] It was not uncommon during and after the Maderista revolution for communities to reclaim lost forested land; what made this case unique was the categorical denunciation of state forestry policies first tested in the Basin of Mexico.[40] To the Forestry Department, this was wholesale rebellion, and they chastised the "ignorant" people of Milpa Alta for believing that Miranda's decrees were legal.[41] Forests were certainly not the only—or even the major—motive for rebellion, but Miranda recognized their importance to the local economy and understood past injustices.[42] By the fall of 1911, hundreds of Zapatista troops roamed the forests of the Ajusco, causing Madero headaches.[43] San Pablo Oxtotepec would remain a bastion of *zapatismo* through 1915—Zapatista generals ratified the Plan of Ayala there in 1914.[44]

Empowered by the revolutionary atmosphere, other villagers of the surrounding mountainous forests joined Milpa Alta in ratcheting up use of the basin's forests. In San Miguel Topilejo, several miles west on the slopes of the Ajusco, officials reported that local authorities had rented twenty-five mules to villagers for the illegal transportation of charcoal and firewood to market in Tlalpan. Officials could do little to curb this type of cutting and, because of the rocky terrain, complained of the difficulty of reforestation there.[45] Similarly, with Zapatistas camped out in the forests of Milpa Alta, campesinos made free use of forest products there and sometimes feuded with each other over access.[46] Illicit extraction of forest products was long-standing practice, but throughout the Ajusco and Sierra de las Cruces ranges, villagers perceived the precipitous decline in state vigilance and began to use the woods as they had before the Forestry Department's interventions.

Armed forest guards, rather than surveilling for illegal cutting, were fast becoming a quasi-military force. Beginning in 1911, they battled "bandits and hordes," Zapatista or otherwise. Quevedo beseeched officials for more arms for his seven small brigades of guards (*monteros*) in Milpa Alta, Xochimilco,

Cuajimalpa, Coyoacán, and San Miguel Topilejo; he boasted that his men guided federal troops and were also "fearless" fighters and "good shots."[47] Quevedo used the threat the Zapatistas posed to public order to win financial and military support for his department, but the vacuum of power in the basin's forests was palpable. The Zapatistas, and other bands labeled Zapatistas by forestry officials, attacked the monteros as government agents and enforcers of anticampesino regulations. Rather than effectively enforcing their department's code, the guards were busy chasing, fighting, or fleeing Zapatistas—who knew how to use the forest cover and steep terrain to their advantage.

While armed force remained the state's primary counterinsurgency strategy, Maderistas heeded Cabrera's warning that restrictive forestry nurtured the insurgency. In January 1913, in the twilight of Madero's government, the Forestry Department, in addition to its military actions against Zapata, experimented with olive-branch politics. They initiated a more egalitarian policy regarding zacatón root, commonly found in the higher elevations of the Ajusco, where Zapatistas had made significant inroads. Zacatón root extraction had been banned in 1910 owing to overexploitation. No longer could Mexico City inhabitants see the fires over the Ajusco range started by extractors, who would burn the giant stalks of the plant to access the roots. But zacatón made a quick resurgence.[48] Quevedo and Minister of Fomento Manuel Bonilla rescinded the ban at the end of 1912: for a small monthly fee, individuals could receive a permit to extract it. Applicants were required to certify "their good conduct, place of birth, and longevity in that place," to ensure that permits went to local villagers and not soldiers of the Zapatista army of Morelos."[49] They assailed those monopolizing and speculating in forest goods, such as Casto de la Fuente y Parres, who despite popular revolt still controlled the extraction and sale of the root. This partial, embryonic reopening of the forest commons signaled a shift in the Forestry Department's outlook. Mexican forestry had at one time appeared to be heading down the same road that French forestry had followed in North Africa (which Quevedo had studied)—wherein a narrative linking native land use to deforestation served to bolster blatant dispossession of those lands by the state and private property owners.[50] By 1913 the tide had turned ever so slightly in favor of forest communities.

Madero's governance of the Texcoco lakebed and hinterland forests, key spaces of urban hygiene, reflected the precariousness of his administration but also offered glimpses of support for villagers. In the face of the onslaught of a campesino army and reformist impulses, he strove to produce a semblance of political legitimacy by addressing the land question and village economies.

Environmental planning was increasingly influenced by campesinos, particularly Zapatista sympathizers south of Mexico City and politicians like Cabrera. Zapata, however, would not provide the coup de grâce against Madero's wobbly government; that distinction belonged to Victoriano Huerta, Madero's top commander, who turned on the president in February 1913.

THE HUERTA YEARS

If the earthquake in June 1911 foreboded shaky times for Madero, the ash that sprinkled the city from the eruption of the Colima volcano in January 1913 portended the explosions that would soon rock Mexico's capital.[51] On the reactionary right, Bernardo Reyes and Felix Díaz, the ex-dictator's nephew, hatched separate plots to overthrow Madero. Each failed on his own, but working together proved more fruitful. They conspired against Madero from prison, and on February 9, 1913, rebels freed Díaz and Reyes and attacked federal troops in the heart of Mexico City. Reyes was killed, but Díaz and his men locked themselves in the city's armory (La Ciudadela). Madero named Porfirian holdover Victoriano Huerta his commander to put down the rebellion. Unbeknownst to the president, Huerta and Díaz secretly colluded to orchestrate their own coup attempt while rebels and federal troops exchanged gunfire and cannon blasts. The battles between the two sides wrecked the upscale Juárez neighborhood and flattened the colonia Obrera.[52] Thousands of civilians perished. On February 19 Huerta hijacked the coup attempt, forcing Díaz into exile; had Madero and Vice President Suárez shot; and declared himself president of Mexico, ending what became known as the Ten Tragic Days.

Huerta, perhaps even more so than Díaz, has long been portrayed as a sinister figure in Mexican history. Four decades ago, the historian Michael Meyer attempted to rescue Huerta from what he saw as the tendentious historiography of the victorious revolutionaries, who smeared him as a counterrevolutionary and Porfirian throwback. Without denying the militaristic and repressive nature of Huerta's government, Meyer argued that Huerta's social policies were in some cases more progressive than Madero's and that, rather than echoing Díaz's oppressive government, they were comparable in spirit to postrevolutionary policies of economic nationalism, land reform, and education.[53] Alan Knight took a different view, putting all suggestions that Huerta was "revolutionary" or "non-counterrevolutionary" to rest. According to Knight, Meyer repeated the postrevolutionary vilification of Díaz without acknowledging that many of Huerta's "progressive" policies arose first under Díaz rather than the revolution; that Huerta's ministers may have discussed some reformist policies, but these were subsumed by Huerta's larger military concerns; and that many of the putative "revolutionary ideals" on which Meyer adjudicated Huerta's authenticity as a revolutionary did not become associated with the revolution until 1917 or even later.[54]

Huerta was indeed a reactionary. He closed opposition newspapers and imposed a compulsory draft to fight the invigorated popular revolution led by Zapata, Pancho Villa, and Venustiano Carranza's Constitutionalists. He carried out targeted political assassinations such as the one that ended the life of Chiapas's senator Belisario Domínguez, and he minimized social expenditures. But government officials enjoyed some autonomy and, sometimes, a willingness to experiment. Huerta was a military man who removed himself from all affairs not concerning the use of armed force. Whether the reactionary leader gave it much thought, officials in public works and forestry shaped expectations of government at the height of the revolutionary fervor and reinforced federal power over territory. In the realm of environmental politics, the shift from Madero to Huerta brought more continuity than change.

Huerta's government continued the Texcoco land reclamation. Both Barragán and Quevedo remained on the junta Madero had authorized. While Barragán continued to preach both forestation and agricultural experiments, Quevedo grumbled that attempting agriculture on the lakebed was futile and offered assistance only in selecting the correct tree species.[55] Nonetheless, the preparation for agriculture continued apace, and by early 1915 over a thousand hectares in several experimental zones had been prepared for drainage and irrigation. Hundreds of those hectares had been planted with crops as well as halophytes such as acacia, joining the tamarixes, eucalyptus, and willows that workers had already planted to fix the loose soil.[56]

This auspicious beginning was overshadowed by numerous obstacles that beset the project. As Huerta lost ground to the revolutionaries, the Bank for Irrigation Works and Agriculture resisted dispensing additional funds. A few engineers doubted the project's feasibility. One noted the "erroneous suppositions" on which the science of reclamation was based.[57] García Lascuraín's "hitherto unknown element"—the impossible hypothetical that could make the project fail—turned out to be the salts, which were not so easily washed away. While Barragán understood that eroded rock washing down the surrounding mountainsides carried sodium compounds into the lakebed, he did not grasp the extent to which these salts, deposited over millennia, would rise through capillary action. Rather than being static and easily manipulated, the salts actively thwarted engineers' plans by limiting the amount of water and nutrients plants could absorb and releasing toxic chloride ions when dissolved.[58]

Salt accumulation through the interaction of rainfall, erosion, and soil mechanics proved to be one obstacle; another was community protest. Locals resisted Maderista expropriations. In April 1913 the peasants of Chimalhuacán, a community on the southern edge of the lakebed, condemned the government for "disappearing" the lake and damaging their interests through the acquisition of land and the cordoning off of the area as federal property. In response to this early popular critique of the drainage and reclamation paradigm, the junta deflected responsibility from engineers onto nature itself, which, they claimed, by virtue of sedimentation, would desiccate the lake regardless, causing "grave consequences" if engineers did not intervene "opportunely."[59] The junta turned the complaint on its head; engineers were doing local inhabitants a favor, controlling an otherwise-injurious "natural" phenomenon.

The contest between Chimalhuacán and the engineers in 1912 and 1913 marked the beginning of a wider set of conflicts over land use and usufruct rights on federal property. Such disputes highlighted not only engineers' struggles to control the lakebed and the people within it but also the notable, if not complete, shift in the locus of social contention in the capital's hinterland. Whereas previous disputes had centered on the private sphere (hacienda and industry), now the primary focus of negotiation was the public (state lands, environmental policy, and infrastructure).

In the short run, revolution proved the greatest obstacle to the Texcoco project. At the end of 1914, Zapatista and Constitutionalist armies pastured their horses in the experimental zones, where they devoured saplings and trampled drainage and irrigation canals. The little money available was invested in maintenance, and when Huerta's demise seemed imminent, Barragán and other project engineers resigned their posts. The Convention, the governing body in power after the fall of Huerta, then disbanded the junta, but the precedent of Texcoco land reclamation, which future revolutionary governments would draw on, had been set.[60]

Forestry constituted Huerta's most significant legacy in environmental politics. The Forestry Department remained militarized—in December 1913 a guard was killed in a skirmish with Zapatistas—and Huerta clung to force as the only solution to the Zapatista uprising. He escalated the war, and the federal army burned villages sympathetic to zapatismo in and around the Ajusco in what one scholar has deemed ethnic genocide.[61] Huerta's war against the Zapatistas was indeed vicious—whether it is understood as genocide or as *guerre à outrance*. But counterinsurgency consisted of more than brute force. Alberto Robles Gil, Huerta's minister of fomento, and Quevedo, head of the Forestry Department until arrested by Huerta, continued the two-pronged strategy to combat zapatismo: on one hand, violent force and, on the other, the binding of the campesinos of the Ajusco to the incipient conservationist state.

The Forestry Department expanded its program in support of village uses and employed more brazen and confrontational rhetoric against exploitative relations. The department permitted poor campesinos to cut trees for firewood and building material without a fee, while officials rejected petitions from those who could not demonstrate poverty. Foresters undercut the monopolizer of zacatón root, Casto de la Fuente y Parres, and permitted root extractors to sell to whomever they wished. Forestry official Luis Corral viewed Fuente y Parres's monopoly with contempt: "in addition to damaging the interests of the indigenous people, it precluded reasonable and important contributions to the Treasury"; another official denounced Fuente y Parres's exploitation of indigenous peasants, who "worked by the sweat of their brow" for a pittance.[62] Corral exaggerated the importance of the thirty-cent zacatón root extraction fee to government coffers (the department grossed 260,754 pesos from 1912 to 1914 from various contributions), but the knot between state conservation and Ajusco villagers had been tied.

Both Quevedo and zacatón expert Ignacio R. Martínez, curiously, pointed to France as a paragon of village forestry, arguing that regulations there existed to promote communal uses along conservationist lines. The conclusions reached by one historian of France refute their perceptions of an inclusive French forestry, but these foresters' understanding of the example across the Atlantic served as an inspiration in 1913. The department organized ten tracts in the zacatón fields of the Ajusco, each with a set number of plots. These were sited on fields with gentle slopes, rather than sharp inclines where extraction might damage the soil, and extraction was rotated so that one tract was harvested per year, permitting regrowth on the other nine. The villages of Santo Tomás Ajusco, San Miguel Topilejo, Xochimilco, and Milpa Alta enjoyed their own tracts and parcels and organized the root's transport to market with foresters' assistance.[63]

The department's promotion of campesino forest production was as much about controlling the people by controlling the forests surrounding them as it was about freeing campesinos from the yoke of exploiters. In effect, the Forestry Department sought its own monopolization, a type of control that paternalistically aimed to protect the campesinos, whom they often referred to as "our Indians"[64]

Paternalism aside, policy changes had a positive effect on campesino forest economies. Controlling zacatón root extraction was a way to "avoid pressures on the indigenous extractors, [allowing] them to work freely and sell their product to the place they wish or to the one that gives them the best price."[65] Fuente y Parres complained that his business was suffering, while the earnings of zacatón root extractors doubled or tripled in some cases. The department granted permits to over sixty-five hundred individuals in the hotbeds of zapatismo immediately south of Mexico City. Forestry officials observed that labor in the zacatón fields (*zacatonales*) reaped a profit of up to two pesos per day; this was admittedly a pittance, but it was substantially more than what they had previously earned as independent sellers or salaried workers employed by Fuentes y Parres.[66] One forestry official expressed that a "liberal, humanitarian, just, and egalitarian government that procures the happiness of its peoples would never benefit a single individual—or the minority—in detriment to the majority."[67] The official's rosy picture of Huerta notwithstanding, he did capture the sentiments of the department as a whole: forest policy should protect poor campesinos against the abuses of anyone who sought to exploit them.

Ordered forest exploitation, the raison d'être of the department, remained a central purpose of the redirected policy. In the interest of order, the department maintained a predilection for large forest concessions whenever enterprises adopted conservationist language, and they continued to be leery of campesino uses. Foresters prevented zacatón root extraction in heavily forested areas and continued to crack down on campesinos who cut down woods for farming and those who toppled trees to burn charcoal.[68] Officials feared that the campesinos of the Ajusco would "follow the example of the hordes of bandits that often roam the Federal District" by plundering the woodlands. In fact, officials and the landowning elite of central Mexico had a tendency to equate campesinos with bandits, and bandits with Zapatistas, and all with forest destroyers.[69]

Foresters attempted to instill in campesinos a conservationist ethic, which several officials claimed they were adopting. One went so far as to say that villagers were not changing their ways by pressure "but by convincing and acceptance."[70] Rather than this being an early example of "environmentality"—

campesino adoption of government conservation—it is much more probable that villagers saw some benefits in participating in the more tolerant forest policies and abided by conservation to advance their own aims.[71] For example, some villagers aided government reforestation campaigns in exchange for the free collection of deadwood.[72] In another case, the community of San Miguel Topilejo allowed residents of neighboring villages to extract zacatón root from their fields as long as they helped detect forest fires.[73]

Did the more open policy stave off zapatismo? According to one forestry official, the policy on zacatón root alone "has brought happiness to many homes, saving many families from ruin, and conserved or reestablished order in some villages that because of a lack of well-remunerated work . . . provided a contingent of individuals to zapatismo or banditry."[74] Another crowed about how "completely grateful peasants were to the government, which in offering continuous work distanced them from the Zapatista army."[75] Motives for joining the revolution were multiple, of course; thus, the policy may have had little overall effect. Indeed, it is easy to imagine that campesinos both participated in the more inclusive forestry and supported zapatismo. However, the historical significance of this more inclusive forestry lies not so much in its overall effect on the revolution—after all, zapatismo helped defeat Huerta, and the policies ended with the collapse of the Forestry Department in 1914—but in the precedent it set for later forest governance. Forestry from the end of Madero through Huerta served as a bridge from Porfirian exclusionism to postrevolutionary community forestry, in which pueblos organized state-sponsored cooperatives to manage communal forests.

TURNING THE CITY INSIDE OUT

Huerta had no coherent plan to unify the divided nation. Desertion depleted his army, while thousands joined Carranza's Constitutionalist forces, Villa's Northern Division, and Zapata's Liberation Army of the South. By the spring of 1914, both Carranza—whose chief military commander was the Sonoran landowner Álvaro Obregón—and Villa were rapidly advancing into central Mexico. Shortly after Villa took Zacatecas, the final federal stronghold in the north, on June 23, Huerta resigned the presidency. Carranza, Villa, and later Zapata agreed to send delegates to meet in Aguascalientes to discuss a resolution of the conflict and the creation of a new government. The military marriage between Carranza's forces and the more rustic peasant armies, however, was one of convenience that obscured profoundly different visions of Mexico.

Villa and Zapata supported local governance, the end of caciquismo, and a set of social rights, most notably agrarian reform, of which Zapata was the most ardent champion. Carranza and Obregón, of elite upbringing, called for political centralization and capitalist development, albeit within a more nationalist and nominally liberal constitutionalist framework than Díaz had pursued. It did not help that Villa and Obregón, the leaders of the two strongest armies, fiercely disliked each other. The Convention of Aguascalientes ended in a cacophony of discord. Obregón again sided with Carranza, who fled to the port city of Veracruz to regroup and ready his forces for an all-out war against *villismo* and zapatismo.

The campesinos Zapata and Villa reluctantly marched into the capital and met for the first time in bucolic Xochimilco in November. Their own regional and political differences resulted in a very tenuous alliance based on a mutual disgust for Carranza rather than a common program of national governance. Mexico City, meanwhile, was being turned inside out. The arrival of peasant and peon armies at the end of 1914 represented the complete breakdown of the old urban hegemony. For decades the city had reached out with its tentacles to mold hinterland landscapes; the revolution temporarily cut those tentacles and submitted the city to the dictates of rural armies. This did not mean that the urban populace was laid prostrate, the victim of forces beyond its control. The urban popular classes suffered from the armies' destruction but also made political alliances, petitioned, and rioted using the language of the revolution, and in the process set new expectations for postrevolutionary governance.

The fragmentation of the Mexican polity during the second half of 1914 induced "local sovereignty," whereby villagers and revolutionary armies seized land, water, and woodlands.[76] Zapatistas confiscated the San Rafael paper mill, which had supplied paper to the reactionary press, to make revolutionary propaganda; they raided Noriega's haciendas for food supplies. Xochimilcans seized hacienda lands, including the estate of Aureliano Urrutia, who had served as Huerta's secretary of state and led the bloody repression of adversaries to the regime.[77] Villagers in the Ajusco range consolidated control over the Eslava and Cañada haciendas.[78] Whereas the Zapatista advance into the immediate Mexico City hinterland emboldened villagers and brought a transitory and fragile peace, in the capital it foreshadowed bleak times.

The Convention government established in Mexico City was well received by the heterogeneous urban working class—many of whom were not far removed from their country roots. Others, especially the anarchist labor move-

FIGURE 2.1 — Zapatistas in the zócalo. COURTESY OF INAH, FOTOTECA NACIONAL.

ment, supported Zapata's agrarian program. Thousands congregated to greet and cheer the Zapatistas as they entered the nation's capital (see figure 2.1). Some Zapatistas were bewildered by their surroundings. One group attacked a fire truck, mistaking it for an enemy machine of war. Another group dined in the upscale Sanborn's restaurant, much to the dismay of its wealthy clientele. While Zapatistas generally avoided banditry, Villistas, who arrived shortly thereafter, were denounced by residents for their waywardness and violence, although their reign of terror in Mexico City paled in comparison to Huertista and Carrancista terror.[79]

The initial honeymoon with the Convention gave way to desperation as the calendar turned to 1915. Rapid price inflation, the forced conversion to Villista currency, frayed rural-urban supply lines, a rising urban refugee population, and depressed production in the countryside, worsened by the machinations of speculators, caused food and fuel shortages.[80] Long lines were frequent sights at meat and other food stores. The dwindling supply of charcoal, the chief cooking fuel, brought in from as far away as Durango and Michoacán and as close as the Ajusco mountains also caused alarm. In December 1914 armed men raided a charcoal dispensary, taking several carts of the "black prince" under the pretext that "the product was meant for the president."[81] Charcoal was being sold at an exorbitant ten pesos per bag, and scarcity compelled many to cut down neighborhood trees or use their household furniture to cook their meager food supplies.[82] That same month Villista Federal District governor Manuel Chao issued penalties against speculators who sold charcoal for more than two and a half pesos per bag, and the police did manage to arrest several violators.[83] These penalties were among the first efforts to regulate privatized food and fuel markets, after a several-decade period of what Amy Chazkel has termed "republican urbanism," in which privatization policies tended to favor commercial enterprises over urban consumers.[84]

The Convention government fled when Obregón's forces knocked on the doors of the capital in January 1915. Upon orders from civic leaders, Zapatistas cut the power of the Xochimilco water-supply system, an act of war that angered city residents and left them short of another basic necessity. What is striking about this event is not that the Zapatistas sabotaged the supply, for they aimed to strangle the city whenever Carrancistas occupied it, but that the Convention, which had just governed the city, placed the order. It was certainly part of a larger military strategy to weaken Obregón's army and to underscore their ineffective control over key sites in the Basin of Mexico. Immediately afterward, however, Convention leadership and top Zapatistas regretted the act. Mexico City, Convention delegates argued, was a city "with all our sympathies," and to deprive the population of water was to bring on "perfectly bad hygienic conditions."[85] Soon thereafter, the Zapatista leadership allowed service to be reestablished.[86]

This restoration did not last. Operating independently of the Convention, Zapatista soldiers cut the Xochimilco water supply twice more over the next eighteen months, whenever their control of that part of the basin permitted it. Many Zapatista rebels and their Xochimilcan campesino supporters, one might imagine, did not understand the sabotage as vandalism, nor as merely a military tactic, but rather as a symbol of resistance to the urban-centered state that had usurped water in the name of growth.

Water shortages had little effect on Obregón's larger military strategy. The Sonoran general foresaw a brief stay since "the damned city"—his term for the capital—did not "constitute a strategic position." The military struggle, he understood, would be settled in the north against Villa, not against Zapata immediately to the south.[87] Politics trumped military logic, however. Obregón likely would have left the capital to the Convention if the Constitutionalists had not begun to recruit workers from the anarcho-syndicalist Casa del Obrero Mundial (House of the World Worker). To garner worker support, Obregón placed the vivacious artist-intellectual and reformer Dr. Atl

(Gerardo Murillo) as well as the former Maderista (and architect of Marroquín y Rivera's pump houses) Alberto Pani in charge of the Revolutionary Committee for the Relief of the Poor. The committee required store owners to hand over 10 percent of all basic goods they possessed to be redistributed to the populace, and gave them forty-eight hours to comply. Store owners resisted this and other measures. Consequently, Obregón forced noncompliant owners to sweep the city streets, to the delight of the populace, which had been petitioning for improved street cleaning since the devastating Ten Tragic Days. This measure had the twin effect of demonstrating an interest in slowing the spread of disease and punishing speculators and price gougers.[88] One denizen appreciated "the material spectacle that I believe the exploited people of many countries have not been able to enjoy."[89] Pani and Dr. Atl also boosted purchasing power by distributing 500,000 pesos of freshly printed Constitutionalist money to the growing mass of indigent peoples at relief centers. The committee's campaign to penalize speculators and blunt the effects of poverty on urban consumption cemented the Casa-Constitutionalist alliance. This in turn led to the formation of the Red Brigades, composed of union workers, who were deployed in the definitive battles against Villa.[90] Once Casa support was assured, Obregón abandoned the capital to the Zapatistas and the Convention.

The constant changes in government and official currency as well as the terrific violence—the revolutionaries battled each other with more ferocity than they battled the old guard—further frayed the lifelines that linked city and country. With the revolutionary armies embroiled in a civil war, there was little the recently arrived Convention could do to ameliorate conditions in Mexico City, even if it had developed a national political program. The incidence of smallpox rose, typhus reached epidemic status, and hunger prevailed. The city entered survival mode. Many residents lined up, restlessly awaiting the arrival of astronomically priced basic goods, while others combed the streets, parks, woods, and nearby farmland for anything that might be edible.[91]

Material want, combined with the vacuum of power and the rising expectation that the government should intervene to secure basic urban rights, generated conditions ripe for protest. Urban popular groups' prerevolutionary concerns for the extension of the sanitary city dropped by the wayside as the focus shifted to survival. Women, as the guardians and purveyors of household consumption, often led riots, ransacking stores and food-delivery vehicles. They targeted food and fuel stores in their working-class neighborhoods and on occasion large city markets such as the Merced.[92] Residents of Santa Julia, who had demanded sanitary improvements during the twilight of the Porfiriato, agitated again in June 1915. When female residents of the colonia snatched grain from a local store to feed their children, Villista soldiers attacked them. The next day, according to the residents, Villistas raided their homes in the vecindades and seized the grain. In response to what they considered an illegitimate act of aggression, the women declared, "It is worth asking: Has the Revolution, the grandiose revolution, brought about in favor of the humble people, triumphed, or are we still in the times of tyranny?"[93] For the urban popular classes, the purpose and ideals of the revolution were embedded in their persistent calls for adequate urban governance. The revolution, by encouraging mass mobilization and strengthening a sense of government accountability around issues of consumption and domestic reproduction, deepened the politicization of city life, a process under way since at least the late nineteenth century.

The rural revolution turned the city inside out. One late afternoon in January 1915, it was as if the hinterland took its revenge for years of plunder and exploitation: a strong wind blew across the Texcoco lakebed, and the city was "enveloped in a cloud of dust so thick that nothing could be discerned at more than a few meters' distance." The dust storm lasted all day, and hungry inhabitants meandered city streets "with their hats tucked over their ears, swallowing dust, and blinking their eyes in anguish."[94] It was in these trying conditions that the urban popular classes shaped the revolutionary struggle. Far from the decisive battles of the revolution, they sought to protect their precarious subsistence and living spaces, in the process shaping more responsive city governance and consolidating conceptions of urban revolutionary rights, which would influence later environmental disputes once elite rule was restored.

THE CONSTITUTIONALIST VICTORY

On April 13, 1915, Obregón's forces routed Villa's Northern Division at the Battle of Celaya. Several years of fighting lay ahead, and the outcome of the revolution was far from clear. But Carranza elaborated a comprehensive national vision that stood in contrast to Villa's and Zapata's localism. Rather than attack Carranza in Veracruz at the end of 1914—which might have changed the course of the conflict—Villa and Zapata reinforced their local power bases, disinclined to venture too far afield. Meanwhile, Carranza built regional alliances, such as that with urban labor, and he tapped Cabrera to write a land-reform law early in 1915, which stole some of the thunder from Zapata's Plan of Ayala.

Constitutionalists took control of the capital for good in the summer of 1915. Securing a steady supply of basic provisions and reducing the frequency of deadly diseases lay at the forefront of their governance. Dire material conditions in a time of raised expectations forced Mexico's new leaders to experiment in order to assert their authority over urban consumption and amass a modicum of consent from the agitated popular classes.[95]

Carranza reconstituted the Federal District's municipal governments (Los Ayuntamientos), which Díaz had reduced to an advisory board in 1903, as a full governing body functioning parallel to the district administration. In 1915, as the government of the Federal District cleaned the city streets, the municipal government of Mexico City confronted the food-supply problem and opened numerous dispensaries around the city that sold basic goods at reduced prices.[96] By June 1916 the city administered thirty-four dispensaries, providing up to nine thousand people with food and four hundred with charcoal.[97] The Regulatory Committee on Prices, another city council creation, inspected stores, fined noncompliant owners, oversaw the arrival of basic goods, and regulated the purchase of clothing and shoes for both the poor and middle classes.[98] Residents of working-class Vallejo hailed the city council for putting "bread to mouths" and petitioned for the improvement of public services as well.[99] The council made at least token gestures by cleaning up parks and assuring the safety and security of the municipal water supply.[100]

In this context of renewed urban governance, following years of popular complaints about urban filth and sanitary deficiencies, Pani vilified Porfirian sanitation. He drew on his experiences working on the Xochimilco waterworks, as the director of public works of the Federal District under Madero, and as the head of the Revolutionary Committee for the Relief of the Poor, to lambaste prerevolutionary public health authorities for failing to improve the city's hygienic standards while spending lavishly "on showy manifestations [like the centennial celebrations, the unfinished capitol, and the national theater] of *a progress purely material and fictitious*, with the inevitable train of vice and corruption."[101] He commended the General Drainage and the Xochimilco waterworks but claimed that Díaz, the so-called modernizer, had flunked the test of "integral progress," allowing Mexico City to languish in disease, dirt, and inadequate housing with higher mortality rates than Madras and Cairo.[102] Pani called the tenements "sinks of moral and physical infection" and advocated "compulsory sanitation" in any Mexican city where the yearly death rate exceeded two per thousand residents (which at the time would have likely been all of them).[103] The enforcement of sanitary policy would be matched with the economic improvement of the people and a *"vigorous and extensive propaganda of the elemental principles of hygiene."*[104] Pani represented both the inclusive version of the Mexican sanitary ideal, solidified by the revolution, and the deep-seated understanding of the urban poor as morally depraved and bereft of education.

Just as there were two sides to Pani's sanitary ideal, there were two sides to the reassertion of urban hegemony. On the one hand, it entailed new government measures to quell popular discontent and mend the supply chains for basic goods; on the other, it resurrected old political practices. Labor's general strike in 1916, led by electrical workers who shut off city power, was brutally repressed, and the Carrancista governor of the Federal District issued tax exemptions for urban developers to build homes and allowed rents to skyrocket without state interference. In 1911 the revolutionaries Gildardo Magaña and Joaquín Miranda—the same militant who had been at the helm of the Milpa Alta peasant rebels—had called for rent controls and affordable, sanitary housing in cities, but Constitutionalist authorities buried this proposal, as well as the Convention's ill-fated rent freezes in the capital.[105] Indeed, Carranza's government differed little from its Porfirian antecedent with regard to urbanization. Rather than suppress real estate speculation, Carranza encouraged it to promote growth in the financially ruined city. From 1910 to 1920 developers established fifteen new colonias, most of which were unauthorized, with the intention of capitalizing on the pitiful conditions in the city center.[106] Indiana native Herbert Lewis bought over 250 hectares of the old hacienda Los Portales north of Coyoacán to establish a residential subdivision. Through newspaper advertisements he coaxed many to escape to his idyllic "sun city," the hygienic and affordable colonia Los Portales, "designed according to the most modern methods."[107] The developers of another subdivision, La Purísima, between San Angel and Mixcoac, trumpeted, "In these times our great metropolis is plagued by infectious diseases, and we bring to your attention a place in the countryside, perfectly healthy and hygienic for you to take your family to live, thus escaping all danger."[108] These kinds of utopian-inspired housing developments perverted the garden-city movement, but the language of escapism drew desperate city dwellers to these communities like iron filings to a magnet. Residents of Los Portales soon discovered that Lewis's company had no plans to install any services whatsoever. Many vacated their lots and lost their investments, while the company resold the properties "to the extent that there are many lots in Los Portales that have been sold up to twenty times" at ever-greater prices.[109] Urban speculation had baleful consequences, but Carranza supported it to restore Mexico City's interrupted economic dynamism and development. Nonetheless, there would be no return to the positivist elite urban dominance of yesteryear.

Carranza called a constitutional convention to legitimate his government and lay the foundation of postrevolutionary rule, and he delivered a rather moderate draft to convention delegates at their meeting in Querétaro. Many of the 220 delegates brought a more radical agenda to the table, and they were vocal.[110] The final version approved in February 1917 mandated a set of rights and government obligations that offered new opportunities for the rural and urban popular classes to make claims on the metropolitan environment. The expansive and comprehensive Article 123 on labor and social security obligated employers to provide hygienic and comfortable homes for workers and considered the construction of affordable and hygienic housing a "social utility." It held urban government responsible for the democratization of hygienic housing and public services and represented a threat to speculative and unequal urban development. Delegates drew on Porfirian achievements to shape the provisions regarding public health but added key clauses concerning working-class hygiene that sprang from popular discontent, Progressive Era housing concerns, Constitutionalist measures to clean up cities, and the intellectual and political work of the prominent Carrancista Pani.[111]

Convention delegates such as Pastor Rouaix and Juan de Dios Bojórquez, in consultation with Molina Enriquez, radicalized Article 27, which provided the legal basis for Mexico's postrevolutionary land reform and the expropriation of foreign oil interests. Article 27 also had important environmental content and consequences. It built on Porfirian decrees and laws that nationalized natural resources; however, by 1917 nationalization had also come to imply a measure of socialization, representing an opening for environmental rights. The article held that lands and waters, "vested originally in the nation," could be appropriated or regulated "as the public interest may demand" in order "to conserve them and to ensure a more equitable distribution of the public wealth."[112] Article 27 bolstered postrevolutionary forest conservation, reaffirmed the nationalization of all the major waterways of the Basin of Mexico, and, under the rubric of nationalization, permitted communities to petition for grants of arable land, forests, and water.[113] The authors of Article 27 shifted the justification for such state powers over the environment from the promotion of private wealth to state-led development and social justice. The right to the commons was etched into the nation's governing document, and subsequent legislation and regulations enacted these progressive elements.[114]

Environmental rights were defined in the revolutionary process and in debates about government accountability—from Madero's Texcoco reclamation and Cabrera's speeches to Quevedo's modified forestry and Pani's role in disease and hunger prevention. In the constitution peoples within the basin found the political framework to demand the more democratic use of the metropolitan environment. Yet Carranza, and later Obregón, would again make Mexico City a center of speculative growth that hinged on control over and transformation of hinterland spaces. To compound matters, environmental planners maintained a powerful disdain for popular appropriations of natural spaces and resources.[115] These two impulses—one revolutionary and potentially emancipatory, the other capitalist-urban and exclusionary—would be at loggerheads in the decades to follow. Much as in the Díaz years, state power remained a double-edged sword, but in Mexico after 1917 the democratizing edge became especially sharp. After 1917 the urbanizing basin acquired a shared institutional and discursive framework of environmental struggle that at the time was unique in Latin America.[116] It did not involve a complete overhaul of the state—the new agrarian bureaucracy and the eventual institutionalization of one-party politics were the most notable modifications to the state's architecture—but reform penetrated the existing state apparatus. The language of rights and the new expectations of governance sedimented over, like the accumulation of eroded soil, the physical infrastructures, the growth model, and the resilient sanitary paradigm of the Porfiriato, forming a new layer that, while not completely covering the old, competed with it for preeminence.

II

———

SPACES OF A

METROPOLITAN ENVIRONMENT

3

Water and Hygiene in the City

Venustiano Carranza, like Porfirio Díaz before him, preferred a centralized Federal District government, and the constitutional proposal he sent to the Querétaro delegates would have extended the Federal District from its limits covering much of the southern portion of the basin to include all of the Texcoco and Chalco lakebeds, mostly situated in the State of Mexico. The proposal would also have suppressed all democratically elected municipalities within its boundaries.[1] The delegates rejected the plan, which, according to one delegate, would have wiped out a government representing those "who anxiously demand of the revolution an authority that cares for them."[2] Democratic municipal government and revolution, many Constitutionalists believed, nurtured each other. Yet over the course of the 1920s, urban experts, government functionaries, and, ironically, wide swaths of the urban populace turned away from this view. The politics of water and hygiene were the focal points of this political transformation. Popular ferment and official responses to it helped reinstall technocratic and centralized environmental governance, albeit under putatively revolutionary auspices.

The municipal government of Mexico City, like its neighboring counter-parts, remained financially beholden to the executive-managed Federal District government and had limited jurisdiction over public services. It maintained nominal authority over the water supply but ceded power to the Porfirian-created Superior Health Council with regard to medical services and disease prevention, and to other federal agencies with regard to drainage infrastruc-ture and forestry. This confused web of city authority stymied action, and the maintenance and extension of water, sewerage, and other health-related ser-vices did not keep pace with growth. The sanitary conditions of the capital, while certainly improved since 1914, led Doctor Enrique de Bosque to quip in 1921, "We are alive [in this city] because of a true miracle."[3]

This chapter is organized around the urban populace's quest for sanitary living spaces. A healthy urban environment depended on the extension and maintenance of Porfirian infrastructure, affordable and hygienic housing, and the enforcement of public health codes, and on all counts the governments of the late 1910s and 1920s failed to deliver. A wide range of city dwellers used myriad tactics—the strike, the street protest, the riot, and the petition—to obtain hygienic homes and neighborhoods. Water and sewer lines for homes and residences fostered private cleanliness and thus a sense of bourgeois individuality, but the provision of sanitary services was also conceived of as fundamentally social, structuring collective politics and residents' relation to the state. In postrevolutionary Mexico City, there was a dynamic interplay between popular demands for affordable, sanitary homes and state forma-tion.[4] At a time when the maintenance and extension of existing sanitary ser-vices were impeded by the political economy of growth, popular mobilization spurred on by new expectations of government accountability foregrounded the environment within urban politics. In particular, two struggles in 1922 for collective consumption stood out: a tenant strike begun in May of that year and a riot in November provoked by the breakdown in the Xochimilco water-supply system. In response, municipal and federal authorities crafted a new urban en-vironmental politics, but a political crisis revolving around municipal gov-ernment negligence ensued. By 1928 such negligence was used to justify the suppression of the municipalities and centralized authority over hydraulic infrastructure.

Census data do not give precise figures, but it is safe to claim that in 1920 the vast majority of the residents of Mexico's capital—likely 85 percent or more—rented their residences; at least a quarter of the inhabitants lived in the dozens of vecindades that dotted the urban landscape.[5] Railway and tobacco-factory workers, skilled craft workers, public employees, domestic servants, and ambulant vendors alike experienced high living costs coupled with atrocious health conditions at home and in the street. Tenancy brought two of the most salient forces of postrevolutionary urban life into stark relief: on the one side, the ineluctable power of landowners and, on the other, the widespread desire to secure an affordable and livable environment—made possible, in large part, by the adequate provision of water and the evacuation of waste.

In the years leading up to and following the passage of the Constitution of 1917, Mexico City was bursting with the energy of revolutionary change. The industrial working class, while small, had a distinct anarcho-syndicalist bent and a penchant for direct action. The general strike of 1916, sectoral strikes before and after, and the socialist experiments of state governors in Yucatán highlighted the open-ended and evolving nature of the revolution. Deeper and more radical changes seemed, if not imminent, then within the realm of possibility. On the international stage, Mexico City represented, at best, an embryonic utopian future; at worst, a refuge from the jingoism north of the border. In this context Mexico City attracted a bevy of foreign travelers and leftist activists like the socialist draft dodger Charles Phillips, progressive journalist Carleton Beals, Italian American photographer Tina Modotti, and Indian nationalist-turned–Marxist revolutionary M. N. Roy.[6] It was also in this context of revolutionary fervor, and after the food scarcities of 1915 waned, that many revolutionaries embraced the politics of healthy and affordable housing.

Their activism had a legal foundation. The constitution mandated that employers provide hygienic housing for workers and charged the Superior Health Council with enforcing the sanitary code, which regulated how many people could reside in a given unit and guaranteed the provision of sanitary services. Although it did not include rent-control provisions, many officials were amenable to curbing landlords' abuses. In 1917 activists created the Tenant League of the Federal District, which lobbied for pro-tenant legislation that was being supported by the radical reformer Francisco Múgica and congressman Filiberto Villareal.[7] This proposal was defeated, but further mobilization followed. The first socialist congress in 1919 placed rent reduction on its national platform, and in May 1921 Melitón Romero and Miguel Ángel Cuevas organized Mexico City's first known tenant union.[8] They condemned property owners who continued to raise rents while forcing tenants to "live in anti-hygienic homes, many in ruins and all with a disagreeable aspect," and claimed that landlords "have not suffered in the least because of the Revolution. . . . The Revolution has respected the tenement buildings." Union leaders pleaded for a "revolutionary" public health that would save "the race" (a mestizo race, one imagines) and require owners to update their properties.[9] However, the tenant union disappeared soon thereafter. Their threat to strike if the government did not act to lower rents and sanitize homes proved to be an empty one.[10]

This auspicious climate for reform was enhanced by worsening material conditions. Refugees from the violent countryside flooded the capital, increasing the population from nearly 500,000 in 1910 to approximately 615,000 in 1921. Landlords took advantage of skyrocketing housing demand by raising rents. By some estimates, rents doubled between 1914 and 1921; others claimed they had nearly tripled.[11] Moreover, the feeble enforcement of the sanitary code of 1903 freed landlords from having to make expensive repairs of domestic sanitary appliances and enabled them to subdivide their buildings into smaller and smaller units. A tenement in Romita, a few blocks from the luxurious Roma subdivision, had ninety-seven rooms with an average of four inhabitants each, and only nine toilets.[12] Tenant activists described buildings that possessed only two or three toilets for over two hundred inhabitants.[13] The previous year, a Department of Labor employee had inspected three tenements and found cramped living spaces that squeezed three or four people into rooms measuring only ten to twelve square meters, with leaky walls and unventilated charcoal-burning stoves. Windows were few, and hundreds of people shared filthy toilets.[14] It was no wonder many city-center residents were enticed by the numerous ads for subdivisions promising a better life—spacious, healthy, and free from abusive landlords. Some who could afford down payments stayed on their new lots; others returned, exasperated and defrauded.

The young firebrand José Valadés invigorated tenant activism from within the city's radical political networks. In 1918, at the green age of eighteen, Valadés was at once enthralled with the Russian Revolution and disappointed in the unfulfilled emancipatory potential of the Mexican Revolution. For Valadés and other young Mexican radicals, Mexico's revolution should have been a stepping-stone to more substantive change of the sort that was unfolding in Russia. In late 1918 Valadés attended a speech by M. N. Roy, who had ventured to Mexico City by way of New York to galvanize support for the cause of Indian nationalism. Roy, who Valadés believed "singularized with his words the birth of a free world," helped found the Mexican Communist Party (PCM) in 1919.[15] Valadés's close ties to Roy and another foreign visitor to the city Sen Katayama, the Japanese liaison to the Comintern, allowed him to gain notable influence within the party, but the party itself, dependent on external support, crumbled once that support vanished. Roy, his mind and heart in Asia, left in 1919, and Katayama departed in 1921. As the PCM struggled to maintain its position, it worked to strengthen bonds to local laborers by helping organize the General Workers Confederation (CGT) to oppose the more conservative Regional Confederation of Mexican Workers (CROM). Luis Morones, the leader of CROM, once a devoted anarchist who opposed the House of the World Worker's alliance with Carranza, by 1922 had become the "pig of the revolution," as one Guadalajaran tenant activist proclaimed, and a formidable foe of leftist activism. In December 1919 Morones had cozied up to General Álvaro Obregón, who was launching his presidential campaign for the elections of 1920. In return for Morones's support, Obregón promised to back the fledgling moderate union and elevate the Labor Department to an autonomous ministry.[16] Before the election, Obregón took up arms, riding a wave of support (including from the CROM) that propelled him to victory over Carranza in the Agua Prieta Rebellion. The CROM's robust growth stood in sharp contrast to the fractured unionism of the Left. At the end of 1921, the PCM and the CGT split, a transatlantic reverberation of the Soviet Union's repression of Russian anarchists, and the Communist Party lost its most important connection to the Mexican labor movement.[17]

The tenant strike of 1922 must be understood in the context of Communist Party decline and Valadés's hopes to revitalize it.[18] He was an impulsive and erratic young man who refused to be corralled by the party leadership, which stressed long-term organization and raising of class consciousness and derided direct action as "infantile."[19] Tenant activism certainly fit Valadés's rebellious personality, but his move to catalyze tenant anger was also inspired by the successes of activists in neighboring cities, particularly Veracruz, where tenants were striking.[20] Valadés and other members of the PCM's Communist Youth organization saw a similar potential wellspring of revolt in Mexico City's hundreds of thousands of renters. Mobilizing tenants, Valadés realized, might be an initial step toward a direct-action revolution.

After the city police dispersed a March rally of nearly five hundred people demanding tenant reform, Valadés and other young Communists established the Tenant Union of the Federal District.[21] The union gained strength over the next month. Communists and their tenant allies held meetings in tenement buildings in the old city center and in the working-class neighborhoods to the north, such as Peralvillo, Guerrero, and Santa María de la Ribera, and other lower-class subdivisions of the Porfiriato, such as La Bolsa and Obrera.[22] Membership ballooned to eight thousand men and women by early April. Emboldened by this rapid growth, the union leadership—a mix of young Communists and older members of the PCM—issued its demands, which if not met would end in a May Day strike. The leadership demanded a 75 percent reduction in rent; the elimination of security deposits, which were rarely returned; the creation of hygiene commissions; the "repair and sanitization of homes, toilets, water connections, etc."; a guarantee that any updates not made could be handled by the union at the owners' expense; and the right of union authorities to name sanitary inspectors who would monitor the conditions of residences.[23] It was a radical set of demands that challenged landlord power and sought to enforce Article 123. Yet apart from placards advising tenants to be "sensible" and not unionize, property owners remained silent through April, perhaps sensing that the movement would stall. Their quiescence likely encouraged further organization, and by the end of May, tenant-union membership peaked at around thirty thousand.[24]

Whereas the strike threat in 1921 had proved empty, the union led by Valadés kept its word in 1922. On May 1 thousands of workers from dozens of labor unions marched in Mexico City as part of three separate May Day rallies. The one organized by the tenant union drew between ten thousand and fifteen thousand participants backed by public employee unions, militant railroad workers, and the bakers' union.[25] As in the food and fuel riots of 1914 and 1915, women participated, joining men in the streets of the historic center. The union claimed that thirty thousand tenants ceased rent payments that same day, and that number may have exceeded fifty thousand by June. With red-and-black flags adorning vecindades across the city, the roughly two dozen members of the Communist Youth organization called hundreds of meetings in plazas and the patios of dilapidated buildings to recruit strikers and volunteers to join neighborhood committees charged with preventing evictions. Women were active participants in the day-to-day strike activities, even if strategy remained the realm of the male-dominated Communist Youth.[26] (See figure 3.1.) Simultaneously, the union organized carpenters, plumbers, and brick workers to repair dilapidated homes, deducting the cost from future rent payments.[27]

FIGURE 3.1 — Rent strikers. COURTESY OF INAH, FOTOTECA NACIONAL.

The strike laid bare the divisive working-class politics of Mexico in the early 1920s. The immense Veracruz strike was led by Herón Proal, a dedicated anarcho-syndicalist and CGT member. However, after initially supporting the smaller-but-growing Mexico City strike, the CGT later withdrew its backing because of the strike's Communist leadership. If the strike was too "statist" for the anarchists within the labor movement, it was much too subversive for the CROM, the ideological brother of the American Federation of Labor. Morones instead worked with Obregón and Federal District governor Celestino Gasca, a representative of the Laborist Party, CROM's political ally, to contain militant tenant activism. These fissures within the tenant movement rendered the mounting opposition against it insurmountable.

While Obregón sent troops to quell the Veracruz strike, he bestowed on Gasca the task of handling the turmoil in Mexico City. Gasca arrested over a hundred participants and provided the muscle to enforce evictions over the strike committees' objections. In some instances violence erupted; a teenage railroad worker died in one attempt to block an eviction, and many others were injured in other union actions.[28] Moreover, the first week of May saw a firmer landowner reaction. Property owners formed two organizations and unleashed a coordinated campaign to smother the movement. They wrote new leases warning tenants that union activity would lead to eviction, sought the assistance of the courts to evict defaulting tenants, and persuaded the government to intervene on their behalf.[29] One organization, the Homeowners League of the Federal District, compiled a blacklist of unionized residents for owners to avoid and founded a commission—led by Miguel Ángel de Quevedo and Manuel Marroquín y Rivera—to design working-class housing. This was precisely the type of work Quevedo believed necessary to reduce class tensions and improve sanitary conditions.[30] The League's response consisted of one part stick and one part carrot.

As evictions rose, the tenant union reinstalled residents in their homes and sheltered homeless tenants in abandoned buildings. In one instance, five hundred unionists reinstalled a family and their furniture, "breaking the seals placed by the judge on the door of the unoccupied apartment."[31] These defiant actions galvanized support for the union but could not keep pace with the evictions being carried out by the city police. They also fueled property-owner reactions. Landlords challenged the legality of the strike, since Article 123 sanctioned only strikes involving the labor force; assailed the union's use of threats against tenants and rent collectors alike; and chided the union as "an association formed to attack both people and property."[32]

The public's response to the strike is hard to gauge but was undoubtedly mixed. Supportive broadsides circulated in working-class neighborhoods. One playful broadside poem read: "They say that the rich man is ungrateful / this is why he acts foolishly / and that he has a few rooms / worse than a dungeon / They're all full of bedbugs / with fleas and ticks / because they never clean them / these ungracious people."[33] One woman claimed to have spoken to many people in the city center regarding the tenant dispute, and "they all agreed that they would be satisfied with a 30 to 40 percent decrease in rent and, with respect to repairs, water, sewerage, and lighting, just the most indispensable."[34] Workers in the construction industry, however, were leery of the movement, concerned that stricter laws would cost them jobs, a powerful argument—regardless of its veracity—that the government, most newspapers, and landlords also utilized to break the strike's momentum.

While the strike alarmed property owners, it never reached the level of participation enjoyed by its counterpart in Veracruz. Amassing some forty-five thousand strikers so quickly was a significant accomplishment, but the strikers remained a minority of city tenants. The challenge presented by orchestrated repression was compounded by the difficulty of maintaining solidarity and compliance among tenants dispersed across the city and with varying political allegiances. Moreover, many small property owners, who often relied on their rent income, opted to negotiate, and tenants took advantage of this opportunity to improve the terms of their leases.[35] These side agreements were likely ephemeral, but they further frayed the movement. The Communist Party, which had tolerated Valadés at the height of the strike, expelled the young Communist once failure seemed inevitable.[36]

The PCM embarked on a more gradualist approach at the end of 1922, reflecting its rapprochement with postrevolutionary reformers. In 1923 another PCM-led tenants' union drafted a bill that pinned rents to a percentage of the property value and called for an autonomous Tenant Department to regulate tenant-landlord relations, just as the Department of Labor did for workers.[37] Obregón, however, argued that the bill threatened to curtail construction. Any tenant bill, Obregón maintained, "should leave a clear path . . . for new entrepreneurs with a more liberal and conciliatory spirit to continue constructing rental units at a reasonable profit."[38] The strike defeated, Obregón stood firm for the propertied class, issuing a decree in September that gave developers tax breaks to build new, affordable rental units but without regulating construction materials or sanitary installations.[39] Housing reform was still not on the horizon. Even the forceful Veracruz strike and the rent law that it spawned failed to bring about lasting reform there due to the resistance of property owners.[40] But the tenant movement of 1922 in Mexico City and other urban centers left its imprint in other ways: it helped bequeath an alternative approach to growth. Indeed, the Mexico City strike shaped the future growth of the city in unforeseen ways.

"TO BE EMANCIPATED FROM THE TYRANNY OF TENANCY"

Although tenant protests throughout Mexico failed to systematically reduce rents or provide adequate water and waste services, they did spark discussions over the provision of affordable, hygienic spaces on the urban periphery. Many residents began to demand that the government provide lots and construct homes.[41] Building companies and planners responded to the social turmoil over housing to push their own schemes, and Obregón turned to land grants to placate frustrated tenants while avoiding a confrontation with urban capital.

The subject of affordable and hygienic homes for the working class pervaded public discussion even after the strike fizzled. Building companies advocated erecting modestly priced houses made of cheaper building materials like reinforced concrete, which used steel reinforcement to strengthen the aggregate of crushed stone and sand.[42] The Homeowners League fulfilled its promise, made at the apex of the strike, to form a commission that would design working-class homes. Commission members Quevedo, Marroquín y Rivera, and Manuel Stampa devised a model economical home, which looked strikingly similar to a suburban U.S. home with yard, picket fence, and eaved roof—a sign of the gradual shift in Mexico toward North American urbanism. However, the League reneged on its commitment to construct the homes. Instead, it displayed the home near the busy entrance of Chapultepec Park in a public relations stunt designed to manifest its concern "for the needs of our people."[43] Other potential developers proposed the formation of new working-class colonias by organizing *sociedades cooperativas* composed of working-class shareholders who would gradually pay the government back for the land concession. One project, led by Ministry of Public Works and Communications (SCOP) engineer Jesus Monserrat, eyed the federal lands of the Ex Hipódromo de Peralvillo (where the first racetrack was located) to reach "the noble goal . . . of realizing the most legitimate longing of the working class: living healthfully under his own roof free of perpetual threats" from landlords.[44]

Obregón had already devised a similar plan for those same lands a few months after the tenant strike ended. In October 1922 the president, in conjunction with the Ministry of Revenue and Public Credit and the SCOP, selected the old racetrack as the site for a new subdivision built solely for tenants.[45] The president assigned his photographer and longtime supporter Jesus Abitia the task of divvying out the lots to beneficiaries and charged SCOP employees with designing the homes and plotting the streets, sewerage, and water. The SCOP planners proposed Mexico's first public housing project: 1,287 lots featuring single-family homes and six-family cooperatives, built in a garden-city design with ample green space and all essential sanitary fixtures.[46] Once residents caught wind of the government's plan, hundreds—perhaps thousands—of lower-class residents sought to be included in the new project, which represented "emancipation from the tyranny of tenancy" and an escape from "the abuses and extortions of those men lacking in conscience known as the HOME-OWNERS."[47] Obregón's colonia Ex Hipódromo de Peralvillo meshed the 1920s planners' dream of bringing hygienic and affordable housing to the urban working class with tenants' dreams of extricating themselves from exorbitant rents and crowded and disease-ridden spaces.

The scop's plans, however, were riddled with complications. Rather than marking the start of a sustained state effort to build housing, the project was gutted. The garden-city housing plan was shelved—even the sewer and water systems were postponed. Instead, Abitia sold lots ranging from under two hundred to three hundred square meters at one and a half pesos per square meter, to be paid in installments. Ex Hipódromo de Peralvillo became Mexico City's first large *colonia proletaria*, a type of subdivision established with varying degrees of state support, independent of large developers but lacking a commitment to housing or sanitation.[48] Hundreds more of these colonias appeared in the decades to come, adding a new interest group—self-help housing occupants—to postrevolutionary politics.

By the beginning of 1923, over a hundred families had begun to construct makeshift homes on ten acres of land in Ex Hipódromo de Peralvillo. The rapid pace of settlement was a testament to how desperate many tenants had become, preferring to live in self-made shacks than in crumbling and expensive tenements. Their desperation was also tinged with a dose of bourgeois aspiration, which was stimulated by planners and other sectors of the elite. A single-family home promised to deliver a private family life and an escape from the stigmas intellectuals associated with tenement life: dirtiness, familial dissolution, moral depravity, promiscuity, and criminality.[49] Here was an opportunity to leave the crowded city center, just as the middle and upper classes had done in previous decades. But their new location on the city's periphery was precarious, and settlers lacked land titles.[50] Insecurity also derived from contention over the property on which they built. In 1918 the self-proclaimed "ex-revolutionary" Macario Navarro laid claim to thousands of acres of land extending from San Lázaro, on the eastern edge of the city, to the outskirts of Guadalupe Hidalgo to the north, most of which had belonged to the disgraced Porfirian hacendado and urbanizer Remigio Noriega. This land, he believed, included most of what Abitia had granted to the lower-class residents. A civil judge agreed with him in 1924, the same year another revolutionary general and ally of Obregón from the state of Sonora, Plutarco Elías Calles, assumed the presidency.

Although Navarro eventually lost his court battle, dozens of residents pleaded for property titles and the right to pay for their lots over five years, as initially agreed.[51] In the mid-1920s, they organized a Junta de Mejoras Materiales (Material Improvement Committee) to represent the settlement's four thousand inhabitants, and the new Calles government ordered that instead of paying a fee per square meter, the residents would cover the costs of "urbanization"—water, sewerage, lighting, and pavement—in exchange for their titles. It was at this point that committee president Roberto Martínez extorted money from the residents. He collected nearly fifteen thousand pesos from settlers with the stated aim of installing essential services, and threatened to evict those who failed to pay. But by 1927 that money had disappeared.[52]

Just as Obregón's friend Abitia had been instrumental in the early stages of planning Ex Hipódromo de Peralvillo, President Calles in June 1927 assigned his own friend, the emerging architect Guillermo Zárraga, to pick up the pieces of the crumbling project. Zárraga, influenced by his father, the eminent Porfirian-era doctor Fernando Zárraga, had completed his thesis "Modern Affordable Housing" at Mexico City's School of Fine Arts and elaborated a plan for the capital that embodied key tenets of the modernist planning vision: the creation of new working-class living environments to foster a healthy citizenry. In tune with Quevedo before him and garden-city planners across the Atlantic, Zárraga envisaged working-class subdivisions replete with urban services, green spaces, and open-air schools. The tenant strike, and Obregón's and Calles's responses to it, gave Zárraga his first experiment, which he hoped would be expanded into a new housing paradigm. Zárraga, like the scop planners of 1923, had an integral vision for the struggling Ex Hipódromo project. He not only set out to monitor the funds collected by the material improvement committee but also designed a less expensive water and sewage system and offered a new design for housing, a market, and parks. But he too ran into administrative constraints. His sewerage and water-supply projects were completed with resident cooperation by 1930, but his broader plan, both for this particular subdivision and for the city in general, fell by the wayside.[53]

The existence of the colonia Ex Hipódromo de Peralvillo was a testament to the tumultuous spring and summer of 1922, when thousands of working-class tenants protested and went on strike. Its problems with nebulous property titles and mismanaged funds would be repeated in later developments. Still, it was in the messy politics of left-wing activism, affordable and hygienic housing, urban planning, and postrevolutionary reform in cities like Veracruz and Mexico City that the peripheral settlement wedded to the ideal of the single-family home was born. As urban living conditions languished and rents rose, the urban working classes called on the state to issue additional land grants that would permit them to create their own neighborhoods independent of developers and landlords.

The housing question in postrevolutionary Mexico raises an unexplored paradox, however. In the 1920s, as housing projects began to take shape across Europe and within Latin America, the Mexican state, emerging from the depths of social revolution and facing off against a boisterous urban working class, repeatedly refused to implement its own planners' public housing proposals. An explanation of Obregón's and Calles's tepid responses to the tenant movement can be found in a comparison with another major Latin American city. Buenos Aires's housing policy was driven by a similar dynamic of tenant protest and government response, but public interventions in housing were more forceful. By 1921 the city had a rent-freeze law, and another that enabled cooperatives to build affordable housing, plus an affordable housing commission empowered to devise new projects.[54] While more profound housing reform occurred during the populist 1940s, public housing construction began in the early 1920s in Buenos Aires.

What explains the different paths? Unlike the Sonoran governments of Mexico in the 1920s, Argentina's government did not claim to represent a revolution, yet party competition spurred the Radicals and the Socialists to court the working class through housing. Party competition in Mexico was fierce at the local and state levels, but Mexico City had little jurisdiction over housing, and national-level politics was steered more by revolutionary caudillos and their camarillas than by electoral politics. In addition, workers in Buenos Aires following World War I were numerous and highly organized around not just production but also collective consumption. The Mexico City working class was also well organized but lacked the sheer numbers of Buenos Aires and thus could put less pressure on the state. Furthermore, as a city increasingly dominated by industrial capital, authorities in Buenos Aires saw in public housing and rent control a means to suppress the factory wages paid by employers, just as Mexican authorities would later in the century. Finally, in Mexico City the revolution redounded on housing in peculiar ways. Carranza and Obregón earmarked a large percentage of their budgets to military needs and, to a lesser degree, the incipient land reform, education, and the renetworking of infrastructure destroyed by violence.[55] The divergent structures of political representation, the differing forces of urbanization, and the counterintuitive consequences of the revolution structured housing policy, and in consequence the living conditions of thousands.

While dreamy-eyed ex-tenants moved onto the lands of the former racetrack at the end of 1922, Mexico City confronted another sanitary crisis: the malfunctioning Xochimilco water-supply system. If the tenant strike of mid-1922 contested capitalist urbanization and its unequal distribution of public services, the water crisis of November 1922 reflected a deep suspicion of democratic municipal governments. The crisis exposed the city's inability to maintain the vital service. The Porfirian culture of water rights converged with rising expectations and a climate of heightened protest, all nourished by dozens of strikes, from the tram operators and textile workers to the tenants. The interplay among an explosive political culture, a prostrate and divided municipal government, and a faulty infrastructure intended to deliver a crucial service detonated the most destructive protest in Mexico City in the 1920s.

The municipal government of Mexico City attempted to govern between the rock of the federal government and the hard place of the urban populace. The odds were against it. The executive dispensed scant funds to the city council at the very time that major investments were needed to maintain and expand services.[56] The same public works that augmented public expectations for decent sanitary services had dire consequences on the city government, which struggled to operate those services in the rapidly growing city. The press relentlessly criticized the drainage and water-supply infrastructure, and rival municipal factions within the broad Obregonista alliance—the Cooperativists, the Laborists, and the Liberals—bitterly contested with one another, destabilizing the political order.

In early 1922 the Liberal Constitutionalist Party mayor, Doctor Miguel Alonzo Romero, a delegate on public health at the Querétaro Constitutional Convention and a supporter of Obregón over Carranza, presciently warned of a pending water calamity because of deteriorating pipes and aging parts in the Condesa pumping station.[57] The mayor's warning underscored the tenuous position of the municipal government. Sewerage, water, and other services remained in neglect years after peace had been restored, and the city owed large debts to its employees.[58] The municipal government managed the Xochimilco water system, which made it responsible in the event of any breakdown—a responsibility magnified by the fact that Xochimilco was the city's lone water source.

On November 19, 1922, disaster struck. According to reports by Mariano Barragán, the former Lake Texcoco engineer who at the time was serving as the city's public works director, a sudden surge in electrical current stalled the Condesa station pumps. A controllable problem quickly turned into a debacle. Without functioning pumps, water levels rose in the aqueduct and threatened to flood the pumping station. Marroquín y Rivera had anticipated such an event by constructing a discharge canal (*canal de desfogue*) at the intersection of the Piedad River and the aqueduct in the southern colonia del Valle. However, the station manager, an employee of the Light and Power Company, failed to promptly notify the guard overseeing the discharge canal. By the time the guard received word of the problem, the pressure in the aqueduct had increased to the point that the gate regulating flow into the drainage canal rose only a few inches.[59] Little water escaped. The manager's vacillation and apparent obtuseness, combined with the guard's poor decision making and the action of the pressurized water, turned a minor interruption into a veritable catastrophe. The Xochimilco water poured into the pumping station, destroying the very technology designed to control it. By the time the employees had drained the floodwaters, the pumps had been damaged and service interrupted. Marroquín y Rivera's design was also implicated. He had failed to place the pumps above potential floodwaters or to provide the station with a natural drainage outlet. One engineer decried the design as "suspending Damocles's sword over the city."[60]

Barragán took emergency measures to ensure a supply of water for the hundreds of thousands of people dependent on the system. He rationed the remaining reservoir water, providing service for two hours each day, one in the morning and another in the evening. With the reservoir completely emptied by November 26, the city reconnected two defunct water sources: the Chapultepec springs and the Desierto de los Leones springs. The city also connected several productive artesian wells to the municipal system. Because of these measures, not a day passed during the monthlong crisis without some water running through the network.[61] Within days, municipal officials also set up a system of twenty-four mule-driven tankers (*pipas*) to deliver water to diverse parts of the city.[62]

Alonzo Romero created a false sense of hope, however, when he declared that the system would be fully restored after six days.[63] The pumps, originally purchased from a U.S. company, could not be replaced expeditiously, a cruel effect of Mexico's technological dependence. The Light and Power Company charged with maintaining the machinery insisted that the motors could be dried. This time-consuming method opened the door for the press to condemn the city government.[64] *El Demócrata* enjoined residents to demand the dissolution of the city council and municipal government, claiming that corrupt councilmen spent the water tax on improving only well-to-do neighborhoods like Roma and Condesa, in which they owned homes.[65] The newspaper invoked the urban protests of the early 1920s and the years of revolution that nourished them, observing that "the people are teaching themselves to reclaim sacred rights thanks to the last liberatory movement."[66] The press spread the notion that the city's accounts of the shortage were "deceiving the populace" and accused the government of scapegoating the canal guard. The accident, according to the papers, was a result of diverted funds, negligence, and illegal trading of replacement parts.[67]

Such accusations were supported by renowned engineers, whose authority reporters rarely questioned. Marroquín y Rivera told *El Demócrata* that the true problem was not the actions of one employee but a long history of neglected maintenance. In an even more scathing commentary, Modesto Rolland, a longtime critic of the municipal government, remarked that "the city council has lied to justify itself and avoid responsibilities"; he placed blame on malfunctioning pump-station valves, whose replacement parts, Rolland claimed, the city had sold "as if they were scrap metal."[68] These engineers' reports, viewed by many as objective, lent credence to the press's antimunicipal narrative.

There is no evidence that the Public Works Department or the SCOP misinformed the public, but there were good reasons to question the city's governance of water service both before and during the crisis. Marroquín y Rivera's project, the sanitary code, and the constitution guaranteeing public health had convinced most, if not all, residents that access to clean, pressurized water was a right, an expectation of modern urban life. Yet the municipal government forsook both the maintenance of the service and the work of extending it to the growing population.[69] At the completion of Marroquín y Rivera's system, the city enjoyed water twenty-four hours per day. By 1922 cracks in the aqueduct and underground, in combination with a growing number of connections, reduced pressure in the system and thus access to water in the shared taps of vecindades and on higher floors. Extrapolating backward from data available from the early 1930s, it appears that in 1922 there were approximately twenty thousand connections for about twenty-seven thousand buildings, comprising about 132,481 residences.[70] Given that official building counts failed to include many irregular developments or accurate information on inhabitants per building, perhaps around 70 percent of the urban population enjoyed safe water, and fewer still enjoyed Xochimilco water.

Thousands of tenants shared taps where declining pressure reduced each person's supply.[71]

Frustration was already mounting over service deficiencies, and the Xochimilco accident triggered a wide range of responses from inhabitants. Residents of the city's east side requested that tanker trucks visit their "more working-class neighborhoods," an indication that not every urban inhabitant was considered equal in terms of emergency water provision.[72] The Lírico Playhouse, one of many popular theaters that often captured the pulse of residents, put on the vulgar improvisational play *Water, I Beg My God* several times, breathing some humor into a desperate situation.[73] The well business boomed as those with disposable income decided to escape this and future crises by privatizing their water supply.[74] While the wealthy had more options to obtain water, large segments of the working and middle classes—those lucky enough to have gained access to city water in the first place—found themselves suffering from the shortage and forced to take water from insalubrious places or solicit it from upper-class homes. It was this urban group—not those who lacked water provision altogether—who were the protagonists of protest.

Partisan conflict also contributed to popular revolt in late 1922. Luis Morones and his powerful CROM, the popular wing of the Laborist Party, parlayed the accident into an opportunity to discredit Alonzo Romero and the Liberal Constitutionalist Party's dominance of the council. The CROM called a rally for November 30, ten days after the accident at the pumping station. Thousands of men, including members of the taxi union (which had just been involved in a bitter strike against the city), the PCM-backed tenant union, shoemakers, brewers, municipal employees, and others, met at the CROM headquarters.[75] Workers, however, were not the pawns of Laborists' political machinations. Weary of years of municipal government negligence and days of water scarcity, their decision to demonstrate constituted a last-resort action to obtain their right to a vital public service.[76] That participants were largely male, unlike earlier protests over matters related to household consumption, suggests that the organizers expected a confrontation.[77]

That evening, about five thousand protesters crying out "Death to the municipal government," "Death to Mr. Romero," and "We want water" reached the municipal palace.[78] (See figure 3.2.) Armed municipal guards closed the palace door, leaving some fifteen members of the Federal District's mounted gendarmerie stranded outside with the vociferous protesters. Saúl Pérez Granja, the captain of the gendarmerie, attempted to calm the crowd by offering to lead a group to the mayor for a "favorable resolution," but one of the protesters

FIGURE 3.2 — Protesters demand water. COURTESY OF INAH, FOTOTECA NACIONAL.

punched him in the face. Others continued shouting "Death to the mayor."[79] Protesters then battered down the palace door, and the municipal guard opened fire, with several armed workers responding in kind. Rioters wrecked the building and started a fire in the Department of Municipal Registry, while another group peeled off to march toward the mayor's residence. Only when federal troops arrived was the plaza evacuated, and the flames extinguished. Up to a dozen people died, and over sixty were injured, including several bystanders.[80] Numerous people were arrested, although nobody dared admit wrongdoing or any political motive behind their presence at the plaza. For example, two men charged with theft and discharge of firearms denied the accusations and claimed they were drawn by mere curiosity.[81]

Rioting had been a forceful—if somewhat uncommon—form of political protest in Mexico's capital for centuries. The riots of 1624, 1692, and 1915 had followed moments of political crisis, and each involved in some way the politics of food provision. In each case, the urban populace saw more traditional political channels exhausted, which led to "bargaining by riot."[82] The tumult of 1922 followed this same underlying grammar, but within the political and social context of postrevolutionary Mexico. The Xochimilco accident unleashed a wave of protest over the right to water, propelled by an antagonistic news media and—as in earlier tumults—political division. In this case, the ruckus over water brought discontent over flailing urban governance to a head.

The restoration of full water service in mid-December did not let the city government off the hook. Even before the November riot, press demands for the dissolution of municipal government—*El Demócrata* called for a corporatist-style "municipal soviet"—resonated with the urban public.[83] In a letter to Obregón in December 1922, a certain Ludovicus Grackus waxed extravagant: "The people that compose the population of the capital of the republic, without class distinction and in the most unanimous form, have condemned the indifferent, inept, and criminal conduct of the city, and the blood spilled by the hit men of this clumsy and criminal [body] was testament to this discontent."[84] He called for the elimination of the municipal government and for the constitution of a "General Public Health Commission." That same day feminist groups proposed that the city be run by a single administrator.[85] Similarly, former Maderista Juan Sánchez Azcona suggested that the city council be replaced by an "administrative advisory board" composed of a few experts. Other civil groups and individuals also spoke out against the municipal government, and the unions demanded punitive measures against the authorities responsible for the loss of their "class comrades." Considering the press coverage, the conspicuousness of signs and slogans spurning the municipality during the November protests, and the flurry of petitions following the riot, there is little doubt that antimunicipal sentiments had wide appeal. But as water was slowly restored, the movement disintegrated. Morones and the Laborists foresaw a devastating loss for the Liberal Constitutionalists in the upcoming elections in 1922, and this likely shaped Obregón's response. He acknowledged that the municipal government "has demonstrated over many years a great ineptitude to efficiently govern the interests of this capital" but refused to seek its annulment.[86] Still, the disruptive three-week period diminished its political capital.

The demands of protesters, strikers, and rioters in 1922 were double-edged. Strikers practiced local democracy in city tenements; others protested and rioted in the streets and the zocalo, making their voices heard. All sought to use direct action to bring about hygienic and affordable homes and neighborhoods, but a large group of them fell back on beliefs in the sanctity of urban expertise and hierarchical organization—Communist leadership, sanitary committees, and technocratic boards. The popular embrace of technocracy had first gathered momentum under Díaz, as complex technological systems and rationalized health care created new expectations of modern life that required the rule of experts.[87] Checked but not stopped during the revolution, technocracy accelerated quickly in city politics during the 1920s. The water protesters sought to convince the president to assign competent experts to manage essential urban services, much as the Porfirian juntas had managed major public works. This seemingly odd popular demand can also be explained through the promises of revolutionary change. Because the central government ostensibly operated under the banner of revolution, residents had faith that a small group of neutral, well-intentioned experts could govern justly. In place of the much-maligned city council, they championed a new, improved revolutionary order, one that would, in Marx's words, "conjure up the spirits of the past" in order to promote a more livable urban environment.[88] By the end of 1922, calls for technocratic governance of the metropolitan environment, putatively free of political maneuvering, took center stage.

THE LAST YEARS OF MUNICIPAL GOVERNANCE

Beginning in 1924, the Laborist Party, with the full backing of Obregón and then Calles, dominated Mexico City politics. In order to establish a popular base, the party harnessed a recurring form of political organization, the neighborhood association. Peralvillo, La Bolsa, Obrera, Romero Rubio, and several other neighborhoods already supported their own associations to advocate for connections to the networked city of sewer lines, water mains, paved streets, and electricity. One Laborist councilman vowed to form similar neighborhood committees under the aegis of the party in "abandoned colonias."[89] Soon thereafter, the council inaugurated the Neighborhood Improvement Committee of Balbuena, a working-class community on the city's east side. Thanks to Quevedo's work on the eve of the revolution, the community boasted a large green space, but it lacked sewer lines. Community donations and city council support led to their installment. The *Boletín Municipal* described the neighbors' mutual assistance as "a good example of public-spiritedness" that would help the city advance toward "modernity."[90] The success of the Balbuena committee encouraged the party to found others in Atlampa, Santa María de la Ribera, and Magdalena Mixhuca.[91] The Laborists initiated a top-down, corporatist form of urban governance entrenched in the history of neighborhood organizing, anticipating future initiatives that would be undertaken by the federal government in the 1930s.[92] Stark inequalities in service provision persisted, but as water and sewerage reached private dwellings in formerly forlorn neighborhoods, nearly everyone, not merely an elite few, shared the expectation of a healthy urban environment. After 1922 the Laborists recognized the political advantage to be gained from sanitizing the living spaces of the lower classes.

The Laborist hegemony led to the payment of outstanding debts and an increase in public works projects, but the spatial inequalities of urban sanitation remained largely unchallenged.[93] Furthermore, despite sanitary works in a few neighborhoods such as Obrera and Balbuena, the municipal government's newfound interest in infrastructure development tended to focus on projects that benefited the central business district and affluent neighborhoods.[94] Moreover, the Federal District government extended the automobile-friendly Avenida de los Insurgentes from the southwestern corner of Roma through the young colonia del Valle to the Bombilla restaurant in the town of San Ángel. Insurgentes symbolized the birth of an urban model oriented around private automobiles over public tramlines.[95]

This kind of street planning encouraged speculation. José G. de la Lama, an urbanizer of Porfirian extraction, capitalized on the expansion of Insurgentes, which increased land values along its trajectory.[96] De la Lama's most renowned development was the colonia Hipódromo Condesa, established in 1925 with his partner, Raul Basurto, on the lands of the Condesa racetrack—a slap in the face to those who were simultaneously settling the unserviced lands of the Peralvillo racetrack. José Luis Cuevas, director of the National Engineering School, designed the San Martín Park where the infield of the track once lay, and gorgeous homes and art deco buildings quickly populated the subdivision, which contained more green space than any other centrally located neighborhood.[97] Only the colonia Chapultepec Heights (now Lomas de Chapultepec), located on a hill above Chapultepec Park in the municipality of Tacubaya, surpassed Hipódromo Condesa in green space. Advertisements by its developer, the Chapultepec Heights Company, boasted that the new subdivision, also a Cuevas design, would become Mexico's first garden city: "Buy in Chapultepec and the Park will be your garden."[98] Cuevas designed winding roads that "followed the hilly contours of the terrain," where the automobile and California architecture predominated.[99] (See figure 3.3.)

The illustrious architect was one of many planners of the post–World War I era who perverted the intentions of Ebenezer Howard's garden city. Cuevas

FIGURE 3.3 — Lomas de Chapultepec (originally named Chapultepec Heights), 1936.
COURTESY OF FUNDACIÓN ICA.

helped turn a utopian form (the garden city) into a speculative endeavor for the prosperous that cemented the spatial segregation of the city.[100] The west and south, around Chapultepec Park and along Insurgentes, boasted hygienic and tree-lined streets; residents in the east and north lived amid dirt and dust, continuously struggling to attain the right to the sanitary city. As important as Ex Hipódromo de Peralvillo was in setting a precedent for future governments, it did not radically alter urban development, which continued to fragment urban life. The mixture of people that had characterized the compact city center during the nineteenth century gave way to a dispersed urban agglomeration in the car-centered twentieth century, in which identity and social worth became increasingly attached to one's residential location and one's access to green space, hygiene, and networked infrastructure.

Suburbanization during the 1920s created conurbations among the adjacent municipalities of Tacubaya, Mixcoac, and San Ángel. At the same time, Laborists endured vitriolic attacks while being financially hamstrung by the Federal District government. Water resurged as the fulcrum of public debate. Newspapers published Health Department accusations that indicted the municipality for water impurities resulting from cracks in the aqueduct. The director of municipal public works, Nicolás Durán, called these accusations "unfounded," reporting that even the bacteriological analysis conducted by that same Health Department had concluded that the water was pure. "It is widely and notoriously known," Durán went on, "that Tacubaya's water, . . . run by different municipal authorities, is a veritable soup of pathogenic germs, and not one word has been said of this."[101] The controversy signaled a widening antagonism between urban experts and the various municipal administrations that had recently been conjoined by urban expansion.

Urban planning further widened the antagonism. Mexico already boasted a long history of planning that featured Quevedo, Roberto Gayol, and José Yves Limantour, among others. But it was not until the late 1920s that it became a clearly demarcated and professionalized discipline in which urbanists identified themselves as planners rather than conservationists, hydraulic engineers, or architects. The steady expansion of Mexico City opened the door for urban experts to draw up an integral plan for growth, and Carlos Contreras was the trailblazer. Contreras bypassed the revolution of 1910 by moving to New York, where he earned bachelor's and postgraduate degrees at Columbia University. During nearly two decades in New York, he absorbed the planning philosophies of Daniel Burnham and studied the zoning regulations of the fast-growing Los Angeles. Upon his return to Mexico City in 1925, he connected with like-minded thinkers and pushed forward a more holistic planning vision for the nation.[102] Aided by experienced minds like Gayol and Quevedo, as well as newer ones like Octavio Dubois and Eduardo Hay, Contreras devised a plan that wove together city and hinterland and offered new prescriptions for transport networks, greenbelts, sanitary services, and industrial zoning. It was a city plan that drew on the capitalist-friendly Burnham plan for Chicago and the regionalist, resource-minded planning of Patrick Geddes.[103] Contreras held firm to a notion that planning must work for the collective good—after all, this was its ideological justification—but beyond its more utopian purpose, Mexican planners envisioned an integral plan of the Basin of Mexico to promote "industrial and commercial growth and the increase of property values."[104] In 1927 Contreras and others launched the journal *Planificación*, which further inscribed the principle that only experts could guide urban development, standing above the political fray and operating under the helm of a revolutionary state. This expert planning vision allowed no room for the Federal District's democratic municipalities, whose independent regulatory powers and partisan divides were seen as undermining planned growth.

Within this context, Obregón, while preparing for a second presidential run in the spring of 1928, sent Congress a proposal to eliminate all the municipal governments of the Federal District. The bill was also a Machiavellian political move. Much of the discussion over the proposal revolved around the need for a centralized administration to improve urban services, echoing the flurry of petitions from the water crisis of 1922. But Obregón also understood that with one shrewd swipe of his pen he could debilitate the powerful Morones and the Laborists, who were embittered by the ex-president's bid for a second term.[105] Indeed, members of the Laborist Party such as Vicente Lombardo Toledano were among the few who spoke out for the municipality. Before becoming the labor leader who would dominate Mexican leftism under the populist Lázaro Cárdenas, Lombardo Toledano was a congressional deputy and an active participant in transnational planning networks.[106] In a meticulous and worldly review of town planning, he hoped to convince fellow urban experts to rally around an alternative plan to create a democratic municipality that would encompass the entire Basin of Mexico. The suppression of the municipality within the Federal District, he argued, would presage the dissolution of municipalities throughout the country, which would violate Article 115 of the constitution, "contribut[e] to civic disassociation," and create "one more ghost within the system of Mexican public justice."[107] In spite of Lombardo Toledano's passion, the deck was stacked against him. The legislative proposal even withstood Obregón's assassination in San Ángel in the summer of 1928, and it comfortably passed the Mexican Congress, controlled by supporters of the Sonorans. The protesters of 1922 finally got what they had requested: the replacement of what was, in theory, the most democratic institution in city politics by an administration dependent on the president.

On January 1, 1929, the centralized Department of the Federal District (DDF)—with the new executive-appointed governor José Manuel Puig Casauranc at the helm—assumed the governance of Mexico City and much of its surroundings.[108] The creation of the DDF had the purpose of transcending political controversy. Planners, for example, believed that more orderly governance would enable a progressive, reformist science of planning to defeat obtrusive politics and the obstacles hinterland nature posed to prosperity.[109] Silvano Palafox, chief of the Architecture Office in the new Public Works Department, captured the spirit: "There is a lack of culture in those who believe that all regulations violate their property rights. It is an axiom that above those rights lie the rights of the collectivity."[110] Unregulated urbanization, it seemed, was in the past, and a new era of urban reform lay ahead.

Mexico City planners anticipated that the DDF would commence a new round of infrastructure projects, designed by themselves, to promote ordered growth and allay sanitary inequalities. Though the new city government did embrace zoning regulations and pioneer a planning department, their dream quickly evaporated. Instead of pursuing massive service extensions to forlorn colonias, the new governor honed in on the vexing problem of water. A service that once operated twenty-four hours a day was now reduced to twelve owing to leaks and extensions, and the city had experienced numerous disruptions of service over the years.[111] With a tight budget, Water Department director Octavio Dubois, one of Marroquín y Rivera's apprentices during the construction of the Xochimilco system, campaigned to replace the station's old valves and purify the water to the level it enjoyed in the 1910s. Workers scoured the lands surrounding the underground aqueduct for sources of pollution. They discovered that despite restrictions on land use along the aqueduct, unserviced homes and garbage dumps surrounded it. The homes were destroyed, the area was cleaned up, and a siphon was constructed to carry the *aguas negras* of the colonias del Valle and Amores away from the aqueduct's surroundings.[112]

In June 1929 workers updating the Condesa station mistakenly cut service to the city. For several days, denizens, still carrying fresh memories of the long November of 1922, suffered from thirst, and *El Universal* reported protests throughout the city.[113] On the heels of the accident the government pronounced Dubois the "Dictador de Aguas," elevating the engineer to the status of a deus ex machina. The announcement could have come straight from the mouths of the petitioners of 1922, as it gave the "dictator" Dubois the political autonomy to reverse what the papers described as the damage done by the old municipal government. The use of the term *dictator*—normally reserved for Díaz—denoted that the promotion was a technocratic advance, and large swaths of the populace seemed to support their new water czar to defeat "the anarchy of water service."[114]

The creation of the post of water dictator was a political performance, however, and the Federal District governor converted the position into yet another water board, with Dubois as its director, in June 1930. The semi-independent committee handled technical studies, the tapping of new water sources, repairs, and the organization of the meter system.[115] In the board's first year, Dubois obtained about a million pesos to improve the most deficient parts of the system and prepare for its future expansion. He ordered the repair of many of the largest leaks in newer subdivisions where developers had used shoddy joints or old piping, and he devoted resources to plugging the holes in the aqueduct, some of which were large enough to put one's hand through.[116] Engineers noted that the new commercial bottled-water operation "Agua Virgen," which had launched the previous year, was, ironically, contaminating the San Juan spring, a potential future source of public water.[117] The board advised the prohibition of all "human gatherings and animal farms within a radius of at least 500 meters" of the spring, and the diversion of canals from the vicinity—just as had been done earlier with the other springs.[118] In their efforts to procure clean water, planners transformed, measured, and regulated the metropolitan environment, sometimes using force.

WATER AND THE ENGINEER

The government's water board, the Engineer and Architect Society that advised it, and other leading engineers debated the merits of different engineering works and water policies. Engineer José Argüelles rejected well perforation, promoted by some as a quick fix to increase supply, as too damaging. He proposed instead the appropriation of water from the Lerma watershed in the Valley of Toluca and the recycling of rainwater through the construction of dams and purification plants—the former began in 1951, while the latter remains a dream of urban environmentalists today. Argüelles was also the first to link land subsidence, an emerging problem that damaged building foundations and other infrastructure, to well use; a few years earlier, Gayol had proved that the city was sinking but believed this was solely the result of lake desiccation and drainage works.[119]

At the beginning of 1930, Dubois, like Argüelles, called for further investments in locating new water sources as well as the timely installation of meters and repairs of the principal mains and pipes. Dubois had plenty of critics within the society, however. Carlos Petricioli, for one, rejected the idea that new sources needed to be tapped and argued that the addition of several wells to the city's supply and repair of leaks could serve the population for decades to come.[120] Petricioli, not coincidentally, was the president of a construction company that specialized in well building and water-supply infrastructure. Dubois fired back that new sources were necessary since the repairs to the network would take years. He brooded over the land subsidence that well drilling might provoke and added that the water surfaced in unhygienic conditions.[121]

Nicolás Durán took aim at consumption practices. He agreed on the need for water meters but doubted that they would be effective at promoting conservation under the current taxation scheme. The remedy, according to Durán, was a private enterprise that would collect usage fees "on an entirely commercial basis" from tenants, who were the ones responsible for "waste." Viewing water waste like a social disease, Durán hoped to teach people that "water has a price" in order to "cure" them of their squandering ways.[122] Durán's privatization solution mirrored events in Puebla, where the city had privatized water service in 1928 under similar justifications.[123] Fernando Beltrán y Puga, an active member of the water board who had come to prominence as the Mexican boundary-waters commissioner from 1906 to 1914, positioned himself on the other end of the political spectrum. The budget of 769,000 pesos, he claimed, was inadequate to address urban inequalities. He sought "to give preference to the most imperious needs, and at least supply those neighborhoods overflowing with the humble population." Given the immense cost of such a task, the engineer implored the water board to first install hydrants so that lower-class residents would cease pumping from clandestine wells and using polluted river water. In the long-term vision of this engineer, meters and increased tariffs would boost income, which then could be used to extend services to needy communities.[124] In a partial victory for Beltrán y Puga, the government refused to pursue Durán's privatization scheme, and the water board agreed to earmark some funds for the installation of public hydrants in some working-class neighborhoods.[125]

Though these were certainly not the only debates over water policy in the postrevolutionary era, the short-lived water board demonstrated the competing models of water provision and the difficulty that engineers faced in pushing through sanitary goals, even in the nation's capital. The government installed meters, which produced a wave of reaction from landlords, homeowners, and other residents. Ultimately, however, city officials followed a more conservative course that tweaked the existing system without radically transforming the way most residents obtained their water. And few people challenged the hardened technocracy in which, it was presumed, neutral planners hired by the government knew what was best for the city.

The 1910s and early 1920s were a vibrant period of mass urban politics, and 1922 witnessed two distinct but related movements for hygienic homes: the tenant strike of May and the water protests of November. The climate of postrevolution informed both the protests and the state's reaction to them. The year ended, however, with a bevy of calls for expert rule to order and better manage an unhealthy and chaotic urban environment. It was a return to Porfirian technocracy, albeit under revolutionary auspices. The hegemony of the engineer and the centralized authoritarianism of city government after 1928 foreclosed popular participation in environmental politics, water policy, and housing conditions in Mexico City, until the Cárdenas sexenio. In this period, the Mexican state assumed greater power over both urban and hinterland landscapes in an attempt to control both unruly nature and unruly people—but rather than embracing a complete makeover of the city that could mitigate stark spatial inequalities, the state made cosmetic changes: the Ex Hipódromo de Peralvillo neighborhood rather than Zárraga's holistic plan; meter installment and well perforation—despite the objections to it—rather than universal service extension.

There existed another continuity from the Porfirian era. Environmental planners continued to discern the interconnections and interdependencies of the urban fabric. The august engineer Roberto Gayol ridiculed the old municipal government for ending his highly acclaimed pipe-flushing scheme, replacing it with an inferior method using the depleted springs of Chapultepec.[126] This predicament led one writer to sardonically warn, "We are going to be flooded for lack of water," since sedimentation in pipes prevented wastewater evacuation.[127] Gayol underscored forest conservation of the hills and slopes of the basin to protect his system from siltation and safeguard the proper functioning of the city's infrastructure, and he also encouraged the government to dredge the flood-prone Lake Texcoco.[128] Gayol's warnings, much like Alonzo Romero's a decade earlier, came true on October 14, 1932, when the entire city center flooded.[129] Gayol construed drainage as an interwoven socionatural imbroglio in which the city's expansion, its hydraulic infrastructure, and the surrounding hinterlands of water and trees were vitally interconnected.[130] It is to this forested hinterland that I now turn.

4

The City and Its Forests

A tapestry of landscapes blanketed the mountains south and west of the city's main water source in Xochimilco. Textile factories, paper mills, and ranchos dotted the diverted and dammed Magdalena River as it meandered toward the basin floor; communal farmland and pastureland as well as a few haciendas covered the foothills and mountain slopes; farther up in the high sierra, vast woodlands of mixed oak, pine, cedar, cypress, and fir gave way to pine and zacatón. According to sanitary planners like Roberto Gayol, the forested mountains were tightly intertwined with the lakes and hydraulic infrastructure. Gayol's close colleague, Fernando Zárraga, cautioned that the sedimentation of Lake Texcoco would hamper the effectiveness of the sewer system and the Gran Canal. He, along with his son Guillermo, recommended a sizable increase in vegetation and open space in and around the capital to promote hygiene and eliminate dust pollution—invoking Miguel Ángel de Quevedo's earlier proposals.[1] Sanitary engineers and architects assumed the environment either vitiated or enhanced human health, and they believed their charge was to modify the environment to engender a healthy urban life. Forest conservation fit neatly into this widespread planning philosophy.

Quevedo had split his career between two interlaced worlds: the hinterland forests of the nearby Ajusco, Las Cruces, and Nevada ranges on the one hand and the city on the other. As a member of various city commissions, he routinely advocated for open, hygienic living spaces to nurture a healthy urban populace, while never losing sight of the city's surrounding forests, which he perceived to be intimately wedded to this lifelong goal. He redoubled his conservationist campaign after the violent phase of the revolution. Quevedo wholeheartedly believed that agricultural and urban development required prosperous forestland, and he feared that the government's agrarian reform would cause irreversible harm to Mexico's already degraded woodlands unless it was channeled within a stringent conservationism.

Postrevolutionary forestry deepened the experiments of the Huertista years. While foresters clung to the old Porfirian script regarding the causes and consequences of forest loss through the radical populist administration of Lázaro Cárdenas (1934–1940), the agrarian reform program emboldened villagers to challenge exclusive forestry and landowner control of woodlands. Foresters were compelled to adapt to this redistributionist phase of the postrevolution. Still, customary forest uses, refashioned as a key component of revolutionary rural justice, chafed against the protection imperative in the mountainous rim of the Basin of Mexico. The friction between agrarian justice and forest conservation turned into a major contradiction within the core revolutionary program of the Cardenistas in the mid-1930s. Pueblos were caught between two countervailing forces. As rising urban demand for fuel, construction material, and zacatón root buoyed their forest economies, and as agrarian reform reverberated across central Mexico, villagers faced a group of urban-focused forestry experts eager to guide and restructure that economy and mold the agrarian reform to their liking. By the end of the Cárdenas sexenio, elitist urbanism had triumphed over the imperfect and halting trials of a more egalitarian form of metropolitan forest governance.

QUEVEDO'S "AGRARIAN PROBLEM"

Quevedo departed Mexico following the fall of Victoriano Huerta. Alberto Pani had accused him of being a reactionary, and a revolutionary general took possession of his *viveros* (tree nursery) in Coyoacán.[2] Once matters with Pani were settled, he returned and gained the support of the Texcoco engineer

Manuel Urquidi upon Venustiano Carranza's rise to power. Quevedo believed Mexico was reaching a defining moment with regard to forest management.

On the eve of the Querétaro Constitutional Convention in 1916, Quevedo penned a text that contributed to the ongoing discussion of Mexico's "agrarian problem," joining the more renowned trailblazers Andrés Molina Enriquez and Luis Cabrera. He wrote that land redistribution should be used as an instrument of rural progress for indigenous pueblos, that cacique monopolies over forests prevented communities from enjoying profits from wood products, and that communal forestry was a viable model for Mexico. Quevedo maintained that the revolution had been caused by Porfirio Díaz's inability to protect and more equitably distribute Mexico's "bienes nacionales"—a view no doubt influenced by his own struggles to conserve Mexico's forest patrimony.[3] He railed against timber companies and hacendados who were permitted to clearcut vast forest tracts that had once been communally held.[4] Despite these populist proclamations, however, Quevedo never embraced agrarian reform as fully as did his colleagues Molina Enriquez and Cabrera, and he only tepidly supported the redistribution of lands to indigenous campesino communities (*indigenous* and *campesino* being essentially synonymous in his view). In particular, he opposed granting forestland to communities, whose "ambition is to extend their crops even to the steepest peaks of our mountain ranges." Since this campesino aspiration was "a severe cause of the great ruin of our forests and our agricultural and hydrological poverty," Quevedo contended that agrarian authorities must redistribute only unforested land suitable for agriculture.[5] He called for higher wages to obviate campesinos' land needs, supported new agricultural settlements of small landowners, and insisted on educating campesinos about proper forest use. Disempowering caciques and imbuing villagers with the science of conservation, Quevedo believed, would allow campesinos to value their forests, and he highlighted the Basin of Mexico villages of Santa Rosa and San Nicolás Totolapan, deemed indigenous despite centuries of mestizaje, as two exemplary communities—islands in a sea of rapacious deforesters.

"THE ONLY ELEMENT WE HAVE TO SURVIVE"

Quevedo's treatise appeared as the National Agrarian Commission, established to carry out Carranza's land-reform law of 1915, was adjudicating the first community land requests. The agrarian reform dislodged landowners' resource monopoly and punctured the urban environmental imaginary that prioritized Mexico City in forestry discussions. Revolutionary elites established land reform as a fundamental building block of national reconstruction, a means of resolving agrarian antagonisms and converting "atavistic" Indians into modern campesinos. The *ejido*, the colonial term designating the pasturelands granted by the Crown, became the highly prized centerpiece of the reform. Although the right to land, forests, and water was etched into the land law of 1915 and enshrined in the Constitution of 1917, villagers faced an uphill climb, maneuvering between recalcitrant landowners, a cumbersome bureaucracy, and a new government wary of radical redistribution.[6] The communities of the basin were among the first petitioners. Geography favored them more than the villages of many other regions. Postrevolutionary rulers had an interest in breaking apart the haciendas of reactionary landowners located close to the capital. Not only were these landowners potentially in a position to threaten the fledgling government, but redistributing their lands also allowed the government to establish a basis of support in the strategically important (mainly Zapatista) hinterlands.[7] Although the process was burdensome, and Carranza, Álvaro Obregón, and Plutarco Elías Calles favored smallholder farming over communal land grants, between 1922 and 1930 a dozen communities on the southern slopes of the basin received small to modest-sized parcels of land, much of it forested (see table 4.1).

The revolutionary violence that had destroyed villages and decimated crops also bequeathed forest communities a legacy of agrarian struggle. On the northern edge of Zapatista influence, the villagers of Santo Tomás Ajusco, San Miguel Topilejo, San Nicolás Totolapan, Milpa Alta, and others learned that while they were suffering the brunt of the Constitutionalist counterinsurgency, the Zapatistas were carrying out land reform in low-lying Morelos pueblos. Beginning in 1916, as zapatismo concentrated its political and military forces in Morelos, and the Constitutionalist forces occupied larger swaths of territory in central Mexico, villagers tilted toward engagement with Carranza's agrarian commission.

Petitions for land that touched on forest use also involved the political frame of urban sanitation. In 1916 the villagers of San Lorenzo Acopilco, a community that had been periodically occupied by the Zapatista forces of Valentín Reyes Nava in 1914 and 1915, denounced the forest guard Ricardo de la Vega for prohibiting use of "deadwood" and "wood waste"—often extracted for domestic use or for production of charcoal for urban markets—within the national protected lands of Desierto de los Leones. Villagers rejected the forester's "calumnious and imprudent imputation" that they were Zapatistas

TABLE 4.1 — Ejidos Created in the Sierra del Ajusco and Sierra de las Cruces,
South of Mexico City, 1922–1940

EJIDO	YEAR CREATED	HECTARES
San Mateo Tlaltenango	1922	250
San Bartolo Ameyalco	1923	78
San Jerónimo Aculco	1923	201
Magdalena Contreras	1923	135
San Bernabé Ocotepec	1924	383
San Nicolás Totolapan	1924	1,300
San Lorenzo Acopilco	1928	356
Magdalena Petliacalco	1930	141
San Andrés Totoltepec	1930	348
San Jerónimo Miacatlan	1930	60
San Francisco Tecoxpa	1930	82
Santa Ana Tlacotengo	1930	350
San Miguel Topilejo	1936	1,374
San Mateo Tlaltenango (extension)	1936	27
San Jerónimo Aculco (extension)	1938	205
San Nicolás Totolapan (extension)	1938	1,405
San Andrés Totoltepec (extension)	1939	145

and protested that the land had "always been theirs," not the property of state foresters as had been argued since the "era of Díaz." Assigned to protect the hydrological system, Vega and his revolutionary credentials came under close scrutiny: "He can't be a man helpful to the Revolution," village leaders declared.[8] Regardless of what the villagers thought, agrarian officials were not authorized to adjudicate conflicts over national forestland.

The leaders of San Mateo Tlaltenango, also situated in the Sierra de las Cruces southwest of the city, faced different circumstances. In 1916 they condemned the "ruinous deforestation" that the Vázquez brothers, owners of the Hacienda Buenavista, were carrying out on their lands and on communal lands. In nearby Santa Fe, community leaders accused the local forestry office of conspiring with landowners to clamp down on their forest uses. Only if villagers acquired permits (*boletos*) from the Vázquez brothers, who acted "as if they were the owners of the whole region," could they use their own woodlands.[9]

This dispute, like many others of the same period, produced new knowledge of conditions in the forests on Mexico City's doorstep. In October 1917 an agrarian inspector entered Buenavista lands with the guidance of forest guards and village representatives. The inspector described an abject sight: "stumps of oak trees turned into charcoal . . . preventing their regeneration"; trees that had been marked by the authorities for cutting that were still standing, with numerous unmarked areas completely devastated; and the Tlaltenango woodlands also leveled.[10] The Vázquez brothers paid some thirty woodsmen from nearby Santa Rosa—ironically, the very community Quevedo had singled out as conservation minded—twenty-five cents per load of wood, and a similar amount for the production of charcoal. Between September and December 1917, inspectors at the Cuajimalpa station recorded 154 loads of charcoal, 3,057 beams, 260 boards, and 42,000 cuts of firewood belonging to the Vázquez operation, with an equal number of products passing through the neighboring Magdalena Contreras station. Later inspections during the 1920s revealed a landscape "where everything has been cut," and where the landowners "don't respect anything," not even shrubs.[11] This was particularly disturbing to forestry officials, who underscored the importance of healthy woodlands to spring output in Desierto de los Leones and Xochimilco, as well as to erosion abatement and flood prevention (see figures 4.1 and 4.2).

Subsequent inspectors' observations suggest that the Vázquez brothers maintained their extractive activities as Tlaltenango's agrarian petition advanced. The landowners may have realized that land expropriation was im-

FIGURE 4.1 — Deforestation
near Desierto de los Le-
ones, no date. COURTESY OF
INAH, FOTOTECA NACIONAL.

FIGURE 4.2 — Firewood
collection in Desierto
de los Leones, around
1920. COURTESY OF INAH,
FOTOTECA NACIONAL.

minent and pursued reckless short-term profit rather than the fruitless defense of their estate. Their methodical destruction of the land bolstered villagers' claims, however. Inspectors noted that village lands "were better conserved than those of the hacienda" and gave villagers permission to extract waste products from the hacienda's cleared lands. The Vázquezes rejoined that the permit violated their property rights: "if I have all the obligations of a property owner, I don't enjoy any of its advantages."[12] But their objections were in vain: the landowners were an obstacle to both community land rights and the urban sanitary imperative.

On occasion, villagers couched their land claims in the urban environmental imaginary. San Nicolás Totolapan's leader Francisco Nava censured the Teresa family, owners of the Hacienda Eslava, for carrying out "a truly unbridled exploitation of the trees that cover the mountainous terrain ... causing the loosening of the soils, which will be swept away as soon as the first rains arrive ... with adverse effects on the lands at the bottom of the Valley of Mexico."[13] Numerous other community missives noted the damage that illegal logging wrought on the climatic and hygienic conditions of the capital, and foresters were sent to halt the practice. Nava was attuned to the science of conservation, and he employed the urban script to whittle away at the power of hacienda owners. His remonstrations were also rather duplicitous, however, as the residents of San Nicolás Totolapan had themselves been illegally extracting forest products from hacienda property even as their leader condemned the destructive activities of the owners.[14] Like many other rural subalterns, Nava walked the tightrope between two intersecting political orders: one urban-centric and exclusionary, the other revolutionary and inclusive. Villagers played the government's game and characterized themselves as the forest's stewards, responsible campesinos deserving of lands rather than reckless Indians.[15]

As hacendados sought to safeguard their landholdings from expropriation, they too mobilized the urban sanitary framework to portray themselves as the true guardians of Mexico's natural resources. The Teresas wrote that the villagers "carry out the absolute logging (*tala*) of Eslava without the forestry officials bothering them in the least," and they grumbled that villagers were seeking an ejido grant to effect "an immoderate exploitation of [our] lands, as has occurred in a great number of ejidos granted [by the government]."[16] Similarly, the owners of the Hacienda Cañada, when faced with losing property to San Bernabé Ocotepec, based their defense on forest utilization. They claimed that their careful tending of the fragile, sloped forests of the Cerro de Judío would go to waste if their lands were handed over to the villages.[17]

Few, if any, villagers of the Ajusco and the Sierra de las Cruces lived solely by tilling the land. The volcanic soils of the Ajusco range were ill suited for farming: the land was precipitous, and water, rather than accumulating on the surface, seeped deep into the substrate, replenishing the springs of the basin floor but leaving little moisture available for crops.[18] The Sierra de las Cruces was slightly more cultivable, despite the prevalence of steep inclines there as well. This mountain ridge possessed less porous soil and more abundant springs and streams, most notably the Magdalena River, which powered numerous textile mills and nourished the crops of San Nicolás Totolapan, Magdalena Contreras, San Bernabé Ocotepec, and San Bartolo Ameyalco, among others. In San Lorenzo Acopilco, villagers cultivated the steep terrain in "zigzags" to avoid landslides, but even so production was limited on the thin layer of soil.[19] Since ejido land grants included large extensions of wooded or partially wooded land, forestry grew in importance within rural economic life.[20] Roughly a third of the 383-hectare grant for San Bernabé Ocotepec was forested including the disputed Cerro del Judío. Even more striking was San Nicolás Totolapan's grant, easily the largest land concession of the 1920s in the Ajusco area, where 1,100 of the 1,300 hectares were forested with a mix of pine, fir and oak.[21] Villagers, however, were not free to use the woods as they pleased but rather were obligated to conserve, propagate, and rationally use them in accord with forestry and agrarian regulations.

Quevedo feared campesinos would clear-cut forestland to expand farming, but around Mexico City this did not take place on a wide scale. Community traditions revolved around making charcoal, cutting firewood, extracting zacatón root and producing turpentine. What the agrarian reform did was afford villagers the opportunity to make better use of nearby urban markets for forest products since most land grants did not satisfy farming needs. In Tlaltenango, for instance, the 250-hectare grant of nonirrigated land translated into less than 2 hectares per eligible family.[22] These forested land grants formed the material basis of the cooperative system that blossomed in the 1930s.

THE BASIN OF MEXICO: A LABORATORY OF SOCIAL FORESTRY

The brief experiment in social forestry under Francisco Madero and Victoriano Huerta was resurrected and recast in the late 1920s. Social forestry sought to blend two major aims of Article 27 of the constitution: the promotion of campesino rights and resource conservation. These dual aims were smoothly synthesized in some Mexican forestlands, but they were at logger-heads in the mountains surrounding Mexico City. The wings of social forestry were clipped before it could take flight. Nevertheless, villagers maneuvered in the interstices of state policies and discourses of wealth redistribution to strengthen communal forest economies.

Forest conservation regained steam during the 1920s thanks to a cadre of urban environmental planners who drew attention to worsening environmental problems. Dry-season dust storms were not a new phenomenon, but they had become more frequent and intense during the 1910s and 1920s. A study of one such storm in 1916 estimated that ten tons of dust had fallen on Mexico City in one day.[23] Dust became an ordinary nuisance of urban life. The storms, labeled "gray ghosts" and "avalanches of soil" by the press, covered market stands and streets, entered homes and businesses, and invaded human bodies, irritating eyes and causing respiratory problems. The Texcoco lakebed was a prime culprit, but urban experts and the media also pointed to the denuded hillsides and mountains surrounding the city. The scientist Julio Riquelme Inda and the engineers Alberto Carreño, Gayol, and Quevedo, among others, promoted afforesting the lakebed with halophyte plants and reforesting surrounding lands to fix the soil.[24] Throughout the 1920s the city's major dailies called for much the same. One predicted that deforestation would transform the basin into a "perpetual dust storm," "presaging the hunger and desolation that already reign in African, Asian, and some European regions where there were once magnificent forests."[25] Another inveighed almost daily against the calamity of deforestation and compared the health of Mexico City to that of cities "on the edge of the Ganges."[26]

The "degradation narrative," which had coalesced in Mexico during the late nineteenth century, proved tenacious after the revolution. The narrative rested on a set of dubious scientific claims that masked a more complex and dynamic ecological reality and justified the exercise of state power over communities. A host of experts and a broadening segment of the general public fixated on their own period as uniquely destructive to the environment, arguing that without swift action, crisis would inevitably turn into catastrophe. This narrative elided the many ways forest cover had changed in the past—for example, the massive forest loss that resulted from intensive colonial mining—and assumed that contemporary Mexico, like its French Algerian counterpart, was suffering a recent breach of a previous environmental equilibrium.[27] In fact, many deforested areas of central Mexico had recuperated after new mining technologies made wood fuel obsolete; by 1910 most ironworks, paper mills, and railroad lines had transitioned from wood to coal or petroleum for their energy needs, offsetting a great deal of the rising urban consumer demand.[28] In addition, there was little attempt to quantify the extent of the problem. Foresters more often than not used the eyeball test to document deforestation, and while some areas of Mexico had unequivocally undergone significant forest loss over the nineteenth and early twentieth centuries, no rigorous, nationwide forest survey had been conducted to measure it. Computations of the national forest cover were more vague estimate than scientific calculation and, like the survey in 1912, were synchronic, not diachronic.[29]

The warnings of impending calamity also stemmed from the presumed axioms linking forests to the wider environment—both built and "natural." Indeed, the rhetoric of calamity was acute in the Basin of Mexico: many urbanites perceived Mexico City's future as intricately interwoven with the fate of its surrounding forests. Without forests, the reasoning went, the city would lack water, urban inhabitants would be deprived of leisurely escapes into nature, the climate of the basin and its agricultural production would deteriorate, flooding would ravage low-lying urban areas, and desertification would result, exacerbating the already severe dust storms.

The story of degradation and desertification surfaced in newspaper articles and pervaded scientific journals and government reports. Yet by the 1920s, from North Africa to the central United States, botanists and engineers alike contended that erosion, torrential flooding, and desertification were complex processes and could not be reduced to forest loss. They suggested a wider focus on the environmental impacts of all types of vegetation, including grasses, shrubbery, and even crops.[30] Mexican scientists alluded to the siltation of the lakebeds, but it remained unclear to what degree the siltation could be attributed to recent forest loss versus particular erosion-inducing grazing and farming practices.[31] Even so, Quevedo and other conservationists around the world failed to modify their understandings of forests, the very foundation of their political power. There is no record that even a single forester inquired whether well-kept pastureland or cropland might offer the same environmental services as healthy, protected forests.[32] To dethrone the forest would undermine the logic of controlling huge extensions of Mexican territory, regulating campesino forest uses, and forbidding all clearing practices— regardless of their environmental impact.[33]

Forest advocacy in Mexico City crystallized, once again, around the steadfast Quevedo. In 1921, with the support of Gayol, the paper industrialist Alberto Lenz, forester Julio Riquelme Inda, and others, he founded the Mexican

Forestry Society, which lobbied for a forestry bill and published the journal *México Forestal*. The Mexican Forestry Society helped reinvigorate conservation throughout the country. Forest degradation, the Mexican Forestry Society narrative went, was brought on by the myopic timber industry and by primitive campesinos with an ingrained culture of destruction. And it spelled doom to urban centers, particularly Mexico City. Many conservationists also understood the inevitability of the agrarian reform and deduced a hard-and-fast reality: if Mexico was going to join advanced conservationist nations like France and the United States, it would be on account of changes in culture as much as legal, economic, or scientific progress. The society sponsored Arbor Day celebrations, filled periodicals with conservation-minded editorials, and, by the late 1930s, broadcast radio transmissions on the importance of trees.[34] Foresters also began to cultivate the new ejido communities as a new ally, even as they questioned whether the agrarian reform gave campesinos too much control over forests. They aimed to instill scientific management in ejido communities and to regulate the production and transportation of forest products.[35] Under the tutelage of experts, they said, forest communities might both extract themselves from dire poverty and conserve woodlands. Economic welfare and forest protection began to be conceived as mutually reinforcing objectives.

The Mexican Forestry Society's activities precipitated the nation's first forestry law. Signed by Calles in 1926, the law charged forestry officials with regulating the use of woodlands on all private, public, ejidal, and communal lands, restricting logging near watersheds and urban areas, and promoting woodland restoration and the creation of reserves.[36] To execute these goals, the law mandated a new Forestry Service (Dirección Forestal y de Caza y Pesca), required forest users to obtain logging permits from this new authority, and authorized the creation of ejido forest cooperatives to assist in governing the use of woodlands in agrarian communities. The cooperative, a unique blend of conservationism and postrevolutionary agrarian justice, became, between 1929 and 1940, the glue that joined foresters to agrarian authorities, and campesino forest users to the state. Working together, if not always harmoniously, the forest and agrarian bureaucracies directed forest extraction on communal lands with the purpose of liberating communities from caciques, a goal first publicized in 1912 during the Zapatista rebellion.

The rise of the Mexican cooperative paralleled the formation of forest cooperatives in India under the British Raj. Both of these historically unique forms of organizing campesino forest economies were the product of social rebellion—the protracted struggle against centralized forest management in India and, in Mexico, a revolution against elite control of land and resources. However, in India the result was a highly decentralized forest management program with much community input, whereas the Mexican cooperative enjoyed less autonomy from state technocrats.[37]

The cooperative system did not develop evenly across Mexico's spaces. The Basin of Mexico served as the testing ground for postrevolutionary social forestry because it was within the limited administrative reach of the newly constituted Forestry Service and because enormous environmental value was placed on the mountainous landscape and watershed south of the city. Forestry policies were, to be sure, forged out of the politicization of the landscape—the many entanglements and disputes among those who sought to conserve, use, or profit from woodlands.[38] The balance of political forces—the influence and strategies wielded by communities, private interests, and state actors—no doubt shifted policy in certain directions. Other variables, however, were also at work. The limited geographic reach of the state hindered the formation of cooperatives and blunted oversight in many regions. Political economy was also a factor; permits for certain users hinged on the exchange value of forest products like charcoal, zacatón root, pine resin, or mahogany. Another was the environmental value experts assigned to a particular forest—its importance in augmenting agricultural and industrial activities and maintaining a balance between health and environment. This final variable held sway in much of central Mexico, and particularly in the Basin of Mexico. Government officials tended to assign greater value to a forest near a key spring, watershed, lakebed, or urban area than to one more distant from a crucial economic activity or population center. Urban and physical geography account for why the limelight beamed on the basin like no other Mexican region during the late 1920s.

While other communities throughout Mexico did not receive official sanction for their cooperatives until the mid-1930s, in 1929 the southern forests of the basin—small but of paramount importance—counted six cooperatives, in San Nicolás Totolapan, Magdalena Contreras, San Bartolo Ameyalco, San Salvador Cuauhtenco, San Mateo Tlaltenango, and San Lorenzo Acopilco. That same year the six united to form the Federation of Forest Cooperatives, under the leadership of Miguel Santibañez.[39] Forestry officials announced that the federation would seek to direct the "irrational and poorly guided" campesinos in their exploitation of forest products and to "free members from speculative practices, intermediaries, and monopolizers": in short, the federation would help stave off the poverty arising from the scarcity of arable lands.[40] Officials divided exploitable woodlands into zones to facilitate both surveillance and management; when forest products were sold, each cooperative would retain 15 percent of the proceeds to invest in community irrigation, public works, and other material improvements. As one forester declared, the cacique, who "eats away at communal usufruct with an insatiable appetite for wealth," would soon be a distant memory.[41] Rather than being subjugated to the cacique, campesinos would manage their own forests in a "rational" way, guaranteeing their optimum health while protecting the climate and hydrology of the basin. The cooperative system in the southern mountains of the Federal District was deemed an instrument to resurrect the forest commons under expert guidance.

Conservationists readily invoked the salvation and liberation of the forest communities surrounding Mexico City, but actual practice belied the lofty rhetoric. The San Nicolás Totolapan cooperative sought permits for the exploitation and transportation of ten thousand beams and thirty thousand lumber pieces (rajas), but the Forestry Service refused to allow the logging of healthy trees.[42] Only deadwood could be collected in the basin, as a means of preventing forest fires—anathema to foresters. Since dead and fallen wood still had exchange value as firewood and charcoal, villagers continued to supply the essential fuels for the thousands of kitchen stoves across Mexico City. Officials also restricted sheep grazing on the edges of forests and on slopes and set aside a number of protected forest zones, among them Desierto de los Leones National Park, established in 1917.[43] Such draconian measures impelled campesinos to cut clandestinely or exploit zones cordoned off as reserves. Vigilance was more aggressive around Mexico City than in most other areas, but local knowledge of trails and the topography, long nights, and some luck allowed many villagers to escape the forest guards and ejidal inspectors.[44] Others, like two campesinos from San Nicolás Totolapan who claimed to be unfamiliar with the procedures for obtaining permission, did not.[45] Once detained, villagers were treated as criminals, charged, and fined or imprisoned, although often a pittance of a bribe was enough to extricate an offender from trouble.[46]

The Forestry Service's binary of rational/irrational and legal/illegal generated a self-fulfilling prophecy. Irrational campesinos necessitated restrictive forestry; so restricted, campesinos invariably resorted to illicit uses that confirmed their supposed lack of rationality, thus perpetuating the same restrictive policies. Incapable of interpreting villagers' forest uses as anything but a vestige of a backward culture, foresters legitimized their own expertise and, ultimately, their power to control resource use. Thus, when officials caught cooperative members logging illegally, their permits, and sometimes those of the entire cooperative, were canceled, as the logging was irrevocable proof that campesinos—understood as a homogeneous group—had not learned a thing.[47] In one extreme case, one forestry official advised the Forestry Service to suspend all permits in the southern basin until the vigilance necessary to combat ongoing illegal logging could be established.[48]

For those attempting to follow the rules, gaining permits to extract and transport forest products was a bureaucratic nightmare. Permits expired monthly, and forestry agents were slow to respond to requests for renewals.[49] In their requests, villagers generally cited their miserable economic conditions and the importance of forests to their livelihoods; on occasion, they declared their support for the government's reforestation and forest-protection objectives. Much like petitioners for agrarian reform, cooperativists walked a tightrope between claims to social justice and acknowledgment of the conservation imperative. The cooperativists of Magdalena Contreras, for example, expressed their desire to aid in government reforestation, locate a convenient spot for a tree nursery, and "clean" the forests of all fire-prone deadwood.[50]

Obstacles at the point of production were matched by obstacles along the distribution line, where monopolies often prevailed. While the cooperatives forbade outsider participation in the production and transportation of forest products, the lack of transport options empowered railroad-company middlemen to charge outrageous prices. In 1929 Magdalena Contreras's cooperative leadership complained that Enrique Valencia, chief of the station there, monopolized the transport of their products.[51] Valencia disappeared from the historical record soon thereafter, but the same leadership later denounced his replacement, none other than the president of the Federation of Forest Cooperatives, Miguel Santibañez. Margarito Ávila, head of the Magdalena Contreras cooperative, accused Santibañez of iniquitous pricing at the station. According to the perturbed Ávila and his supporters, the federation president owed the local cooperative 1,705 pesos out of a total 13,076 pesos' worth of recent cooperative products.[52] The cooperative members' pleas to be allowed to sell their products "to whomever will pay us the most" and to disassociate themselves from the federation fell on deaf ears. Yet a few cooperatives were able to sell enough product to free themselves from outsider control. In 1932 San Nicolás Totolapan cooperative members were transporting their products using Chevrolet trucks.[53] In the adjacent state of Morelos, a forest cooperative in Tepoztlán also managed to organize its own transport to urban markets. They sold an impressive 1,209,430 kilograms of charcoal in 1934 and used part of the profit to fund various community improvements.[54] However, these were exceptional cases, as most cooperatives were unable to sidestep middlemen.[55]

Although cooperative leaders struggled to eliminate monopolies in transport and delivery, they increasingly dominated the forest economy within their own communities, establishing their own surveillance systems (many of which replicated policies imposed from above) and cracking down on independent activities. Membership soared: in 1931 the San Mateo Tlaltenango cooperative counted fifty-two members, with forty-two more seeking to join, and the San Nicolás Totolapan cooperative grew from a small handful of members in 1930 to eighty-one in 1935.[56] Coercion played a role in the rise, but many villagers recognized that their cooperative established a more methodical and organized economy that would benefit the community. This is not to say that illicit forest uses disappeared; corruption, rampant in postrevolutionary Mexico, penetrated Mexico's forests. Villagers frequently bribed inspectors to let them extract and transport forest products; forester Agustín Castro observed that "every time [villagers] wanted to remove wood without permission or make charcoal, they would give a reward (*gratificación*) to the inspector, who would let them do whatever they wanted."[57] On occasion, cooperative leaders even negotiated with inspectors to carry out illegal operations.

It is likely many campesinos believed in the importance of protecting forests to maintain the hydrological balance while simultaneously cutting down trees to make charcoal. Such are the contradictions between actions and beliefs. But the cooperative system introduced forest conservation—the same urban vision villagers once vehemently opposed—as a fount of political power within communities. Participating in official conservation held the promise of improving relations with high-level functionaries while also shoring up the authority of village leadership. At the same time, as a new expression of local power, the cooperative was a frequent vehicle of abuse. In February 1934 thirty-three members of the San Mateo Tlaltenango cooperative leveled misconduct charges, "all well founded and confirmed," against cooperative director Marcelino González. Since his election in 1930, the disgruntled campesinos claimed, González had stolen money from sales and charged fees that were not placed in the cooperative safe deposit.[58]

Given the high stakes of controlling the organizations, competition for leadership roles often turned fierce. Jesús Nava (a relative of the earlier agrarian leader Francisco Nava), Prisciliano Mendoza, and Ramón González all jockeyed to run the San Nicolás Totolapan cooperative during the late 1920s and 1930s. González won, and Mendoza's and Nava's failed attempts to take over the cooperative resulted in the cancellation of their permits in 1929. Three years later, a forest inspector discovered unauthorized logging near a spring that inhabitants planned to utilize for drinking water. Mendoza exploited the opportunity to discredit his rivals and informed the inspector that Nava and another community member were to blame.[59] Whereas foresters harnessed the cooperative to conserve the woodlands surrounding the city by regulating campesino economies, community caciques used the new institution to bolster their influence, excluding some and including others. Everyone, however, played by the rules of the same game, a contest between local rights to land and resources and the stringent conservation program. Promoters of each dueled, accommodated, and negotiated, resulting in tepid official support of local commons governance while bribery loosened the noose of state restrictions. Yet foresters—even at the height of revolutionary populism under Cárdenas—did not fully entrust campesinos with forests considered fundamental to the capital's prosperity.

CÁRDENAS AND AGRARIAN REFORM

Calles relinquished the presidency in 1928, but he continued to influence the Mexican political system from behind the scenes in a period known as the Maximato (1928–1934). Agrarian reform came to a virtual halt, and rural policies favored commercial agriculture and smallholders over land-poor peasants. Similarly, militant unions were subdued, and the CROM continued to mitigate worker radicalism and circumscribe shop-floor demands. Calles, however, was no dictator. His extended stays outside of Mexico gave certain leeway to each president, particularly Abelardo Rodríguez (1932–1934), who made overtures to renew land and labor reform. Then, as the election of 1934 approached, Calles went along with left-wing momentum within the party to nominate Michoacán's ex-governor Lázaro Cárdenas.[60] Still, Calles assumed he could be Cárdenas's puppeteer, turning the country to the right or left as needed.

Cárdenas, however, was not the marionette Calles had expected. Rather than bending to Calles's moderate program, Cárdenas plotted a more radical path, mobilizing support from worker and peasant organizations, ousting Callistas from positions of power, and, eventually, exiling Calles himself. Between 1935 and 1940, Cárdenas redistributed nearly eighteen million hectares of land to 800,000 people (four times more than all previous presidents combined) and supported workers' demands—most famously in the oil strike of 1938 that precipitated the expropriation of foreign oil companies.

Recent interpretations of *cardenismo* rest on the premise of an inherently progressive (even radical), coherent, and consistent political-ideological core of revolutionary goals: land and labor reform, support for unionization, resource nationalism, and the adulation of popular culture, including indigenous culture. Cárdenas himself may have defeated *callismo* and solidified his authority through sometimes uncomfortable alliances, but such political opportunism, the historiography hints, stood in contrast to the movement's truly progressive core. For these historians, the core of Cardenista policy and ideology was epitomized by the six-year plan, which began as a party platform and was soon elevated to the unquestioned agenda of the whole sexenio. The limits of cardenismo were to be found outside this core political project, within political-economic structures or the contingencies of regional political dynamics. In the words of Nora Hamilton, cardenismo was unable to complete its agenda owing to the capitalist nature of the Mexican state.[61] Other historians have emphasized the political challenges from the periphery, where the core program was remodeled, diluted, and, in some instances, defeated entirely. In this perspective, the messy local politics that played out in a state, region, or locale constituted cardenismo and determined its success, limits, and failures. Where empowered local groups pushed core Cardenistas to enact reforms, the likelihood of far-reaching progressive change increased.[62]

My interpretation of cardenismo fuses these political, structural, and spatial approaches while questioning the coherence, consistency, and inherent progressivism of the core political program. Rather than addressing cardenismo's tensions and limits in terms of core–periphery (where the core tends to be homogenized and rendered uniform and the periphery perceived as the sole locus of conservative elements), a focus on the ideological core and spatial center of cardenismo throws new light on the dynamic process at work in the sexenio. The core Cardenista agenda was rife with political contradictions along the urban-hinterland axis: between producers' and consumers' rights, between urban hygienic housing and agrarian justice, and between conservation and popular rights to forests. These contradictions became open fissures when materialized as policy, program, and practice in different spaces around the Basin of Mexico. Cardenista politics amplified existing interests, concretized new (and conflicting) bases of social power, and encouraged groups marginalized by official policy to mobilize around discourses of revolutionary justice, stretching the limits of the possible but also aggravating the tensions in the original platform.

Forestry embodied one of cardenismo's central contradictions. Like the Constitution of 1917, the six-year plan promoted forest conservation, authorizing the creation of an autonomous department while promising a more equitable distribution of land and woods. The Cárdenas administration, rather than dissolving the contradiction between forest protection and community uses, magnified existing divisions, as cooperatives faced additional challenges from a new Forestry Department and its creation of a national park system.

Shortly after assuming the presidency in December 1934, Cárdenas invited Quevedo to head his Forestry Department, intended to replace the Forestry Service. Quevedo vacillated, perhaps doubting the president's commitment, but finally accepted the post to further his already substantial work in Mexican forestry. Thus began the golden age of Mexican conservationism and its uncomfortable marriage to revolutionary populism. The prominent forester and past president of the Mexican Forestry Society Edmundo Bournet argued that the new department's aim was the "consolidation and organization of campesinos for the better utilization of the country's natural resources."[63] Many Cárdenas-era foresters, like Bournet, steeped in revolutionary nationalism, were more generous to campesinos than their predecessors and more critical of large-scale exploiters, at least rhetorically. Radical politician Francisco Múgica declared conservation a new venue of working-class struggle against forest "despoilers," while Salvador Guerrero remarked that the cooperative system transcended capitalism entirely by ousting middlemen and placing the means of production in the hands of workers.[64]

These statements suggest a seamless overlap between social change and reinvigorated conservationism, and there is some evidence that rhetoric lived up to reality. In 1937 there were close to 500 forest cooperatives operating in Mexico—most created under Cárdenas—and by 1940 that figure had increased to 866.[65] Historians know far too little about the vast majority of these cooperatives, but while many surely suffered the hardships typical of the original ones in the basin's southern forests, a handful of others were as productive as the Tepoztlán cooperative.[66] Yaqui communities in the state of Sonora, with a history of violent resistance to the state, adopted a more conciliatory pose toward the Cardenistas and gained new communal revenue from producer cooperatives.[67] Quevedo boasted of the success of the fifty cooperatives in the Sierra de Puebla, a region with a long tradition of engagement with the Mexican state, and he singled out the cooperative of Río Frío as particularly profitable.[68] The Forestry Department also planted fruit trees on community lands in central Mexico and stocked highland lakes with protein-rich fish to improve campesino resource economies.[69]

Cardenismo and forest science coexisted uneasily, however. As much as some foresters sought to promote campesino rights, a majority, including the influential Quevedo, continued to oppose community control in the central Mexican highlands. Foresters spoke grandiosely about educating and directing campesinos to profit from forests in a rational way, but ejidal production never amounted to a significant portion of the national forest economy. And within the Basin of Mexico, all uses took a back seat to forests' environmental services, specifically their benefits to the capital. Accordingly, a special division, the Forestry Delegation of Central Mexico, was created within Cárdenas's new Forestry Department; in this new delegation's view, preservation and recuperation of woodlands trumped use.

There were a few new land grants in the mountains above Mexico City. The village of Magdalena Petliacalco received 622 hectares of forestland in the Ajusco range and in 1938 set up a forest cooperative.[70] San Nicolás Totolapan received a sizable ejidal extension of forestland that roughly matched its first grant from the 1920s and extended the territorial reach of its cooperative.[71] San Miguel Topilejo received land for the first time in 1936. Nestled deep in the highlands, this pueblo was surrounded by the nearly two thousand–hectare property of Jesús Casto de la Fuente y Parres, a member of the same family reproached by the foresters during the revolution. While Fuente y Parres cultivated zacatón root for a world market, San Miguel Topilejo had 271 hectares of arable land for 377 families, and about five hundred hectares of woodlands. People's occupations in San Miguel Topilejo corresponded to the land available; there were 136 charcoal producers, 116 firewood collectors, 64 zacatón root extractors, and 61 farmers.[72] The grant of thirteen hundred hectares expropriated from Fuente y Parres, agrarian authorities hoped, would convert the village into the center of communal zacatón production, a small-scale version of what Cárdenas had in mind for workers in the cotton-growing region of La Laguna and the henequen fields of Yucatán.

Those were the most important land grants in the mountains around Mexico City under Cárdenas, a far cry from the massive holdings found in other Mexican regions. Certainly the relatively small size of the haciendas in the basin accounts for some of the difference. Several haciendas had already been reduced to small, legally undividable properties by the land grants in the 1920s, but plenty of additional land went undivided.

Foresters opposed the powerful Cardenista agrarian reform for the repercussions it might have on woodlands. Antonio Sosa applauded forest communities in the state of Tlaxcala that ostensibly melded conservation with use, while scolding other communities that lacked a "forest mentality"—a view shared by Quevedo.[73] In the 1920s Quevedo had contended that forests should not be redistributed as part of an agrarian reform, but he indicated that certain communities could, through "ordered exploitation," use forest-land grants to their economic advantage.[74] He hardened his position a decade later, however. Quevedo recoiled at agrarian authorities' intemperate practice of handing over forests to one community after another at the beginning of Cárdenas's term, and he specifically assailed land-reform requests in the watersheds and heavily urbanized areas of central Mexico. He came to believe that all land grants must exclude forests, which should be managed solely by forestry experts; if hacienda owners, knowing their lands would be expropriated, did not decimate their woodlands for short-term profit, the newly constituted ejidos surely would.[75] Technocratic forestry ebbed amid the flows of campesino organization and state-sponsored land reform, but it was far from exhausted.

In the spring of 1935, Quevedo rebuked San Mateo Tlaltenango's request to extend its ejido. The pueblo had received a small land grant in the early 1920s, in part because they successfully cast the owners of the Buenavista hacienda as rampant forest destroyers. This time, Quevedo turned the tables, contrasting the rich and "well-conserved vegetation of Buenavista with the battered woods belonging to the pueblos of San Lorenzo Acopilco, San Pablo Chimalpa, and San Mateo Tlaltenango."[76] The other dividable estate, La Venta, belonged to Quevedo's friend, the paper industrialist Alberto Lenz, whom the head of the Forestry Department acclaimed for his important reforestation work and orderly extraction methods. Because the forested land "provides great services from a hydrological perspective," given its location adjacent to the Desierto de los Leones National Park, Quevedo adamantly opposed San Mateo Tlaltenango's request for an extension.[77] The village agrarian representatives accused Quevedo of supporting a "Spanish landowner, not even nationalized"—the owner of Buenavista—but with no apparent irony the forestry chief argued that the government had to protect the woods for the benefit of the pueblo, which had recently begun receiving piped water from hacienda lands. The village, in effect, had to be protected from itself, and thus the same hacendado maligned for his unbridled deforestation just two decades earlier remained the owner of the springs from which the village received water.[78] Quevedo butted heads with agrarian authorities, but his efforts paid off: San Mateo Tlaltenango received a measly twenty-seven-hectare extension. At the beginning of Cárdenas's term, the inclusion of woodlands in land grants was determined on a case-by-case basis, and San Mateo Tlaltenango's bid bowed to urban concerns. Quevedo's preconceptions about community forestry also limited ejido extensions on the northern edge of the basin. He underscored the case of the pueblo of Espíritu Santo, whose land use, he claimed, obstructed Mexico City's plans to capture nearby river water. Quevedo convinced Cárdenas to reconsider the parcel grant "due to the simple fact that the public interest supersedes the unilateral interest of the particular community."[79]

CARDENISMO AND NATIONAL PARKS

The intermingling of conservation science and the nationalist intent to possess and protect Mexico's natural and cultural patrimony also led Cárdenas to create numerous national parks. Parks were spaces where foresters could foster the rational use of nature through education and tourism, and they doubled as national landmarks and areas designated to protect watersheds, urban areas, and agricultural zones. Cárdenas created thirty-four of these parks over his term, to join the six that already existed. Eight were located within the basin or along the mountains that formed it. Some, such as Tepeyac, Insurgente Miguel Hidalgo, and Molino de Flores de Nezahualcóyotl, were designed primarily as cultural landmarks; the Ajusco, Desierto de los Leones, and the Iztaccíhuatl-Popocatépetl parks served specific urban environmental purposes. However, through the lens of postrevolutionary conservation, the protection of natural patrimony was inextricable from the protection of cultural patrimony. Some parks, such as Iztaccíhuatl-Popocatépetl, Ajusco, and Tepeyac, had a dual function as nature reserves and cultural emblems of the nation. The discourse around the parks also drew parallels between prevailing notions of the rural Indian—primitive, close to nature, and in desperate need of care—and the trees themselves. The experienced forester Salvador Guerrero went so far as to declare the protection of the Indian and the protection of nature one and the same: "It is impossible to try to protect natural resources without sheltering the Indians, who are most worthy of pity and protection."[80] Indians and the landscapes they inhabited composed the building blocks of the Mexican nation, elements to be respected, protected, and cultivated.

In their broader social and political project, Cardenista foresters fused nature and culture. In addition to presuming that healthy forests begat healthy and prosperous humans, the foresters of postrevolutionary Mexico aimed—whether by principle or political necessity—to accommodate existing communities within park boundaries. Rather than dispossessing communities and suppressing their economic activities within a declared park, as was commonly done in colonial contexts, or declaring a park a wilderness, as was frequently done in the western United States, the Forestry Department sought to educate campesinos and regulate their economic activities without completely outlawing local uses of parklands.[81]

These adaptations, however, hardly meant that park creation fundamentally entailed social justice—such an assumption holds only if our point of comparison is the United States or colonial Asia. The political climate of postrevolutionary Mexico gave forest communities some leverage over land policy, but community leaders nonetheless struggled mightily to protect their economic activities within recently created parks. A significant portion of the Ajusco range south of San Ángel, which had been declared a protected forest zone in 1932, was declared a national park in 1936. Officials considered the Ajusco "one of the most marvelous and significant ranges because of its physical contrasts and its immediate proximity to the most populated centers of the Republic," and they emphasized the need "to protect at all costs its soils against degradation, maintaining its forests in good state and its beautifully contrasting meadows as a guarantee of healthy climate and drinking water to the capital of the Republic."[82] The Forestry Department exempted populated areas and cultivated land with less than an 8 percent incline from expropriation but (like elsewhere in the mountains around the basin) rejected all requests to topple trees and delayed permit approvals. Officials often granted permits for deadwood with the reasoning that the revolutionary government should aid "the needy classes," but delays in renewals followed each expiration date.

Because granting of permits was erratic, campesinos took advantage of inadequate vigilance in the national parks, much as they did within their own communal or ejidal forests. One forestry employee keenly observed, "Experience has shown us that, far from obtaining conservation of the forest stands, [the regulations] have fomented a spirit of rebellion" in the Ajusco National Park. "It is illogical to assume," he added, "that [villagers] are going to respect dispositions that go against their right to survival."[83] The Ajusco "spirit of rebellion" was apparent in Ocuilan, where community members used arson and other tactics to claim forest rights that they believed preceded the formation of the park, which lay adjacent to village lands. Ocuilan leaders managed to win preferential access to deadwood in the park as well as to fruits produced by park trees.[84] Few communities around central Mexico's parks won concessions to this extent, however, and many resorted to the covert extraction practices that were well documented around the Basin of Mexico.

Quevedo's campaign to curb agrarian reform in Mexico's forestland triumphed in June 1937, when Cárdenas decreed that forestland and national parks were exempted from all ejido grants.[85] Communities around the basin were especially hard hit. Emboldened by the executive order, the Forestry Department challenged the provisional land grant of over a thousand hectares that San Nicolás Totolapan had received, but the agrarian commission was permitted to follow through since the community's petition had been processed before the presidential decree.[86] Other potential reform beneficiaries around the Ajusco and other national parks were not as fortunate. San Bartolo Ameyalco's extension grant of fifty-four hectares fell far short of the need— over two hundred individuals were eligible to receive a plot—likely because a large portion of the Hacienda Eslava lay in the Ajusco National Park.[87] San Miguel Topilejo, which had received 1,373 hectares in September 1936, requested another extension the following year. Agrarian authorities authorized that 922 hectares of pastureland belonging to Ángel Entrambasaguas's nearby El Fraile hacienda be distributed among 448 campesinos. A year later, in March 1939, however, Cárdenas repealed the decision, citing its location within the Ajusco National Park. The decree tilted forestry policy toward the exclusive, urban-centered conservationism to the detriment of social forestry and restrained the redistributive reach of the agrarian reform around Mexico City.

No town in the area was more affected by Cárdenas's decree than the village of Santo Tomás Ajusco. In February 1937 representatives of the town of 860 demanded fifteen hundred hectares of El Fraile hacienda land. Entrambasaguas, like so many landowners before him, appealed to conservation science: "What the inhabitants of Ajusco seek is the deforestation of El Fraile lands, now . . . in the Ajusco National Park."[88] The Forestry Department implicitly supported the hacendado's anticampesino position, warning against the land grant "owing to the important biological role that the Ajusco forests play in regulating the output of the springs that supply this capital with water."[89] Agrarian authorities approved a 648-hectare parcel for 293 heads of household, only to see it buried by the Federal District governor for violating the decree of 1937.[90] Santo Tomás Ajusco, on the receiving end of anti-Zapatista violence during the revolution, bore the consequences of that violence in the ensuing decades as urban scientific forestry took precedence over local land needs.

Mexico City conservationists understood the greater public interest in the Basin of Mexico as a series of biophysical relations that sustained urbanization. These understandings seeped into the urban middle-class and popular sectors, who imbibed Arbor Day celebrations, natural history museum exhibits, radio broadcasts about conservation, and other government propaganda espousing the urban environmental imaginary. The president of the Excursionist Club pleaded with the Forestry Department to revoke all cooperatives' permits. On another occasion, he claimed to have caught residents who "do not care about the forest" cutting on a hillside near Magdalena Contreras and felt compelled to inform the president by "elementary duty of culture and patriotism."[91] One resident of Coyoacán similarly fretted over deforestation carried out by the Santo Tomás Ajusco cooperative that, she maintained, was sneaking carloads of wood past forest inspectors. Evoking the urban logic of conservation, she argued that "the scarcity of Xochimilco water, climate change, and the loss of beautiful places for recreation" were caused by felling.[92]

Such complaints came from the forested hinterland as well. Proletarianization reconfigured social relations in communities adjacent to the Magdalena River, whose constant water flow, cascading from mountaintop to basin floor, had powered textile and paper mills since the mid-nineteenth century. Twenty-four workers in factories along the Magdalena River condemned what they saw as the "ruthless deforestation" in areas under cooperative authority. These workers feared the exhaustion of water resources in their communities and in the factories—"the pillar of thousands of workers"—owing to the links between deforestation and water loss.[93] Several other residents of Magdalena Contreras implored the government to curtail logging, citing government plans to provide drinking water to various towns in the area using the Monte Alegre springs of the Sierra de las Cruces.[94] The urban environmental imaginary linked city and hinterland politically and forged a new sociospatial hierarchy around the use of resources. Campesino forest use came under attack not only by foresters but also by broader sections of the population who, through consumption practices or relations in the means of production, embraced what had been a rather elite-centered vision of the metropolitan environment.[95]

Those for whom forestlands were a vital part of a larger hydrological, soil, and climatic system, or a site of recreation, rather than a resource with use and exchange value, tended to excoriate the cooperatives and blame them for environmental deterioration. Those who lived off the forests had two choices: they could navigate conservation's complex set of scientific axioms and Kafkaesque regulations, or they could conduct clandestine operations with the risk of fines and possibly imprisonment. Most opted to do both.

CONCLUSION

If community leadership looked to comply with postrevolutionary forestry to sustain their livelihoods—battling regulations, forest guards, and corrupt officials—Quevedo's Forestry Department struggled to forge a unity between conservation science and Cardenista populism. Forest workers circulated a placard on Mexico City streets questioning why "Quevedo systematically opposed the ordered exploitation of forests when 90 percent of ejidal grants comprise forestland."[96] The 90 percent figure may have been hyperbole, but by 1939 conflicts between forest users and the Forestry Department had exploded into a full-blown crisis. Cárdenas had been a steady supporter of Quevedo and a staunch conservationist in his own right, but the department he founded was, rather than tying peasants to his progressive agenda as he had wished, threatening to undermine popular support for his finely crafted Party of the Mexican Revolution (PRM), founded in 1938. This compelled Cárdenas to dissolve the young Forestry Department and demote the aging conservationist. There was an unintended consequence to the president's action: with the department the whole rationale behind cooperative forestry went down.

During its five-year existence, the Forestry Department had placed conservation at the center of public debate, both in cities and in their hinterlands. The department had promoted education about the role of vegetation—especially the tropical deciduous vegetation of the central plateau—in the Mexican economy and human health. It also encouraged city folk to camp and explore Mexico's natural wonders and, in its greatest achievement, created over thirty national parks and numerous other forest-protection zones. To a lesser degree, the Forestry Department, and the Forestry Service that preceded it, established a bureaucratic system of regulations and permits that brought ejido communities within the state's fold and, ideally, enabled them to maximize their income from their woodlands. On the outskirts of Mexico

City, this amounted to a partial recovery of the forest commons in which communities had a voice and organizational leverage in the management and use of crucial elements of the metropolitan environment. Thousands of hectares of forestland once enclosed or trampled on by expanding industries and haciendas were, by means of the agrarian reform, repossessed by the surrounding pueblos, which operated cooperatives in collaboration, and at times outright conflict, with Forestry Department officials. Yet the seeds of cooperative forestry, a potential instrument to bury technocratic forestry, were not allowed to germinate. The nineteenth-century urban-elitist roots of forestry, which disdained customary uses, were simply too deep. Revolutionary justice under Cárdenas, circumscribed in the forests above Mexico City, shone more brightly in another hinterland space, Lake Texcoco, where urban sanitary planning melded more smoothly with local campesino interests.

5

___

Desiccation, Dust,
and Engineered Waterscapes

In 1945 Diego Rivera began his patio corridor murals that now grace the halls of Mexico City's National Palace. Rivera's brushstrokes traced a nationalist history that culminated with the revolution of 1910 but whose beginnings were found within the Basin of Mexico hundreds of years earlier. Rivera depicted a prosperous Tenochtitlan surrounded by Texcoco's waters and a verdant Xochimilco of neatly ordered chinampas. Indian life and waterscapes were stitched together seamlessly.

Rivera's nationalist mythology of pre-Columbian Indian grandeur and subsequent collapse paralleled the story well-off Mexicans and foreigners told themselves about the basin's lakes. Lake Texcoco had become a thing of the past, moribund and backward like those who lived around it. Most viewed the lake in opposition to the modern city: as the city expanded, the lake and the indigenous lifestyles it sustained receded. The Lake Xochimilco environs were a living relic of the imagined past, geographically close to but culturally distant from the modern metropolis, a quaint vestige of Indian authenticity rooted literally and figuratively in the chinampa soil beds. The American journalist and novelist Katherine Anne Porter, who visited Mexico City in the early 1920s, depicted Xochimilco as a romanticized "earthly Eden," an original Mexico of unrealized dreams.[1] In 1926 José Montes de Oca described the "innumerable national and foreign tourists who immerse themselves in the nature of Xochimilco and receive the gentle caress of the colors and scents of roses, the lushness of its fanciful agaves, and its emerald, quiet waters."[2]

Whether romantic or gloomy, representations of the basin's waterscapes concealed their tight connection to the growing metropolis—the urban markets full of lake-based foodstuffs, the process of desiccation brought on by hydraulic infrastructure, and dust storms. Much like in the forest communities above, urbanization represented both boon, for the close proximity to markets, and curse for lakeshore residents. Manuel Marroquín y Rivera's Xochimilco aqueduct was the city's lifeline, but the transfer of ever more water to a thirsty urban population jeopardized chinampería. The Texcoco lakebed constituted a threat to urban modernity, not its lifeblood. Experts fretted over the tortuous relationship the city maintained with the lake; it was as if the more they attempted to efface the city's lacustrine past, the more it came back to bite them. Whereas blinding dust and summer floodwaters constantly reminded urban inhabitants of this past, the residents around the two lakebeds struggled to redefine their livelihoods in the midst of changing environments. Both waterscapes remained at the crux of urban civilization—just like they had been for the Mexica. They were artifacts of the sanitary city and hinterland economies, and the product of water runoff, the output of springs, and soil movement.

Following the revolution, these were deeply politicized spaces as well. Intentionally or not, Porfirian hydraulic engineering furthered desiccation and dust storms, environmental changes that postrevolutionary engineers debated and disputed with much hand-wringing. Desiccation, in turn, altered land uses and molded the ways in which villagers engaged with the agrarian reform, resulting in a campesino political culture that reinforced the extractivist paradigm. Much as with the forests discussed in the previous chapter, the agrarian reform empowered the communities around the lakebeds to redefine their relationship with their changing ecology and establish their rights to use the metropolitan environment. Lakeshore villagers shifted strategies in the late 1910s, from protesting lake desiccation and seeking to sustain a living from the dwindling lacustrine ecosystem to embracing conventional dryland farming in these highly engineered environments. Around Lake Xochimilco, the agrarian reform, rather than uniting local agriculturalists, drove a wedge between them, as the newly empowered community ejidos formed a counter-weight to chinamperos' water-conservation interests. Cardenismo did nothing to change the unequal relationship between Xochimilco farmers and the city. Around Lake Texcoco, however, the winter dust bowl and summer flooding predisposed Cardenista engineers to sketch out a plan that wedded urban health to rural revolutionary justice. Postrevolutionary engineering was determined by interlocking social and environmental forces, from everyday popular politics and high statecraft to the dynamic movements of water and soil.

SALVAGING A LACUSTRINE LIVELIHOOD

The surface area of the basin's lakes diminished by approximately 50 percent between the conquest and the mid-nineteenth century. It halved again over the next hundred years.[3] Such absolute statistics tell a story of inexorable desiccation but obscure the fluctuations in the hydrological system within that overall progression. At the end of the nineteenth century, a long dry season might reduce Lake Xochimilco to a shadow of its former self and cause Lake Texcoco to disappear entirely, but the lakes would rebound when the rains returned. By 1920, though, only heavy rains made the lakes a formidable presence within the basin. Sedimentation, a problem aggravated by widespread ranching and other erosion-inducing land uses, reduced the carrying capacities of both Lakes Xochimilco and Texcoco. Moreover, city wells siphoned water from the aquifer, causing land subsidence under Mexico City. By the 1940s the bottom of Lake Texcoco, once the lowest-lying area of the basin, stood higher than the zocalo. The similarities in the two lakes' desiccation ended there, however. Texcoco's reduced size was also due to drainage infrastructure, whereas Xochimilco's more gradual recession increased over the course of the twentieth century as Mexico City's hydraulic works extracted ever-greater quantities of water for domestic and industrial use. Facing these changing conditions, villagers harnessed the resource nationalism of the postrevolutionary period to ensure access to aquatic environments.

In the Texcoco lakebed, the fertilization efforts launched under the aegis of Mariano Barragán succumbed to toxic salts and the storm of revolution. Barragán's original experimental zone, the drainage works, and the rest of the lakebed remained under federal control, but Venustiano Carranza, and later Álvaro Obregón, opted to sell small parcels on the condition that buyers would prepare the lands for farming. This scheme proved unrealistic, as few buyers were interested in making the outlays necessary to turn a profit on the barren land.[4] Purchasing parcels was out of the question for most villagers, who instead employed a variety of tactics to contest the state's ongoing presence and negotiate rights to land and water.

In 1918 local residents from Magdalena Salinas, Peñón de los Baños, and Tocuila used the petition to air their grievances to the Carrancista government. They called for the conservation of the lake environment in a fierce rebuke of the inequalities brought on by the hydraulic infrastructure and land federalization. The villagers explained that even with proper agricultural knowledge, the transformation of the lands from saline to fertile would be slow. Astutely embedding their argument in urban health, they explained that "the uncovered lands that remain after desiccation produce with harm to this capital those suffocating clouds of dust so damaging to the eyes and throats of the residents of the capital as well as completely changing the atmospheric conditions of the area."[5] The moribund lake and its associated threats—both real (dust storms) and debatable (climate change)—in combination with failed attempts to fertilize the land, afforded villagers the opportunity to defend their customary means of subsistence. Although ostensibly willing to become farmers, they were leery of such endeavors, as their own efforts had not borne fruit.

The petition triggered the first debates within the Carrancista state over the efficacy of Texcoco drainage and soil fertilization. In response, a project engineer issued a report to the head of the Texcoco Improvement Works head Joaquin M. Alegre that parsed the pros and cons of drainage. On one hand, a regenerated lake would have many advantages, the engineer noted. It would suppress the dust storms that damaged nearby farms and the health of city residents, facilitate cloud formation and increase humidity, preserve local subsistence patterns that depended on lake water, and help prevent the capillary action that drew salts to the surface once waters receded. On the other hand, the engineer asserted, a continually drained lake basin made it possible to embark on a fertilization project at any moment, curbed flooding of the city, and allowed for better maintenance of existing desagüe works.[6]

With this report in hand, Alegre conferred with President Carranza, who ordered that the gates that regulated the water flow from the lakebed to the Gran Canal remain permanently open, as they had been since the initiation of Barragán's work in 1912, "it being his wish that all the water that arrives in the lake be given a quick exit."[7] The more flexible Alegre countered with a compromise to maintain a certain level of water in the bed during the dry season so that "the residents can collect and capitalize off [lake] products."[8] This proposal was rejected, and the centuries-old drainage pattern continued. Neither the specter of the dust storm nor the needs of local subsistence could outdo drainage and reclamation for agriculture.

Lakeshore residents also challenged the public works indirectly by claiming dried or marshy federal lands for their own purposes—as they had done as early as 1909 when federal surveyors arrived on the scene—or by seeking usufruct rights within the federal zone. In 1917 Carranza reaffirmed state authority over the lakebed, decreeing that all land formerly under water belonged to the nation unless village or personal property rights could be confirmed.[9] Carranza continued Francisco Madero's policy of purchasing privately held lands, believing them beneficial to the public works. Project engineers encountered some locals who had occupied land they had previously sold to the state and sought to punish them for "dispossessing the Nation."[10] It was common for villagers residing on the shore to extend their holdings as the waters receded, whether they rightfully owned that land or not. The villagers of San Pedro Xalostoc appealed to their right "of accession to those lands . . . by virtue of the simple withdrawal of the waters."[11] The lake had been their source of sustenance for centuries, and no federal decree was going to usurp their rights to it. Such ongoing conflicts, dating back at least to 1909, evinced the nebulous and contested property relations in and around the lakebed, a struggle that curtailed state sovereignty over a space just miles from the seat of political power. Government-contracted engineers not only struggled to transform the lakebed but also engaged in a pitched battle to keep federal property.

Land tenure was at stake in the federalized lake basin, as was the use of that land and its natural resources. In the late 1910s and 1920s, villagers from Peñón de los Baños, San Juan de Aragón, Ixtacalco, San Pedro Xalostoc, and other communities negotiated with the postrevolutionary state for usufruct rights to federal lands and waters. Villagers and small landowners won over four hundred contracts authorizing fishing, hunting, salt extraction, and bug collection in the lakebed as long as no disorder or damage was caused to existing works.[12] Even where permissions were not granted, it is easy to surmise that many locals, like their counterparts in the forested Ajusco, would have ignored the rules in order to sustain their livelihoods. That guards were placed around the hydraulic infrastructure and experimental zone indicated as much.[13] Engineers sought first and foremost to control and transform the lands, and government officials were willing to acquiesce to rural demands when they did not undermine reclamation efforts.

Several communities around Lake Xochimilco hitched their water-based means of subsistence to the agrarian reform and federal water policy. The fundamental issue at stake was that of whom water federalization served. The community of Tláhuac held 722 hectares divided into small parcels— insufficient acreage to meet local needs, in spite of the productivity of its chinampas. Obregón approved a transfer of nearly a thousand hectares of Hacienda Xico, Remigio Noriega's rich estate, along with seventy-one hectares of the federally owned Tláhuac marsh. Tlahuacans targeted the marsh as a site to rejuvenate the communal economy. What is more, in 1926 the ejido received water from the federally owned Magdalena spring to irrigate 666 hectares.[14] New federal water policies favored Tláhuac, whose ejido encompassed a productive parcel of Xico's rich lands as well as a sizable aquatic environment where fishing and chinampería prospered.[15]

Tlahuacans similarly petitioned for the nine-hectare San Andrés pond, fertile ground for chinampería. This battle proved more onerous; its alleged owner was not the federal government but the influential Simón Ruíz Morelos, a magistrate on the military tribunal. Dozens of chinamperos contested Ruíz Morelos's drainage rights, arguing that the pond was, in reality, national property. If not for threats of "taking them to jail if they sign[ed] the petition," community leaders maintained, other chinamperos in a similarly desperate situation would have endorsed the letter.[16] As far as they were concerned, Ruíz Morelos had committed "theft of the nation," and they exhorted the government "to reproach an act similar to Noriega's in the time of Porfirismo." Another petition invoked Article 27 and the equitable distribution of resources.[17] However, about fifty other Tláhuac farmers—not chinamperos—backed Ruíz Morelos's actions, claiming that draining the pond was a public health necessity.[18] Both chinamperos and conventional agriculturalists claimed to represent the entire community, and such contrasting demands foreshadowed coming agroecological disputes between these two groups in the lacustrine space.

Ruíz Morelos defended his ownership of the San Andrés pond, which was confirmed by a Supreme Court decision in 1931 that held that Zapatistas had formed the pond by breaking dams constructed by Noriega. Because it was not a natural body of water, the verdict read, the pond was not national property.[19] The political clout of Ruíz Morelos shone through here. Most government accounts determined that the pond water originated in a nearby spring, which was connected to a much larger pond within the Chalco lakebed, thus making San Andrés national property. These reports implied that Ruíz Morelos's drainage works lacked authorization.[20] The production of knowledge about the basin's nature, whether forest cover or the process of lake formation, occurred within the context of ongoing social disputes over regulated and engineered environments.[21] In the particular quarrel over the San Andrés pond, the democratic applications of resource nationalism were thwarted; the Tlahuacan struggle for San Andrés ended in community defeat.

Resource nationalism gave water-dependent and land-deprived villagers a useful political tool. The Texcoco lakebed had been federalized before the revolution, and the specifically urban and elite-conceived functions of it clashed with villagers' priorities. Nonetheless, many campesinos managed to gain land and usufruct rights to what remained of the waterscape. Around Lake Xochimilco, the line between federal and private waters was even blurrier, and communities at times sparred with powerful landowners over which lands and waters belonged to the nation.

ADAPTING TO A CHANGING ENVIRONMENT

Campesino efforts to salvage their lake-based economies stalled in the face of desiccation, compounded by a resource crunch resulting from population growth. Land reform offered a way out. From San Gregorio Atlapulco at the edge of Lake Xochimilco to San Juan Aragón on the banks of the old Lake Texcoco, villagers entrusted their hopes of reconstructing rural life to the agrarian reform, that is, conventional dryland agriculture. Ejido grants and water recession coupled to boost conventional farming over other uses of the lakebeds.

The experiences of two communities on the western shore of the Texcoco lakebed, San Juan de Aragón and Santiago Atzacoalco, underscore the interplay between agrarian politics and changing ecologies. In 1917 over forty residents from Santiago Atzacoalco protested the Porfirian government's "unrightful" expropriation of lands for the relocation of the Remedios River, a project linked to the general drainage of the basin.[22] They demanded access to the restricted federal lands east of the Gran Canal, which had created a barrier separating their village from the lakebed.[23] Dozens of villagers from San Juan de Aragón related a similar tale of dwindling resources: "This pueblo has sustained itself principally from the salt marsh and from the different products of Lake Texcoco. . . . Now all those resources have been exhausted, as much from the desiccation of the lake as from the diversion of the Guadalupe River, which

TABLE 5.1 — Ejidos Created around Lake Xochimilco, 1917–1924

EJIDO	YEAR CREATED	HECTARES
San Juan Ixtayoapan	1917	406
San Andrés Mixquic	1918	558
Xochimilco	1918	820
San Gregorio Atlapulco	1922	476
Santiago Zapotitlan	1922	244
Tulyehualco	1923	407
Santa Cruz Xochitepec	1923	60
Tláhuac	1923	1,049
Xochimanca	1924	53

provided us, apart from irrigation water, the land that we used for the extraction of the salts."[24] For these petitioners, the agrarian reform constituted the last ray of hope for a life in the countryside.

Most communities received lands of varying quantity and quality in the 1920s, after years of waiting (see table 5.1). Santiago Atzacoalco, a village that possessed scant fertile land, received 50 hectares from the Hacienda Risco and 209 from federal Texcoco lands.[25] A few years later, engineers built a canal through the village's new ejido without installing a bridge for the *ejidatarios* (ejido members) to cross, turning the short jaunt back to town into a nine-kilometer journey. Ejidatarios recognized that the drainage work was "of the utmost importance" but sought to defend their own needs, much as the villagers of Magdalena Salinas, Peñón de los Baños, and Tocuila had done in their petitions in 1918: "just as you search for a solution either to the floods or the dust storms that rise from Lake Texcoco, we should be offered the easiest means of communication."[26]

The land available to residents of San Juan de Aragón was similarly pitiful in the early 1920s; the community nominally possessed 148 hectares, but 39 were in the hands of outsiders.[27] Remigio Noriega had acquired the midsized Hacienda Santa Ana Aragón, which encircled the village's lands. After agrarian officials announced the expropriation of over a thousand hectares from the hacienda in 1921, Noriega fought back. He deceived the campesinos into believing that they would have to reimburse him for the land, or "he would seize our land, even our homes."[28] Fear of destitution compelled community leaders to decline the government's offer, but the hacendado's subterfuge took him only so far. The villagers soon realized their mistake and renewed their land request, which agrarian officials approved.

Undaunted, the landowner drew on government reclamation goals, property rights, productivist rhetoric, and the reality of a shifting peri-urban population to continue his defense. Formerly under water, the land, according to Noriega, had been made productive through costly works and large investments. Noriega claimed to have "created" fertility and was furious that his efforts would "benefit those who have not put forth any effort."[29] He cynically labeled the villagers urbanized workers without knowledge of farming, arguing that the ejido would be abandoned. Obregón rubber-stamped the 1,074-hectare grant, but the tract the villagers received was not the one they had requested but rather a poor-quality parcel that lacked Noriega's irrigation and drainage network.[30]

Since farming the dried lakebed produced little without substantial investments, many continued to fish, hunt, and extract salts. These enterprises were diminishing in value, however. The ducks and geese that once covered the Basin of Mexico's skies no longer arrived as before, victims of habitat loss and the unsustainable hunting practice of the armada.[31] The ejidatarios of Peñón de los Baños asked officials to revoke a ban on the armada and declared that, without maize, "the only hope is from the duck."[32] Fishing declined as the water receded, and salt production, which increased in some areas as patterns of humidification and drying brought salts to the surface, was an ancillary activity. In 1913 residents sold a thousand metric tons of tequesquite to market vendors, soap factories, and haciendas, but competition from foreign trade and Pacific coastal production squeezed small producers out of the market during the 1920s and 1930s. Moreover, tequesquite's scant exchange value made it unsuitable for large-scale exploitation.[33]

Lakeshore residents stood between the half-fulfilled promises of the agrarian reform and the malaise of the floundering fertilization project. And since the state held ownership of ejido lands, campesinos could not offer their land as collateral to obtain credit for machinery and other tools to prepare the soil for farming.[34] Communities possessed land where one could "dig over a meter deep to bury the salts and still not obtain [productivity]."[35] Their situation resembled writer Juan Rulfo's descriptions of the troubles other agrarian reform recipients faced decades later: lands like "a sizzling frying pan" where "they want us to plant some kind of seeds to see if something will come up and take root. But nothing will come up here. Not even buzzards."[36]

Whereas the ejidatarios surrounding the Texcoco bed confronted a degraded environment, the inhabitants around the Xochimilco lakebed became embroiled in conflicts over relatively productive land, albeit lands also subjected to years of drainage and drying. As Lake Xochimilco receded, numerous marshes (*ciénegas*) took its place. These wetlands, including the Ciénega Grande and Ciénega Chica in the village of Xochimilco, the San Gregorio Atlapulco marsh in Atlapulco, the Huexocoapa marsh bordering Santa María Nativitas, and the San Andrés pond in Tláhuac, remained active chinampería sites. Villages and haciendas competed for these prized environments, which landowners coveted for conventional farming.

Composed of sixteen barrios and the town center, Xochimilco had a population of around eight thousand people in 1910 and over twelve thousand by the mid-1920s.[37] The town was more than an agricultural community—craftworkers government functionaries, and merchants also populated it—but farming and a variety of lake-oriented activities figured prominently. Agrarian representatives asserted that the Haciendas Coapa and San Juan de Díos had dispossessed villagers of hundreds of hectares during the nineteenth century. The owners of Coapa had drained large tracts of their newly acquired lands to practice conventional farming and sold the rest to locals who maintained chinampa plots.

Aureliano Urrutia had also drained the San Gregorio Atlapulco marsh, but following Victoriano Huerta's ouster, community members occupied the former wetlands, which Luis Cabrera had considered as a small property. Carranza had the Atlapulqueños expelled, but over 180 villagers quickly turned to the promise of land reform, requesting the 280-hectare ciénega as well as 500 additional hectares of Urrutia's holdings.[38] The landowner resorted to two common tactics: subdividing the land to create inalienable holdings and appealing to productivist rhetoric. Targeting chinampería, Urrutia maintained that "the only way to improve [the lands] . . . is to keep them in the power of a single owner who will make new works and improvements that increase their value."[39] As if mimicking urban environmental planners' intentions for the basin as a whole, drainage and forestation topped his list of priorities.

In Santa María Nativitas, intercommunity land disputes and the Xochimilco waterworks frustrated community leaders' agrarian demands. The community claimed the eighty-one-hectare Huexocoapa marsh and the smaller Acapixtla marsh, but these lands had been occupied by nearby villagers, and the agrarian authorities, by law, could not adjudicate competing community claims.[40] Neither were the authorities going to tamper with the Xochimilco water system, another point of contention. The aqueduct, pumping station, and tree nursery, chinamperos complained, "cut as if it were the Great Wall of China all communication" between the center of town, local woods, and chinampa plots.[41] Even before the urban waterworks began to deplete the springs and the surrounding water bodies, the physical structure itself threatened communal economies.

The agrarian reform passed Santa María Nativitas by, but San Gregorio Atlapulco and Xochimilco received early land grants.[42] The Xochimilco grant in 1918, one of the earliest partitions in the basin, consisted of 820 hectares comprising the Ciénega Grande and Ciénega Chica marshes. In June 1922 Obregón granted 476 hectares to San Gregorio Atlapulco, much of which was taken from Urrutia's properties, including the marshland. In both cases the nationalization of water resources worked in favor of villagers, but it is unclear to what extent they used them for chinampería. Some evidence suggests that in San Gregorio Atlapulco chinampería persisted on some of the more humid ejidal land, but most of the parcel, including parts of the drained San Gregorio marsh, was too dry most of the year. The ejidatarios of San Gregorio Atlapulco thus aimed to continue the drainage initiated by their hacendado nemesis. These efforts were delayed for over a decade, however, because of the machinations of indignant small property owners who had bought land from Urrutia when he fled the revolution. Xochimilco's ejidal authorities continued their wetland drainage in 1919, a year after taking definitive possession.[43] Soon thereafter, the ejido obtained a pump and used a system of ditches to conduct water toward a nearby canal.[44]

Land reform and water nationalization emboldened Xochimilcan communities to reassert control over productive environments strained by urbanization and intensifying land uses. Yet much of the area, too dry for chinampería but composed of rich alluvial soil, was used for conventional agriculture, which further altered the agroecology of the lakebed and undercut the pervasive association of Xochimilco with a vibrant water-based economy. By compelling many campesinos to practice conventional agriculture, land reform generated intercommunity disputes between chinamperos and conventional farmers.

ENGINEERING, REVOLUTIONARY POLITICS,
AND ENVIRONMENTAL CHANGE

Engineering, of course, rearranges social relations by altering environments, but it is no one-way street. Engineers operate amid ecological change and divergent social interests, and they respond to both social and environmental forces in accord with the interests they represent, in this case, urban-sanitary and class-inflected political interests.[45] A comparison of Lake Texcoco and Lake Xochimilco reveals that this is not a story of high modernism run amok.[46] Local political culture, national political assemblages, elite environmental imaginaries, and vibrant natures intersected to mold urban engineering schemes, which, in a dialectical relation, modified local environments and political strategies and objectives.

By the 1920s Lake Texcoco still extended up to twelve thousand hectares during portions of the wet season but was too shallow to navigate. For most of the year it was a cracked and dry expanse dotted with intermittent ponds and marshes. It was the saline soil, inhospitable to plant growth, that so worried urban experts. It was as if Lake Texcoco was taking revenge for centuries of drainage; instead of floodwater, the lakebed sent the city tons of irritating dust. Lake Xochimilco had also undergone desiccation, if more slowly and less extensively than its neighbor to the north. Chinampería output had steadily declined, but the lake and its canal system endured. Like the proverbial frog sitting in a pot of heating water, most urbanites assumed that the beloved "land of flowers" had not reached the boiling point of crisis—no matter how much some locals disagreed. Whereas the Lake Texcoco problem persisted and, in some minds, worsened, spurring further engineering, most assumed that the Xochimilco waterscape needed management, not radically reworking. The Cassandra call of the chinamperos was ignored.

Engineering practice in the lakebeds was not determined solely by planners' representations. Local social relations, appropriations of nature, and politics also mattered. Communities on the western edge of the Texcoco lakebed had won significant land grants that desiccation had impoverished. Their pleas for productive land coincided with the state's resolve to vanquish the rampant social and environmental ills around Lake Texcoco. This set the stage for the Cardenista project to transform the Texcoco lakebed for both agrarian and urban interests. The residents living around the Xochimilco lakebed, in contrast, held no such unified vision as their counterparts to the northeast did. Villagers diversified their economic activities in response to

FIGURE 5.1 — Trajineras on a Xochimilco canal. COURTESY OF INAH, FOTOTECA NACIONAL.

population growth and slow but steady desiccation. Further, the tourism boom—enabled by readily available land transport, the flourishing *indigenista* discourse, and the expansion of the middle class—allowed countless urbanites and foreign travelers to revel in the waterscape as an emblem of authentic Mexicanness without venturing too far into the so-called primitive countryside.[47] Locals embraced the boom, taking up work on one of several docks as vendors or *trajineros* (oarsmen of the traditional canoe-like transport vessel called a *trajinera*) to cater to curious and party-seeking arrivals (see figure 5.1).

Other Xochimilco residents turned to conventional farming on new ejido lands. But the desiccationist engineering policies advocated by conventional farmers often conflicted with chinampero interests. In 1926 the residents of the former Hacienda San Juan de Díos experienced flooding from a nearby stream and the "infiltrations of Lake Xochimilco." They beseeched the government for a technical solution to lower the lake level and recanalize the stream. However, they did not put all their eggs into the basket of official aid and purchased a pump to redirect floodwater toward a nearby canal.[48] During a rainy summer in 1934, the Xochimilco ejido experienced a heavy dose of flooding, which they also blamed on the neighboring lake and "chinampa infiltrations." In September of that year, the ejidal leadership reached an agreement with the scop to periodically dredge the Canal Nacional and open its floodgates. These actions forestalled the inundation of ejidal fields and recently urbanized land at the canal's end point in Jamaica but endangered chinampería, which required consistently high water levels in canals.[49]

Ejidos and chinampas lay side by side, and conflict over water was inevitable.[50] While the ejidal authorities of Xochimilco convinced the scop to reduce the lake through floodgate management, the Campesino Social League of the Federal District demanded the full drainage of all of Xochimilco's canals, which they claimed were "stagnant" and thus "a public health threat."[51] Another conflict erupted when chinamperos extended their domain by breaking the boards of Xochimilco's canals, resulting in the inundation of neighboring ejido lands.[52]

Because of the lakebed's volatile hydrology, chinamperos could not agree among themselves on water management. Some feared an overabundance of water. The chinampas of Xochimilco flooded in 1925 owing to heavy rainfall and the closure of sluice gates that blocked the passage of water to the Canal Nacional. The scop, in response to chinampero petitions, opened several gates to direct water into the canal.[53] Others on the outskirts of the lake or on secondary canals faced desiccation. Scarce rains and the dredging of the Canal Nacional reduced water levels, dried out some chinampas, and left many chinamperos unable to farm.[54]

The same Federal District campesino league that called for the drainage of all of Xochimilco's canals—which would have amounted to the coup de grâce for chinampería—also issued an unequivocal statement denouncing the effects of canal dredging on local chinampería. What appears an outright contradiction on the surface was more the balancing act of an organization that sought to represent the agroecological practices of all its members. The two practices, moreover, were not altogether mutually exclusive. Some ejidatarios held chinampa plots of their own, and still others continued to rely on the chinampa nurseries to plant their seeds.[55] The government played up the emerging divisions, however. Ceasing canal dredging, officials affirmed, would meet with resistance from "the immense majority of Xochimilco residents."[56] Ejidatarios supported dredging to prevent flooding, some chinamperos unaffected by desiccation approved it to preserve their transportation routes, and other chinamperos worried about altered water levels. Water governance in Xochimilco was as unstable and mushy as the lakebed soil, a reflection of diverse, often contradictory, farming interests, even as chinampería remained the central component of Xochimilco's picturesque imaginary.

Xochimilco tourism, spawned by nationalist indigenismo, required chinampería's survival. The national centennial celebration of 1921 saw the inauguration of a new boat dock and the planting of traditional *ahuehuete* trees. A boat trip through Xochimilco's chinampa-lined canals became a sine qua non for prestigious international visitors and well-to-do residents of the capital.[57] Workers in tourism, like chinamperos, sought to conserve the canal and lake system, and during the 1930s several local organizations began to vouch for the water environment. In the late 1930s, Xochimilco's Neighborhood Improvement Committee teamed with several architects and engineers to promote lake conservation over urban water needs.[58] At stake was not merely chinampería but a tourist economy that faced extinction. Lake proponents worried that "Xochimilco's beauty and life are soon to disappear within no more than five years; and then in Mexico's Venice, [visitors] will not find more than dry chinampas and the desolation and ruin of a beautiful town."[59] Mexico City's water-supply system incurred the sharpest scorn as a visible and symbolic marker of environmental usurpation. This same group of Xochimilcan lake conservationists proposed that the city water authority make use of the basin's streams rather than the springs on which their town depended. In a more confrontational statement, they boldly exclaimed, "Thirty years of desiccation has been enough."[60]

Not all farmers in the region felt threatened by the waterworks. Some residents of Santiago Tepalcatlalpan—a community of predominantly dry agriculture—suggested that the principal cause of desiccation was sedimentation, not water extraction for Mexico City. They supported dredging the lake bottom to maintain tourism and "the extraordinary farming [our indigenous race] does in the chinampas."[61] Here, the pro-lake argument centered on leisure and the food supply. In this view, environmental protection was the equivalent of the protection of indigenous peoples, a social category with which the petitioners did not identify. Their proposal eulogized chinamperos and endorsed lake conservation but also glossed over emerging divisions over the governance and engineering of waterscapes.

Whereas objections to the waterworks gained little traction, those that inveighed against sedimentation were addressed, if rarely sufficiently. Sedimentation certainly contributed to desiccation, but, more important for conventional farming communities, it also contributed to flooding. Since siltation limited the carrying capacity of the Xochimilco lakebed and the various rivers that fed it, fields turned into muddy swamps after heavy rains. Accordingly, Santiago Te-palcatlalpan residents sought to convince the government to dredge the Amec-ameca, Tepalcatlalpan, and San Luis Xochimanca streams.[62] Government engineers understood that tackling this threat was much more cost-effective and perhaps more popular than revamping the capital's entire water-supply system. The scop dredged the Canal Nacional to much fanfare in 1926, con-tinued dredging the rivers that flowed into the lakebed up until the late 1920s, and in 1935 dredged the lake itself.[63]

Ejidos composed, according to one agronomist, 60 percent of the land in the lakebed in 1940. Needless to say, flooding constituted an imminent threat, and to counter it, ejidos centered dam construction within their agrarian poli-tics.[64] A local agrarian community league regularly demanded the dredging of the Amecameca and the construction of an upstream dam.[65] The league la-mented that "year after year" the nine ejidos and a multitude of other commu-nities in the Xochimilco and Chalco lakebeds "irremissibly suffer from floods originating in the overflowing of the Ameca[meca] River."[66] They submitted an astonishingly meticulous plan about how to construct the dam, so detailed that one wonders whether an engineer had been hired for the task. The scop accepted the proposal but gave no timetable for its construction.

Dams constructed to protect crops might have also saved lives. On Sun-day, June 2, 1935, a severe rainstorm struck the Ajusco range, and walls of water cascaded down the Amecameca River and other nearby streambeds. The mountain community of San Pedro Actopan, located in a gully adjacent to a stream, was devastated by water three meters high in some areas (see figure 5.2). Community members had sought sanctuary in the church when the storm began. The structure "received the unstoppable force of the flood," which broke through the doors and windows to drown the dozens of people huddled inside.[67] The wreckage of dozens of adobe and straw homes washed down the mountain slope, and the floodwaters took out additional buildings and homes in San Bartolomé Xicomulco, San Pablo Oxtotepec, Milpa Alta, and the lakeshore community of San Gregorio Atlapulco before overflowing Xochimilco's canals. Newspapers reported that 114 people perished—66 in San Pedro Actopan—while the government claimed 96 deaths, all but 10 in Actopan.[68] Once the roads became passable, Lázaro Cárdenas sent medical supplies, food, and coffins to the affected communities and spent a full day touring the wreckage and offering consolation to victims.[69]

The flood galvanized support for the dam and construction began in the late 1930s but was suspended soon thereafter. One government engineer

FIGURE 5.2 — Aftermath of the San Pedro Actopan flood, 1935.
COURTESY OF AGN: ENRIQUE DÍAZ 97/4.

explained that the land set aside for it was highly permeable, thus unsuitable for water storage and potentially harmful to several important downstream springs that were nourished by the river overflow.[70] A dam would certainly have mitigated sedimentation, but according to engineer Carlos Betancourt, it would also have imperiled a significant source of future urban drinking water. Even the Amecameca, at the intersection of the Ajusco and Sierra Nevada ranges, was entangled within metropolitan resource politics, and elite urban interests again prevailed at the apex of Cardenista populism.

As engineers dithered over how to accommodate diverse local interests while dealing with the dual threats of flooding and desiccation, the city increased the Xochimilco system's output from 2,000 liters per second to nearly 3,600 liters per second by the late 1930s. In 1912 Marroquín y Rivera had justified his engineering feat by arguing that aquifer recharge rates eclipsed the system's output.[71] For this esteemed engineer, the springs were of value only insofar as their yield ran unimpeded through city pipes. All other water was superfluous or, worse, wasted since it would be lost to evaporation. But it was this excess water that made Xochimilco a bastion of chinampería and a cherished landscape bursting with meaning and memory. Aquifer recharge rates determined spring output, which did not increase just because engineers tapped the springs. It was a zero-sum game; the more water was extracted by the urban waterworks, the less water was available to sustain the remaining lakes, wetlands, and canals.[72]

In the absence of studies that measured overall spring production in the Xochimilco lakebed, eyewitness accounts from myriad sources and academic reports indicate that urban water appropriations affected the lacustrine environment. The German geographer Elisabeth Schilling reported that shortly after the completion of the waterworks, traffic on the Canal Nacional was suspended for twenty days on account of low water levels.[73] The anthropologist William T. Sanders observed rather despondently in his travels to the chinampa zone that whereas the four hundred hectares of chinampería in San Gregorio Atlapulco, which relied on spring water untapped by the waterworks, flourished well into the 1950s, historically productive chinampa areas in Xochimilco, Santa María Nativitas, and some locations near the extraction zone had begun to decline in the 1930s.[74] Chinamperos from the Barrio de Guadalupita in Xochimilco linked water abatement to the "decreased volume of water that the nearby springs bring up" and suggested that the city should tap water from Lerma instead.[75] These accounts corroborate what two geophysicists found in the early 1970s: "the pumping of water from Xochimilco's springs resulted in the decomposition of the hydrological regime [and a] considerable decline in lake levels, which affected local agriculture."[76]

The communities of Lake Xochimilco hold an admirable place in Mexico City's imagination. They have, it is understood, wobbled but not yet fallen to the bulldozer of urbanization, uniting heroically, if not always successfully, in defense of their indigenous lifeways and the precious water on which those lifeways depend, maintaining a small and fragile oasis in a sea of pavement. Such a view holds some weight. Whereas other hinterland communities have long been subsumed by the city, chinampería continues, albeit more tenuously now than ever before, and water, although heavily polluted, continues to fill the canals. Without downplaying the political achievements of Xochimilcans, however, this story of a unified, heroic fight needs qualification. The cultural and leisure services Xochimilco continues to provide the urban middle and upper classes have placed the area and its preservation closer to the top of the priority list for governments since 1940. In addition, Xochimilcans themselves held (and continue to hold) different and conflicting agroecological interests and environmental demands. While urban water expropriation was seen as a major evil, many locals were more preoccupied with flooding and sedimentation. State engineering practices reflected messy local social relations, shifting among contradictory interests while refusing to reroute the urban water supply. In general, officials tended to support works to allay sedimentation rather than protect chinampería. Lakeshore residents may have perceived Xochimilco to be in environmental crisis as early as the 1930s, but until the esteemed waterscape faced imminent desiccation, few would concern themselves with conservation.

A CITY OF BLINDING DUST

Around Lake Texcoco the environmental conditions, cultural imaginary, and social relations interacted to bring about a different brand of engineering. Environmental planners responded differently to the lakebed's changing ecology, and, encouraged by a relatively cohesive campesino population intent on farming the saline lands, they revived the Maderista plans to reclaim Texcoco lands for agriculture, this time to favor ejidal communities.

Scientists and engineers believed dust counts in the basin were rising precipitously, with nasty effects on health. Intense heat over the lakebed during the spring combined with dry conditions and strong northeasterly winds to produce the ideal conditions for swirling clouds of dust, hence the popular refrain "febrero loco, marzo otro poco."[77] Urban experts associated dust with deforestation, but the drying Lake Texcoco received most of the blame. In 1923 scientists at the Tacubaya Observatory began measuring "dust events" and counted an average of seventy-four per year through 1939, with most occurring between February and June.[78] These dust storms irritated lungs and could carry germs that caused respiratory or gastrointestinal illnesses.

The dust storm captured the urban imagination. On June 1, 1923, a dust cloud from the lakebed advanced quickly through the city, first engulfing the poor neighborhoods on the eastern fringe and then moving into the city center. It was so intense that "the cars, trams, and carriages that traveled through the city's streets were obliged to turn on their headlights to defeat the dense, black mist, to the point that it was difficult to make out the silhouette of a person from three or four meters away."[79] The storms often lasted an hour or more; they blocked sunlight, paralyzed traffic, covered pedestrians with a layer of brown filth, and gave the city an ominous look.

In 1917 the Mexican Society for Geography and Statistics convened a conference on the "Lake Texcoco problem," inviting members to issue their opinions on the dust-swept city. One critic, the engineer Julio Riquelme Inda, referred to the small agricultural experimentation camp, a vestige of Maderista reclamation, as "an oasis in middle of the desert"—but in the same breath rued the prohibitive cost of draining the lands of accumulated salts.[80] Instead, Riquelme Inda, along with Alberto Carreño, proposed a massive afforestation effort using salt-resistant plants. This conference marked the beginning of the next phase of the incessant debate over how to respond to the changing ecology of the Texcoco lakebed and its desiccation, the flailing agricultural project, dust storms, and sedimentation.

While many engineers, including Felipe Ruíz de Velasco, Mariano Barragán, and Alonzo Patiño, continued to uphold fertilization as a viable objective, during the 1920s others joined Riquelme Inda in seeking alternative solutions to the persistent Texcoco problem. Miguel Ángel de Quevedo defended the drainage project he had helped build but roundly rejected the agricultural solution. According to Quevedo, reclamation authorities erred in leaving open the floodgates, draining too much of the lake and causing an uptick in the dust count. He urged respect for the desagüe's original intent, the evacuation of only potential floodwaters. Aware that sediment was steadily filling the lakebed, he continued to push for forest-conservation measures in the surrounding area as well as retention dams that could limit torrential flows. To curtail the dust storms, he insisted on the expansion of his earlier afforestation project using halophytes.[81] (See figure 5.3.) Prominent urban thinkers such as Fernando Zárraga; his architect son, Guillermo; and the engineer Ricardo de la Vega drew up similar forestation plans that would fix the soil and create "windbreaks" against advancing dust clouds.

Luis Careaga's critique of the agricultural project went far beyond anything Quevedo could support. Harking back to Manuel Balbontín and Ladislao de Belina a half century earlier, Careaga envisaged the regeneration of Lake Texcoco and the entire lacustrine system. He asserted in 1922—several years before Roberto Gayol's major study implicating subsidence in the decreasing efficacy of the city's sewer system—that the desiccation of the basin's lakes caused land subsidence, which damaged buildings and important infrastructure. According to Careaga, subsidence, not rising dust, was the most dangerous effect of lake drainage.[82]

Quevedo dismissed Careaga's claims and asserted that the damage was not the result of sinking ground but of buildings with unstable foundations (they

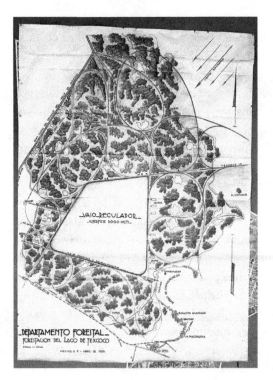

FIGURE 5.3 — Texcoco forestation plan. COURTESY OF INAH, FOTOTECA NACIONAL.

were both correct). Quevedo was tenacious in his disapproval of lake regeneration. He declared it contrary to hygiene and impractical, since it would require the excavation of enormous quantities of soil sediment. Regeneration, he said, was a utopian solution "that can only sustain itself through the complete ignorance of the problem at hand."[83] These experts advocated divergent solutions, for sure, but they came to understand the intricate connections between urban infrastructure and the nonhuman natural elements that composed the larger metropolitan environment, particularly that of the Texcoco lakebed. They aimed to remedy an urban ecology that they perceived to be in crisis, roiled by past engineering practices.

"FROM PARIAHS TO CITIZENS": REENGINEERING LAKE TEXCOCO

After a decade-long hiatus, during which the state failed to interest landowners in purchasing Texcoco land, President Pascual Ortíz Rubio (1930–1932), a former SCOP minister, reinvested in Texcoco land reclamation. In 1930 he authorized the Mexico City Agricultural Park, in which engineer Angel Peimbert and architect Augusto Petricioli, brother of the builder Carlos Petricioli, promised to create a canal system in the Texcoco lakebed that would connect villages to each other and to markets in Mexico City. Washed of its salts, the lakebed would become another cradle of agriculture in the basin and, according to some technicians, of chinampa agriculture. The plan also included a "Lake City" to serve as a hub of trade for the newly created small farms, which would be sold at thirty pesos per hectare to recuperate the costs of reclamation. The planned park bridged the agricultural and the water-recuperation visions of the lakebed in an attempt to jumpstart local agrarian capitalism.[84] Yet, like its predecessor, it was another failure: first, because its benefactor, Ortíz Rubio, resigned from office in consternation over Calles's overbearing influence and, second, because funding from the National Agrarian Credit Bank failed to materialize.

Disasters tend to reshuffle government policies and cause radical swings in how leaders conceptualize social and environmental problems.[85] The recurring dust storms of April 1933, while comparatively minor as disasters go, provided just that impetus. The press, a cadre of foresters, and Mexico's leading planner, Carlos Contreras, renewed calls for a resolution to the irritating dust storms, and the Department of the Federal District (DDF) under Aaron Sáenz responded.[86] Sáenz integrated Lake Texcoco, one-fifth of which fell under his jurisdiction, into his larger environmental program.

Under the aegis of city engineer and planner Felipe Sánchez, the DDF set aside over a hundred ejidal hectares of Peñón de los Baños and San Juan de Aragón to experiment with various crops and tree species.[87] Like Barragán, Sánchez first washed the land through controlled flooding, but unlike in earlier trials, which utilized river water, Sánchez constructed a pump and canal system that carried city sewage from the Gran Canal to the saline fields. After two weeks of washing, workers planted corn, barley, beetroot, and alfalfa on soil fertilized by part of the city's waste; the rest was channeled through the Gran Canal and corresponding tunnel to the vegetable fields of the Otomí ejidos in the arid Mezquital Valley north of the basin—exchanging the city's waste for vegetables in a practice that continues today. Yet whereas the farmers of the nearby Mezquital enjoyed productive lands irrigated with wastewater, the Texcoco salts again worked insidiously. Sánchez reported that only beetroot and alfalfa accompanied by eucalyptus, tamarix, and willow trees withstood the obstinate sodium compounds. Neither Sánchez nor any other reclamation engineer of the 1930s referenced the Sisyphean struggle to fertilize the lands that Barragán had undertaken in the 1910s. Whether it has been a matter of ignorance or a calculated decision to evade discussions of past failure, efforts to engineer Lake Texcoco have always been rather myopic.

The Pollyannaish Sánchez saw the glass of land reclamation as half full. He warned against large-scale reclamation of the entire lakebed owing to the high cost of continual washing and draining, plus his belief that part of the lakebed must be maintained as a regulating reservoir. But he promoted using fertilization on a smaller scale to grow beetroot and fodder, which could be marketed to local ranchers. He also supported the planting of eucalyptus and tamarix to fix the soil and form windbreaks against the tormenting dust storms. Sánchez may have envisioned some economic advantage for local ranchers, but his plan did little to improve locals' means of subsistence. Indeed, he showed nothing but contempt for the ejidatarios on whose lands he was experimenting. He berated them for their "war against the tree," blaming them for destroying recent plantations, and accused residents of San Juan de Aragón of allowing their animals to trample the experimental fields and eat the saplings.[88] That Sánchez and the government of the federal district made no overtures to support ejidal production surely contributed to the unwelcoming reception engineers received. This is not to say that no government authority strove to foster ejidal production. Agrarian officials hoped the works would be redirected to improve the two ejidos' farmland and enjoined President Abelardo Rodríguez (1932–1934) to authorize a more sustained and dedicated reclamation effort.[89] Rodríguez wrote a new decree but never signed it.[90]

Cárdenas took the reclamation ball and ran with it. He embarked on the most diligent effort yet to transform the land for productive use and use afforestation to prevent dust storms. Large-scale reclamation under Cárdenas had different priorities than Barragán's original project or Sánchez's defunct proposal. The expansion of ejidos in the early 1920s had reduced the portion of the lakebed under the state's direct management, so any major governmental effort to fertilize the lands needed to consider their interests. Cárdenas's election on a groundswell of agrarian activism certainly lent itself to a reclamation project more attuned to local needs.

Yet there were other situational reasons for Cárdenas to endorse state-driven land reclamation as the solution to the Texcoco problem. The timing was auspicious. State developmentalism was cresting around the world, irrespective of political ideology. In 1932 Benito Mussolini charged engineers and soldier-peasants with the task of draining and reclaiming for agriculture the vast Pontine marshes, an environment that some well-read Mexicans compared to Lake Texcoco. Adolf Hitler followed a similar path in draining wetlands for race and nation, while in the United States Franklin Delano Roosevelt's Tennessee Valley Authority and Bureau of Reclamation reengineered rivers to bring power and electricity to booming cities and agricultural enterprises.[91] It comes as no surprise, then, that the authors of Mexico's six-year plan (1934–1940) underscored the importance of reclamation. But, international trends aside, state-led reclamation served a unique domestic purpose. Although the plan emphasized wide-ranging social aims spanning urban and rural concerns and issues of both production and consumption, when plan turned to action the Cárdenas administration heavily favored two key constituencies: agrarian and industrial workers and landholding peasants. This generated a number of enemies. One of these was the urban middle class, which increasingly felt alienated by the administration's rural and labor reforms. Cárdenas seemed to devote much more attention to the surrounding countryside, carrying out agrarian reform, fomenting producer cooperatives, and installing potable-water service, sewerage, lighting, and roads in far-flung towns, than to the capital's infrastructure needs. Whereas in Xochimilco the political contradiction between urban water and rural production could not be attenuated, the fertilization of Texcoco lands presented Cárdenas an opportunity to satisfy ejido demands on the city's doorstep while appeasing disquiet in the capital by eliminating the reviled dust storms once and for all. Like most public works, reclamation for agriculture served a legitimizing function for the Cardenista state, but this project was especially important in smoothing over emerging divisions between the urban and the rural. Cárdenas used reclamation to reconcile urban development with his rural revolutionary program, linking environmental politics (both freedom from unhygienic dust and freedom to work the improved land) to the state.

Opposition to fertilization endeavors persisted, however, mostly arising from concerns that capillarity would continue to draw harmful salts to the surface. Experts in this camp called for nonagricultural uses of the land. Gilberto Galindo envisaged turning "the spongy saline desert into a giant Xochimilco . . . with wider, longer, and deeper canals" for its "enormous aesthetic and health advantages."[92] He, in concert with the engineer Rafael de la Cerda, regularly condemned fertilization and repeatedly sought audiences with Cárdenas, but top government officials wrote them off as minor players in the profession.[93] Others hoped to resuscitate the lake and build a tourist playground featuring hotels, urban developments, and sports fields.[94] Quevedo, as head of the Forestry Department, was the most powerful among the vocal opponents of fertilization. He never condoned lake regeneration, and Cárdenas called on him to create a "silvo-pastoral park" in the lakebed.[95]

These and other members of the professional class denounced the agricultural project as hubristic and fundamentally flawed owing to the action of alkali salts. Yet their alternative proposals for lake conservation, difficult to achieve in their own right because of the diminishing carrying capacity of the lakebed and the constant threat of flooding of valuable lands, and for afforestation were devoid of concern for lakeshore populations. Agriculture, it seemed, could solve the social and the environmental problem at hand. The fertilization project conformed to the political moment; it assured state-led economic productivism and agrarian revolutionary justice.

Project engineers did not initially champion ejidos, even if the work would be done in their name. They sought first to drain, fertilize, and reforest the lands in and around the ejidos of San Juan de Aragón and Peñón de los Baños, as this area in the southwestern portion of the lakebed was situated next to the fertile waters of the Gran Canal and close to several freshwater streams— the ideal place to start if reclamation was to succeed. At the end of 1934, the government planned to indefinitely expropriate four hundred hectares from the ejido of San Juan de Aragón and three hundred hectares from Peñón de los Baños, in exchange for five-year permits and subsidies for the communities' use of the Gran Canal's rich waters.[96] In a meeting in 1935 with a regional ejido organizer concerning the public works, the ejidatarios of San Juan de Aragón were seemingly unaware that the project entailed expropriation, conveying tremendous gratitude that at last "the government shares in their desire to work the land."[97] Once the ejidatarios caught wind that the government planned expropriation, however, they rejected the offer, and the authorities returned to the drawing board.

Negotiations between the government and the ejidos yielded a compromise in early 1936. Villagers provided the Forestry Department with access to part of their ejido in exchange for government-funded irrigation works on their barren lands utilizing the sewage of the Gran Canal—the very infrastructure that had so deteriorated their means of subsistence a mere generation earlier. The concession to the city's life-giving *aguas negras* (wastewater) was instrumental in the transformation of the briny soil. Once, communities such as San Juan de Aragón and Peñón de los Baños had looked askance at the monumental Porfirian drainage project, but under Cárdenas the villagers embraced it to revitalize rural subsistence. In addition to providing irrigation water, engineers helped ejidatarios install drainage systems and plow the land.[98]

FIGURE 5.4 — Texcoco reclamation project. COURTESY OF INAH, FOTOTECA NACIONAL.

In total, the government assigned 1,400,000 pesos over two years to execute the works for the two ejidos.[99] (See figure 5.4.) In garnering the support necessary to fertilize the lands, villagers had managed to negotiate a degree of autonomy from engineers to ensure that state aid would not result in another form of dispossession. Cardenista engineering projects, much like the administration's forestry policies, were as much the product of negotiation, politics, and environmental change as they were an exercise of centralized political power or modernist ideology. The government was obligated to adapt to the local political culture, highlighting the importance of the ejidatarios' claims on the metropolitan environment.

Cárdenas attempted to turn marginalized, resource-poor campesinos into productive citizens. Between 1936 and 1938, the Texcoco fertilization project spread to include other ejidal lands from a variety of lakeside towns. By the spring of 1937, 375 hectares of reclaimed ejido land were under cultivation, and another 5,367 were undergoing preparation in ejidos within and immediately surrounding the lakebed, including Tulpetlac in the north and Santiago Acahualtepec in the south.[100] The Texcoco project affected regions beyond the Basin of Mexico. The Cardenista agrarian reform had unlocked new

Mezquital Valley lands for Otomí use, and Manuel Gamio and other leading indigenistas equated the expansion of Tula River wastewater irrigation with Otomí cultural revival. The Texcoco project posed an obstacle, however. Once workers commenced washing the saline Texcoco bed, Mezquital ejidatarios received less water and, most likely, more salts.[101]

Although the project interfered with plans for increasing wastewater irrigation in the Mezquital, by 1938 it was reaping immense political dividends for Cárdenas, who that same year stated that the reclamation works would prioritize ejido production over all other "social interests."[102] The lakeshore campesinos' unremitting support of the project became evident when José Favela, the director of the works and a prominent city planner, became embroiled in a political scandal involving three fired union workers that led to his own dismissal. The leadership of various ejidos vociferously defended the engineer, who, they claimed, had terminated the workers because they had destroyed machinery and shirked on the job. The fate of the three fired workers is unknown, but the incident sparked an outpouring of appreciation for Favela's labor. The ejidal commissioner of Santiago Atzacoalco declared that his work "has resulted in the immediate benefit for the comrade campesinos of these villages, which have provided their labor contingents, winning the means of subsistence for their families." "In the future," he added, the campesinos would "continue realizing the extensive agrarian program of the Government of the Republic [and] respond with all the necessary diligence to the development of these works."[103] The commissioner from San Salvador Atenco championed Favela for "fully guaranteeing the program that the Revolution turned Government is carrying out."[104] Additional support of Favela followed. Many ejidatarios had developed a strong personal bond with the director and associated his downfall with the expiration of the project itself and thus of the gains made over several years.[105]

Despite Mexico's well-known conservative turn after 1940, land reclamation for the ejidos flourished during the first few years of the Manuel Ávila Camacho sexenio (1940–1946). Ignoring engineers such as Quevedo and Careaga who belittled fertilization schemes as counterproductive—especially given the available tracts of arable land elsewhere—the government justified the project as "elevating the cultural and economic level of fifty thousand families."[106] As one campesino organization put it, the works—most notably the concession to use the city's wastewaters—transformed villagers "from pariahs to the category of citizens."[107] The public works aided dozens of villages in the fertilization of their land, but not every ejido received equal treatment.

Because they were crucial forestation sites and prime beneficiaries of the drainage waters, San Juan de Aragón, Peñón de los Baños, and San Pedro Xalostoc on the western shore enjoyed the vast majority of the improved farmland. Other ejidos, although they fervently supported the works, were not as fortunate; government claims of uplifting fifty thousand families were obvious exaggerations. Santiago Atzacoalco, Iztapalapa, Ecatepec, and others were left more with empty promises than concrete results.[108]

CONCLUSION

Mexico City's surrounding lacustrine environment withdrew significantly over the course of the first half of the twentieth century. This converged with a vibrant period of popular politics as different constituencies sought access to the basin's receding waters. The mounting political leverage enjoyed by lakeshore campesinos reshaped the socio-ecological relations of the Xochimilco and Texcoco spaces, as well as the way engineering was conceived. Whereas city engineers attacked sedimentation and flooding around Lake Xochimilco with a host of minor works—engineering measures that were more economical than reconfiguring the city's water supply—they faced a much graver urban threat in the Texcoco lakebed: the dust storm. There, more homogeneous local agrarian objectives coincided with a dystopian imaginary of a dust-drenched city to convince Cárdenas to try to transform a menacing space widely portrayed as a symbol of a once-magnificent Indian civilization into an agricultural oasis. Technical interventions in diverse waterscapes rarely obeyed a purely ideological or institutional logic; rather, they were constituted by and deeply enmeshed in interlocking social and environmental forces, the unintended consequences of previous technical applications, and the changing contours of politics and power at different spatial scales.

6

The Political Ecology of
Working-Class Settlements

Eliminating the dust storms that rose from the dried Texcoco bed and the surrounding denuded land was part and parcel of planners' larger quest to secure
sanitary living spaces for the city's population. The dust storms pelted the capital's working-class neighborhoods first, before sweeping through the colonial
center and dissipating over the wealthier western subdivisions. The same
planners who promoted the afforestation and fertilization of the saline
lands in the 1930s also exhorted the government to build hygienic worker
housing and extend essential sanitary services.[1] As working-class settlements
spread eastward, closer to the dried lakebed, dust became a daily menace for
the urban poor and a chief cause of respiratory illnesses.[2] Dust was only one
of the problems menacing the health of these settlers. They also experienced
flooding, less from the rising waters of Texcoco than from the many seasonal
rivers that emptied into the lakebed as well as from deficient or nonexistent
drainage. Even as water and drainage pipes connected ever more city residents enmeshing city and hinterland in an environmental codependency, new
working-class settlements faced the underbelly of urban environmental en-

gineering: makeshift water supplies and flood-prone lands on the edge of a dried lakebed spewing forth tons of swirling dust. In this context, such settlements became hotbeds of political mobilization under Lázaro Cárdenas. The urban-reformist language that Cardenistas spouted outstripped their concrete actions, however, which dragged under the weight of real estate capital, contradictory political priorities, and an atomized urban political culture.

This chapter extends chapter 3's analysis of Mexico City's postrevolutionary experience through the 1930s and deepens the reinterpretation of the Cárdenas sexenio begun in chapters 4 and 5. It delves into the living environment of the urban working class, uncovers the intense conflicts that at times emerged across these spaces, and explores how grassroots political mobilization to improve living conditions became intimately tied to state policies and infrastructure development.

In the midst of Mexico City's astonishing population explosion after World War II, a slew of social scientists studied the social relations and political consequences of peripheral urban settlement.[3] The booming urban slums seemed to hold the key to the urban experience writ large, but scholars treated these informal settlements as if they had no history. The origins of these later settlement patterns, I argue, lie in the political ecology of urban settlement immediately before and during the presidency of Cárdenas: changing land uses and property ownership, community politics and state intervention, and environmental disputes. Peripheral settlement involved a host of actors within the urban fabric, including developers, state functionaries, architects and engineers, villagers, and the urban poor themselves. Deciphering the interactions among these actors reveals a complex and contested web of urban environmental politics and their central role in postrevolutionary state formation.

ENVIRONMENT AND URBANIZATION
IN THE "EMBARRASSMENTS OF MEXICO"

The suppression of the tenant rights movement in 1922 fortified real estate capital, and the municipal government of the late 1920s failed to address the city's unequal sanitary conditions. Vecindad living, much maligned for its misery and moral depravity, spread from the city center to outlying neighborhoods, where builders and landowners made a lucrative business off urban squalor (see figure 6.1). In the early 1930s, individual units generally ran between five and seven pesos per month and often consisted of one poorly ventilated room

FIGURE 6.1 — Tepito vecindad. COURTESY OF INAH,
FOTOTECA NACIONAL.

with a highly polluting charcoal-burning stove (*brasero*) and, at best, a shower and a bathroom shared by all residents of the vecindad. In the early 1930s, to rent an apartment with a bathroom with a shower, a sink with a faucet, and a toilet cost between twenty and thirty pesos per month, significantly more than the average monthly salary. Fewer than half of the city's residents could afford to spend twenty or more pesos on rent, although some families moved in together and split the rent of a single more hygienic apartment. Others decided to escape the dense communal living quarters of the vecindad, setting up their own homes on peripheral lands, as the settlers of Álvaro Obregón's Ex Hipódromo de Peralvillo had done in 1923, but here too residents generally faced atrocious conditions.

In 1930 the city comprised roughly ninety square kilometers, yet about half of this area lacked drainage, drinking water, and paved streets.[4] Vacant lots and streets were used as garbage dumps, and unpaved roads made transit nearly impossible during the rainy season and encouraged dust clouds during the dry season—in addition to the hinterland dust that laced the air. Without sewerage, the water found above and below ground teemed with bacteria, and flooding of low-lying settlements near riverbanks was a constant concern. Women and children fetched water from nearby subdivisions, local streams, or unregulated wells. These deplorable conditions fostered malaria and gastro-intestinal illnesses—the most fatal diseases in Mexico—and forced residents to use scarce resources "to perforate artesian wells, build septic tanks, and pay for posts and cables for electrical hookups."[5]

Postrevolutionary urbanization followed a strikingly similar track to that of its prerevolutionary predecessor. The new colonias of Lomas de Chapulte-pec, Hipódromo Condesa, and Guadalupe Inn offered, as their developers were quick to boast, reliable and pure drinking water, drainage, clean air, and paved, tree-lined streets.[6] Architects—whether they designed in the Cali-fornian or the neocolonial style—followed sanitary and building codes, and these wealthy colonias often had covenants restricting construction to single-family homes.[7] In so-called middle-class colonias, however, services were not always shining examples of urbanization. Parts of Nápoles, del Valle, San Miguel Chapultepec, and Roma Sur lacked many basic services, much to the dismay of their inhabitants, who aspired to a higher class status through hy-gienic homes and clean neighborhoods. Yet even these deficiencies paled in comparison to the conditions in the subdivisions to the east, north, and south of the center, where more than a hundred thousand people lived in colonias lacking all sanitary services. In 1930 the governor of the Federal District, José Manuel Puig Casauranc, listed at least eighteen colonias as lacking any ser-vices whatsoever and about thirty-five others as having extremely deficient ones, for instance, limited sewer hookups but no other amenities. He declared the colonias Buenos Aires and Obrera "the embarrassments of Mexico," but he could easily have conferred that title on many others.[8] The new Depart-ment of the Federal District (DDF) established in 1929 inherited the daunting task of sanitizing the city in the name of revolutionary reform, and achieving that would take much more than naming water czars.

MEXICO CITY AS A "REFLECTION OF OUR BIOLOGICAL AND CIVILIZED NEEDS"

The DDF responded during the early 1930s with a set of initiatives to ensure that more people had access to public hygiene, or, in the words of Governor Aaron Sáenz, to satisfy people's "biological and civilized needs."[9] These efforts were circumscribed by the global depression, and results were mixed.

The first initiative, passed in 1930, was a revised building code, the strictest of a series of sanitary codes dating back to the 1880s. It established new regulations requiring that each unit of current and future housing—including the crowded vecindades—include a toilet and a water connection. Property owners sparred with government officials over these clauses, claiming that the code amounted to nothing short of economic disaster. Their association predicted that 172 million pesos would be needed to bring all the buildings of the city up to standard, an indication of just how unhygienic residences were in 1930. They also declared every toilet "a site of infection" and claimed, paradoxically, that it was thus "not necessary to increase them."[10]

The government held its ground against property owners in this battle, but enforcement was the Achilles's heel for city and public health authorities alike. Also, in those units where owners abided by the new code, rents tended to rise, forcing many tenants into cheaper, unhygienic apartments. As long as the state failed to universalize sanitary services through massive infrastructure development, the market determined who could access them.

While the building code attempted to regulate the housing market, the growing public housing movement took center stage. The city tapped the bubbling intellectual optimism of the rising modernist architects. Juan O'Gorman and Juan Legarreta, both trained by Guillermo Zárraga, espoused functionalism as the panacea for housing the masses and fulfilling the revolution's promise. Architectural modernism found a safe home in 1930s Mexico, where the labor code, the legislative arm of Article 123, stipulated the construction of affordable and hygienic homes for the working class. Sáenz authorized Mexico's first public housing project of over three hundred single-family homes. The houses were designed by Legarreta and located in Balbuena in the east, in San Jacinto in the north, and on La Vaquita, an old ranch between the Rastro meat market and the federal prison on the city's northeastern edge (see figure 6.2). The neighborhoods included parks and provided drainage, pavement, water, and other services. The San Jacinto development alone cost more than a million pesos.[11] The project succeeded in providing hygienic homes to those who could otherwise not afford them and thus lent a degree of legitimacy to the state's social justice claims. Those citizens fortunate enough to purchase one of the homes no doubt escaped crowded apartments and, in some cases, the insalubrity of collective tenement living, where, as elites scoffed, dirtiness accumulated, disease multiplied, and promiscuity reigned. But amid a sea of poor tenants, several hundred homes hardly made a dent in the sanitary segregation and housing inequality. Indeed, salaried state bureaucrats who could afford

FIGURE 6.2 — Single-family public housing in Balbuena.
COURTESY OF INAH, FOTOTECA NACIONAL.

the monthly installments bought most of the homes.[12] Promoted as working-class housing, they afforded struggling lower-middle-class residents entrance into bourgeois culture, where premium value was placed on single-family homes, the privatization of waste, and efficient domestic sanitary appliances.[13]

The housing project was part and parcel of a wider public works program. While the promotion of urban infrastructure palliated the worst effects of real estate speculation, it did not challenge the hierarchies inherent in urban development. Like characters in a Carlos Fuentes novel, former revolutionaries joined the new urban affluent class. Officeholders such as the presidents Plutarco Elías Calles and Pascual Ortíz Rubio, Federal District governor Sáenz, and Alberto Pani offered up plans and modest investments to alleviate sanitary inequalities and simultaneously took advantage of the existing growth machine. They used government contracting and construction to enrich themselves. Ortíz Rubio built roads in the 1930s, including a major avenue; Calles used his control of the city government to aid his construction firm; and in 1925 Pani, a tireless supporter of urban sanitary improvements since his diatribe in 1916, invested in the very tenements he abhorred and bought an old hacienda to resell it as residential lots at a huge profit.[14] In 1933, moreover, Pani helped found the National Urban Mortgage and Public Works Bank to assist in state funding of important urban infrastructure, and ten years later he became the owner of the ritzy Hotel Reforma, designed by his nephew, the budding architect Mario Pani. Sáenz, owner of a construction firm and (starting in 1932) president of the Bank of Industry and Commerce, took out a loan from Pani's bank to support his own business ventures.[15] In addition to increasing investments in drainage and water, he also used his post to acquire contracts for his paving company.[16] Environmental planning and Mexico's budding state capitalism went in lockstep, creating a new economic elite and shoring up existing hierarchies.

It was up to residents to solve their own problems. Homeowners—and in some cases neighborhood organizations—followed the example of the mobilization in the colonia Balbuena in 1926 to demand urban improvement by petitioning for infrastructure projects and offering to contribute funds and labor. Generally such petitions were authored by middle-class property owners, but homeowners in working-class colonias occasionally followed suit. In Obrera, for instance, a dozen residents of the principal street offered to provide all the materials necessary to introduce drinking water into their houses as long as the government supplied the labor.[17] Citizen donations for all kinds of infrastructure skyrocketed during the late 1920s and early 1930s.[18]

The Department of the Federal District administration appropriated this citizen *cooperación*, a practice in other Mexican cities as well, by creating the Contribution Office to receive the funds and carry out the requests.[19] Between 1931 and 1932, hundreds of contributions, ranging from a few pesos to hundreds, flooded into the office. Thereafter, such contributions became mandatory government policy.[20] In 1932 Sáenz promulgated the Contribution Law for Public Works of the Federal District, which paid for specific public works projects through localized taxes on the property owners of a neighborhood or district, if a 51 percent majority approved the project.[21] The government thus avoided using general tax revenue to install essential services and pitched the law to property owners as a vehicle for increasing the value of their properties.[22]

The new policy divided urban resident associations; some applauded it, whereas others decried it. The Iztapalapa Neighborhood Improvement Committee deemed it "just and equitable that the owners have to contribute," and the Balbuena committee encouraged the law's passage so that works could begin.[23] In Obrera, in contrast, residents protested the law because "it relieves companies of their duty to contribute to urban services, with damage to workers." Residents of Los Portales insisted that it would destroy any hope that they could become homeowners because of the rising land rents the projects would bring, and a small property organization considered the law "disastrous."[24]

A mainstay of urban policy, the Contribution Law resulted in the completion of many public works projects throughout the city. Residents who could afford to pay enjoyed more hygienic living spaces, as well as higher property values, while the DDF took credit for the work done. By 1934 the city had invested in urban improvements, including sanitary services and housing. But a hygienic home and neighborhood required the ability to pay. Despite official discourse to the contrary, sanitary services remained in practical terms less a social right guaranteed by the state and more a privilege accessed through one's purchasing power. It should not surprise, then, that a variety of urban actors disputed how such services would be accessed and how the urban environment would look. These disputes underscored the immense gap between government claims of representation and justice on the one hand and concrete actions on the other. This was a gap that many residents, increasingly organized in neighborhood associations, hoped the populist Cárdenas would bridge.

THE CÁRDENAS CONJUNCTURE

During the 1930s, the fervent political mobilization in the Texcoco lakebed and the forests of the Ajusco was matched by organizational drives in Mexico City proper around urban environmental rights, culminating in a citywide urban social movement. Unlike in 1922, when tenants and their Communist sympathizers called the shots, this movement was spearheaded by a new urban popular actor: the *colono proletario* (worker-settler). These settlers of the expanding urban periphery called on the Cardenistas to bring revolutionary justice to their streets and homes, for the six-year plan promised precisely that.[25] In the process they exposed a central contradiction within the Cardenista program over questions of production in factory and field and questions of consumption in neighborhoods and homes.

Until the early 1930s, urban expansion had been dominated by developers and their subdivisions, legal or fraudulent. Several factors altered this settlement pattern. Vecindades became ever more crowded as migrants from the countryside streamed into central city quarters. Here residents developed strong community ties, the kinds of networks and associations that poor people rely on to scrape by. They also joined tenant leagues, which resurged a decade after the suppression of the rent strike, or neighborhood associations, and it was from within this vibrant organizational milieu that they plotted out alternatives. Obregón's Ex Hipódromo de Peralvillo neighborhood and the Balbuena housing project plan made it more plausible to dream of a middle-class homeowner ideal in which residents could experience bourgeois family life and escape from insalubrity, stigma, and exploitative landlords. Some tenants, of course, stayed put in the vecindades and demanded reform. Others, such as members of the Sánchez family made famous by Oscar Lewis, revolted with their feet.[26] A new and politically volatile form of urban settlement was born: land invasions to form what were labeled *colonias proletarias* (literally "worker subdivisions" although most settlers were not members of the industrial proletariat), composed of unauthorized single-family homes built on the city's barren outskirts, many adjacent to the fetid Gran Canal. If, as John Womack Jr. put it in writing about zapatismo, the Morelos peasants "did not want to move and therefore got into a revolution," thousands of working-class residents saved a little money and packed their belongings in the hope that the postrevolutionary government might ensure them a better future.[27] (See map 6.1.)

The documentation is fuzzy on how and when the first self-help housing occupations took place. The colonia proletaria Paulino Navarro, named after the former revolutionary commander who encouraged its settlement, was located along the Canal Nacional on the city's southeastern periphery. It may have been founded as early as the mid-1920s, but most—if not all—of the other occupations occurred in the 1930s.[28] Some colonias proletarias were better organized than others, and in a few cases, funds were raised to purchase private land. In 1930 residents of colonia proletaria Pro-Hogar, encouraged by the ruling National Revolutionary Party, formed the Pro-Hogar Employee and Worker Cooperative to buy over ninety acres of land along the Consulado River to the north of the city. On an installment plan, the cooperative bought 1,792 two hundred–square–meter lots for a total of 82,721.80 pesos, suggesting that these were not the poorest of the city's residents and that the cooperative may have been promised party funding.[29]

In a few cases, colonias proletarias were formed by invitation from individuals pursuing more political influence. The self-proclaimed revolutionary Macario Navarro created colonias to defend his property claims, including a big chunk of Remigio Noriega's old Hacienda Aragón. While Navarro claimed that the lands had been a gift from Obregón, the Noriega succession and a

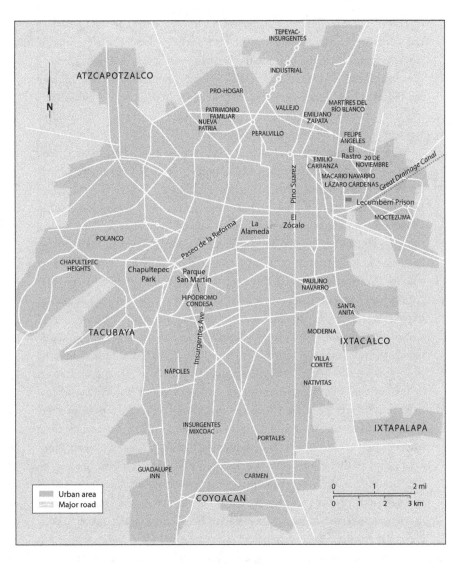

N

TEPEYAC-
INSURGENTES

ATZCAPOTZALCO

INDUSTRIAL

PRO-HOGAR

PATRIMONIO
FAMILIAR

VALLEJO

MARTÍRES DEL
RÍO BLANCO

NUEVA
PATRIA

EMILIANO
ZAPATA

PERALVILLO

FELIPE
ANGELES

El
Rastro

20 DE
NOVIEMBRE

EMILIO
CARRANZA

Pino Suarez

MACARIO NAVARRO
LÁZARO CÁRDENAS

Great Drainage Canal

Lecumberri Prison

MOCTEZUMA

POLANCO

Paseo de la Reforma

La
Alameda

El
Zócalo

CHAPULTEPEC
HEIGHTS

Chapultepec
Park

Parque
San Martín

PAULINO
NAVARRO

HIPÓDROMO
CONDESA

SANTA
ANITA

Insurgentes Ave

TACUBAYA

MODERNA

IXTACALCO

VILLA
CORTÉS

NÁPOLES

NATIVITAS

IXTAPALAPA

INSURGENTES
MIXCOAC

PORTALES

GUADALUPE
INN

CARMEN

COYOACAN

0   1   2 mi

0   1   2   3 km

Urban area
Major road

MAP 6.1 — Mexico City around 1940. COURTESY OF BILL NELSON.

myriad of other landowners challenged his titles in a dispute dating back to the 1920s. The Noriega estate had the "usurper" Navarro jailed eleven times. Navarro struck back, denouncing the Noriega heirs as "Gachupines ladrones" (Spanish thieves).[30] One of these men, Alejandro Romero, who had founded the Industrial and Emiliano Carranza colonias on lands claimed by Navarro, was fast becoming a key developer of Mexico City's working-class outskirts. Romero proved to be Navarro's biggest threat.

Whereas Romero engaged in classic land speculation, charging desperate city dwellers inflated urban prices for unimproved lands, Navarro took a different tack. Under constant harassment from local police over his contested claims, Navarro, desperate for support to fend off the local police, invited hundreds of former soldiers and evicted tenants to settle on La Vaquita, which he claimed, the same lands where public housing had been built and where Romero's colonia Emiliano Carranza was located. Navarro ingratiatingly named his first colonia Lázaro Cárdenas and donated the land to the settlement's cooperative; in a self-aggrandizing move, he also formed another settlement nearby, named Macario Navarro. In Lázaro Cárdenas, Navarro entrusted Ángel Ladrón de Guevara with the organization of the cooperative that would distribute the lots and raise the money to improve the colonia. In May 1935 the cooperative leader picked up "evicted families" and "brought them in trucks to the colonia, where they were given lots as an act of humanity and justice." In total, 237 lots were handed to evicted families, 139 to poor workers (obreros), 52 to unemployed government workers, and 47 to families from Michoacán and Tamaulipas. The cooperative had accumulated over six thousand pesos in donations, with five hundred pesos coming from Ladrón de Guevara himself, for improvements such as public washbasins, water tanks, and pack animals for transporting materials like brick, wood, and sheets of metal, the preferred construction materials before the popularization of concrete in the 1950s.[31] By donating land rather than selling it, Navarro hoped to secure the support of the settlers and undercut the power of Romero and his allies. Within a year, thousands of people depended on his success against the likes of Romero to guarantee that their new homes would remain free of developer intrusion.

Romero shifted tactics from pursuing Navarro to coordinating with the police and *pistoleros* (hired gunmen) to stem the invasions. Attempts to raze homes were legion.[32] In this context the residents petitioned Cárdenas to resolve the situation by expropriating the land.[33] One group of ex-soldiers called on Cárdenas to create a giant military colony on the disputed land, which would also serve as a counterweight to the Spanish developers.[34] In June 1935 Cárdenas did expropriate fifty-eight hectares for the residents of Lázaro Cárdenas and Macario Navarro, although disputes over land rights continued.[35]

Similar calls for expropriation, authored by citywide resident organizations founded by the leaders of neighborhoods and colonias proletarias, abounded. The General Union of Colonos proposed the expropriation of all abandoned colonias. The leadership of another citywide organization recognized "the ideals of the improvement of the proletarian element" under Cárdenas, lamented the lack of works "that could make their lives more humane," and championed investments that would "secure the hygiene of the capital."[36] Settlers of colonias proletarias and more established colonias, along with their leaders, who looked to exploit new power nuclei, aimed to achieve a healthier and secure living environment on the city's periphery, a goal that rested on the more democratic distribution of water, land, and infrastructure. Residents of the capital were not alone in crafting an urban social movement for improved environmental conditions. In 1937 Confederation of Mexican Workers laborers in San Luis Potosí struck to bring attention to the scarcity and unhygienic condition of the municipal water supply, a conflict in which Cárdenas intervened directly to support the strikers.[37]

But despite Cárdenas's avowed revolutionary credentials, the budding urban social movement did not translate into immediate action. Workers and peasants who organized around production concerns formed the administration's major base of support, and the twin pillars of land and labor reform aimed to please this base—the president's intervention in San Luis Potosí likely resulted from the Confederation of Mexican Workers' heavy involvement. The government's six-year plan made references to urban housing and hygiene but prioritized the needs of rural communities over urban ones, and sanitation in towns and small cities was privileged over new works in the capital.[38] These priorities have led one scholar to identify a "rural bias" inherent in cardenismo.[39] Under Cárdenas, expenses on sanitary services in the Federal District on average declined slightly compared to expenses under previous administrations, and these expenses represented a smaller percentage of the city budget, which otherwise expanded. A federal official called the Cárdenas term "the sexenio of drinking water," but rather than focusing on major cities as Porfirio Díaz had done, the government directed funds to secondary cities and large towns.[40] One resident lamented that while the president supported the "campesinos so that they live well," thousands of tenants "vegetate in truly lamentable conditions."[41] Mexico City's housing and sanitary infrastructure

FIGURE 6.3 — Family in a Mexico City colonia proletaria.
COURTESY OF INAH, FOTOTECA NACIONAL.

were not a major priority for an administration with resources tied up elsewhere (see figure 6.3).

Cardenista programs stalled urban reform in other ways too. The radicalization of the agrarian reform and the threat—both real and exaggerated—of nationalization further urbanized Mexican capitalism. Urban land rents and construction served as important "spatial fixes" for capital investment.[42] Landowners found in Mexico's cities both a safe haven for their capital and a new opportunity for investment. Hacendados close to the expanding city jumped at the opportunity to divide and sell their lands, especially since urbanized land was exempt from ejido claims. One agrarian representative accused the owner of the Hacienda Narvarte of reaching an accord with the government for the urbanization of lands that his pueblo had claimed, "even though they are being farmed and there is no sign of urbanization."[43] The colonias Aragón, Los Portales, and Moderna were also formed under the lurking specter of redistribution. Construction during the mid-1930s flourished, increasing 40.3 percent between 1936 and 1940, while the value of the new buildings doubled over that same span.[44] To explain the spike in urban construction during the Cárdenas administration, one editorialist wrote, "Whenever they [capitalists] could salvage what they had invested in works of the countryside, they found refuge inside the city."[45] The government, with its resources invested in dealing with the rural elite, judged it prudent not to attack their counterparts in the cities. Cárdenas had forged a dynamic in which political priorities urbanized Mexican capitalism, a process that in turn reinforced those priorities and the position of the urban elite at the expense of tenants and colonos proletarios. Cardenismo's political agenda and the state's limited autonomy from capitalism, in the words of Nora Hamilton, collided with popular ferment emanating from tenements and peripheral settlements.[46] The collision aggravated an existing tension that the administration sought to resolve beginning in 1936.

EXPROPRIATION, HOUSING, AND THE URBAN SOCIAL MOVEMENT

Between 1935 and 1939, a burst of popular residential mobilization, several legislative proposals, landowner discontent, and three major housing and planning conferences placed urban land and environmental rights in the limelight. As the engineer and then secretary of foreign relations Eduardo Hay remarked at one of the conferences, "The family has an inalienable right to live well, not with ostentation and luxury but with decency, in hygienic and healthy conditions. . . . To fulfill such necessity has been one of the constant concerns of the Mexican Revolution."[47] Hay, like Pani before him, distinguished the revolutionary government from the Díaz regime, in which decent living conditions for people "with scarce resources" were forgotten. These were strong words from a government official, particularly given the persistently egregious sanitary and housing conditions of hundreds of thousands of people in the nation's capital. However, the very fact that such concerns were voiced by a leading minister signaled just how far housing and environmental rights had come in official circles since the early 1920s.

The city budget belied Cardenista rhetoric about inalienable rights and the revolution's objective of "suppressing urban inequalities and privileges."[48] Yet authorities had in mind a different path to attenuating inequalities. In 1935 the minister of the economy and revolutionary theoretician Francisco Múgica proposed the Expropriation Law, which Congress debated in 1936.[49] Expropriation, or the execution of eminent domain, was not innovative or radical per se. Similar laws authorizing expropriation had existed since the mid-nineteenth century and were strengthened under Díaz. This particular bill, however, expanded the legal boundaries of expropriation as well as the cases under which it could be employed. Múgica wished to break the power of the landowning elite by redefining property not as an "absolute right" but rather as a "social function." Whereas past uses of eminent domain aimed to build public works or provide public services, Múgica explained, from this point on expropriation would have a "social character," pegged to the collective interest and particularly "the needs of a determined social class," since "an individual does not have the right to maintain his property unproductive."[50] Through the fulfillment of working-class interests, Múgica argued, society as a whole would benefit. Expropriation, he argued, could be applied to "the division of the great Latifundios or their colonization as much as the division and ur-banization of lands destined for affordable and hygienic homes for workers."[51] Múgica widened the doors of eminent domain to debilitate capital, although in some instances his proposal repeated existing laws. It sought to authorize expropriation in order to beautify and sanitize cities; construct parks, schools, hospitals, or any work destined to provide services; to conserve, develop, and use natural resources and to redistribute the public wealth; and to create and improve factory towns.[52] While the immediate political reality of agrarian hotbeds such as the cotton-rich La Laguna may have provided sufficient mo-tivation for the proposal, Múgica also had in mind an urban reform to re-distribute land and resources and thus create an urban commons that would complement the extensive agrarian commons.

Property owners fulminated against the proposal, as did the two major Mexico City dailies, *Excélsior* and *El Universal*. These two newspapers had harangued the municipal government for years over the squalid conditions in abandoned colonias, but it was clear they favored top-down technical so-lutions and public works over radical legislation. *Excélsior* deemed the law a grave threat to private property, and *El Universal* asked rhetorically, "What confidence can there be, where because of an expropriation law suspended like Damocles's sword over owners, nobody knows what may become of their assets?"[53] A homeowners organization warned that the law would strangle urban capital, leaving "not a cent" for urban projects, and would result in fifty thousand unemployed workers.[54] Top officials alluded to the long history of eminent domain in Mexico, predating the revolution, but property owners were not appeased, being well aware of the difference between the intentions of nineteenth-century liberals and those of Cárdenas.[55]

Their concerns went unheeded. In fact, the bill that Cárdenas signed into law in November 1936 was more expansive than Múgica's original. An article to conserve national patrimony was added, and the article concerning the creation and improvement of factory towns was changed to include all "population centers," thus paving a clearer path for the expropriation of peripheral urban settlements. By placing the expropriation of urban property on par with that of rural property, the bill represented a major legislative victory for the city's working-class residents, yet it did not spell doom for urban capital as the propertied classes had warned. Urban construction and property values increased steadily between 1936 and 1940.[56]

Encouraged by the new law, House Deputy Cosme Riva Palacio proposed an amendment to Article 27 of the constitution that would have allowed workers to acquire urban lots to build homes in the same way that peasants could expand their communal land.[57] Supporters of the amendment, however, overestimated the revolution's urban reach. *Excélsior* ripped the proposal on practical grounds, claiming that workers would then have to build on the land and, lacking capital, would build derelict homes without services. In a similar vein, the developer Raul Basurto argued, rather self-servingly, that the problem was not land but capital to build on the land—without mentioning that his company was constructing several colonias for the wealthy.[58] Political leaders preferred to avoid another standoff with urban capitalists on the heels of the Expropriation Law, and the amendment was soundly defeated.

Even without this additional boost, the urban social movement of colonos proletarios and poorer homeowners grew stronger after the passage of the Expropriation Law, and over the following two years their organizations pushed for further social rights. The General Union of Residents of the Federal District demanded a muscular new urbanization law and the provision of "cheap and hygienic homes destined for workers."[59] The union, moreover, implored the state to expropriate abandoned colonias and develop them "when they lack urban services or when the sale price is an obstacle."[60] The General Union of Colonos joined the mounting voices for a more just urbanization law. Claiming to represent groups from over a dozen poor working-class colonias in Mexico City, the front devised its own legislative proposal, which called for the revocation of numerous contracts between Arthur Braniff's Mexican Land Company and residents who had paid off their homes without receiving sanitary and other services. Article 7 of the proposal mandated that "as reparation for the damage caused to the purchasers of lots and to the public health," the government would demand the complete "urbanization" of the colonias, to be paid for by developers.[61] Working-class organizations fused public health and revolution to put forth a more inclusive and just vision for their city. They aimed to fundamentally alter the social and environmental conditions of the capital by replacing private developers with the state as the principal agent of urban development in Mexico City. The proposals made little headway in Congress, however.

The tenants of the old vecindades organized as well. They held boisterous meetings in the patios of decaying tenement buildings, decried their landlords, and draped red-and-black flags from their units—just as they had in 1922. Periodic rent strikes troubled property owners, and activists rehoused evicted tenants in their old units. The Tenant Defense League, founded in 1933, demanded the promulgation of a new law to control the "despicable landlords" and set up a "sanitary dictatorship"—a familiar technocratic demand in postrevolutionary Mexico City.[62] The league also called for a state-run bank that would protect tenants from abusive landlords, "the enemies of the revolution"; promote new housing developments; and repair apartments "in support of hygiene, comfort, and sanitation."[63] The National Tenant Confederation, the main player in strike organization and other direct actions, placed more hope in expropriation. They longed for the creation of a garden city on a small part of the federal Texcoco lakebed and other privately held lands. The garden city would house five thousand tenants in new, hygienic homes sponsored by government-issued mortgages and supplied with government-funded drinking water and sewer systems.[64] Pro-tenant legislation reached the House of Deputies in late 1938 but received minimal support. The alarmism of property owners won the day, and the House rejected the bill two years after the passage of the Expropriation Law.[65]

The interest in enacting wide-reaching housing and sanitary reform went beyond Congress. In 1938, as politicians debated the merits of the tenant bill, leading planners Carlos Contreras and José Luis Cuevas convened the Sixteenth International Planning and Housing Conference in Mexico City, which hosted hundreds of the world's leading urban professionals. Registration included an excursion to the Desierto de los Leones sponsored by Miguel Ángel de Quevedo, lunch in the trajineras of Xochimilco, and a visit to Balbuena public housing. Several presentations discussed sanitary-service extension to abandoned areas and workers' housing in the nation's capital—including an impassioned talk by Adolfo Zamora, a spokesman of the National Urban Mortgage and Public Works Bank.[66] For a sanitary engineering conference held the same year, the government invited Hannes Meyer, the Swiss socialist architect and former director of Bauhaus, to speak on hygienic housing for workers.[67] Meyer was encouraged by the interest in state-sanctioned worker housing in

Cárdenas's Mexico, and he found a comfortable home among a host of radical planners and architects. These professionals included the founders of the Union of Socialist Architects, Enrique Yañez and Alberto T. Arai, who had proposed at the planning conference a utopian *ciudad obrera* (worker city) to solve the capital's hygienic housing shortfall. The Union of Socialist Architects also held its own conference on worker housing in 1939.[68] One speaker, Gabriel Oropesa, a civil engineer involved in the Texcoco reclamation, devised a project "to alleviate the situation of four thousand poor families who now live in filthy pigsties because they cannot afford better housing."[69]

The three conferences between 1938 and 1939 marked the pinnacle of a brewing discussion over affordable hygienic housing among urban experts who were witnessing the disordered and fraught transformation of pastureland, farmland, and former waterscapes into unsanitary shantytowns. Together, the conferences marked a shift in thinking about public housing. Zamora and Meyer, in particular, denounced the government's single-family, resident-owned housing projects. Zamora claimed that the only realistic way to house the city's lower class was to build vertically, while Meyer, a former activist in Germany's Communist Party, glorified collective tenement living as having planted the seeds of socialism.[70] Planners sought to build homes and provide healthy environments for the very "workers who give expression to [their] designs," but their activism temporarily marginalized the notion of single-family public housing, for which so many residents longed, and foreshadowed a lengthy experiment in large complexes of rental housing.[71] This era of public rental housing was still a decade away, however, and, like its single-family predecessor, had more success housing middle-class bureaucrats than the city's industrial workers—much less its underclass. In retrospect, 1938 was the pinnacle of Cardenista radicalism, not its inception. By 1940 there had surfaced an air of disillusionment with government inefficacy and the very methodology of a functionalism centered on inexpensive materials such as concrete. The optimism of Meyer's urban socialist revolution was fading into O'Gorman's creeping pessimism concerning the ways in which functionalism was serving capitalism more than socialism. The government seemed to be investing more in "architectural monuments [and] decorative street dividers [e.g., the Monument to the Revolution and Avenida de los Insurgentes] than in "the fundamental needs for housing and of worker struggle."[72]

Notwithstanding the absence of an urban revolution in line with what socialist architects from O'Gorman to Meyer envisioned, the Expropriation Law rearranged the balance of forces in Mexico's capital. By creating a political and legal opening for further government intervention in the urban land-scape, the law extended the social rights of the revolution to urbanization itself. Land expropriated from the Hacienda Narvarte formed a colonia for schoolteachers, while unemployed workers were granted expropriated land in Azcapotzalco along with 500,000 pesos for the construction of homes and artesian wells, among other projects.[73]

It was easier, however, for Cardenistas to pass the law than to implement it. The obstacles to expropriation were numerous. Government funds were al-ready heavily allocated, first to the agrarian reform and in 1938 to oil national-ization, and blurry property lines on the urban periphery, a product of rampant speculation, complicated the questions of what could be expropriated and who should be indemnified. Moreover, many peripheral communities were divided internally, with multiple organizations claiming to represent them. It was rarely clear that expropriation would end up benefiting the people it was supposed to. Rather than engage in risky expropriations of privately held lands, the Cardenista government of the late 1930s more frequently assisted in—or at least tolerated—the formation of colonias proletarias on vacant lands. Cárdenas's urban agenda—support for new colonias proletarias and minimal use of expropriation—brought the urban poor into the PRM fold without requiring huge investments in housing or infrastructure, a venture that would have run afoul of political priorities and stretched the limits of the capitalist state.

POLITICAL CULTURE IN URBAN COMMUNITIES

The colonias proletarias became both the bedrock of urban governance and sites of social tumult. So far I have presented a largely political-structural ex-planation of the limits of urban reform. These limits had a political-cultural component as well. Cardenista policies within the colonias proletarias also emerged out of the contingencies of community politics, a common denomi-nator for interpreting cardenismo throughout the Basin of Mexico. In other words, a bird's-eye political-economic explanation needs grounding in the daily experience of urbanization and the interactions, actors, and interests it created. The settlement process divided communities as much as it united them, and these divisions weakened the urban social movement. Authorities parlayed disunity and divisiveness for political profit.

The colonias proletarias facilitated the rise of what Wayne Cornelius termed the "urban cacique."[74] Residents, many of whom had not-too-distant roots in rural towns with their own caciques, needed organizational leadership and someone to wield enough power to negotiate with authorities and combat landowners and developers who might threaten their settlement. Caciques emerged from within communities and from without, and they sought to strengthen their power and influence through representation while also enriching themselves. Much like community politics in other times and places, there was a constant tug-of-war between leadership and base that reflected and determined community cohesion. In the case of Mexico City's colonias proletarias, caciques often overstepped their boundaries.

Macario Navarro was one of these caciques. His influence over his putative lands in and around La Vaquita waned in the mid-1930s. Navarro lost numerous indemnity claims, including one to reimburse him for La Vaquita lands used by the state to erect housing. In 1938, in a last-ditch effort to solidify his claim to part of the lands on the northeastern fringe of the city he hired pistoleros to evict squatters from the banks of the Consulado River.[75] Navarro had sought to use urbanization as a weapon to defend his property, but his weapon turned against him. The central locus of power in the colonias proletarias in the city's northeastern corner shifted away from Navarro and toward internal community power dynamics and relations with an increasingly interventionist state.

Navarro had assigned Ladrón de Guevara the task of donating lots in Lázaro Cárdenas. The donation was consummated on Christmas Day in 1934, but the infelicitously named Ladrón de Guevara (*ladrón* means "thief" in Spanish) turned the Christmas present into a nightmare. As he distributed hundreds of lots, new residents denounced a variety of abuses. One group labeled him "an eternal exploiter of the proletarian classes who gives much honor to his last name."[76] He charged residents twelve and a half pesos for each lot, opened sales to lands not authorized by Navarro, and, to draw in more revenue, divided the property into smaller units than Navarro had intended. Margarito Tejeda, a deposed leader of the colonia Macario Navarro, latched onto the settlement process in Lázaro Cárdenas and formed his own community organization to counter Ladrón de Guevara there. While Tejeda lauded Navarro as a hero of the working class, he urged residents to "repel the aggressions and continual arbitrariness" of Ladrón de Guevara. Furthermore, over the course of 1935 and 1936, the residents also accused Ladrón de Guevara of selling the same lots up to three times by evicting previous occupants. He also used these multiple sales to harass his enemies. One day in June 1935, Tejeda was told to abandon his lot within twenty-four hours.[77]

Despite various abuses, Ladrón de Guevara maintained his hold on the newly formed colonia for a time by mobilizing his base and disarming his adversaries. He organized meetings in favor of government services; founded the Revolutionary Bloc of Federal District Colonias, a key proponent of the urbanization law that brought together many of the colonias proletarias in La Vaquita; and named Tejeda its treasurer.[78]

The colonia Lázaro Cárdenas, lacking government oversight and clear property lines, remained ripe for financial exploitation. In late 1936 Salvador Martínez Lira sought to represent residents subjected to the abuses of Ladrón de Guevara and, in doing so, managed to lay claim to thirty lots in the colonia. As tensions between the two men escalated, the colonia's women's organization beseeched Cárdenas to send someone "of confidence" to resolve the dispute and expropriate the land.[79]

Before arriving in Lázaro Cárdenas, Martínez Lira himself had been expelled from the colonia Pro-Hogar, where he had been a victim of that colonia's leader, Alfonso Ruíz Velasco. The colonia Pro-Hogar had originated in negotiations between the PRM and the Tenant Defense League, in which the league purchased land on the banks of the flood-prone Consulado River. In 1932, to wield influence in Pro-Hogar, Ruíz Velasco took control of the distribution of pulque, the city's most popular alcoholic beverage. He created a clique of supporters around the sale and distribution of the drink, and this support lifted him to the presidency of the cooperative the following year. Ruíz Velasco rewarded his supporters, but his suspect practices as head of the community cooperative bred discord. Dissident residents accused Ruíz Velasco of embezzling fifty-four thousand pesos of community funds that had been set aside to purchase the land. Despite the opposition, he managed to maintain his authority throughout Cárdenas's term. As a PRM member and a delegate of Azcapotzalco (one of sixteen delegations in the Federal District), he had friends in high places, including the deputy Jesús Vidales and the wealthy Callista senator Ezequiel Padilla.[80]

Intercommunity divisions frequently distracted settlers from the reasons they had mobilized in the first place: to withstand developers and secure a healthy living environment. While residents were mired in internal disputes over La Vaquita's lands, the former governor Sáenz's construction company, in cahoots with Alejandro Romero, removed residents in order to lay down streets and resell the lots.[81] Another case involved the colonia Río Consulado, formed in 1937 when Tomás Alonso, Trinidad González, and others purchased land from Navarro to create a colonia of some eight hundred working-class families. The land apparently belonged to the developers of the colonia Industrial, however, and the Industrial developers, backed by the city government, destroyed the squatters' homes. Ousted from the land, González and Alonso split into separate factions and each led their own groups to occupy the same neighboring land—also property of the developers. On March 5, 1939, a fight erupted between the rival factions, and several people were seriously wounded. The battle with the company over the right to the land and the many removals residents faced were overshadowed by tensions between leaders and, occasionally, bloodshed.[82] Community power and the privileges that accompanied it often eclipsed taking on the common adversary.

As evidenced by the case of Río Consulado, evictions happened, but usually only on the property of wealthy developers. The most publicized case of removal occurred on the edge of Chapultepec Park, where José G. de la Lama and Raul Basurto, the developers of Lomas de Chapultepec, planned Chapultepec Morales (now Polanco), an upper-class colonia of tree-lined streets. Former peons and recent squatters occupying the ex-hacienda land stood in the developers' way, and Cárdenas had them removed. Invasion of unimproved vacant land or small properties might be tolerated—and even encouraged in some cases—but it would be punished on the lands of prominent entrepreneurs.[83]

Urban caciques used land invasions as a springboard to power within communities, but these leaders also became a source of intercommunity conflict. Hilario García split with the leadership of the colonia Macario Navarro to lead an invasion of nearby land, naming the new settlement Socialista Hilario García. García saw the land that supported his power threatened by other communities, which he labeled "counterrevolutionary."[84] Frequently, threats turned into battles on the city's periphery. In 1939 two hundred members of the squatter settlement Martíres del Río Blanco, armed with "clubs and rocks," tried to commandeer the administration of the colonia Felipe Ángeles, located on the north side of the Rastro market.[85] Their motives were not disclosed, but given that city officials were contemplating granting titles to settlers of Felipe Ángeles, it is likely they hoped to disrupt its legalization, which would have invalidated their own claims.

During the 1930s, abandoned or marginally productive rural land became immensely profitable, not only for established developers but also for ordinary residents capable of leading occupations. These individuals employed a wide repertoire of tactics, such as economic controls, land invasions, and political influence, to establish local authority. Once they had established power, they resorted to double-dealing, the collection of unnecessary taxes or quotas, and embezzlement of funds to extract wealth from the marginalized poor. Urban caciques reproduced many of the same hierarchies that beset more established colonias. Yet they often held onto power because they were able to obtain environmental services and land titles for their constituents—Pro-Hogar, Macario Navarro, and 20 de Noviembre, for instance, received drainage systems soon after their founding.[86] That success translated into leaders' continued authority, even if they engaged in exploitative practices and generated conflicts that curtailed the effectiveness of the larger, antisystem movement they themselves had helped create.

Sanitary-service extension was another key bone of contention between communities. The political economy of urbanization, in tandem with dominant ideas of status and distinction, weighed heavily on popular environmental protest in postrevolutionary Mexico City. The real estate market and the Contribution Law sustained cultures of status, whereby access to enough money could secure one's place in the sanitation hierarchy. Money bought cleanliness, purity, and the ability to privatize one's bodily functions; money bought the distinction of living the urban sanitarian ideal. The city's marginalized population, those who lived in the crowded tenements without access to clean water and without adequate drainage, were the antithesis of this ideal (see figure 6.4). Because access to water and drainage had not been universalized, the idea of achieving cultural distinction by gaining access *was* universalized. Cleanliness was a state achieved in the privacy of home, but it was constituted relationally (who was and was not clean), and its pursuit was a collective act. Many thus saw water as their right, but a right that might simultaneously reinforce privilege.

Discrepancies in sanitary service highlighted the extent to which identification with a neighborhood molded the making of environmental claims. Roberto Guerrero Grosso of the colonia Nápoles expressed his expectation that the supposedly middle-class subdivision should have water and drainage, given its proximity to well-serviced neighborhoods. He complained of tourists to the neighborhood taking photos of "ten to twenty people who at all hours are found in the middle of the street carrying out their needs [*haciendo sus necesidades*], something that cannot be avoided due to the lack of water and drainage." Guerrero Grosso's argument centered on the idea that an honorable colonia in the respectable part of town required privatized waste removal and cleanliness. To deny the request would tarnish Mexico City's image.[87] Residents of Peralvillo, on the opposite side of the city, had been waiting since the

FIGURE 6.4 — Flooding in the colonia Vallejo. COURTESY OF INAH, FOTOTECA NACIONAL.

beginning of the century for water hookups and, in the words of *El Universal*, had looked "with distrustful and envious eyes upon their neighbors who had attained modernity and comfort."[88] The residents of the colonia Industrial in the north, numbering ten thousand by 1940, considered that they had "as much right as the inhabitants of La Villa de Guadalupe to receive Xochimilco water and more right than the colonia Tepeyac-Insurgentes, where the Xochimilco water would only serve to irrigate the gardens of the uninhabited homes."[89] Other neighborhood associations and individuals likewise invoked what other neighborhoods or subdivisions enjoyed and what they deserved as respectable citizens.[90]

This parochial colonia-first mentality merits an explanation. In part, it was a logical response to decades of suburban development and spatially selective environmental planning. Developers announced new colonias with their own services, amenities, and vibes that would cater to particular classes: the affluent, the middle class, or the working class. Sometimes developers failed to match amenities with class aspirations, as in Nápoles, hence Guerrero Grosso's tirade. Where essential infrastructure was lacking, the city government intervened selectively, negotiating with the residents of each colonia separately, rather than connecting whole areas at once.

There were practices internal to each subdivision or neighborhood that also strengthened community identification, particularly within the new colonias proletarias. The neighborhood (analogous to a colonia), according to sociologist Pierre Mayol, is an urban dweller's appropriation of a public space within a larger, more anonymous city, established through cultural practices such as political engagement, daily walking routines, encounters and relations with neighbors, and economic exchange. The neighborhood becomes a kind of familiar safe haven, a privatized public space and a place of comfortable withdrawal.[91] As a linchpin between the totally privatized home and the impersonal city, the neighborhood attracts strong sentiments of community solidarity forged through social interaction. In colonias proletarias, home and neighborhood were not simply reproduced or refashioned via cultural practice but were physically produced from scratch—built out of metal, brick, adobe, or cement or fashioned through the improvisational construction of common infrastructure like wells, septic tanks, or drainage canals. Such production added another layer of social connection and reciprocity within the colonias proletarias. In colonias proletarias the neighborhood did not follow the private home as an "outgrowth." Instead, the private home followed the building of the neighborhood; homes were individual "marks" on a new public space already inscribed through community ties and solidarity.[92] However, neighborhood solidarity also bred isolation, creating a sense of belonging that excluded outsiders and fed envy, especially if certain neighborhoods progressed at a faster pace than others in similar conditions. A colonia's ties of solidarity and neighborly behavior were likely stronger in times of high interaction or negotiation with outsiders (when other colonias, officials, or developers threatened the community's right to the urban space). Nonetheless, factional disputes within colonias proliferated wherever the boundary between legal and illegal was blurry and the opportunities for easy profiteering great.

There were fleeting moments of trans-colonia solidarity, represented by the numerous umbrella organizations that cardenismo spawned, but these organizations came and went with time. A confluence of factors tended to atomize popular political culture: a sense of neighborhood (or colonia) identity, cacique practices, land competition, and the social distinction acquired through sanitary infrastructure. The city was socially, geographically, and culturally divided in ways that rendered a cohesive trans-neighborhood urban environmental movement difficult to sustain. The postrevolutionary government exploited these divisions to exercise authority on the city's periphery.

Rather than confront the system that real estate speculation perpetuated, the government intervened in individual settlements on an ad hoc basis. Through the Contribution Office, the DDF responded to popular demands for land and infrastructure, but officials retained the colonia-first mentality that the urban political culture generated and shied away from widespread expropriations. They also saw themselves as saviors. Authorities like Rafael de Villa, appointed by Cárdenas to head the Contribution Office, aimed to rescue communities from their own abusive representatives. Villa made a list of enemies of the city government, including Hilario García of Socialista, Eliezer Lezama of Patria Nueva, Margarito Tejeda of Macario Navarro, and Ángel Ladrón de Guevara of Lázaro Cárdenas. He formed alliances with embittered residents while using the local police force to oust these leaders. In Lázaro Cárdenas a police sergeant replaced Ladrón de Guevara as head of the community cooperative, and Tomás Calvo replaced Lezama in Patria Nueva. Tejeda was later arrested for leading an invasion of a local ranch. Government intervention in these settlements failed to eradicate exploitative practices. The new leaders were no less corrupt. Calvo, in particular, faced accusations of land hoarding and speculation in 1938 and 1939.[93] Other government interventions followed in the twilight of cardenismo. Jorge Muñoz Cota, president of the local PRM, gave the green light for the land invasions that formed Mártires del Río Blanco and Felipe Ángeles, ratified colonia proletaria Emiliano Zapata ex post facto, and supported Alonso's invasions on behalf of Consulado River squatters, against the community's other leaders. Muñoz Cota also founded the Federation of the Colonias Proletarias of the Eastern District to tie various community organizations to the state.

Authorities did more than encourage or lead the formation of colonias proletarias and meddle in their leadership. In some cases, the government purchased land to then sell back to the urban poor.[94] In places with ill-defined property lines, the government declared itself the owner, ceding titles to squatter settlements. The process of title transfer went slowly in places like Lázaro Cárdenas and Macario Navarro where it was unclear whom to indemnify, but more quickly in Emiliano Zapata and Felipe Ángeles, where the government had already set aside vacant lands for this very purpose. In Patria Nueva, Muñoz Cota's Federation of the Colonias Proletarias threw a party when the government officially rewarded the residents with contracts to acquire land titles, and Muñoz Cota deemed the land transfer a "positive triumph."[95] The

Contribution Office administered service extensions—just as it did legal titles—on a piecemeal, colonia-by-colonia basis. In this way, the Cárdenas administration circumvented the urban growth machine while simultaneously fulfilling a commitment to provide land and sanitary services to the urban poor. By formalizing peripheral settlements and shaping their political organization, the PRM and the Department of the Federal District administration brought thousands of previously marginalized inhabitants within the state's fold.

State intervention also had a darker side. The Contribution Office was targeted for malfeasance and abuse of power. In one egregious case, a government engineer not only charged residents for water and drainage services that had not yet been installed but also repossessed lots and impounded homes on the basis that residents had not paid for the nonexistent services.[96] Rafael de Villa also came under fire. The residents of Paulino Navarro accused him of selling land at exorbitant prices, keeping the money he charged for services, and installing his allies in the community's cooperative. He was cast as "an accomplice of the bourgeoisie" who visited cabarets, "spending the money that we poor workers make with our sweat and labor."[97] Such charges were difficult to corroborate, and colonos proletarios, dependent on these officials to legalize their land claims, were nearly powerless against abuse.

Poor communities on the periphery of Mexico City were sites of protest and intense political mobilization but equally sites of abuse and internal dissension. Many settlements were dogged by speculation, wealth extraction, political maneuvering, and unaccountable leadership. The discord within and between communities diverted energy that could have driven more universal change. Rather than attacking the roots of spatial and environmental inequality, the government used colonias proletarias as escape valves. Officials intervened along the fissures of the urban social movement, taking advantage of community divisions to assert their own authority. Urban state formation sprouted from the grassroots of environmental politics: the multifarious, but fractured, popular claims to land and a healthy living environment.

CONCLUSION

A new era of urban reform dawned when the Department of the Federal District replaced the old municipal system and promised to bring the revolution to the nation's capital. The government quickly enacted housing and sanitary reforms, but urban environmental inequalities persisted. Public expectations for reform only increased with the rise of Cárdenas, who, despite laws, plans, and codes mandating action on questions of hygiene and housing, grounded his populist project in issues of production, specifically agrarian land and workplace demands. This program of rural expropriation and nationalization sent Mexican capital into the cities, reinforcing the structural limits of urban reform. Yet the president did not ignore the environmental demands of the urban poor, and the Expropriation Law put environmental rights at the center of public discussion. In the spirit of expropriation, the government pursued a set of policies that encouraged and supported colonias proletarias. The government's urban policy reflected structural constraints but also popular political culture, and urban state formation was born out of the dynamic relationships between political authorities and peripheral settlements. Officials successfully channeled popular demands within an institutional structure with established rules and routines. No matter how progressive or radical the popular demands were during the 1930s, the privileged tactics of social protest were the same: the petition, the demonstration, and the hearing. Direct action rocked some cities such as Oaxaca in the 1940s—events more akin to the ongoing protests over collective consumption in Rio de Janeiro throughout much of the twentieth century than to urban politics in Mexico City.[98] Cárdenas's approach proved advantageous, and future administrations borrowed from it as millions of campesinos migrated to Mexico's capital looking for a hygienic home and a refuge from the exploitative practices of landlords and developers.

A brief comparison between the agrarian reform and the politics of urban settlement helps clarify the limits of Cárdenas's urban agenda. At least as far back as Andrés Molina Enriquez, the Mexican elite had viewed the agrarian community as a cohesive entity with shared communal interests.[99] This vision—romantic, simplistic, and founded in common notions of Mexican indigeneity—entailed a clear enemy, the landowner, and a clear ally, the peasant community. Expropriation in the countryside therefore had an unmistakable objective. However, in new urban settlements—particularly the colonias proletarias—and across the urban landscape, urban planners and other officials perceived pure division, dissension, and multiple adversaries. Expropriation was a political weapon not so easily brandished, as officials were rarely able to ascertain who its beneficiaries would be. In these fraught spaces, Cardenista officials saw themselves as providing order and banishing corruption.

Speculative and abusive practices abounded in these new urban settlements, and they eroded people's organizational capacities to pursue social and environmental reform. Peripheral settlements multiplied, nonetheless, and by the early 1940s, they were beginning to encroach on ejidal lands, introducing new actors to the story of Mexico City's urbanization.

7

Industrialization and
Environmental Technocracy

From the outbreak of the revolution through the 1930s, the popular classes employed a wide repertoire of tools—riots and community organizing, petitions and occupations, and clandestine extraction—to claim rights to the metropolitan environment: waters, forests, sanitary infrastructure, and the urbanizing periphery. These rights, etched in the constitution, the agrarian and civil codes, and the Expropriation Law of 1936, promised a productive environment for hinterland villagers and healthy, affordable living spaces for the urban working classes. However, official rhetoric exceeded action, and laws and regulations were honored more in the breach than in the observance. Subaltern populations saw uneven results. The urban lower classes did gain some respite from city-center tenements, although relatively few were able to attain healthy living spaces; forest communities won the right to extract wood products from their forest commons, if under the watchful eye and restrictions of the Forestry Department; and ejidatarios in the Texcoco and Xochimilco lakebeds used agrarian legislation, urban discourses of health, and perceptions of indigeneity to reinvigorate their means of subsistence in the baneful context of lake desiccation, albeit with varying degrees of success. Environmental governance in the basin was far from democratic, but avenues to shape the nature of its urbanization existed.

In the years leading up to the PRM's conversion to the PRI in 1946, conservative forces gained the upper hand. Small landowners, a small but influential middle class, conservative Catholics, and business elites expressed discontent over Lázaro Cárdenas's reformism, and the final two years of the sexenio, which ended in 1940, witnessed a marked conservative retrenchment. As the balance of power tipped rightward, former allies of the president began to turn. The radical Left, under the leadership of Marxist labor leader Vicente Lombardo Toledano, certainly would have preferred that Cárdenas support Francisco Múgica as the party's presidential candidate in 1940, but with the political winds shifting, they acquiesced (not without some perturbation) to nominating the moderate minister of defense, Manuel Ávila Camacho. Nonetheless, the election was tight. Dissatisfaction coalesced around the wealthy mine owner and longtime general Juan Andreu Almazán, who carried Mexico City but lost the bitterly contested election. Ávila Camacho and his successor, Miguel Alemán Valdés (1946–1952), tacked back to a more moderate, pro-business course that facilitated rapid urban industrialization.

The Mexican state at midcentury resembled its Porfirian predecessor: technocratic, selectively violent, bereft of popular empowerment, and pursuant of policies that exacerbated social inequality. But this was not history repeating itself. Unlike its Porfirian antecedent, the postrevolutionary regime endured owing to its plasticity, its strategic concessions to popular demands, its institutionalized rule, and its caciquismo and repression of autonomous organizations. The durability of the PRM/PRI had much to do with its tripartite corporatism, comprising ejido peasants under the National Campesino Confederation, workers under the Confederation of Mexican Workers, and the consumer-centered popular organizations and middle classes under the eclectic National Confederation of Popular Organizations. These manifold strategies of rule underwrote the policy of import substitution industrialization, which flooded the cities, particularly Mexico City, with rural migrants.

The rightward turn and the drive to industrialize cemented a techno-bureaucratic alliance of corporatist politicians and environmental planning experts. These state authorities buried the more egalitarian and democratic visions of the urbanizing basin and instead applied a limited set of top-down concessions to city residents that buttressed the industrialization of the metropolitan environment. Technocratic rule had crumbled somewhat following the revolution of 1910, chipped away by democratic and redistributive forces, but citizens had rarely questioned the making of expertise and technical applications per se. Rather, they disputed how knowledge and technology would be employed, and in whose benefit. At times, popular demands had paradoxically fed into the logic of technocracy, and by midcentury its star shone brighter—as it did around the world.[1]

The urban-industrial path to modernity embraced by officialdom after 1940 came at the expense of hinterland inhabitants. The state slowed the agrarian reform and divested from the ejido and cooperative sector of the rural economy, which had gained some stability from supplying cities with food and fuel. The urban model also imposed great costs on the hinterland environments from which raw materials and resources could be extracted. Cooperative forestry collapsed under the weight of paper manufacturing and Pemex's promotion of stove oil, Xochimilcan farmers witnessed their lands dry up from urban water use and saw floodwaters wash away their crops, and the reclaimed Texcoco land reverted to its alkaline state once the government abandoned fertilization schemes for ejidatarios. Productivity declined, and life in the countryside proved unsustainable for many. After 1940 governance set up a vicious circle of urbanization in which ejidal divestment, natural resource transfers, and rural-urban migration reinforced each other. Ejidatarios on the outskirts of Mexico City, once hopeful of fertile fields, yielded to urban developers and central-city squatters while navigating the rugged political terrain to obtain maximum compensation for their alienated lands. Old ejido tracts stood at the front lines of urban settlement, where the residents of colonias proletarias and more traditional subdivisions followed the political scripts written under Cárdenas and expanded by Ávila Camacho to demand land tenure and environmental services. In 1950 the city's population had climbed above three million and continued to balloon. Political legitimacy shifted toward the demands of urban consumers, whose concerns had largely not been addressed by Cárdenas, but the door to a more equitable urbanization had closed.

"FORESTS NOW DENIED US"

In 1940 Cárdenas eliminated the Forestry Department and subordinated forestry to the Ministry of Agriculture and Development. He justified this move by pointing to the strain on the budget caused by oil expropriation, but the Forestry Department had funded itself through contracts and concessions.

The actual reasons were political. Miguel Ángel de Quevedo, seen as having failed to balance conservation and revolutionary reform, found his reputation damaged. Department employee Ernesto Sánchez denounced the "family oligarchy"—a nonliteral claim pointing to cliquish hiring—that Quevedo had established at the expense of foresters Sánchez deemed to be better qualified.[2] Dozens of communities, including Santo Tomás Ajusco, San Nicolás Totolapan, and Magdalena Contreras, accused Quevedo of corruption and nepotism, and department employees of bribing forest users. "The Forestry Department, from its elderly head [Quevedo] to the last employee of the lowest category," forest users griped, "is our worst enemy"; despite "shedding our blood for the Revolution, for the ideals of the return of lands, forests, and water . . . [these rights] are now denied us."[3] In the spring of 1939, dozens of cooperative members from south of Mexico City marched in the capital to expose the apostle of the tree.[4] Campesino discontent from without and corruption and "anti-revolutionism" charges from within the department proved too much for Cárdenas to ignore.

Disbanding the Forestry Department gave the president a unique victory: he could appear to be slashing government expenditures and reaffirming his revolutionary credentials at a time when the core Cardenista agenda was flagging and conservatives were in ascendance. Yet, in doing so, Cárdenas did away with the very agency that had supported cooperative forest economies—if only tepidly. Not only the contentious national park movement but also much of the official legitimacy conferred on popular forest economies went down with the department. The termination of the Forestry Department augured a new direction in forestry, toward industrial interests at the expense of the cooperative.

Throughout the Cardenas sexenio, the production of fuelwood, especially charcoal, for Mexico City's expanding market had been a major component of campesino forest economies in central Mexico. Before the Cardenista land redistribution, about 7.5 percent of the charcoal consumed in Mexico derived from the ejidos of central Mexico. Ejido production had risen to an estimated 40 percent by 1940.[5] During this period, the Forestry Department issued permits to each ejido cooperative for tree felling or deadwood collection. Campesinos targeted oak trees (*encinos*), which were relatively rare (accounting for only about 20 percent of central Mexico's forests) but made the most valuable charcoal.

The process of transforming wood into charcoal was time-consuming and dangerous. Whereas metal kilns were commonly used in Europe, most Mexican charcoal producers would build fire pits formed by a frame of three or four thick logs anchored vertically into the ground.[6] Sticks, grass, leaves, and soil filled in the walls of this wooden frame, with openings for oxygen carved out around the bottom. Carbonization required constant vigilance and patience. The entire process took several days, and dangerous mixtures of hydrocarbons could cause the makeshift ovens to explode.[7] Once the logs inside the pit had fully carbonized and then cooled, cooperative members took the product to the nearest train depot to sell to a wholesaler (*introductor*), although occasionally cooperatives were able to evade middlemen. The wholesaler oversaw the delivery of charcoal to the capital, where independent retailers would line up daily to purchase the combustible. In the mid-1930s there were hundreds of carbonerías and hundreds more ambulant charcoal vendors announcing their product, a staple of the domestic economy as prevalent as the tortilla. Nearly every home possessed a brasero (charcoal-burning stove), and women, whether housewives, food vendors, or maids, obtained charcoal on a daily basis.

Because charcoal was essential for the daily subsistence of thousands of families in Mexico City, disruptions in the commodity chain ignited social disputes and concerns over its viability as a cooking fuel. While adulteration— increasing "the weight of the charcoal with soil and on occasion with stones painted black"—was common practice, charcoal shortages arose as a serious problem only in the mid-1930s.[8] Lines outside dispensaries regularly stretched around street corners, and women and children often returned empty-handed. The charcoal scarcity coincided with Cárdenas's creation of the Forestry Department, and foresters were quick to blame the shortages on campesino forest destruction and to promote alternative fuels. Charcoal production caused forest decline, the argument went, and forest decline, most palpable in central Mexico, led to a host of environmental problems. Environmental degradation was, in part, caused by urban energy demand. The city, in effect, was imperiling itself.[9]

Accusations that campesino charcoal production was destroying the forest commons of the Basin of Mexico were overstated. Although the Mexican Forestry Society estimated (and *El Universal* reaffirmed) that the forests of the Federal District had shrunk from twenty-two thousand hectares in 1913 to six thousand hectares in 1935, this assessment of drastic forest loss is contradicted by archival evidence regarding forest cover on community lands and in national parks.[10] Deforestation was unequivocally a reality between 1910 and the 1930s, but it was not as severe as widely asserted and was due less to charcoal production than to the expansion of farmland, paper production, and railway needs. Indeed, government officials and the press exaggerated the amount of charcoal produced in the basin's southern mountains and overestimated the havoc the charcoal economy was wreaking on forests in general.[11] Charcoal producers defended their practices, noting that oak trees regenerate over time; in addition, many campesinos preferred to cut branches instead of the entire tree, and still others gathered dead logs and fallen branches from the forest floor. Local use customs, species regeneration, and government regulations prevented outright destruction. Forest loss was not so much a natural limit on overall production as a factor in pricing. As the forestland closest to Mexico City was logged for a variety of purposes, charcoal producers were forced to exploit woodlands more distant from railways, thus increasing the sale price in Mexico City. Scarcity, according to the agronomist Efraín Jaimes Piñeda, was not "due only or exclusively to the lack of production" but rather to a multitude of factors, including the machinations of powerful wholesalers.[12]

This was precisely the line of reasoning city charcoal vendors adopted to explain the charcoal scarcity. Backed by the Regional Worker and Campesino Federation, vendors campaigned against wholesalers whom they labeled as "hoarders," "speculators," and "monopolizers." In the summer of 1937, Cárdenas countenanced the sellers' assertions regarding the cause of the charcoal scarcity. The president decreed that the shortage was "due not so much to the dearth of the product as to the devious scheming of individuals interested in excessive profit making to the damage of the urban consumer." He called charcoal "a public utility," demanding the release of hoarded product, equitable distribution of charcoal to all sellers, and the fining of storeowners who sold charcoal at exorbitant prices. Article 5 of the decree granted the government powers to set up a central depository that would purchase charcoal directly from producers.[13] This represented a potential death knell to monopolizers and a boon to the forest cooperatives, but there is no evidence it was ever realized. The government's fixed price per kilogram for charcoal doubled between 1932 and 1938, while wholesalers like "the king of charcoal," Ramón Nieto, who owned dozens of dispensaries, regularly priced the product higher than officially sanctioned.[14]

The sellers' framework, seconded by some producer cooperatives and upheld by Cárdenas, counteracted the foresters' argument about the causes of scarcity by highlighting charcoal's social production. According to the sellers, scarcity was not a natural outcome; rather, it was a reflection of power along the transport network that brought charcoal from the forests to the urban market.

In vindicating their industry, vendors temporarily sustained the link between small-scale rural production and urban fuel consumption, even as hoarding and price gouging continued. Once Cardenista populism gave way to the more conservative presidency of Ávila Camacho, the environmental frame provided the lethal ammunition to debilitate this campesino-dependent energy economy.

Slowly yet inexorably, during the 1940s and early 1950s Mexico City's cooking fuel began to be drawn more from Mexico's rich petroleum reserves than from its forests. State officials promoted the transition for several reasons. First, purportedly wasteful campesinos and unpredictable wholesalers dominated the charcoal enterprise. Oil—nationalized by Cárdenas in 1938—lay in the government's hands, could be transported via pipeline free of the vagaries of labor and weather, and was a symbol of national pride. Second, petroleum, as a substance fueling industrial growth in the North Atlantic, represented Mexico's passage into modernity, and the petroleum-derived kerosene used for cooking burned more cleanly. State and private firms also regularly represented the petroleum stoves as the savior of Mexico's woodlands.[15] Cleaner and healthier homes meant healthy forests.

During this period, state and federal administrations once again besieged the campesino charcoal economy, this time ordering a series of forest-related bans around central Mexico. A ban in 1941 on cutting in the Federal District was followed by a decree from Hidalgo that no forest products could leave the state and a presidential ban in 1944 on cutting in all of central Mexico.[16] After the end of World War II logging bans proliferated throughout the nation. In pueblos such as San Miguel Topilejo, authorities shut down charcoal ovens.[17] The bans, which attempted to sever important production spaces from Mexico City's market, arose from the spurious assumption that prohibiting forest use would conserve Mexico's woodlands. Feeble enforcement diminished the effects of the bans, but the amount of charcoal entering Mexico City declined steadily during the 1940s, while the state oil company, Pemex, sold petroleum stoves at discounted prices.[18] The minister of agriculture, the agronomist Marte Gómez, championed cheap petroleum-based energy and readily compared Mexico's situation with that of England during the late eighteenth century when, many presumed, an overreliance on wood devastated the English countryside.[19] Gómez's pedigree was that of an ardent agrarian reformer, but after 1940 he increasingly served as a booster for agribusiness. His denigration of the fuelwood economy, in which cooperative production had gained ground over more capital-intensive production during the 1930s, mirrored his broader ideological change.[20] Others joined Gómez. The rising biologist and forester Enrique Beltrán, generally a vituperative opponent of Quevedo, nonetheless shared with the august conservationist a fervent disapproval of charcoal production. On his National Autonomous University of Mexico radio broadcast in 1941, Beltrán encouraged the development of fossil fuels, blaming heavy flooding across central Mexico during that year's rainy season on widespread deforestation. Urban consumer groups likewise hailed the switch from charcoal to petroleum as a sign of progress.[21]

Charcoal consumption in the capital declined precipitously. Scarcity was again in part manufactured. During World War II, store shelves lay bare of dozens of goods, including charcoal, a result of the bans and a war economy that incentivized speculation and hoarding.[22] As the consumption of charcoal decreased (down 60 percent in Mexico City between 1940 and 1951), the use of stove oil in kitchens and restaurants increased.[23] By early 1942 over twenty thousand city residents had bought the cheaper Pemex stoves, and the company boasted that fifty thousand families had bought them in 1943 alone—although it is unclear whether this referenced sales nationwide or only in the Federal District.[24] Stove sales by Pemex and private retailers continued apace throughout the 1940s, and by the end of the decade many poor families living in Mexico City's tenements had one, including anthropologist Oscar Lewis's Sánchez family.[25] (See figure 7.1.)

The charcoal economy did not disappear completely, but Mexico's charcoal and firewood producers confronted a harsh reality of inhospitable policies and a changing market. A forest workers' union in central Mexico denounced the existing forest policy that punished the charcoal industry and left thousands of workers associated with it jobless. In an eloquent defense of their much-maligned forest practices, union representatives claimed that their use of the regenerating oak did not harm the woodlands and criticized the paper mills' destruction of most of the less renewable pine stands around the major volcanoes of Popocatépetl, Iztaccíhuatl, and Ajusco.[26] This somewhat-overstated accusation represented the last stand of a debilitated occupation against the industrial turn in policy. Thereafter, the union's periodic requests focused on acquiring agricultural land and other forms of employment for its members.[27]

The environmental rhetoric seen in the transition from wood to oil also accompanied the industrialization of agriculture during the same period. Government officials blamed the rural poor for central Mexico's degraded soils and stimulated irrigation and agribusiness in the arid north. The promotion of agribusiness, combined with the popularization of stove oil, broke the

FIGURE 7.1 — Advertisement in *El Universal*, October 9, 1950: "Mexico's current progress is due to the open defense of its production. You, Madam, as a Mexican, can protect one of Mexico's great resources, its forests, and contribute to its national progress by NOT USING ANY MORE CHARCOAL" (author's translation).

bonds established during the 1930s between peasant producer and urban consumer. Fewer and fewer peasant producers supplied cities with goods. In the transition to industrial agriculture and to stove oil, the Mexican state shone the spotlight on the conditions of production primarily to highlight natural limits—degraded soils and destroyed forests—and to justify a putatively modernizing change in policy.[28] Environmental narratives helped lead to industrialized food, which was cooked with industrialized fuel on top of stoves increasingly manufactured in an industrializing Mexico City, which was filling rapidly with migrants from the unproductive countryside. Resource conservation and economic nationalism masked the power relations behind the transition to oil. Two notable casualties of the shift were the ejido forest cooperative of central Mexico and other campesino fuelwood producers.

The rising production capacities of the San Rafael and Loreto y Peña Pobre paper mills, supported by administrations after 1940, further abraded community forest economies. The German immigrant Alberto Lenz merged the Loreto and Peña Pobre paper mills in 1928.[29] He had purchased a denuded property in the Sierra de las Cruces and reforested it for the application of "scientific forestry," itself a nineteenth-century German invention that spread around the world.[30] Alberto Lenz, and his son Hans, joined the Mexican Forestry Society, ascribed to the belief in the environmental services of forests, and became good friends of Quevedo's. The Lenz family's solid reputation among foresters kept obstreperous campesino activists and their land claims at bay during the Cárdenas years, but no major concessions were forthcoming. Alberto Lenz and the owners of the San Rafael mill were obligated to purchase wood products from villagers, who, they ranted, "destroy [the forests] quickly . . . damaging climatic conditions [and] health and altering the water regime" with their primitive techniques.[31]

World War II helped provide the impetus for the industrialization of Mexico's forests. Logging companies used sawmills, large trucks, and skidders and built sawmills and paper mills to meet wartime needs and satisfy a growing urban market. In anticipation of rising production, the Lenz family expanded the Loreto y Peña Pobre mill in the southern delegation of Tlalpan.[32] The forestry law of 1943, to which Alberto Lenz was a key contributor, disempowered the cooperatives, sanctioned operations like the basin's paper mills while exempting them from federal bans, and gave the president the authority to create Industrial Units for Forest Development (UIEFs), within which large corporations would be granted exclusive purchasing rights for forest products.[33] In 1947 the Lenz family became the beneficiary of one of the first UIEFs granted by the Alemán government: eighty-two thousand hectares of woodlands stretching across the Ajusco range.[34] The San Rafael mill received two UIEFs the same year, one in the forested mountains around the volcanoes and the other in the Nevado de Toluca National Park west of the Basin of Mexico. With the pretext that campesinos were poor stewards of the land—the decree stated they were "the cause of great damage to forests"—Alemán granted the two major paper mills ejidal and communal woods to supply the raw material for their booming enterprises.[35] Foresters in tune with the industrial goals of the government insisted that these and other companies would provide jobs for locals while also maintaining the forests in good health owing to more efficient technologies and reforestation practices. The regulations guiding the UIEFs also stipulated that the companies had to pay a "just price" to landowners and ejidos in return for their forest products and to fund public works projects in communities. There was little oversight, however, and few infrastructure projects materialized.[36]

Most communities fought the new forestry regime. The agrarian leadership of Magdalena Contreras pleaded that their ejido be excluded from the jurisdiction of the Loreto y Peña Pobre UIEF, knowing that the company would control pricing and exert more authority over extraction. Like the charcoal union, the leadership of Magdalena Contreras employed the durable conservationist frame against the paper mill, which they said "converts the woods into sterile plains to the detriment of agriculture and the textile industry."[37] Their fight was largely in vain, however: only one community in Morelos was granted exclusion from the UIEF.

This policy turn defanged the state-sanctioned cooperative system, but the villagers living within the UIEFs and banned woodlands were not hapless victims. Clandestine logging flourished, and many communities within banned territories took advantage of industrialized forestry by illegally selling their lumber to sawmills and paper companies.[38] Some manufacturing jobs were created at the productive paper mills on the slopes of the Basin of Mexico, and villagers in the UIEFs doubtless found employment selling wood (at chronically low prices) to be converted into pulp for bags, paper, and packing material. Indeed, the decrease in demand for charcoal and fuelwood, in tandem with the industrial forest program, supplied the Lenz family and other concessionaires with a steady labor supply, often from members of the old ejido cooperatives.

The fledgling forest commons of peasant producers organized in cooperatives succumbed to industrialized forestry and an energy policy that severely restricted forest use and shrank the fuelwood market. The shift from popular and communal to industrial capitalist forest use may have inadvertently accelerated deforestation; it certainly increased the wage-labor force.[39] Many of those who chose not to work for the mills turned to farming and ranching, activities that often required clear-cutting. Others almost certainly moved to Mexico's booming postwar cities, particularly Mexico City, where they would eventually have settled in the colonias proletarias of the urban periphery.

FROM MEXICO'S VENICE TO MEXICO'S LOVE CANAL

In 1919 the town of Xochimilco received the first ejidal grant in the Xochimilco lakebed, the first of many that reinvigorated community agricultural production. Ejidal lands on the old lakebed were highly productive during the 1920s and 1930s, and thousands of villagers from pueblos such as San Gregorio Atlapulco, Tláhuac, San Andrés Mixquic, San Luis Tlaxialtemalco, and Santa María Nativitas farmed fertile lands—and chinampas in several cases—to supply the bustling urban market. Desiccation and floodwaters were constant threats, however, and campesino political organizations pushed the Cárdenas government to address them. The contradiction between hinterland production, dependent on abundant, well-managed water, and the urban need for water became more glaring during the 1940s.

A host of political, technical, and ecological forces converged to deteriorate agricultural production around the lakebed. Mexico City's water service was already stretched thin in the 1930s. Urban land speculation required the extension of water service to peripheral zones, and the state's promotion of import substitution industrialization depended on fixing defunct infrastructure— leaks were incessant, and nightly service suspensions the norm—and locating new sources. In the early 1940s, the city government increased pumping of the Xochimilco springs, replaced miles of the old reinforced concrete aqueduct with a new cast-iron one, and perforated deep wells just north of Xochimilco to tap the prodigious underground aquifer.[40] Extraction soon exceeded the aquifer recharge rate, which had already been decreased by drainage, vegetation loss, and the spread of concrete and pavement, which prevented rainwater from filtering underground.[41] As urban water flowed through aqueducts and pipes, hinterland water rushed down mountain slopes, flooding Xochimilco's farmland. The water came laden with sediment, which replenished the topsoil but also settled in the old lakebed and aggravated flooding. And dropping water tables wreaked havoc on crops. Desiccated lands harbored the *chahuixtle*, a black fungus that thrives in dry farming conditions. The fungus plagued ejidos' maize crops, which were less susceptible to the mold when grown in chinampas.[42] Moreover, by 1940 the Canal Nacional, one of the emblems of "Mexico's Venice," held insufficient water for transportation, and sections of it were shut down that year. While the closure went unnoticed by most city inhabitants, it forced villagers to find land-based transport to Mexico City's markets.

The consequences of the changing political ecology were dire. In the mid-1950s the ejidal authorities of Tláhuac informed the young anthropologist William T. Sanders that their crops "had been totally lost" because of the chahuixtle.[43] As early as 1940 the League of Agrarian Communities calculated that the ejidos in the Xochimilco/Chalco basin had lost 720,000 loads of maize (worth 11 million pesos) to floodwaters in the eleven years since engineers had stopped dredging the Amecameca River, and they expected future losses to increase.[44] An ejidatario of Xochimilco lamented the large investments needed to "just remove the salts" that surfaced with drying and pined for the days when the lands "gave huge maize harvests."[45] Ejidal production declined further as the dropping water table caused subsidence, a phenomenon that further worsened floods. Ejidal corruption and environmental mismanagement made a tough situation worse. The ejidal commissioner of Xochimilco rented communal pastureland to outside livestock holders, whose roaming cattle prevented springtime field preparation. Worse, he pocketed the profits, despite the urgent need for money to build flood walls.[46] Conventional farming communities faced seemingly incongruent environmental extremes: severe flooding in the summer and dried-out, saline, and fungus-infested lands in winter.

There is some truth to the notion that Xochimilco was the victim of a rapacious urban perpetrator, but midcentury lakebed governance was shaped by local political pressures as well. In 1949 the Xochimilcan water crisis turned calamitous: the famous canals, plied by hundreds of tourist-filled trajineras weekly, turned into scattered puddles, and the lake nearly vanished.[47] It was this desiccation, more than flooding and fungus, that put Xochimilco in the national spotlight. Neighbors formed the Lake Xochimilco Conservation League, supported by a host of professional planners, and President Alemán promised the restoration of the lacustrine environment.[48]

Engineers concocted a water-diversion plan using the nearby Churubusco River. Once the diversion was completed in 1957, a leading hydraulic engineer averred that Xochimilco would have water levels comparable to those found during the early 1940s. However, given the seasonal nature of river flows in the basin, water levels rose only during the rainy season, and the injection of muddy mountain water increased lakebed and canal sedimentation.[49] Even during the rainy months, the addition of Churubusco water failed to compensate for the rapid rate at which water was being extracted. Chinampería persisted precariously only in communities with surviving springs and ponds, most notably in Xochimilco and San Gregorio Atlapulco but also parts of San Andrés Mixquic, Tláhuac, and several other nearby pueblos.[50]

As engineers celebrated Xochimilco's dubious rebirth in 1957, the government set in motion a second project to demonstrate its commitment to conserving chinampería: the injection of treated wastewater into the canals. The wastewater received only primary treatment, which did not (and still does not) remove most bacterial and industrial pollutants. Studies found both in the few remaining chinampa plots, which produced food that eventually made its way onto the plates of city inhabitants. The polluted water, moreover, brought on a plague of water lilies, which choked the canals, suffocated the area's rich biological life, and snarled water-based transit.[51] Attempts to cure the ills of Xochimilco inverted Marx's famous dictum about Napoleonic France: Churubusco water was the farce, the treated water the tragedy. Mexico's Venice had become Mexico's Love Canal avant la lettre. Through the replenishment of the canals and wetlands—the fundamental ingredients in chinampa agriculture—the indigenous agricultural technique continued, but its output declined, and the health risks to chinamperos and the consumers of their products escalated. Whereas charcoal producers were stigmatized for destroying Mexico's forests, Xochimilco's chinamperos were denounced for exposing the populace to gastrointestinal disease.[52]

Writings about Xochimilco focus on the agonizing death of Lake Xochimilco and the loss of chinampería as a uniquely Mexican tradition. The farmers of Xochimilco have surely been the victims of rapid urbanization, but they have also been actors with heterogeneous interests. Environmental degradation meant different things to different people residing around the lakebed, and only during the late 1940s and early 1950s did a broad-based movement involving locals and concerned urbanites emerge to defend the waterscape. This was too little and far too late; a new round of high-powered deep wells built in the 1950s sucked water out of the aquifer at higher rates than ever before, and pollution from new industries and settlements seeped into the once-flourishing canals. Country life became a bigger challenge to sustain than ever before.

If Xochimilco experienced gradual environmental impoverishment over a half century, the Texcoco lakebed underwent successive rapid transformations during the same period. The fertilization schemes of the 1930s and early 1940s aimed to turn dried, alkaline lands into verdant, productive ejidos, dependent on a benevolent government. But by the century's halfway mark, engineering had left communities like San Juan de Aragón and Magdalena Salinas in the lurch.

Although Ávila Camacho continued to invest in the reclamation of the alkaline lands for the ejidos, the project to industrialize Texcoco's salts suggested harsher times were near. In October 1943 Ávila Camacho granted a fifty-one-year lease to the parastatal company Sosa Texcoco to exploit the dissolved salts on the northern edge of the lakebed, where the saline content was highest, using a solar evaporation pond. The state provided the infrastructure necessary for the enterprise, and the company was exempted from all tariffs on machinery and other supplies. Sosa Texcoco commenced operations soon thereafter and became the largest producer of alkali in Latin America.[53]

Alemán terminated Texcoco reclamation. As of 1946, 3,300 of the lakebed's 27,000 hectares had been drained and readied for cultivation, and, in total, land reclamation had consumed nearly 14 million pesos over an eleven-year span.[54] (See figure 7.2.) Government priorities, however, had turned elsewhere, and the Ministry of Hydraulic Resources, acknowledging fertilization's high costs, considered other schemes in the lakebed. Drawing on engineer Miguel Brambilla's proposal to flood a vast area of the lakebed to curtail the dust storms, the ministry occasionally filled the southern part of the lakebed with stream water, though perhaps more to ward off urban settlement on federal property than to prevent the dust storms.[55] Still, the majority of funding for Texcoco works after 1943 was funneled to industrializing the deposits of sodium carbonate. As a result, the dust storms, which had persisted even at the height of the fertilization campaign, worsened. By the late 1960s, they tormented Mexico's capital at the rate of over sixty per year. Officials frequently closed the international airport because of the blinding dust, and one estimate put the average yearly costs of the storms at 419 million pesos.[56]

The experiences of San Juan de Aragón brought into focus how the defunding of the fertilization project and the changing environment interacted with campesino economies. The public works project constituted a major source of employment for villagers, and some of the distress over its termination revolved

FIGURE 7.2 — President Miguel Alemán visits the Texcoco project, 1948.
COURTESY OF AGN: HERMANOS MAYO 3.260.

around employment expectations. It also, of course, promised fertile fields. In 1938 the ejido had turned over ninety-four hectares to the National Irrigation Commission for an agricultural experimentation camp in exchange for a government promise to return the parcel "with all the uses that were obtained." Five years later, the ejido received just a small portion of the reclaimed tract, at which point some community members decided to occupy and work the larger portion of land. But in the summer of 1949, police forces evicted the occupants. Meanwhile, the ejidatarios anxiously appealed for the continuation of the Cardenista project, from which "all the machinery and agricultural instruments [had been] sold," leaving only part of the irrigation services in order.[57] Farming in the lakebed was analogous, as one local peasant quipped, to cultivating on a "hot comal"[58]

Alemán supported a smallholder regime in the Texcoco lakebed. Large sections of the unimproved federal land southeast of the major ejido beneficiaries were sold at bargain-basement prices to ex-military personnel, and several urban developers claimed chunks of unclaimed, dried-out lands bordering the federal zone to the south.[59] These areas soon formed the sprawling Ciudad Nezahualcóyotl, whose population soared to over a million by the

FIGURE 7.3 — Colonia del Sol in the Texcoco lakebed, 1959. COURTESY OF FUNDACIÓN ICA.

early 1970s (see figure 7.3). The proliferation of small landowners with urbanizing intentions affected San Juan de Aragón, which in 1947 was denied an ejidal extension on the grounds that there were no dividable (that is, large) properties nearby. Driven by alkalizing lands and the ejido commissioner's accumulation of multiple tracts, six ejidatarios occupied a plot owned by David Arías, one of the beneficiaries of Alemán's sell-off. Arías, protective of his land, notified agrarian officials that the ejidatarios had planted seeds "without any rights whatsoever," and the police moved to expel the ejidatarios from the disputed property.[60] Between the near-complete dearth of arable land and a corrupt ejidal administration accused of hoarding land, the populous San Juan de Aragón experienced a precipitous decline.[61] Many inhabitants migrated to one of the colonias proletarias or to the nearby developments of Ciudad Nezahualcóyotl.

The ejido itself was also soon beset by urbanizers. In 1955 the much-despised ejido commissioner received a bribe to permit Manuel Guadarrama to illegally fence off land for a colonia proletaria. Guadarrama removed vital

irrigation pipes to clear the way for settlers. Several ejidatarios refused to transfer their titles to other, less hospitable parcels, and they too likely left the ejido.[62]
The remaining ejidatarios continued to fight for a productive environment
on the edge of the lakebed, invoking the halcyon years when Cárdenas aimed
to turn their sterile fields into fertile farms.[63] Not long thereafter, the authorities expropriated the entire ejido to construct public housing. The story of
San Juan de Aragón typified dozens of ejidos around the Basin of Mexico. As
communal land deteriorated, urban developers moved in.

"BECAUSE THE LAND IS BAD"

During the immediate postrevolutionary period, the urban poor began settling on vacant federal lands, and hacendados viewed the urbanization of
their property, or the mere intention of it, as a source of immediate wealth
and an underhanded way to evade agrarian claims.[64] During the 1940s the
advancing city also crept onto the nearby ejidos of the formerly rural Federal
District delegations Iztacalco, Iztapalapa, Gustavo Madero, and Azcapotzalco.
Ejidatarios turned into chief protagonists of urbanization, with the political
leverage to negotiate deals to privatize dried, eroded, or saline lands abandoned by the state. In the delegations Iztapalapa and Iztacalco in the southeast
and Gustavo Madero in the northeast, ejidatarios courted private interests to
enclose their communal holdings. The insatiable demand for housing combined with environmental deterioration to make the urbanization of ejidos
inevitable, but the process was highly contested and the specific outcome contingent on the maneuvering and negotiating strategies of conflicting interests.

In 1940 the National Campesino Confederation discerned the imminent
threat to ejidos on the outskirts of Mexico City and counseled all community
authorities to defend their common lands against speculators, their government allies, and eminent domain.[65] Expropriation decrees, regularly issued
by Cárdenas to strengthen communal landholding, could also serve as potent
weapons against the commons. Ejido enclosures were outlawed by the agrarian code and planning laws, but there were three ways of legally circumvent-
ing these obstacles: an ejidal land transfer (*permuta*) if acceded to by the
ejidatarios, eminent domain in the "public good," and, starting in 1954, expropriation for the creation of an urban ejido zone.[66] Eminent domain was the
most frequent method of alienation, exercised by the state to build the high-
ways and power lines that were essential infrastructure for the modern city.
Corruption and collusion between private developers and agrarian officials

provided another means to alienate ejidal lands, made all the easier when the ejidatarios themselves supported privatization.

Speculation, government interest in providing land for city-center inhabitants, and infertile communal fields fueled extensive settlement on the basin's ejido hinterlands. Iztapalapa, for example, grew 250 percent between 1930 and 1950, to a population of over 75,000, while the minuscule Iztacalco tripled over the same stretch, reaching 34,000. Gustavo Madero, centered on the old Villa Guadalupe Hidalgo, had a population of 41,585 in 1940 but ten years later boasted 204,833.[67] Ejidatarios, rejecting their confederation's orders, conceded to the inevitable and embraced land sales as a kind of bittersweet victory.

The small delegation of Iztacalco, to the south of the city, was home to several ejidos and lay at the front lines of urban expansion starting in the late 1930s. In fact, one of the first government-sanctioned privatization acts was carried out at the tail end of Cárdenas's sexenio. The ejidal leadership of the pueblo Iztacalco bemoaned saline soils and flooding in an area that once had supported chinampas, and they did not equivocate when developer Ramón Rivera Torres offered to pay the community 500,000 pesos in exchange for a twenty-hectare tract where he planned to build the Villa Cortés. The large sum, both parties agreed, would be reinvested in home construction and service provision for the ejidatarios. Existing law stipulated that land transfers were the only path to privatizing ejido land, but Cárdenas made a crucial exception, recognizing that transfers within the highly populated and environmentally degraded Basin of Mexico were impracticable and undesirable.[68]

By the beginning of Alemán's term, the Iztacalco ejido was surrounded by subdivisions, including Rivera Torres's Villa Cortés and other illicit settlements, and there is no evidence that much of the 500,000 pesos had been invested for community development. Instead, the rapid settlement of communal land broke the rhythm and routines of agrarian life. Home builders erected fences around their property, blocking paths to fields and disrupting communal bonds, and they dug sewage canals that threatened public health. Denser settlement also made long-standing practices like going to the bathroom outside into shameful acts.[69] These were signs that agricultural life on Iztacalco lands was doomed. In this context, the ejido assembly approved developer Agusto Santamarina's proposal to develop a 133-hectare subdivision on the remaining ejido lands in exchange for an indemnity payment of 3.75 pesos per square meter.[70] As long as the government refused to grant an ejido extension or provide financial support to improve the existing land, the villagers' best option was to bargain the terms of urbanization.

Although some functionaries evidently supported Santamarina and the ejidatarios' urbanization scheme, the Agrarian Department blocked the agreement as illegal. Santamarina countered that the campesinos were "laborers and small traders," not farmers, and thus not worthy of retaining their ejido.[71] This kind of argument had not worked for Remigio Noriega in his bid to defeat community land claims in the 1920s, nor did it work for Santamarina. There were strong countervailing positions within the government that held firm to the principle of protecting communal land. One agronomist chastised his coworkers for even considering flouting the law; clearly rattled, he argued that "to approve the petition . . . [,]apart from following an illegal procedure, would establish a dangerous precedent since any person or company could obtain ejidal expropriations for subdivision development."[72] This agronomist's stand prevailed, but urbanization by one means or another was imminent. Denied the land transfer, Iztacalco's ejido leadership resorted to illegally leasing lots to fraudulent urbanizers and land invaders wishing to set up colonias proletarias, While Iztacalco's ejidatarios hoped their leaders would collect some income for the community or at least keep out land squatters unwilling to pay rent, the breakup of communal holdings generally spawned new divisions within communities and allowed wealth to accumulate in the hands of a few townspeople who were well positioned to exploit land sales or leasing agreements.[73]

The expropriation of Santa Anita, a village on the banks of the defunct Canal Nacional, once made famous by Fanny Calderón de la Barca as a bucolic place, exemplifies the parts played by the numerous actors involved in the privatization of communal lands. Santa Anita, a short jaunt from the colonia Moderna on the southeastern outskirts of the city, was prime real estate. The well-connected José C. Madrazo and Jorge Jiménez Moral were handed seventy-six hectares of Santa Anita's ejido in 1940, over the petitions Agrarian Department workers had made for the same land.[74] Santa Anita's leadership initially developed a positive relationship with Madrazo, but it turned sour in 1941 when he failed to fully pay off his enclosure. Madrazo and Jiménez Moral owed the ejido 600,000 pesos, all earmarked for home construction and service installation, but had paid only 40,000 and had, according to ejido authorities, turned the town into a trash heap. Ávila Camacho revoked the expropriation decree in 1943, and the community leadership began courting other suitors. A healthy dose of competition raised the compensation. Agrarian department employees offered 743,000 pesos, but private developers approached the ejido with even more. Alejandro Romero, a major developer of Ciudad Nezahualcóyotl, Iztapalapa, and Iztacalco, offered over 900,000 pesos. Another appealing offer came from Ricardo Rodríguez y Soriano, who had pending development deals with two other communities. He offered to transfer the ejido to an old hacienda in Querétaro valued at 1.3 million pesos, in addition to providing funds for an urbanized settlement there.[75]

These enticing bids folded. The Supreme Court granted an injunction to Madrazo and Jiménez Moral, salvaging their urbanization project. Santa Anita authorities had, however, gained greater leverage through their astute bargaining. The community managed to increase the indemnity from Madrazo and Jiménez Moral to over a million pesos, a sum the developers paid fully in 1949, and the following year water and drainage works were completed for the ex-ejidatarios.[76] The ejidatarios of Santa Anita had learned how to play developers off against each other. If the ejido was useless for productive farming, its value as prime urban land was climbing.

Ejidatarios in Santa Anita, Iztacalco, and elsewhere were adept negotiators. Agreeing to land commodification made sense for ejidatarios, who responded pragmatically to environmental and social forces beyond their control. This is not to say that villagers always obtained exactly what they wished or that the negotiation process was not riddled with inequalities. Still, ejidatarios were a force to be reckoned with because of the exchange value of their land. Ejido land may have been bulldozed, but ejidatarios were often able to force the bulldozers to open an otherwise-rocky path to urban living for them. Even when the government blocked expropriation, as it often did in this period, many ejidatarios illegally leased their land to developers or the caciques of colonias proletarias.[77] During the 1950s and 1960s, the city's expansion reached the ejidos of San Bernabé Ocotepec and Magdalena Contreras on the slopes of the Sierra de las Cruces, where the workers who were building the new campus of the ambitious National Autonomous University of Mexico, the high-end subdivisions surrounding it, and the extension of the Periférico highway constructed their homes. In 1976, 40 percent of Mexico City's surface area had once been ejido land.[78]

ENVIRONMENTAL POLITICS IN THE INDUSTRIALIZING CITY

In the last days of Ávila Camacho's term, the Magdalena Salinas ejido, which had supported the agricultural reclamation of the Texcoco lakebed, surrendered to the housing demands of the urban working class. The state expropriated fifty-five hectares of the ejido and transferred the land to the

Agrarian Department employee union, the same workers who had coveted Santa Anita. The paradox of state employees receiving ex-ejido lands while ostensibly working on behalf of the ejido sector was not uncommon in this political moment. Cárdenas had made overtures to address housing demands, service extensions, and consumer shortages, but his reformism petered out at the city's gates and at the shop-floor exit. Production mattered more than consumption. Juan Andreu Almazán's strong showing in several major cities in the presidential election of 1940 exposed the holes in the PRM's worker-peasant base. With campesinos firmly entrenched in the National Campesino Confederation and the pugnacious tendencies of the organized working class tamed under the Confederation of Mexican Workers, Ávila Camacho turned his attention to extending urban institutional authority through the National Confederation of Popular Organizations and implementing specific policies regarding urban consumption. He and his successor Alemán froze rents to attenuate the rising costs of living and appease the small shopkeepers who were drawn to Almazán, ramped up food-distribution programs, established new bus lines, and promoted cheaper stove oil.

The new urban alliance was as much about placating urban popular demands as it was about propping up industrial capital and the construction industry.[79] Stabilized living costs enabled General Motors, Ford, General Electric, Kelvinator, and other new foreign and national industries across the city's northern periphery to hold down salaries and assure themselves a higher and more stable profit.[80] Expropriation also played a key role in the new alliance. It had a radical redistributionist provenance, but it quickly became a means of purchasing political legitimacy, fostering urban construction, and containing the rising cost of living for the industrial working class, whose power to negotiate wages was diminishing rapidly. Expropriation, conceived by Múgica as a path to social justice and universal hygiene, served to guide urban industrialization.

Expropriation decrees proliferated to provide housing for the growing industrial working class, government employees, shopkeepers, and informal-sector workers. Between December 1941 and December 1943, the Office of Colonias distributed over seventeen thousand lots, and the Ávila Camacho administration issued thirty expropriations for the formation of colonias proletarias. Between 1940 and 1946, the same office issued expropriation decrees in 72 of the 107 colonias it regularized, amounting to 28,272 housing lots.[81]

Ávila Camacho also expropriated lands in established colonias. The developer of the colonia Buenos Aires (now Doctores), founded in the 1920s and billed as one of "the embarrassments of Mexico" by the Federal District governor at the time, had sold lots to six hundred people without providing services. No remedy was in sight, and the new owners of the colonia stripped many residents of their property titles in the 1930s.[82] In 1941 Ávila Camacho expropriated the colonia, "invaded by shacks [and] bereft of absolutely all hygiene," to provide sanitary services and beautify and widen the streets.[83] The decree involved more than neighborhood improvement, however. Word spread that expropriation was a pretext to raze much of the neighborhood and erect, ironically, an enormous medical center for the new Health Ministry. Hundreds of homeowners presented an injunction request to the Federal District court.[84] The Defense Committee of Buenos Aires led the charge, skeptical of the decree's purpose. Expropriation, they recognized, had been a "weapon in social struggles for the improvement of the disadvantaged classes," but they feared that now it was being used against them.[85] Later in the year, health minister Gustavo Baz released details of his plan for fourteen hospitals equipped to hold forty thousand patients. The Defense Committee exposed what they saw as the contradiction between expropriation to sanitize the neighborhood and the building of an enormous medical center filled with contagious patients in the heart of a residential neighborhood.[86] Resistance postponed the hospital project, and in 1944 the state abrogated its earlier expropriation decree, although the hospital complex, named Centro Médico, was eventually constructed there in the early 1960s.

Expropriation in the 1940s met with varying degrees of success; concrete actions stoked the fires of urban dispute as much as they demonstrated government authority. Yet, in the many cases in which the government ended exploitative speculation and granted lots to the urban poor, expropriation was indeed a symbol of the state's benevolence, and peripheral residents remained beholden to the government for their titles and services. Moreover, modernist public housing projects for government workers were constructed around the city, drawing the attention of left-leaning architects like Hannes Meyer. Whereas Meyer's and other socialist architects' plans to solve the housing crisis through "worker cities" fizzled, Mexico's Le Corbusier, the modernist and decidedly nonsocialist architect Mario Pani, designed the two most famous public housing complexes at midcentury: the Presidente Alemán and Presidente Juárez Towers, intended to be semiautonomous villages with open spaces separate from the hustle and bustle of the anarchic city.[87]

Expropriations, rent freezes, public housing, and service extensions were accompanied by organizational changes in the corporatist state, building on the experiments with city government under Cárdenas. A presidential decree in 1941 integrated neighborhood improvement associations more firmly into the PRM while discouraging transcity alliances over urban environmental concerns. Under the guise of defending residents from the "abuse" and "speculation" committed by some association leaders, the regulation mandated that all neighborhood improvement associations be registered with the Contribution Office. The government authorized one organization in each colonia and strictly forbade it from intervening "in concerns related to other colonias."[88] The parochial tendencies of the improvement associations were inscribed in the architecture of the postrevolutionary state and merged into the National Confederation of Popular Organizations, the diverse, multiclass, and largely urban prop of the PRI. The party consolidated its urban base through selective—and often ad hoc—reforms, co-optation, and organizational reform.[89]

CONCLUSION

Urban developers, state officials, industrialists, and hydraulic engineers consolidated the power to control, appropriate, and improve the metropolitan environment. Hinterland campesinos shouldered the costs of rapid urban industrialization. Industrial policy and the environmental deterioration of the mostly rural Basin of Mexico during the 1940s and 1950s severed ties between local production and urban consumption and precipitated speculative urbanization. Urban inhabitants, in turn, faced a government that reinforced key components of Cárdenas's urban strategy. But whereas Cárdenas promoted, at least rhetorically, if not always in practice, social justice and popular mobilization, Ávila Camacho pursued a more activist program to foster capitalist industrialization and turn the multifarious urban popular classes into key cogs of the PRI machine.

Suffice it to say that rent freezes, expropriations, and public housing did not thwart private speculation on the urban periphery. Instead, industrialization at any cost, in combination with the capital's cultural and political magnetism, led to speculative housing development for the working classes and the well-to-do. Mexico City's two most renowned midcentury architects, Luis Barragán and Mario Pani, designed the subdivisions Jardines del Pedregal and Ciudad Satélite, respectively—both on expropriated ejido lands.[90] Located adjacent to the imposing new campus of the National Autonomous University of Mexico on the city's southern edge, the gigantic Pedregal subdivision contained scattered homes for the affluent amid a striking landscape of volcanic rock, the remnants of an eruption nearly two millennia earlier. Pani, advised by his planner friend José Luis Cuevas, designed Ciudad Satélite to be a well-ordered, modernist, automobile-friendly garden city for the middle class. But over-development made it part of the problem rather than the solution to urban woes; it had more in common with American suburbia than with a Euro-pean garden-city ideal.[91] Mexico City's reliance on the automobile was born in Lomas de Chapultepec and on major thoroughfares such as Insurgentes in the 1920s, and it reached maturity following World War II in new developments like Pedregal and Satélite and along the Periférico highway. City engineers also placed the Churubusco, La Piedad, and Consulado Rivers—polluted and flood prone as new settlements sprang up around them—into concrete and metal tubes to make way for east–west speedways named after the riverbeds in which they were built. Mexico City, quite literally, drove down the path to becoming Latin America's largest metropolis.

CONCLUSION

The modern utopian dream was alive and well in postwar Mexico. The anxiety about nuclear apocalypse did not discomfit Mexicans in quite the same way it did other Western nations, and an expectation of unfettered progress suffused much of Mexico City, particularly its middle and upper classes, who purchased new cars and a plethora of other industrial consumer goods. José Emilio Pacheco's *Battles in the Desert* captured the spirit of the time: "For a still unimaginable 1980, a future of plentitude and universal well being was predicted, without specifying just how it would be achieved. Clean cities without injustice, poverty, violence, congestion, or garbage. Every family with an ultramodern, aerodynamic (words from that era) house. . . . Streets full of trees and fountains, travelled by silent, non-polluting vehicles that would never collide. Paradise on earth."[1] This vision, however outlandish, rested on the premise of the benevolent PRI state effectively conducting capitalist industrialization through the control, appropriation, and transformation of the natural world.

It was a future Mexico City would not come close to attaining. The social contradictions that led to the Mexican Revolution festered in the years that

FIGURE C.1 — The flooded colonia Aurora in Ciudad Nezahualcóyotl. COURTESY
OF AGN: HERMANOS MAYO/CRONOLÓGICA 22.335.2.

followed, and urban development—the same model of development offered
up as a utopian promise—chafed against the redistributive, democratic ideals
of the Constitution of 1917 and its backers. Modernity's project of conquering
nature for universal welfare also proved unrealistic, and no place displayed
this better than the Basin of Mexico. By the early 1950s, the city on a lake, the
city Porfirian planners had reengineered—the "most transparent region of the
atmosphere"—had become a city of raging dust and stubborn floods, a city
literally sinking into desiccated land, a city of revived hierarchy, segregation,
and exclusion.[2] (See figure C.1.)

The Mexico City that people know today, with its seemingly intractable
socio-environmental predicaments, came to be in great part through the suppression of more egalitarian (albeit ephemeral and often disarticulated) alternative visions, and through the promotion of capitalist land speculation and
industrialization dependent on the rapid reengineering of nature. Urbanization for much of the twentieth century was deeply contingent and contested,
a power-laden process by which different actors vied for their own place in the
urbanizing basin by disputing the appropriation, regulation, and transformation

of what I have called the *metropolitan environment*—the lands, woods, and waters encompassed in sanitation projects and new settlements.

Urbanization was also mostly a top-down practice at the turn of the century. Urban experts and positivist officials aimed to create a sanitary city amenable to capitalist growth within and beyond the Basin of Mexico. The Mexican Revolution of 1910 opened new legal and organizational possibilities for a variety of peoples to demand more democratic use of the metropolitan environment. Ejidatarios, forest cooperative members, and city residents disputed the very nature of urbanization, and the ecological change it engendered, with state officials, planners of different stripes, and developers, and at times with one another. State and city danced in tandem, supporting each other and creating networks of power—both material and discursive—through which the popular classes claimed rights, adapted to new conditions, and helped shape environmental planning. Within these spaces of contention, however, a techno-bureaucratic environmental politics prevailed, similar in many respects to its Porfirian predecessor. While sometimes promoted by popular groups, this politics was driven by a postrevolutionary elite bent on smothering a more democratic urbanization by means of co-optation and petroleum-centered industrialization.

This environmental and spatially specific lens on the urbanizing basin throws new light on the Cardenista years. Most discussions regarding the limits of cardenismo have revolved around either the negotiations and open conflicts between a progressive "center" and a conservative "periphery" or the "limits of state autonomy" under capitalism. Yet the platform of core Cardenistas harbored its own contradictions once diverse popular classes seized the political moment. Forest communities revealed the exclusionary dimensions of conservationism, the communities of the Xochimilco lakebed confronted the water-drafting imperative, and the city's colonos proletarios and tenants were constrained by the government's agrarian and workplace priorities. The city revealed a great paradox of the revolution: agrarian reform, pro-labor policies, and the nationalization of industry (real and feared) reinforced real estate speculation and exclusive urbanization at a time when working-class residents were demanding the right to the city.

Cardenismo did result in certain gains, but a deeper analysis of specific spaces shows that Lázaro Cárdenas exacerbated postrevolutionary inequalities and furthered the desiccation of the expanding metropolis. He tolerated the paternalistic and elitist underpinnings of the Forestry Department, and although he dissolved the department as a gesture of revolutionism, he failed to replace it with a more inclusive, pro-campesino entity. Cárdenas approved the fertilization of ejido lands in the saline Texcoco bed, but waterscape advocates helped derail the project, denouncing it as hubristic and fundamentally flawed. One might surmise that Cárdenas missed a chance to fuse lake regeneration with revolutionary justice, but he received no assistance from lake conservationists, whose vision of "turn[ing] the spongy saline into a giant Xochimilco . . . with wider, longer, and deeper canals" ignored the concerns of lakeshore populations.[3] It is no wonder that Cárdenas, who fostered forest conservation, roundly rejected its lake counterpart, favoring instead the engineering marvels of agricultural productivism, which coupled well with ejido land claims. Industrial uses of the lakebed were not far behind; Cárdenas earmarked funds to industrialize Texcoco salts at the expense of small-scale peasant production, a plan in sync with the emerging policies of import substitution industrialization in the early 1940s.

Xochimilco lakebed agriculturalists may have been better off at the start of the sexenio than their Texcoco counterparts, but they were largely forsaken as competing agroecological interests precluded the formation of any unified policy on lakebed production. Xochimilco continued to be more important as a source of metropolitan water than a source of food and flowers. City government rhetoric, meanwhile, embraced the rights of the urban poor, but, if anything, rentier and construction-sector capital strengthened during the Cárdenas sexenio, and urban spatial segregation mounted. Cárdenas preferred colonia-specific interventions that facilitated the urban corporatism of the 1940s and deflected more universal challenges to urban capitalism.

One July afternoon in 2008, I sat at a table in the National Agrarian Archive in Mexico City, researching the land disputes between San Juan de Aragón and Remigio Noriega's adjacent hacienda. The building had been noisier than usual that day, but, engrossed in documents, I hardly noticed. At 2:30, with my stomach screaming for lunch, I hurried down the stairs and discovered to my surprise about forty-five men, young and old, some wearing sombreros and others baseball caps, standing in the foyer, blocking access to and from the building. One man explained that the government had refused to pay their ejido for land it had expropriated for public housing over forty years ago. Then, naturally, I asked where they were from, and he replied, "San Juan de Aragón." For better or worse, I decided not to discuss the irony of being trapped by the same community whose conflictive past I had researched that day. After another hour of waiting, an agrarian official agreed to meet with them, and the building emptied.

To understand their protest one must excavate over a century of environmental history. The land for which they had demanded compensation was seasonally underwater in 1880, on the western edge of Lake Texcoco. Drainage and fertilization works dried the land, part of the quest to remake the environment for Mexico's capital. The briny, barren land made manifest the growing rifts between the city and its surroundings, but it also glistened with hope for an agrarian future. The lakebed became the centerpiece of a united elite-popular imaginary of verdant, fertile fields free of dust and next to the largest single market in the country. When the state withdrew support for this and other popular environmental visions, the city began a period of staggering growth. Mexico City reached a population and industrial output that had seemed impossible at the beginning of the century, even as briny soil swept across the deforested hills and the dried Texcoco floor, forcing inhabitants to perpetually wash floors, cars, sidewalks, and clothes.[4] "We bite the fine sand with disgust," the great essayist Alfonso Reyes proclaimed in his eulogy for the lacustrine Basin of Mexico in the late 1940s. "It wants to suffocate us, it wants to strangle us."[5] The dust storms are now a distant memory—mostly eliminated and since overtaken by the pollutants produced by millions of vehicles—but for decades they were part of a package of ecological woes to which urban experts sought answers. They were a constant reminder for virtually all inhabitants, regardless of class, of the injurious environmental consequences of Mexico's development model.

At the dawn of Mexico City's postwar boom, the city engineer Fernando Madrid Mendizábal, from the newly minted Ministry of Hydraulic Resources, wrote a long report on the many hydraulic works that had made Mexico City "habitable."[6] It was a paean to decades of hydraulic engineering: canals, collectors, dams, dikes, aqueducts, pumps, storage tanks, and more. This is what quenched Mexico City's thirst and prevented it from drowning in its own effluents. This is what protected life and property and opened up great expanses of land to development. *Chilangos* (as residents of Mexico City became known in the latter half of the twentieth century) were totally dependent on the proper functioning of a mostly invisible hydraulic infrastructure. Many people, in fact, wanted to be even more closely bound to these technical networks crisscrossing the city. In order to make their communities and homes more livable, they continued to demand more of the expertise and the technics that had defined early twentieth-century urban environmental planning.

Other urban experts, however, thought quite differently about the city's hydraulic engineering and long-term habitability than did the engineer of the

Ministry of Hydraulic Resources or much of the urban public. They espoused a decidedly more ecological vision of the urbanizing basin, one that apprehended the many interdependencies between nature and city. The ideas of this small but important group of engineers and scientists, rather than being diametrically opposed to the traditional sanitary approach to urban governance, were incubated within it. Sanitary engineers in Mexico and elsewhere had "long been taught to recognize limits presented by nature," so many urban experts questioned Mexico City's environmental health as the capital turned into a juggernaut using more and more resources.[7] Concerns about deforestation, desiccation, dust, and land subsidence, first articulated by prominent planners early in the century, such as Luis Careaga, Octavio Dubois, Roberto Gayol, and Miguel Ángel de Quevedo, were echoed by both younger and older urbanists with a more forceful sense of urgency and a more profound understanding of the interconnectedness of built and natural environments. The relation between city and nonhuman nature defied outright control; it was one of mutual constitution and interdependent evolution, not separation.

For decades, indeed for centuries, Mexican scientists, from Juan de Torquemada to the many thinkers influenced by Alexander von Humboldt, had posited some degree of interdependency and interconnectivity between nature and culture. The linchpin of interconnectivity had been forests and their role in the hydrological system, climate, and soil protection. So, in a way, forest conservationists like Quevedo were already ecologically minded. I do not wish to exaggerate the differences between 1930 and the 1960s. But I do contend that midcentury Mexico witnessed a noticeable intellectual change regarding humans' place in nature and a more overt use of the terminology of modern environmentalism. Scientists and urban experts from Gonzalo Blanco Macías and Enrique Beltrán to Guillermo Zárraga and Miguel Rebolledo embraced a more profound ecological thinking that revolved around the quest to restore a broken equilibrium between nature and city. They championed forest conservation but just as adamantly soil and water conservation, and they tended to reject large and conventional sanitary engineering projects. They perceived an urban ecology in crisis, an interconnected set of problems of deforestation, sedimentation, desiccation, dust storms, land subsidence, and overpopulation that was in large part the product of past planning errors. They condemned the long-standing extract-and-expel (or draft-and-drain) water policy, warned of humans "going against nature," and feared that deforestation, erosion, and water loss would lead to the desertification of the Basin of Mexico. By the 1960s and early 1970s, even Pablo Bistraín and Eduardo

Chávez, stalwart defenders of orthodox sanitary planning and large-scale hydroelectric and irrigation dams, were publicly advocating the return to a city of lakes. Once deemed a threat, the old lake was more and more conceived as a victim of deforestation and a misguided drainage philosophy.

Mexico City seemed headed toward catastrophe, but it was, for this influential group, also a space where ecology might join forces with engineering to rework Mexico City once again—this time to create not the sanitary city but the ecological city. The city they had in mind, however, was a homogenized entity, a place of harmonious political and economic interests that, if properly directed by environmental expertise, could continue the march of progress. This was a mirror image of the PRI's portrayal of the capital and, indeed, of the PRI's own role in Mexican politics.[8] It was also indicative of a more general political shift in which experts would direct urbanization unshackled by bottom-up pressures. Mexican urban experts and scientists acquired a more comprehensive knowledge of ecological interconnection just as revolutionary populism's moment was fading. Despite the lofty ecological rhetoric of top government officials from the 1950s onward, official interest in reforming the unequal developmental goals of import substitution industrialization was low. Their solutions were technical—only experts could implement them—and in this respect these planners did not differ much from their predecessors. But they lost many of the politically progressive aims that had pervaded the minds of earlier planners such as Hannes Meyer, Gabriel Oropesa, and Fernando Beltrán y Puga.

By the 1950s the draft-and-drain infrastructure that Madrid Mendizábal extolled included an updated and expanded version of Gayol's sewer system. New collectors and sewer lines reached into the vast suburbs, several wide drainage canals emptied into the original Porfirian canal, riverbeds were covered with cement and turned into freeways, and a vast network of deep wells and pipelines distributed water to over two million residents. The most remarkable midcentury hydraulic addition was the Lerma River water system, completed in 1951. A flourish of Mexican engineering, the system was designed to offset the alarming subsidence of the ground under Mexico City, caused by an overreliance on the aquifer.[9] Subsidence had reached forty-five centimeters per year in some areas, and downtown Mexico City, three meters above Lake Texcoco in 1900, was over a meter below it at midcentury owing to sinking soil underneath the city center and lakebed sedimentation. As the first city water service to pump the liquid from one watershed to another, the Lerma system expended a huge amount of energy. It also extended socio-environmental degradation outside the Basin of Mexico to communities around the river. Regardless, the Lerma system only slowed subsidence; population growth ensured that deep wells would continue to take water from the aquifer, causing the volcanic and unstable lakebed soil to compress and the ground to sink unevenly. Subsidence intensified flooding in low-lying areas and damaged buildings, sewage collectors, and, more ominously, water piping. Historically, as much as 40 percent of the city's water has been lost to leaks, and the solution has been more drafting—a worrisome positive feedback loop. As subsidence reared its ugly head, the drainage infrastructure and a flailing fertilization project brought on the implacable dust bowl.

The devastating summer floods of 1950 and 1951 and the ongoing dust storms of late winter and early spring exemplified Mexico City's extreme— even paradoxical—condition. Downtown streets remained flooded for weeks at a time, invoking the Mexico City of the nineteenth century or, according to *El Universal*, "Tenochtitlan, surrounded by water on all sides . . . with canoes, oarsmen and all the rest."[10] Just a few months later, schoolchildren would return home from school covered in dust (see figures C.2 and C.3). This was the material environmental reality that served to legitimize and bolster ecological thought. Ecological ideas received an additional push from the Pan-American dialogues after 1940 and their reverberations within a transnational scientific community.

Several scientists from the United States traveled through Mexico City during and after World War II and contemplated the relationships among population, overconsumption, and environmental crisis. A central figure was William Vogt, an ornithologist and a friend of the conservationist Aldo Leopold. Vogt spent several years studying guano bird populations in Peru during the late 1930s, where he fused the new science of ecology with Malthusian population theory, and then followed that up with several years touring Latin American countries and studying their environmental challenges.[11] He had a long stint in Mexico City in 1943, during which he associated with Enrique Beltrán (they cohosted a popular radio broadcast on conservation) and the equally influential agronomist and hydraulic engineer Gonzalo Blanco Macías. During his stay, he published *El hombre y la tierra*, a forerunner to his best seller *The Road to Survival* (1948), a neo-Malthusian environmentalist manifesto that linked irrational production to overconsumption and stressed ecological limits, the balance of nature, and conservation of water, soil, and forests.[12] The renowned ecologist Paul Sears, whose seminal *Deserts on the March* (1935) had attempted to explain the Dust Bowl in terms of an imbalance between

FIGURE C.2 — Rodrigo Moya, *Dust Storm*, Mexico City, 1958. COURTESY OF THE ARCHIVO FOTOGRÁFICO RODRIGO MOYA.

FIGURE C.3 — Mexico City flood, 1951. COURTESY OF AGN: ENRIQUE DÍAZ 97/4.

nature and culture, spent a few months in Mexico City just a couple of years after Vogt's departure, studying the relationship between sedimentation and climate in the dried Texcoco lakebed. His time in Mexico helped form his prediction of widespread global desertification if people refused to live by ecological principles. Former secretary of state and president of the Mexican Society for Geography and Statistics Juan de Díos Bojórquez invoked Sears in stating that only water and trees would save the city from "this uncontainable march to the desert."[13] Díos Bojórquez warned against "going against nature" and called the desiccation of the lakes and the attempts to fertilize their lands "a capital error."[14] Tom Gill, another celebrated environmentalist who spent time in Mexico, helped Beltrán y Puga fund his Mexican Institute of Renewable Natural Resources. Enrique Beltrán went on to publish *El hombre y su ambiente*, a thorough interpretation of the Basin of Mexico's ecological imbalance, evocative of Vogt's earlier *El hombre y la tierra*. Gill, who had worked with Gifford Pinchot and at the United Nations Food and Agricultural Association, later published *Land Hunger in Mexico*, his chief contribution to postwar environmentalism.[15]

Beltrán and Blanco Macías, in particular, led the charge for a more ecological approach. They decried the basin's "ecological disequilibrium," bemoaned the "destruction of natural resources," and pined for a more ecologically balanced city replete with forests, lakes, and canals.[16] In 1948 Vogt organized the Pan-American Union's Conservation Congress, along with Leopold, whose excursions into mountainous northern Mexico helped spawn his famous "land ethic." At the conference, held in Denver, Blanco Macías explained Mexico City's predicament to scientists from around the world: "In view of all the evident and catastrophic effects of deforestation, soil misuse, of the opening of the [Grand] Canal, of poor use of the land, and of the excessive extraction of underground water, it seems inexplicable their origin has not yet been identified with the ecological imbalance of the watershed that began with the 16th century; and that instead of correcting original mistakes, deforestation continues with an accompanying tenacious insistence on the drilling of wells."[17] Blanco Macías envisioned a sophisticated water-treatment and purification system to replenish Mexico City's aquifer, provide irrigation, and fill the former lakebeds, thus preventing "the dust storms that cause so much discomfort and disease among the city's inhabitants, and [helping] reestablish fish populations and other aquatic fauna."[18] Three years later, Blanco Macías went on to found Amigos de la Tierra (Friends of the Earth), an organization dedicated to advancing the cause of soil conservation and the veneration of nature.

Three distinguished urban designers joined the midcentury discussion. Miguel Rebolledo, the architect of several prominent buildings in the city center, rebuked the entrenched draft-and-drain policies by offering one simple command to resolve flooding, dust storms, and water shortages: "not one drop of water out of the valley, not one deep well working."[19] Guillermo Zárraga, who had played a key role in the creation of Ex Hipódromo de Peralvillo, by midcentury was turning his eye to the city's threatened environment. He most cogently captured the tenor of a budding urban ecological thought: "The different issues that constitute the problem of the Valley of Mexico are interconnected in such a way that one cannot refer to one of them without alluding to the rest. Water and subsidence, for example, are intimately united, just as water and sewerage are and the latter to flooding. Deforestation, erosion, and dust storms are other threads of the same warp." This urban ecological crisis arose, Zárraga wrote, from uncontrollable population growth—a nod to postwar Malthusian environmentalism—and the "accumulation of past engineering errors."[20] Zárraga held that flooding, deforestation, dust storms, water waste, and subsidence were tied together in a vicious circle. Under the pseudonym Diego Cañedo, he took the findings of his articles to an apocalyptic conclusion, in which the poorly planned, cancerous megalopolis scourged with migrants (and homosexual deviants) would fall victim to the "gran planificador" (the great planner), the Popocatépetl volcano, whose violent eruption would destroy the city.[21] Zárraga, like most ecologically minded urbanists, wedded environmentalism to social control and stigmatization. Another urbanist, Alberto T. Arai, a founder of the Union of Socialist Architects, did not express the same contempt for the city's populace. He did, however, abandon the class analysis of his earlier worker city. Even so, his proposal was the most radical of all: the sunken historic center would be converted into a historic garden-park while much of the population would be moved to one of five smaller urban centers rimming a revitalized Lake Texcoco, which would serve as "the principal center of interest for the region, like the bays of Rio de Janeiro and San Francisco are today."[22]

In June 1951, with the city bracing itself for another flood season, Miguel Alemán created the Hydrological Commission of the Basin of Mexico, the first government organization to approach the city's vast hydraulic system in an integrated fashion.[23] The commission conceived of the city's hydrological problems as necessarily interdependent. The restoration of the basin's disrupted "hydrological balance" was paramount, and the commission's engineers called for several projects that challenged the status quo, including the construction of wells through which treated water would be injected into the aquifer to check subsidence and prevent flooding—a plan that was assiduously pursued in 1952, albeit with little success. In 1953 the engineers called for a ban on new wells, as well as the retention and conservation of water for reuse in agriculture and reforestation to regenerate lost soils, reduce sedimentation of dams and lakebeds, and conserve springs.[24] The commission unlocked debate over ecological proposals, some of which became official policy, and invited scientists such as Beltrán to discuss the problems of the basin. Still, most commission members shunned lake recuperation. Adolfo Orive Alba, for example, mocked the myriad proposals of "engineer ecologists."[25]

Despite the political conservatism of much ecological thinking, it had quite radical implications for urban environmental planning. Blanco Macías, Arai, and others threatened to lay waste to the engineering investments based on which a host of political and social interests flourished. Government positions and private-sector engineering contracts relied on the continual maintenance and extension of hydraulic infrastructure. And the bigger the project to be constructed, the bigger the payoff. Experts battled over the types of knowledge that the government would value most, and those attached to state agencies tended to argue for the fundamental correctness of current hydraulic policy and merely tweak it around the edges rather than explode decades of expertise and investments that might drive a dagger through the whole development model. In short, Mexico City was a living example of path dependency—defined loosely as sticking with current planning practices even when better alternatives may exist. It is no surprise, then, that the hydrological commission advised the completion of the second drainage tunnel (to replace the original one from the Porfiriato) and oversaw the repair of collectors and sewer pipes. The commission also recommended the continuation of Texcoco reclamation for agriculture and studied additional water sources outside the Basin of Mexico, beyond the Lerma watershed.

The architect Mauricio Gómez Mayorga gave an environmental twist to Mexico City's path dependency. He considered the mammoth deep drainage project, then under construction to supplement and ultimately replace the Porfirian drainage, to be a necessary evil, required because the sedimentation of the lakebeds and the land subsidence in the city made the "hydrological ideal" of restoring the lost lakes impracticable.[26] Furthermore, flood control and desiccation had freed new lands for millions of settlers—Ciudad Nezahualcóyotl and Ecatepec were two prime examples—and these sprawling settlements depended on the existing drainage infrastructure.[27] Mexico City, according to Gómez Mayorga, could never return to its lacustrine past, an idea he shared with Quevedo. Such were the restrictions on the city's environmental planners. The commission's agenda therefore comprised a heavy dose of the old sanitary ideal with a small portion of the new ecological ideal, an ambivalent policy that typified environmental planning after 1950.

Big engineering continued to underlie techno-bureaucratic governance. In the late 1960s, construction of the deep drainage system, comprising "the world's longest tunnel," commenced. The system represented a retrenchment into conventional engineering, but there were powerful detractors as well.[28] The former minister of hydraulic resources, Eduardo Chávez, venerated for his earlier work damming the Papaloapan Basin, lambasted the "expelling fury" of city engineering and called for an immediate halt to the "absurd" works.[29] The about-face of the influential Chávez was a testament to Lake Texcoco's role in pushing forward ecological planning ideas.

Nabor Carrillo, a rising star in soil science and hydraulic engineering, helped turn ideas into government-sponsored action. In 1965 Carrillo convinced president Gustavo Díaz Ordaz to finance studies of his proposals for the remaining Texcoco federal lands, which Carrillo hoped would end the dust storms, forestall flooding, and conserve valuable water. Perhaps the first scientist to definitively prove subsidence was caused by water extraction—he followed up his study of the basin with another of subsidence in Long Beach, California—Carrillo aimed to re-create a large portion of the lake with treated urban wastewater.[30] To avoid the flooding that Quevedo and Gómez Mayorga feared, Carrillo proposed to pump water from underneath the lake to sink the lakebed, create an artificial reservoir, and alleviate many of the most serious environmental problems by recycling wastewater.[31]

Carrillo's project promised to solve environmental woes without undoing years of megaprojects, and it was not derailed by his untimely death. The project did, however, sound the death knell for agricultural experimentation in the lakebed, which had cost the government over 14 million pesos between 1912 and 1946. Since the project's inception in 1971, Project Texcoco engineers have achieved the afforestation of a significant portion of the saline bed, built dams and diversion canals to control and conserve water, and reforested surrounding hillsides. The original reforestation plan barred local terrace farming techniques, but campesino protest convinced project officials to integrate such community practices alongside the reforestation effort.[32] Later, in the early 1980s, engineers renewed a portion of the old lake, although the surface area remains minuscule in comparison to the original plan. Lake Nabor Carrillo

FIGURE C.4 — Lake Nabor Carrillo, 2008. PHOTO BY AUTHOR.

and three other artificial lakes, all smaller than Carrillo had intended, now cover over three thousand hectares of the lakebed with treated wastewater.[33] (See figure C.4.) The project curtailed the mighty dust storms, but some two hundred tons of dust still fall on the city daily, mainly on working-class settlements.[34]

As the metropolis of five million turned into the megalopolis of fifteen million, ecological planning became an integral part of urban discourse, if seldom of actual governance.[35] In 1989, amid Mexico's market-friendly and privatizing neoliberal reforms, and two years following the UNESCO's designation of Xochimilco as a world heritage site, president Carlos Salinas de Gortari (1988–1994), along with the Federal District's governor Manuel Camacho Solís, planned to expropriate 257 hectares of the San Gregorio Atlapulco ejido and 780 of the Xochimilco ejido in the name of "ecological balance." Echoing similar work done in Texcoco, the Lake Xochimilco Rescue Plan aimed to rejuvenate the lake and canals, treat water for reuse, and install "regulation ponds" to curb flooding. This was more ecological façade than anything else, obscuring the plan's neoliberal impulse. The city government also planned the extension of the Periférico highway, Mexico City's not-quite-circular freeway, as well as opening the northern section of Xochimilco to high-rises and building an exclusive theme park replete with private clubs, golf courses, and hotels.

Ejidatarios, chinamperos (then 5 percent of the local population), academics, environmental groups, and other popular organizations challenged this "rescue." Protesters rallied around Xochimilco's indigenous and revolutionary identity. This was an identity that obtained its force, in part, through chinampería, the agricultural practice that years of desiccation had forced the ejidatarios to abandon. Placards at one protest rally read "History is not sold," a reference to an "ethic of place" in which the ejido embodied the triumph of the revolution and the persistence of local agriculture, especially the mythologized chinampería.[36] The alliance proved formidable. Camacho Solís reduced the area of the proposed lake from 360 to 52 hectares and offered ejidatarios 230 hectares of irrigated farmland outside the theme park. Although tourism remained a central objective, the revised plan stressed making more affordable activities available in the park. These concessions divided the movement. One organization continued the fight, calling attention to the persistent problems locals faced: contaminated and dwindling canal water (which they claimed was siphoned off for the tourist zone), the disproportional effects of subsidence in the well-heavy lakebed, and urbanization pressures.[37] Undoubtedly, the Xochimilco rescue was more accountable to local populations than its Texcoco counterpart—where one still needs special permission to enter the grounds. The environmental technocracy was robust, but it could not always keep local populations in check.

Even as path dependency encouraged adhering to the status quo, ecological planning figured prominently at the end of the twentieth century, forged through the dynamic interplay between planners' varying responses to a threatened urban environment and global scientific trends following World War II. Urban experts ascertained the interdependencies of nature and human artifice and in the process carved out a technocratic urban environmentalism amenable to capital accumulation. Mexico City's official environmentalism matured within a top-heavy PRI development plan in which, as in its Porfirian conservationist predecessor, environmental protection often equaled social control and marginalization. Instances when squatter settlements have been razed to protect forests while luxury suburbs were left intact are another case in point.[38]

This story about the making of an expert-led environmentalism may not be so unique to Mexico City. Environmental ideas have traversed national boundaries and penetrated other megacities, where planners, engineers, and scientists, embedded within power-laden urban structures and, more recently, neoliberal governance, encounter both conditions universal to the modern urban experience—chaotic development, population booms, polluting effluents, and the squandering of resources—and other conditions specific to city, region, and nation. Moreover, throughout the Global South, environmentalism has tended to bifurcate along two lines: the environmentalism of the poor and bourgeois environmentalism. Around the latter, scientific experts, environmental nongovernmental organizations, the affluent, and corporate capital have come together to beautify urban spaces, arrest environmental decline, and diversify consumption and recreation options with the objective of achieving sustainability and enhancing their city's position in a competitive global economy. Their efforts, however, have often neglected urban working-class communities in ways that parallel the consequences of recent restoration projects in Mexico City.[39] This framing of the rise of environmentalism within urban ecologies and a global intellectual and political-economic milieu also contributes to scholarship that resituates its provenance, not as a reflexive reaction against urbanization but as a set of ideas that incubated within urbanism and developmentalism.[40]

Many chilangos have now pinned their hopes for a sustainable Mexico City on the water-nostalgic plans of architects Alberto Kalach and Teodoro González de León or the latest proposal by Iñaki Echeverría to reconnect Mexico City with its lacustrine past in a more profound way than Carrillo ever imagined. Kalach has promoted land development along a revived Texcoco lakeshore for almost two decades, while Echeverría is now calling for an enormous urban wetland park crisscrossed by biking trails. As admirable as these plans seem on paper, they would require a massive reform in urban land speculation and democratic accountability—yet Kalach has called for expert commissions along the lines of those during the Porfiriato. Absent this, the plans would impose, not new urban utopias, but more likely, in the words of Mike Davis and Daniel Monk, "evil paradises" that, in rejuvenating lost spaces, reproduce the inequalities that preceded them.[41] Such an undertaking would likely displace hundreds of thousands of working-class residents in the vast eastern settlements to make room for commercial and residential development drawn to the rejuvenated public space and waterfront. Neither are these fresh proposals; Manuel Balbontín had a similar idea in the 1870s, as did Arai in 1950, at moments when the city was much more scalable and eastern settlement sparse.

A new layer of history will soon be added to Lake Texcoco, joining the alkali soil sediment, the drainage infrastructure, the failed fertilization schemes, the colonias proletarias, and Project Texcoco. In 2015 ground was broken on the eastern flank of the dried lakebed for the ultramodern $9 billion international airport. Between 2002 and 2006, the residents of San Salvador Atenco had managed, not without struggle and the spilling of blood, to defeat an earlier plan for an airport on their ejido. This time, the call to capitalize on the mostly barren federal lakebed has been too strong for them to weather, and a new era of development potentially more transformative than all preceding eras awaits Mexico City's eastern margins.

One might conclude that it is too late to salvage Mexico City from social and environmental ruin, and that deurbanization is the only recourse. Time, it would seem, has run out. As David Harvey puts it, cities "become more and more fixed with time, more and more sclerotic, precisely because of the way they incrementally add things on rather than totally shedding their skins."[42] But deurbanization is ultimately misguided. Mexico City, like other megacities, could use a descaling, but the solution to environmental crisis does not lie in an escape from the urban. The repurposing and reworking of cities must be at the heart of any social justice and sustainability project. As for Mexico City, which has its unique challenges, the odds are long, but perhaps all is not lost. The city's most recent environmentalist architects, engineers, and planners have been well-meaning, working to shape mentalities and promote water recycling, river regeneration, and lake revival.[43] This kind of incremental change is necessary, but it must also be fixed to a progressive political project and a class critique of urbanization and the ever-expanding resource hinterlands with which it is bound.[44]

Too often, environmental sustainability, similar to its sanitary forebear, has been packaged with social control and the refortification of power. What is missing is an ecological critique that integrates the social, a political ecology that lays bare the interactions, dependencies, and relations among unequal groups and classes and the ways in which those inequalities are reflected in and entrenched in material environments. The built environment, as an expression of state making, capitalist growth, and environmental philosophies, constitutes a set of barriers to social justice, but the city also contains within it past struggles that have left imprints on landscapes and in collective memory.[45] These imprints harbor alternative worlds. My hope is that this book offers some ideas as to how urban expertise might coalesce with and enable popular empowerment to create a more environmentally just Mexico City.

NOTES

INTRODUCTION

1 See Adriana Zavala, "Mexico City in Juan O'Gorman's Imagination," *Hispanic Research Journal* 8, no. 5 (December 2007): 491–506.

2 Ana Isabel Pérez Gavilán, "Chávez Morado, destructor de mitos: Silencios y aniquilaciones de la ciudad (1949)," *Anales del Instituto de Investigaciones Estéticas* 87 (2005): 83–89.

3 Arturo Sotomayor, *La metrópoli mexicana y su agonía* (Mexico City: UNAM, 1973).

4 Octavio Paz, "Return to the Labyrinth of Solitude," in *The Labyrinth of Solitude*, trans. Lysander Kemp (New York: Grove, 1985), 344.

5 Jorge Ibargüengoitia, "Call the Doctor," in *The Mexico City Reader*, ed. Rubén Gallo and Lorna Scott Fox (Madison: University of Wisconsin Press, 2004), 195–196.

6 Carlos Monsiváis, "Identity Hour," in *The Mexico Reader: History, Culture, Politics* (Durham, NC: Duke University Press, 2002), 616. See also Carlos Monsiváis, *Apocalipstick* (Mexico City: Debate, 2009), 19–21.

7 I will generally use the term *Basin of Mexico*, rather than *Valley of Mexico*, to better represent the geographical features of the area of study.

8 G. F. Lyon, *Residencia en México, 1826: Diario de una gira con estancia en la República de México* (Mexico City: FCE, 1984), 200.

9 Carl Christian Becher, *Cartas sobre México: La República Mexicana durante los años decisivos de 1832-3* (Mexico City: UNAM, 1959), 77–79. See also Fanny Calderón de la Barca, *La vida en México* (Mexico City: Porrúa, 1979), 37–38.

10 Brantz Mayer, *México: lo que fue y lo que es*, trans. Francisco Delpiane (Mexico City: FCE, 1953), 53–56.

11 Ramón I. Alcázar, *Poesias de Ramón I. Alcázar* (Mexico City: Imprenta de I. Cumplido, 1860), 96–98.

12 Antonio García Cubas, *Cuadro geográfico, estadístico, descriptivo e histórico de los Estados Unidos Mexicanos* (Mexico City: Secretaría de Fomento, 1885), 234;

Geografía e historia del Distrito Federal (Mexico City: Murguía, 1892), 44–75. For an environmental angle on Velasco, see Jorge Cañizares Esguerra, *Nature, Empire, and Nation: Explorations of the History of Science in the Iberian World* (Stanford, CA: Stanford University Press, 2006); Peter Kreiger, ed., *Transformaciones del paisaje urbano en México: Representación y registro visual* (Mexico City: MUNAL, 2012).

13 See Alexander von Humboldt, *Ensayo político sobre el Reino de la Nueva España* (Mexico City: Porrúa, 1984), 369–370; Calderón de la Barca, *Vida en México*, 371.

14 William Denevan, "The Pristine Myth: The Landscape of the Americas in 1492," *Annals of the Association of American Geographers* 82, no. 3 (September 1992): 369–386; Ángel Palerm, *Obras hidráulicas prehispánicas en el sistema lacustre del valle de México* (Mexico: INAH, 1973); J. A. Poumarede, *Desagüe del valle de México* (Mexico: Imprenta de I Cumplido, 1860), 23; William T. Sanders, Jeffrey R. Parsons, and Robert S. Santley, *The Basin of Mexico: Ecological Processes in the Evolution of a Civilization* (New York: Academic Press, 1979), 284; Vera Candiani, *Dreaming of Dry Land: Environmental Transformation in Colonial Mexico City* (Stanford, CA: Stanford University Press, 2014).

15 Jesús Galindo y Villa, *Historia sumaria de la ciudad de México* (Mexico City: Editorial Cultura, 1925), 209.

16 Galindo y Villa, *Historia sumaria*, 210.

17 *Metropolitan environment* is an adaptation of *metropolitan nature*, explained by Matthew Gandy, *Concrete and Clay: Reworking Nature in New York City* (Cambridge, MA: MIT Press, 2002), 2; Stéphane Castonguay and Michèle Dagenais, introduction to *Metropolitan Natures: Environmental Histories of Montreal*, ed. Stéphane Castonguay and Michèle Dagenais (Pittsburgh: University of Pittsburgh Press, 2011), 1.

18 Henri Lefebvre, *The Urban Revolution*, trans. Robert Bononno (Minneapolis: University of Minnesota Press, 2003).

19 Lewis Mumford, quoted in Andrew C. Isenberg, "New Directions in Urban Environmental History," in *The Nature of Cities: Culture, Landscape, and Urban Space*, ed. Andrew C. Isenberg (Rochester, NY: University of Rochester Press, 2006), xii.

20 Manuel Orozco y Berra, *Memoria para la carta hidrográfica pare el valle de México*, ed. Manuel Orozco y Berra (Mexico City: A. Boix, 1864), 143.

21 Roberto Gayol, *Proyecto de desagüe y saneamiento para la ciudad de México* (Mexico City: Fomento, 1892), 31.

22 Orozco y Berra, *Memoria*, 108–115; Antonio Peñafiel, *Memoria sobre las aguas potables de la capital de México* (Mexico City: Secretaría de Fomento, 1884), 129; Leopoldo Río de la Loza, "Un vistazo al lago de Tetzcoco: Su influencia en la salubridad de México," in Orozco y Berra, *Memoria*, 179.

23 Peñafiel, *Memoria*, 129.

24 Quoted in Moíses González Navarro, "México en una laguna," *Historia Mexicana* 4 (1955): 507.

25 Peñafiel, *Memoria*, 23–24; Luis Salazar, "On the Distribution of Water in the City of Mexico," trans. Alfred Sears, *Transactions of the American Society of Civil Engineers* 3, no. 1 (1892): 336–338.

26 José Lorenzo Cossio, "Las aguas de la ciudad," *Boletín de la Sociedad Mexicana de Geografía y Estadística* 45 (1935–1937): 40.

27 Cossio, "Aguas de la ciudad," 40; Ariel Rodríguez Kuri, "Gobierno local y empresas de servicios: La experiencia de la ciudad de México durante el Porfiriato," in *Ferrocarriles y obras públicas*, ed. Priscilla Connolly and Sandra Kuntz Ficker (Mexico City: Instituto Mora, 1999), 172; Alain Musset, *El agua en el valle de México, siglos XVI–XXVIII* (Mexico City: Pórtico de la ciudad de México, 1992), 87.

28 See José Lorenzo Cossio, *Guía retrospectiva de la ciudad de México*, 2nd ed. (Mexico City: Segumex, 1990), 139. The number of public fountains is from 1887. See Archivo Histórico del Distrito Federal (AHDF): Ayuntamiento, Aguas, Fuentes Públicas, 59/143, "Informe de la Comisión de Agua," April 19, 1887.

29 Angus Wright, *The Death of Ramón González: The Modern Agricultural Dilemma* (Austin: University of Texas Press, 2005), 159.

30 María Eugenia Terrones López, "La ciudad de México y su hinterland: El círculo virtuoso," in *Problemas de la urbanización en el valle de México, 1810–1910*, ed. Mario Barbosa and Salomon González (Mexico: UAM-Cuajimalpa, 2009), 94.

31 Orozco y Berra, *Memoria*, 149.

32 Terrones López, "Ciudad de México," 107; Richard Conway, "Lakes, Canoes, and the Aquatic Communities of Xochimilco and Chalco, New Spain," *Ethnohistory* 59, no. 3 (summer 2012): 547.

33 Ignacio Pozo, *Informe sobre el ramo de aguas presentado al ayuntamiento de 1887* (Mexico City: Ireneo Paz, 1888), 7–14; AHDF: Ayuntamiento, Aguas, Desierto de los Leones and Santa Fe, 53, 22, "Dictamen del Ayuntamiento de Santa Fe," May 21, 1880; AHDF: Ayuntamiento, Aguas, Cuajimalpa, 50, 25, "Guardamontes to Comisión de Agua," March 1, 1874.

34 For a similar perspective, see Claudia Agostoni, *Monuments of Progress: Modernization and Public Health in Mexico City, 1876–1910* (Calgary: University of Calgary Press, 2003), 41.

35 See Mark D. Szuchman, "The City as Vision: The Development of Urban Cultures in Latin America," in *I Saw a City Invincible: Urban Portraits of Latin America* (Wilmington, DE: Scholarly Resources, 1996), 1–32; Eric Zolov, "Notas sobre la capital en su contribución hegemónica," in *Los últimos cien años, los próximos cien . . .* , ed. Ariel Rodríguez Kuri and Sergio Tamayo Flores Alatorre (Mexico City: UAM, 2004), 111–126. There were certain conservative elements that idealized country living and vilified city life. Politician and writer Federico Gamboa best illustrated this take on Porfirian Mexico in his popular novel *Santa*. Gamboa, *Santa: A Novel of Mexico City*, trans. John Charles Chasteen (Chapel Hill: University of North Carolina Press, 2010).

36 For the purpose, design, and construction of sanitary infrastructure in U.S. cities, see Martin M. Melosi, *The Sanitary City: Urban Infrastructure in America from the Colony to the Present* (Baltimore: Johns Hopkins University Press, 2000).

37 For Mexico, see, among others, Pablo Piccato, *City of Suspects: Crime in Mexico City, 1900–1931* (Durham, NC: Duke University Press, 2001); Katherine Bliss, *Compromised Positions: Prostitution, Public Health, and Gender Politics in Revolutionary Mexico City* (University Park, PA: Penn State University Press, 2001); John Lear, *Workers, Neighbors, and Citizens: The Revolution in Mexico City* (Lincoln: University of Nebraska Press, 2001); Andrew Grant Wood, *Revolution in the Street: Women, Workers, and Urban Protest in Veracruz, 1870–1927* (Wilmington, DE: SR Books, 2001); Michael Snodgrass, *Deference and Defiance in Monterrey: Workers, Paternalism and Revolution in Mexico, 1890–1950* (Cambridge: Cambridge University Press, 2003); Ariel Rodríguez Kuri, *Historia del desasosiego: La revolución en la ciudad de México* (Mexico City: Colegio de México, 2010); María Dolores Lorenzo Río, *El estado como benefactor: Los pobres y la asistencia pública en la ciudad de México, 1877–1905* (Mexico City: Colegio de México, 2011). For the rest of Latin America, see, for example, Ernesto Capello, *City at the Center of the World: Space, History, and Modernity in Quito* (Pittsburgh: University of Pittsburgh Press, 2011); Brodwyn Fischer, *A Poverty of Rights: Citizenship and Inequality in Twentieth-Century Rio de Janeiro* (Stanford, CA: Stanford University Press, 2008); Silvia Arrom and Servando Ortol, eds., *Riots in the Cities: Popular Politics and the Urban Poor in Latin America, 1765–1910* (Wilmington, DE: Scholarly Resources, 1996); Germán Mejía Pavony, *Los años del cambio: Historia urbana de Bogotá, 1820–1910* (Bogotá: Universidad Javeriana, 2000).

38 See Manuel Perló Cohen, *El paradigma porfiriano: Historia del desagüe del valle de México* (Mexico City: Porrúa, 1999); Agostoni, *Monuments of Progress*; Lise Sedrez, "The Bay of All Beauties: State and Environment in Guanabara Bay, Rio de Janeiro, Brazil, 1875–1975" (PhD diss., Stanford University, 2004); Germán Palacio Castañeda, ed., *Historia ambiental de Bogotá y la Sábana, 1850–2005* (Bogotá: Universidad Nacional de Colombia, 2008).

39 Mark Healey, *The Ruins of the New Argentina: Peronism and the Remaking of San Juan after the 1944 Earthquake* (Durham, NC: Duke University Press, 2011); Patrice Olsen, *Artifacts of Revolution: Architecture, Society and Politics in Mexico City, 1920–1940* (Lanham, MD: Rowman and Littlefield, 2008).

40 Chris Otter, "Locating Matter: The Place of Materiality in Urban History," in *Material Powers: Cultural Studies, History and the Material Turn*, ed. Tony Bennett and Patrick Joyce (New York: Routledge, 2010). For another important theoretical exegesis on the materiality of urban life, see Ellen Stroud, "Does Nature Always Matter? Following Dirt through History," *History and Theory* 42, no. 4 (2003): 75–81.

41 See Marina Alberti, *Advances in Urban Ecology: Integrating Humans and Ecological Processes* (Boston: Springer Science, 2008); Ingrid Leman-Stefanovic and Stephen B. Scharper, eds., *The Natural City: Re-envisioning the Built Environment*

(Toronto: University of Toronto Press, 2012); Jared Orsi, *Hazardous Metropolis: Flooding and Urban Ecology in Los Angeles* (Berkeley: University of California Press, 2004); Anna Zimmer, "Urban Political Ecology: Theoretical Concepts, Challenges, and Suggested Future Directions," *Erdkunde* 64, no. 4 (October–December 2010): 343–354; Gandy, *Concrete and Clay*; Nik Heynen, Maria Kaika, and Erik Swyngedouw, eds., *In the Nature of Cities: Urban Political Ecology and the Politics of Urban Metabolism* (London: Routledge, 2006); Matthew Klingle, *Emerald City: An Environmental History of Seattle* (New Haven, CT: Yale University Press, 2007).

42 Hillary Angelo and David Wachsmuth, "Urbanizing Urban Political Ecology: A Critique of Methodological Cityism," in *Implosions/Explosions: Towards a Study of Planetary Urbanization*, ed. Neil Brenner (Berlin: Jovis, 2014), 372–385.

43 For the founding text of socionatural hybridity, see Bruno Latour, *We Have Never Been Modern* (Cambridge, MA: Harvard University Press, 1993). Recent works by Erik Swyngedouw, Nik Heynen, and other urban political ecologists have politicized the notion of hybridity along Marxist lines. A key text on hybridity within environmental historiography is Richard White, "From Wilderness to Hybrid Landscapes: The Cultural Turn in Environmental History," *Historian* 66, no. 3 (2004): 557–564.

44 Several environmental historians have dissected city-hinterland relationships. See, for example, Ellen Stroud, *Nature Next Door: Cities and Trees in the American Northeast* (Seattle: University of Washington Press, 2012); Karl Appuhn, "Friend or Flood? The Dilemmas of Water Management in Early Modern Venice," in *The Nature of Cities*, 79–102; Andrew C. Isenberg, "Banking on Sacramento: Urban Development, Flood Control and Political Legitimization, 1848–1862," in *The Nature of Cities*, 103–121; Castonguay and Dagenais, *Metropolitan Natures*; William Francis Deverell and Greg Hise, eds., *Land of Sunshine: An Environmental History of Metropolitan Los Angeles* (Pittsburgh: University of Pittsburgh Press, 2005); Andrew Needham, *Power Lines: Phoenix and the Making of the Modern Southwest* (Princeton, NJ: Princeton University Press, 2014); Andrew Needham and Allen Dieterich-Ward, "Beyond the Metropolis: Metropolitan Growth and Regional Transformation in Postwar America," *Journal of Urban History* 35, no. 7 (2009): 944–969. These works took up William Cronon's earlier assertion about Chicago that the urban and the rural "created each other [and] transformed each other's environments." Cronon, *Nature's Metropolis: Chicago and the Great West* (New York: W. W. Norton, 1991), 384.

45 In my analysis of and conclusions regarding postrevolutionary state formation, I borrow from the neopopulist school of thought on the Mexican Revolution. The classic text is Gilbert M. Joseph and Daniel Nugent, eds., *Everyday Forms of State Formation: Revolution and the Negotiation of Rule in Modern Mexico* (Durham, NC: Duke University Press, 1994).

46 Peter Vandergeest and Nancy Lee Peluso, "Territorialization and State Power in Thailand," *Theory and Society* 24, no. 3 (June 1995): 388.

47 For the importance of material nature to state formation in relation to forest management, see Karl Appuhn, "Inventing Nature: Forests, Forestry, and State Power in Renaissance Venice," *Journal of Modern History* 72, no. 4 (2000): 861–889.

48 On the question of the state system and the ways legitimacy is obtained through sanction and affirmation, see Philip Abrams, "Notes on the Difficulty of Studying the State," *Journal of Historical Sociology* 1, no. 1 (March 1988): 58–89; Goran Therborn, *The Ideology of Power and the Power of Ideology* (London: Verso, 1999). There is a growing list of works that engage the environmental history of the Mexican Revolution, although rarely through the lens of urbanization. See Christopher R. Boyer and Emily Wakild, "Social Landscaping in the Forests of Mexico: An Environmental Interpretation of Cardenismo, 1934–1940," *Hispanic American Historical Review* 92, no. 1 (February 2012): 73–106; Alejandro Tortolero Villaseñor, "Water and Revolution in Morelos, 1850–1915," in *A Land between Waters: Environmental Histories of Modern Mexico*, ed. Christopher R. Boyer (Tucson: University of Arizona Press, 2012), 124–149; Luis Aboites Aguilar, *El agua de la nación: Una historia política de México (1888–1946)* (Mexico City: Centro de Investigaciones y Estudios Superiores en Antropologia Social, 1998); Myrna Santiago, *The Ecology of Oil: Environment, Labor, and the Mexican Revolution, 1900–1938* (Cambridge: Cambridge University Press, 2006); Mikael Wolfe, *Watering the Revolution: An Environmental and Technological History of Agrarian Reform in Mexico* (Durham, NC: Duke University Press, 2017); Emily Wakild, *Revolutionary Parks: Conservation, Social Justice, and Mexico's National Parks, 1910–1940* (Tucson: University of Arizona Press, 2011).

1. THE PORFIRIAN METROPOLITAN ENVIRONMENT

1 Raymond Craib, *Cartographic Mexico: A History of State Fixations and Fugitive Landscapes* (Durham, NC: Duke University Press, 2004), 22.

2 Mauricio Tenorio-Trillo, *I Speak of the City: Mexico City at the Turn of the Twentieth Century* (Chicago: University of Chicago Press, 2012).

3 In a similar vein, Karl Offen employs the term *geographical imagination* in his history of Mosquitia, Nicaragua, to underscore elite ideas of how nature should be used to support economic progress over so-called backwardness. See his "The Geographical Imagination, Resource Economies, and Nicaraguan Incorporation of the Mosquitia, 1838–1908," in *Territories, Knowledges, and Commodities: Latin American Environmental History in the Nineteenth and Twentieth Centuries*, ed. Christian Brannstrom (London: Institute of Latin American Studies, 2004), 51–52.

4 Antonio Peñafiel, *Memoria sobre las aguas potables de la capital de México* (Mexico City: Secretaría de Fomento, 1884), 78–79.

5 In this chapter I use the terms *sanitary planners* and *environmental planners* interchangeably.

6 See Manuel Perló Cohen, *El paradigma porfiriano: Historia del desagüe del valle de México* (Mexico City: Porrúa, 1999); Priscilla Connolly, *El contratista de don Porfirio: Obras públicas, deuda y desarrollo desigual* (Mexico City: Fondo de Cultura

Económica, 1997); Claudia Agostoni, *Monuments of Progress: Modernization and Public Health in Mexico City, 1876–1910* (Calgary: University of Calgary Press, 2003).

7   Junta Directiva de Desagüe y Saneamiento, *Report on the Valley Drainage Works and the Sanitation Works of Mexico City, November 1, 1896* (Mexico: Tipografía Artística Ramón F. Riveroll, 1896), 4–5; Roberto Gayol, "The Drainage of Mexico City," *Public Health Papers and Reports* 17 (1891), http://www.ncbi.nlm.nih.gov /pmc/articles/PMC2266410/?page=1.

8   See Stephen Graham and Simon Marvin, *Splintering Urbanism: Networked Infrastructure, Technological Mobilities, and the Urban Condition* (London: Routledge, 2001).

9   Vera Candiani, *Dreaming of Dry Land: Environmental Transformation in Colonial Mexico City* (Stanford, CA: Stanford University Press, 2014).

10 Marcela Dávalos, *Basura e ilustración: La limpieza de la ciudad de México a finales del siglo XVIII* (Mexico City: INAH, 1997).

11 Connolly, *Contratista*, 206.

12 The classic studies are Leopoldo Zea, *Positivism in Mexico* (Austin: University of Texas Press, 1974); Charles Hale, *Transformation of Liberalism in Late Nineteenth-Century Mexico* (Princeton, NJ: Princeton University Press, 1989).

13 See Mauricio Tenorio-Trillo, *Mexico at the World's Fairs: Crafting a Modern Nation* (Berkeley: University of California Press, 1996).

14 María Teresa Gutiérrez de McGregor and Jorge González Sánchez, *Geohistoria de la ciudad de México (siglos XIV a XIX)* (Mexico City: UNAM, 2002), 121; Jeffrey M. Banister and Stacie G. Widdifield, "The Debut of Modern Water in Early 20th-Century Mexico City: The Xochimilco Potable Water Works," *Journal of Historical Geography* 46 (2014): 40.

15 Edward Beatty, *Technology and the Search for Progress in Modern Mexico* (Berkeley: University of California Press, 2015), 195–196.

16 Norberto Domínguez, "Discurso pronunciado en honor de Manuel Marroquín y Rivera," *Revista Mexicana de Ingeniería y Arquitectura* 5 (1927), 265.

17 AHDF: Ayuntamiento, Colonias, 520/44.

18 The Federal District was divided into over a dozen municipalities during the Porfiriato, including the municipality of Mexico City, which covered the historic city center and its immediate surroundings. Each municipality had its own city council (Ayuntamiento).

19 AHDF: Ayuntamiento, Colonias, 520/44. See also María Dolores Morales, "La expansión de la ciudad de México en el siglo XIX: El caso de los fraccionamientos," in *Ciudad de México: Ensayo de construcción de una historia*, ed. Alejandra Moreno Toscano and Carlos Aguirre (Mexico City: Secretaría de Educación Pública, 1978), 190.

20 Myrna Santiago, *The Ecology of Oil: Environment, Labor, and the Mexican Revolution, 1900–1938* (Cambridge: Cambridge University Press, 2006), 65.

21 AHDF: Ayuntamiento, Colonias, 519/27; Edgar Tavares López, *Colonia Roma* (Mexico City: Clío, 1996), 28.

22 Michael Johns, *The City of Mexico in the Age of Díaz* (Austin: University of Texas, 1997), 55.

23 T. Philip Terry, *Terry's Guide to Mexico* (New York: Houghton Mifflin, 1911), 257; John Lear, *Workers, Neighbors, and Citizens: The Revolution in Mexico City* (Lincoln: University of Nebraska Press, 2001), 45; Jeffrey Pilcher, *The Sausage Rebellion: Public Health, Private Enterprise, and Meat in Mexico City, 1890–1917* (Albuquerque: University of New Mexico Press, 2006).

24 "Las colonias de los alrededores," *El Imparcial*, April 9, 1902.

25 See John Coatsworth, *Growth against Development: The Economic Impact of Railroads in Porfirian Mexico* (DeKalb: Northern Illinois University Press, 1981).

26 The Díaz government encouraged the use of coal-burning locomotives, and with the ratcheting up of coal extraction, most locomotives traveling in and out of Mexico City had switched to coal by the end of the century. Díaz also ordered that new ties be of iron rather than wood, but it is unclear when this switch was completed. Diplomat and politician Matías Romero estimated that by the end of the nineteenth century, 44 million ties had been laid across the nation, made of 22 million trees. See Lane Simonian, *Defending the Land of the Jaguar: A History of Conservation in Mexico* (Austin: University of Texas Press, 1995), 63; Coatsworth, *Growth against Development*, 134; Germán Vergara, "Fueling Change: The Valley of Mexico and the Quest for Energy, 1850–1930" (PhD diss., University of California, Berkeley, 2015).

27 See Coatsworth, *Growth against Development*.

28 Manuel Payno, "Bosques y arbolados," *Boletín de la Sociedad Mexicana de Geografía y Estadística* 2 (1870): 77–94; Vergara, "Fueling Change."

29 See Daniel Rodgers, *Atlantic Crossings: Social Politics in the Progressive Era* (Cambridge, MA: Belknap, 1998); Paul Ross, "Mexico's Superior Health Council and the American Public Health Association: The Transnational Archive of Porfirian Public Health, 1887–1910," *Hispanic American Historical Review* 89, no. 4 (2009): 573–602; Gerardo G. Sánchez Ruíz, "Epidemias, obras de saneamiento y precursores del urbanismo: La ciudad de México rumbo al primer centenario," *Secuencia* 78 (September–December 2010): 123–147; Alfonso Valenzuela Aguilera, *Urbanistas y visionarios: La planeación de la ciudad de México* (Cuernavaca: Universidad Autónoma del Estado de Morelos: Mexico City: Porrúa 2014). Prominent nineteenth-century and early twentieth-century planners such as Raymond Unwin, Ebenezer Howard, and Jean-Claude Nicolas Forestier influenced Mexican urban experts.

30 Paul Ross, "From Sanitary Police to Sanitary Dictatorship: Mexico's Nineteenth Century Public Health Movement" (PhD diss., University of Chicago, 2005).

31 Manuel Marroquín y Rivera, *Proyecto de abastecimiento y distribución de aguas potables para la ciudad de México* (Mexico City: Secretaría de Fomento, 1901), 107.

32 Marroquín y Rivera, *Proyecto*, 101, 116; José Alvarez Amezquita et al., *Historia de la salubridad y de la asistencia en México* (Mexico City: Secretaría de Salubridad y Asistencia, 1960), 86.

33 I agree with Howard Platt that bacteriology fueled the sanitary revolution of the turn of the century, but I argue, in contrast to Platt, that it had a deterring effect on equalizing services. See Platt, *Shock Cities: The Environmental Transformation and Reform of Manchester and Chicago* (Chicago: University of Chicago Press, 2005), 303.

34 Carol McMichael Reese, "Nacionalismo, progreso y modernidad en la cultura arquitectónica de la ciudad de México," in *Hacía otra historia del arte en México: La amplitud del modernismo y la modernidad*, ed. Stacie G. Widdifield (Mexico City: Conaculta, 2004), 177, 181. For discussions of networks, hybridity, and adaptations in Latin American science, see Regina Horta Duarte, "Between the National and the Universal: Natural History Networks in Latin America in the Nineteenth and Twentieth Centuries," *Isis* 104, no. 4 (December 2013): 777–787; Mariola Espinosa, "Globalizing the History of Medicine, Disease, and Public Health in Latin America," *Isis* 104, no. 4 (December 2013): 798–806.

35 Gerardo Aldana Martínez, "Degradación y recuperación de suelos en el pie de Monte Alto Texcocano," in *Mundo rural, ciudades y población del Estado de México*, ed. Manuel Miño Grijalva (Toluca: Colegio Mexiquense, 1990), 317.

36 Richard Grove, *Green Imperialism: Colonial Expansion, Tropical Island Edens and the Origins of Environmentalism, 1600–1860* (Cambridge: Cambridge University Press, 1995).

37 Alexander von Humboldt, *Political Essay on the Kingdom of New Spain* (Longman, 1811), 31; see also Jorge Cañizares-Esguerra, "How Derivative Was Humboldt? Microcosmic Narratives in Early Modern Spanish America and the (Other) Origins of Humboldt's Ecological Sensibilities," in *Nature, Empire, and Nation: Explorations of the History of Science in the Iberian World* (Stanford, CA: Stanford University Press, 2006), 112–128. For Alzate's ideas on the role of forests in public health, see Graciela Zamudio Varela, "La imagen de la naturaleza en la obra de José Antonio Alzate," in *José Antonio Alzate y la ciencia mexicana*, ed. Teresa Rojas Rabiela (Michoacán: Universidad Michoacana, 2000), 86.

38 Christopher R. Boyer, *Political Landscapes: Forests, Conservation, and Community in Mexico* (Durham, NC: Duke University Press, 2015), 53–54.

39 Payno, "Bosques y arbolados," 77; Simonian, *Defending the Land*, 59–60; Christopher Woolley, "Conservation against Justice: Environment, Monarchy, and New Spain's Council on Forests" (paper presented at the annual meeting of the Rocky Mountain Council for Latin American Studies, Tucson, AZ, April 11, 2015).

40 Diana K. Davis, "Desert 'Wastes' of the Maghreb: Desertification Narratives in French Colonial Environmental History of North Africa," *Cultural Geographies* 11 (2004): 359–387; Archivo General de la Nación (AGN): Lázaro Cárdenas del Río (LCR) 502/12.

41 See Luis González Obregón, *Memoria histórica, técnica y administrativa de las obras del desagüe del valle de México, 1449–1900*, 2 vols. (Mexico City, 1902); *Desagüe del valle de México: Documentos relativos al proyecto de ejucación* (Mexico City: Secretarín de Fomento, 1888).

42 Roberto Gayol, *Proyecto de desagüe y saneamiento para la ciudad de México* (Mexico City: Secretaría de Fomento, 1892), 40.

43 Gilbert M. Joseph and Alan Wells, "Modernizing Visions, 'Chilango' Blueprints, and Provincial Growing Pains: Mérida at the Turn of the Century," *Mexican Studies/Estudios Mexicanos* 8, no. 2 (summer 1992): 167–215.

44 In his study of Humboldt in the United States, Aaron Sachs has argued that the Prussian geographer developed an early ecological consciousness. See his *The Humboldt Current: Nineteenth-Century Exploration and the Roots of American Environmentalism* (New York: Viking, 2006). Also see Ulrike Leitner, "Humboldt's Work on Mexico," *Quipu* 13, no. 1 (2000): 23.

45 For a similar take on the hygienists of this era, see Mikael Hard and Andrew Jamison, *Hubris and Hybrids: A Cultural History of Technology and Science* (New York: Routledge, 2005), 228; Linda Nash, *Inescapable Ecologies: A History of Environment, Disease, and Knowledge* (Berkeley: University of California Press, 2007); Joachim Radkau, *Nature and Power: A Global History of the Environment* (Oxford: Oxford University Press, 2008).

46 Agustín Aragón, "Palabras dichas en el entierro del Ing. Manuel Marroquín y Rivera," *Revista Mexicana de Ingeniería y Arquitectura* 5 (1927): 224.

47 Comisión especial para estudio de abastecimiento de aguas de la ciudad de México, *Informe sobre el proyecto del Ing. Marroquín y Rivera, Estudio sobre las proposiciones del Sr. Mackenzie* (Mexico City: Secretaría de Fomento, 1902), 48–49.

48 Comisión especial, *Informe sobre el proyecto*, 71; Carlos A. Medina, *Exposición que hace el ingeniero a todos los habitantes de la ciudad de México* (Mexico City: Dublán y cia, 1884); Ariel Rodríguez Kuri, "Gobierno local y empresas de servicios: La experiencia de la ciudad de México durante el Porfiriato," in *Ferrocarriles y obras públicas,* ed. Priscilla Connolly and Sandra Kuntz Ficker (Mexico City: Instituto Mora, 1999), 172–174.

49 For the quote, see Comisión especial, *Informe sobre el proyecto*, 71. See also Rodríguez Kuri, "Gobierno local," 172.

50 José Antonio de Alzate y Ramírez, *Periodismo científico en el siglo XVIII* (Mexico City: UAM-Xochimilco, 2001), 119–125.

51 See his Proyecto de desecar la laguna de Tescuco y las de Chalco y San Cristóbal (Mexico City: Gobierno de la Ciudad de México, 1998).

52 Alexander von Humboldt, *Political Essay,* 173, 170.

53 Humboldt, *Political Essay,* 52.

54 Examples of works hinting that the desiccation paradigm was dominant, see Perló Cohen, *Paradigma porfiriano*; Gobierno del Distrito Federal, *Vuelta a la ciudad lacustre: Memorias del congreso, octubre 1998* (Mexico City: Instituto de la Cultura de la Ciudad de México, 1998; Agostoni, *Monuments of Progress.*

55 Manuel Balbontín, "El lago de Texcoco," *Boletín de la Sociedad Mexicana de Geografía y Estadística* 1 (1873): 375; see also Ladislao de Belina, "Influencia de la altura sobre la vida y salud del habitante de Anáhuac, por el socio Dr. de Belina," *Boletín de la Sociedad Mexicana de Geografía y Estadística* 4 (1878): 298–303.

56 Humberto Urquiza García and Luz Emilia Aguilar Zinser, "El tlacuache, el coco y el eucalipto," *Nexos en línea*, June 17, 2013, http://registropersonal.nexos.com.mx /?p=3826.

57 Jorge Cañizares-Esguerra, "Landscapes and Identities: Mexico, 1850–1900," in *Nature, Empire, and Nation*, 129–168.

58 See Simon Schama, *Landscape and Memory* (New York: A. A. Knopf, 1995).

59 For the Central Valley, see Nash, *Inescapable Ecologies*; for drainage under Frederick the Great, see David Blackbourn, *Conquest of Nature: Water, landscapes, and the Making of Modern Germany* (New York: W. W. Norton, 2007), 31–46.

60 Alejandro Tortolero Villaseñor, "Los usos del agua en el valle de Chalco: Del Antiguo Régimen a la gran hidráulica," in *Tierra, agua, y bosques: La historia medioambiental en el México Central*, ed. Alejandro Tortolero Villaseñor (Mexico City: Instituto Mora, 1996), 219–251; Tony Morgan, "Proletarians, Politicos, and Patriarchs: The Use and Abuse of Cultural Customs in the Early Industrialization of Mexico City, 1880–1910," in *Rituals of Rule, Rituals of Resistance: Public Celebrations and Popular Culture in Mexico*, ed. William H. Beezley, Cheryl English Martin, and William E. French (Wilmington, DE: Scholarly Resources, 1994), 151–172.

61 Paul Friedrich, *Agrarian Revolt in a Mexican Village* (Chicago: University of Chicago Press, 1977), 43–44.

62 AGN: Secretaría de Comunicaciones y Obras Públicas (SCOP) 546, 1.

63 Alejandro Tortolero Villaseñor, "The Drainage of Central Mexican Waterscapes," in *Territories, Commodities, and Knowledges: Latin American Environmental Histories in the Nineteenth and Twentieth Centuries*, 121–147.

64 AGN: SCOP 546/4, "Opinión a Liceaga," December 9, 1894.

65 This was one of many hydraulic projects the government conceded to private investors after 1888. See Luis Aboites Aguilar, *El agua de la nación: Una historia política de México (1888–1946)* (Mexico City: Centro de Investigaciones y Estudios Superiores en Antropologia Social, 1998), 67.

66 See Fernando Altamirano, "Estudios relativos a la evaporación del lago de Texcoco," 11–40; José Terres, "Influencia del desagüe del valle de México en la higiene de la capital," 63–81; Domingo Orvañanos, "Geografía y climatología del lago de Texcoco," 83–96, all in *Estudios referentes a la desecación del lago de Texcoco, año de 1895*, ed. Instituto Médico Nacional (Mexico City: Secretaría de Fomento, 1895).

67 Peñafiel, *Memoria*, 69.

68 Conservationists in Europe and the rapidly urbanizing northeastern United States shared this understanding of forests. See Ellen Stroud, *Nature Next Door: Cities and Trees in the American Northeast* (Seattle: University of Washington Press, 2012).

69 Miguel Ángel de Quevedo, *La cuestión forestal* (Mexico City: Secretaría de Fomento, 1908), 8, 21 (quote on 21).

70 Quevedo, *Cuestión forestal*, 3.

71 See AGN: Secretaría de Agriultura y Fomento (SAF), Bosques 70, 1; Simonian, *Defending the Land*, 73, 75; Miguel Ángel de Quevedo, *Relato de mi vida* (Mexico City: n.p., 1943).

72 AHDF: Ayuntamiento, Desagüe de la Ciudad, 744, 148, Roberto Gayol, "Breve descripción del proyecto de desagüe y saneamiento de la ciudad de México," December 14, 1895.

73 Gayol, *Proyecto de desagüe*, 138.

74 Jane Bennett, *Vibrant Matter: A Political Ecology of Things* (Durham, NC: Duke University Press, 2010).

75 Connolly, *Contratista*, 264.

76 Luis Espinosa and Isidro Díaz Lombardo, "Reseña técnica de la ejecución del Gran Canal y de las obras de arte, 1886–1900," in Luis González Obregón, *Memoria histórica, técnica y administrativa de las obras del desagüe del valle de México, 1449–1900*, vol. 1 (Mexico City: Oficina Impresora de Estampillas, 1902), 473.

77 See Luis Espinosa and Isidro Díaz Lombardo, "Reseña técnica," 486–488, for the Texcoco flood; AGN: Desagüe del Valle, box 8, vol. 11, "Informe por Marroquín y Rivera," May 17, 1898; box 8, vol. 2, "Irrupción del Río del Consulado sobre el talud del Gran Canal," August 29, 1900.

78 Ernesto Lemoine Villicaña, *El desagüe del valle de México durante la época independiente* (Mexico City: UNAM, 1978), 70.

79 On the architectural and visual history of the potable-water infrastructure, see Jeffrey M. Banister and Stacie G. Widdifield, "The Debut of Modern Water in Early 20th Century Mexico City: The Xochimilco Potable Waterworks," *Journal of Historical Geography* 46 (2014): 36–52.

80 Manuel Marroquín y Rivera, *Memoria descriptiva de las obras de provisión de agua potable para la ciudad de México* (Mexico City: Müller Hermanos, 1914), 256–259.

81 See Perló Cohen, *Paradigma porfiriano*, 27; González Navarro, "México en una laguna," 516.

82 Jesús Galindo y Villa, "Las obras públicas en el valle de México," *Boletín Municipal*, May 29, 1903; González Obregón, *Memoria*, 1:xv.

83 Quoted in Paul Garner, *British Lions and Mexican Eagles: Business, Politics, and Empire in the Career of Weetman Pearson in Mexico, 1889–1919* (Stanford, CA: Stanford University Press, 2011), 64. In terms of scale, the General Drainage was certainly on par with Chicago's twenty-eight-mile Sanitary and Drainage Canal inaugurated the same year as, according to one historian, "the biggest earth-moving project in history." Platt, *Shock Cities*, 375.

84 Jesús Galindo y Villa, "Las obras públicas en el valle de México"; AHDF: Ayuntamiento, Desagüe de la Ciudad, 744, 150, "Eduardo Liceaga a Gobernación," February 15, 1896.

85 S. Graham and Marvin, *Splintering Urbanism*, 47.

86 Villicaña, *Desagüe del valle*, 120–121.

87 Tenorio-Trillo, *World's Fairs*, 172–173.

88 Shawn William Miller, *An Environmental History of Latin America* (Cambridge: Cambridge University Press, 2007), 143–144.

89 Adrián de Garay, *Juicio sobre las obras de desagüe del valle de México: Triunfo de las ideas del ingeniero Francisco de Garay* (Mexico City, 1930).

90 Carlos Contreras Servín, "La desecación del lago de Texcoco," *Relaciones* 76 (fall 1998): 137.

91 Alain Musset, *El agua en el valle de México, siglos XVI–XVIII* (Mexico City: Pórtico de la Ciudad de México, 1992), 218; Charles Gibson, *The Aztecs under Spanish Rule: A History of the Indians of the Valley of Mexico, 1519–1810* (Stanford, CA: Stanford University Press, 1964), 306.

92 Tortolero Villaseñor, "Drainage," 131–132.

93 Alfonso L. Herrera, "Fauna del lago de Texcoco," in *Estudios referentes a la desecación del lago de Texcoco, año de 1895*, ed. Instituto Médico Nacional (Mexico City: Secretaría de Fomento, 1895), 45–47.

94 Herrera, "Fauna," 48.

95 Rafael de Zayas Enríquez, *Los estados unidos mexicanos: Sus condiciones naturales y sus elementos de prosperidad* (Mexico City: Secretaría de Fomento, 1893), 448; Roberto Gayol, *Dos problemas de vital importancia para México: La colonización y el desarrollo de la irrigación* (Mexico City: Montes de Oca, 1906).

96 See Archivo Histórico del Agua (AHA): Aguas Superficiales (AS) 32, 411, for a case of a petition to drain Lake Xochimilco being denied.

97 Juanita Sundberg, "Placing Race in Environmental Justice Research in Latin America," *Society and Natural Resources* 21, no. 7 (2008): 579.

98 See Julio Guerrero, *La génesis del crimen en México: Estudio de psiciatría social* (Paris: Bouret, 1901).

99 Consejo Superior de Salubridad, *Informes rendidos por los inspectors sanitarios de Cuartel* (Mexico City: Imprenta del Gobierno, 1898), 12.

100 Consejo Superior de Salubridad, *Informes rendidos*, 11.

101 Marroquín y Rivera, *Proyecto*, 7–9.

102 Miguel Ángel de Quevedo, *Espacios libres y reservas forestales de las ciudades: Su adaptación a jardines, parques y lugares de juego; Aplicación a la ciudad de México* (Mexico City: Gomar y Busson, 1911), 13.

103 Moreover, city council members and Federal District government officials drew from the ranks of the Grupo Científico, the inner circle of positivist politicians who held power during the Díaz regime, and they often had personal interests in the success of these companies. See Ariel Rodríguez Kuri, *La experiencia olvidada: El Ayuntamiento de México; Política y gobierno, 1876–1912* (Mexico City: Colegio de México, 1996).

104 AGN: Desagüe del Valle, box 8, vol. 1, no. 6, "Puente de Atzacoalco," March 7, 1899.

105 See, for example, AGN: Desagüe del Valle, box 6, vol. 2, no. 19.

106 Bonifacio Contreras Tirado, *El doctor Aureliano Urrutia: Ciencia y política durante el Porfiriato y el Huertismo* (Mexico City: Centro de Estudios Históricos sobre el Porfiriato, 2003), 16.

107 Miguel Santamaría, *Las chinampas del Distrito Federal: Informe rendido al director de agricultura* (Mexico City: Secretaría de Fomento, 1912), 36. The author stated that some lands were leased out to those who lacked other means but emphasized that this practice affected less than 15 percent of producers.

108 For an exposé of inter- and intracommunity strife, see Sostenes Chapa, *San Gregorio Atlapulco, Xochimilco, D.F.* (Mexico City, 1959).

109 See Marroquín y Rivera, *Memoria*, 57, 68, 73, 80, and 188.

110 Marroquín y Rivera, *Memoria*, 69.

111 Marroquín y Rivera, *Memoria*, 31.

112 Simonian, *Defending the Land*, 72.

113 AGN: SAF, Bosques, 70, 7, "Quevedo a secretario de Fomento," June 20, 1910.

114 See Secretaría de Fomento, *Memoria de la Secretaría de Fomento, años de 1911–1912* (Mexico City: Secretaría de Fomento, 1913).

115 Mario Trujillo Bolio, *Operarios fabriles en el valle de México (1864–1884): Espacio, trabajo, protesta y cultura obrera* (Mexico City: Colegio de México, 1997), 53; Gerardo Camacho de la Rosa, *Raíz y razón de Totolapan: El drama de la guerra zapatista* (Mexico City: Gobierno del Distrito Federal, 2007), 21.

116 Francisco Torentini, *El florecimiento de México* (ill. ed.) (Mexico: Bouligny and Schmidt, 1906), 122; Roberto Martínez Baca, *La raíz de zacatón: Su explotación y comercio exterior* (Mexico, 1938), 20; José Juan Juárez Flores, "Besieged Forests at Century's End: Industry, Speculation, and Dispossession in Tlaxcala's La Malintzin Woodlands, 1860–1910," in *A Land between Waters: Environmental Histories of Modern Mexico*, ed. Christopher R. Boyer (Tucson: University of Arizona Press, 2012), 107.

117 Miguel Ángel de Quevedo, *Algunas consideraciones sobre nuestro problema agrario* (Mexico City: Victoria, 1916), 15–16.

118 See Quevedo, *Cuestión forestal*, 32–38.

119 AGN: SAF, Bosques, 3, 23.

120 AGN: SAF, Bosques, 3, 27, "Beltrán y Puga a La Junta de Aguas Potables," March 22, 1905.

121 See for example, AGN: SAF, Bosques, 14, 4, and 70, 14.

122 AGN: SAF, Bosques, 70, 18, "Quevedo a vecinos de San Salvador Cuauhtenco," September 2, 1910. Also see Ignacio R. Martínez, *La raíz de zacatón y su explotación* (Mexico: Secretaría de Industria y Comercio, 1914), 7.

123 AGN: SAF, Bosques, 70, 17, "Oficio de Quevedo a Agricultura," October 5, 1910. Even without the help of the Rurales, the guards suppressed illegal extraction. In one case, thirty-six peasants were charged with extracting the root on the mountain slopes of Milpa Alta. For the revitalization of zacatón, see I. Martínez, *La raíz de zacatón*, 18.

124 The system cost 16 million pesos, more than either the desagüe (13 million) or the sewage system (12 million).

125 Marroquín y Rivera, *Memoria*, 31–32.

126 Jesús Galindo y Villa, *Reseña histórica-descriptiva de la ciudad de México* (Mexico City: Díaz de Leon, 1901), 8.

127 AHDF: Ayuntamiento, Consejo Superior del Gobierno del Distrito Federal, Aguas, 586, 33, La Junta de Provisión de Agua Potable, "Instrucciones a los propietarios de casas," August 28, 1912.

128 AHDF: Ayuntamiento, Consejo Superior del Gobierno del Distrito Federal, Aguas, 586, 33, La Junta de Provisión de Agua Potable, "Instrucciones a los propietarios de casas," August 28, 1912.

129 AHDF: Gobierno del Distrito Federal, Aguas, 1328, 1497, "Vecinos al Gobierno del Distrito Federal," January 28, 1905.

130 AHDF: Ayuntamiento, Colonias, 520, 37, "Las colonias de la municipalidad de México y en el Distrito Federal," 1906.

131 AHDF: Ayuntamiento, Colonias, 519/22.

132 AHDF: Ayuntamiento, Colonias, 520, 38; AHDF: Ayuntamiento, Colonias, 591, 7. Rents were rising in the city, and hygienic homes were difficult to obtain, without any public housing option, that is, unless one was fortunate enough to be a midlevel worker in the Buen Tono cigarette factory, whose owner, Ernesto Pugibet, hired Quevedo to build worker homes furbished with modern amenities. See Morgan, "Proletarians, Politicos and Patriarchs," 157–158.

133 Valenzuela Aguilera, *Urbanistas y visionarios*, 101–114.

134 "Estudio de la Comisión de Ingeniería Sanitaria," *Boletín del Consejo de Salubridad* 14, no. 5, November 30, 1908.

135 AHDF: Ayuntamiento, Colonias, 593, 37.

136 William Roseberry, "Hegemony and the Language of Contention," in *Everyday Forms of State Formation*, ed. Gilbert M. Joseph and Daniel Nugent (Durham, NC: Duke University Press, 1994), 360–361.

137 See AHDF: Ayuntamiento, Desagüe y Saneamiento, Junta Directiva, 758, 81, various documents.

138 See AHDF: Ayuntamiento, Desagüe y Saneamiento, Junta Directiva, 758, 81, "Gayol a los vecinos de La Bolsa," June 28, 1899; "Vecinos de La Bolsa a la Junta," September 2, 1899.

139 AHDF: Ayuntamiento, Consejo del Gobierno del Distrito Federal, Desagües y Albañales, 605, 12, "Obras Públicas a Consejo de Gobierno," December 7, 1911.

140 For popular protest and organization for urban services in Morelia, see Christina Jiménez, "Popular Organizing for Public Services: Residents Modernize Morelia, Mexico, 1880–1920," *Journal of Urban History* 30, no. 4 (2004): 495–518.

141 For similar perspectives on urban nature, see Jared Orsi, *Hazardous Metropolis: Flooding and Urban Ecology in Los Angeles* (Berkeley: University of California Press, 2004); Ari Kelman, "Boundary Issues: Clarifying New Orleans's Murky Edges," in *Cities and Nature in the American West*, ed. Char Miller (Reno: University of Nevada Press, 2010), 195–204.

2. REVOLUTION AND THE METROPOLITAN ENVIRONMENT

1 Virginia García Acosta and Gerardo Suárez Reynosa, *Los sismos en la historia de México* (Mexico City: UNAM, 2001), 620–624.

2 Alan Knight, *The Mexican Revolution* (Cambridge: Cambridge University Press, 1986), 1:247.

3   See Thomas J. Campanella, *The Concrete Dragon: China's Urban Revolution and What It Means for the World* (New York: Princeton Architectural Press, 2008).

4   Ted Steinberg, "Down to Earth: Nature, Agency and Power in History," *American Historical Review* 107, no. 3 (2002): 802–803.

5   See Ariel Rodríguez Kuri, *Historia del desasosiego: La revolución en la ciudad de México* (Mexico City: Colegio de México, 2010), chap. 1; Knight, *Mexican Revolution*, 1:390.

6   Stanley Ross, *Francisco I. Madero: The Apostle of Democracy* (New York: Colombia, 1955), 248–249.

7   Mariano Barragán, "Memoria del saneamiento y cultivo del lago de Texcoco" (1910), in "El crecimiento urbano de la ciudad de México y la desecación del lago de Texcoco," by Carlos Contreras Servín, *Relaciones* 76 (1998): 150–153; Mariano Barragán, *Proyecto de bonificación de las tierras del vaso del lago de Texcoco* (Mexico City: Secretaría de Comunicaciones y Obras Públicas, 1913), 8–9.

8   See AGN: SCOP 544/95 Mariano Barragán, "Informe," May 6, 1912.

9   Roberto Gayol, *Dos problemas de vital importancia para México: La colonización y el desarrollo de la irrigación* (Mexico City: Montes de Oca, 1906).

10   S. Ross, *Francisco I. Madero*, 231.

11   Abdiel Oñate Villareal, "Banca y agricultura en México: La Caja de Préstamos para Obras de Irrigación y Fomento de la Agricultura, 1908–1926" (PhD diss., Colegio de México, 1984), 99–102.

12   Felipe Ávila Espinosa, *Los orígenes del zapatismo* (Mexico City: Colegio de México, 2001), 225.

13   Along the edges of the lakebed, Remigio Noriega and the family of former president Manuel González owned two haciendas (Aragón and Chapingo, respectively), but their holdings were dwarfed by the expansive haciendas of nearby states.

14   Concerned about the city's food supply, Manuel Schwartz optimistically declared that Lake Texcoco "would be transformed into a fertile agricultural colony." See Schwartz, "La desecación del lago de Texcoco," *Boletín Oficial del Consejo Superior del Gobierno del Distrito Federal* 27, no. 2 (1913): 417–420; Diego López Rosado, *Historia del abasto de productos alimenticios a la ciudad de México* (Mexico City: Fondo de Cultura Económica, 1988), 192.

15   "Será desecado y repartido el lago de Texcoco," *La Nueva Era*, May 2, 1912.

16   Quoted in S. Ross, *Francisco I. Madero*, 233.

17   To put the figure of 4 million pesos in perspective, the entire budget of the Federal District in 1910 was 9.5 million pesos. See José Romero, *Guía de la ciudad de México y demás municipalidades del Distrito Federal con los datos más recientes de su régimen político como asiento de los supremos poderes de la Federación* (Mexico City: Librería de Porrúa Hermanos, 1910), 35–37.

18   Miguel Ángel de Quevedo, *Relato de mi vida* (Mexico: n.p., 1943), 49.

19   See AGN: SCOP 544/63, 544/93, 544/135, and 544/101 for descriptions of the project.

20 See AGN: SCOP 544/134, Meletino Nava, "Informe General y sintético de los experimentos llevados a cabo para la reforestación de las tierras del antiguo lago de Texcoco, 1912–1916," April 12, 1916.

21 AGN: SCOP 544/98, "Barragán a Urquidi," March 1913.

22 AGN: SCOP 544/116, "Estudio," June 15, 1912.

23 AGN: SCOP 544/70, "Informe de Escobar," March 13, 1913; 544/153, Clarence Dorsey, "Alkali Soils of the United States: A Review of Literature and Summary of Present Information."

24 See AGN: SCOP 544/273.

25 See AGN: SCOP 544/285.

26 Barragán, *Proyecto*, 15.

27 AGN: SCOP 544/87, "Informe," July 26, 1912; Myrna Santiago, *The Ecology of Oil: Environment, Labor, and the Mexican Revolution, 1900–1938* (Cambridge: Cambridge University Press, 2006), 263.

28 Luis C. Campoamor, editorial, *El País*, August 16, 1912.

29 AGN: SCOP 544/134, "Informe general y sintético de los experimentos llevados a cabo para la reforestación de las tierras del antiguo lago de Texcoco de los años 1912–1916," April 12, 1916.

30 For the belief in community rights, see, for example, Andrés Molina Enríquez, *Los grandes problemas nacionales (1909) y otros textos* (Mexico City: ERA, 1979), 176–183.

31 Luis Cabrera, "Carta abierta a Presidente Francisco Madero April 27, 1911," in *Obras políticas*, ed. Eugenia Meyer (Mexico City: INERHM, 1985), 1:286; Gabriella de Beer, *Luis Cabrera: Un intelectual en la revolución mexicana*, trans. Ismael Pizarro y Mercedes Pizarro (Mexico City: Fondo de Cultura Económica, 1984).

32 Quoted in Knight, *Mexican Revolution*, 1:422. For Cabrera's speech, see Luis Cabrera, "La Revolución es la Revolución," in *La Revolución es la Revolución: documentos*, ed. Luis Cabrera and Humberto Hiriart Urdanivia (Guanajuato: Gobierno del Estado de Guanajuato, 1977), 137–145.

33 Luis Cabrera, "The Restoration of the Ejido," in *The Mexico Reader*, ed. Gilbert M. Joseph and Timothy J. Henderson (Durham, NC: Duke University Press, 2002), 348.

34 Marco Antonio Anaya Pérez, *Rebelión y revolución en Chalco-Amecameca, Estado de México, 1821–1921* (Mexico City: INERHM, 1997), 2:120–122.

35 Luis Cabrera, "La reconstitución de los ejidos de los pueblos como medio de suprimir la esclavitud del jornalero mexicano," in *Revolución e historia en la obra de Luis Cabrera*, ed. Eugenia Meyer (Mexico City: Fondo de Cultura Económica, 1994): 133–134.

36 Luis Cabrera, "La reconstitución de los ejidos," 143.

37 Luis Cabrera, "La reconstitución de los ejidos," 143.

38 John Tutino, "The Revolutionary Capacity of Rural Communities: Ecological Autonomy and Its Demise," in *Cycles of Conflict, Centuries of Change: Crisis, Re-*

form, and Revolution in Mexico, ed. Elisa Servin, Leticia Reina, and John Tutino (Durham, NC: Duke University Press, 2007), 211–268.

39 AGN: SAF, Bosques, 72, 40, "Jefe Sección Forestal del Sureste a la Guardería de Milpa Alta," August 4, 1911.

40 Paul Eiss, In the Name of El Pueblo: Place, Community, and the Politics of Community in Yucatán (Durham, NC: Duke University Press, 2010); Boyer, Political Landscapes, 66–67.

41 AGN: SAF, Bosques, 72, 40, "Jefe Sección Forestal del Sureste a la Guardería de Milpa Alta," August 4, 1911.

42 It is worth noting that one of Zapata's leading generals, Genovevo de la O, was a charcoal and firewood producer in Morelos before joining the revolution. See Ávila Espinosa, Zapatismo, 104.

43 Gerardo Camacho de la Rosa, Raíz y razón de Totolapan: El drama de la Guerra Zapatista (Mexico City: Gobierno del Distrito Federal, 2007), 25.

44 See Iván Gomezcésar, Pueblos arrasados: El zapatismo en Milpa Alta (Mexico City: Gobierno del Distrito Federal, 2009), 35–36.

45 AGN: SAF, Bosques, 72, 40, "Quevedo a Dirección General de Agricultura," August 5, 1911.

46 Gomezcésar, Pueblos arrasados, 87; AGN: SAF, Bosques, 38, 11, "Informe de Quevedo," February 27, 1913; 37, 22.

47 AGN: SAF, Bosques, 13, 18, "Quevedo a Secretario de Gobernación," n.d. Throughout his career Quevedo believed that guards should be armed to protect the forests by violent means if necessary. See Christopher R. Boyer, "Revolución y paternalismo ecológico: Miguel Ángel de Quevedo y la política forestal en México, 1926–1940," Historia Mexicana 57 (2007): 102–103; AGN: LCR 432/806, "Memorandum de Quevedo," March 1939.

48 Ignacio R. Martínez, La raíz de zacatón y su explotación (Mexico City: Secretaría de Industria y Comercio, 1914), 17.

49 AGN: SAF, Bosques, 77, 1, "Corral a Manuel Palafox," January 29, 1913.

50 Diana K. Davis, Resurrecting the Granary of Rome: Environmental History and French Colonial Expansion in North Africa (Athens: Ohio University Press, 2007), 89–130.

51 "Cenizas se cayeron en la ciudad," La Nueva Era, January 25, 1913.

52 Katherine Bliss, Compromised Positions: Prostitution, Public Health, and Gender Politics in Revolutionary Mexico City (College Station: Penn State University Press, 2001), 70.

53 Michael Meyer, Huerta: A Political Portrait (Lincoln: University of Nebraska Press, 1973).

54 Knight, Mexican Revolution, 2:94–100.

55 AGN: SCOP 544/82, "Respuesta de Quevedo," July 17, 1913.

56 See AGN: SCOP 544/63 and 544/132, Eduardo Borbolla, "Ideas generales sobre las obras del lago de Texcoco," August 29, 1914.

57 Tomás Rosales, "Las obras del lago de Texcoco," El Radical, January 6, 1915.

58   See Tomás Rosales, "Las obras del lago de Texcoco," *El Radical*, January 6, 1915; Gonzalo González Hernández, "El problema agrícola en los terrenos del antiguo vaso del lago de Texcoco," *México Forestal* 11 (July 1933): 133–142.

59   AGN: SCOP 544/73, "Actas de la Junta Directiva," April 21, 1913.

60   See AGN: SCOP 544/63; SCOP 544/116, "Suspensión de obras," August 1914.

61   Francisco Pineda Gómez, *La revolución del sur, 1912–1914* (Mexico City: ERA, 2005).

62   AGN: SAF, Bosques, 77, 1, "Corral a Quevedo," June 7, 1913; I. Martínez, La raíz de zacatón, 16.

63   I. Martínez, La raíz de zacatón, 18–21; Miguel Ángel de Quevedo, *Algunas consideraciones sobre nuestro problema agrario* (Mexico City: Victoria, 1916), 13–14; Kieko Matteson, *Forests in Revolutionary France: Conservation, Community and Conflict, 1669–1848* (Cambridge: Cambridge University Press, 2015).

64   AGN: SAF, Bosques, 81, 11, "Informe del jefe de la Segunda Sección," March 30, 1914. While the department blocked the monopoly of zacatón root in Milpa Alta and its surrounding area, it was less successful at blocking monopoly control over forest products by caciques in some other communities. In early 1914 one forestry official lamented that the department could not wrest control of the monopoly held in Santiago Tepalcatalpan, Xochimilco. See AGN: SAF, Bosques, 81, 11, "Informe del jefe de la Brigada de Xochimilco," January 3, 1914.

65   AGN: SAF, Bosques, 81, 11, "Informe del jefe de la Brigada de Xochimilco," January 3, 1914.

66   AGN: SAF, Bosques, 81, 11, "Informe del jefe de la Brigada de Xochimilco," January 3, 1914.

67   AGN: SAF, Bosques, 81, 11, "Informe del jefe de la Brigada de Xochimilco," January 3, 1914.

68   AGN: SAF, Bosques, 81, 11, "Informe del jefe de la Brigada de Xochimilco," January 3, 1914.

69   AGN: SAF, Bosques, 81, 11, "Informe del jefe de la Brigada de Xochimilco," January 3, 1914; AGN: SAF, Bosques, 76, 1, "Jacinto Pimentel a Quevedo," December 29, 1911.

70   AGN: SAF, Bosques, 81, 11, "Informe del jefe de la Brigada de Xochimilco," January 3, 1914.

71   See Arun Agrawal, *Environmentality: Technologies of Government and the Making of Subjects* (Durham, NC: Duke University Press, 2005); James C. Scott, *Domination and the Arts of Resistance: Hidden Transcripts* (New Haven, CT: Yale University Press, 1990).

72   AGN: SAF, Bosques, 81, 11, "Informe del departamento," July 16, 1913.

73   AGN: SAF, Bosques, 81, 11, "Informe del jefe de la Segunda Sección," March 2, 1914.

74   AGN: SAF, Bosques, 81, 11, "Informe del jefe de la Segunda Sección," March 21, 1914.

75   I. Martínez, *La raíz de zacatón*, 24.

76   See James C. Scott, foreword to *Everyday Forms of State Formation: Revolution and the Negotiation of Rule in Modern Mexico*, ed. Gilbert M. Joseph and Daniel Nugent (Durham, NC: Duke University Press, 1994), ix.

77 Bonifacio Contreras Tirado, *El doctor Aureliano Urrutia: Ciencia y política durante el Porfiriato y el Huertismo* (Mexico City: Centro de Estudios Históricos sobre el Porfiriato, 2003).

78 See Camacho de la Rosa, *Raíz y razón*, 45–51; Archivo General de la Nación, *Documentos inéditos sobre Emiliano Zapata y el cuartel general: Seleccionados del Archivo de Genovevo de la O* (Mexico City: AGN, 1979), 125–127. These were mostly unofficial seizures of land; in the heartland of zapatismo in Morelos, Zapata had more consistent military control between 1914 and 1918, carrying out a more systematic land reform in what Adolfo Gilly has called "the Commune of Morelos." See Gilly, *La revolución interrumpida* (Mexico City: ERA, 1994).

79 See Frederick Katz, "Violence and Terror in the Russian and Mexican Revolutions," in *A Century of Revolution: Insurgent and Counterinsurgent Violence during Latin America's Long Cold War*, ed. Greg Grandin (Durham, NC: Duke University Press, 2010), 45–61.

80 See Rodríguez Kuri, *Historia del desasosiego*, 157–159.

81 Rodríguez Kuri, *Historia del desasosiego*, 159.

82 Jorge Basurto, "La conciencia tranquila: Entrevista con Ignacio Torres Vda. de Álvarez," in *Vivencias femeninas de la Revolución*, ed. Jorge Basurto (Mexico City: INERHM, 1993), 29.

83 "Se acabarán los abusos que cometían los carboneros," *El Sol*, December 11, 1914; "Varios carboneros en las oficinas de policía," *El Sol*, January 19, 1915.

84 Amy Chazkel, *Laws of Chance: Brazil's Clandestine Lottery and the Making of Urban Public Life* (Durham, NC: Duke University Press, 2011), 22; Jeffrey Pilcher, *The Sausage Rebellion: Public Health, Private Enterprise, and Meat in Mexico City, 1890–1917* (Albuquerque: University of New Mexico Press, 2006).

85 AGN: Fondo Emiliano Zapata (El Cuartel General), box 4, file 2, leaflet 195; *Crónicas y debates de las sesiones de la Soberana Convención Revolucionaria* (Mexico City: Biblioteca del Instituto Nacional de Estudios Históricos de la Revolución Mexicana, 1965), 2:157.

86 AGN: Fondo Emiliano Zapata, box 4, file 194.

87 Obregón, quoted in Rodríguez Kuri, *Historia del desasosiego*, 107; Jorge Jiménez Muñoz, *La traza del poder: Historia de la política y los negocios urbanos en el Distrito Federal, de sus origenes a la desaparición del Ayuntamiento* (Mexico City: Codex, 1993), 130.

88 Alberto J. Pani, *Apuntes autobiográficos* (Mexico City: INEHRM, 2003), 227–229; John Lear, *Workers, Neighbors, and Citizens: The Revolution in Mexico City* (Lincoln: University of Nebraska Press, 2001); Rodríguez Kuri, *Historia del desasosiego*. For petitions on street cleaning, see AHDF: Ayuntamiento, Gobernación, Limpia 1726, 74; 1726, 66.

89 Eduardo Sánchez Vargas, "La ciudad de México de 1900 a 1920," in *Mi pueblo durante la revolución*, ed. Alicia Olivera Sedano (Mexico City: Museo Nacional de Culturas Populares, 1985), 1:181.

90 Lear, *Workers, Neighbors, and Citizens*, 256–262.

91   Francisco Ramírez Plancarte, *La ciudad de México durante la revolución constitu-cionalista* (Mexico City: Botas, 1941), 366.

92   Lear, *Workers, Neighbors, and Citizens*, 305–308.

93   Quoted in Lear, *Workers, Neighbors, and Citizens*, 311.

94   Ramírez Plancarte, *Ciudad de México*, 321.

95   Rodríguez Kuri, *Historia del desasosiego*, 141–177.

96   AHDF: GDF, Bandos, leyes y decretos, box 81, file 4, Jesús Acuña, secretario de Estado y del Despacho de Gobernación, "Reglas de Prevenciones Contra la Epidemia del Tifo," December 9, 1915.

97   Rodríguez Kuri, *Historia del desasosiego*, 167–169.

98   See Rodríguez Kuri, *Historia del desasosiego*, 170; AHDF: GDF, "Junta Reguladora de Precios del Comercio," box 1, file 5; AHDF: GDF: Reguladora de Comercio: 3857 and 3860, various files.

99   AHDF: Ayuntamiento, Colonias, 520, 58, "Vecinos de Vallejo a Ayuntamiento," March 25, 1915.

100 See Ariel Rodríguez Kuri, "Desabasto de agua y violencia política: El motín del 30 de noviembre de 1922 en la ciudad de México, Economía moral y cultura política," in *Formas de descontento y movimientos sociales, siglos XIX y XX*, ed. José Ronzón and Carmen Valdes (Mexico City: UAM-Azcapotzalco, 2000), 158; Douglas W. Richmond, *Venustiano Carranza's Nationalist Struggle, 1893–1920* (Lincoln: University of Nebraska Press, 1983), 170.

101 Alberto J. Pani, "The Sanitary and Educational Problems of Mexico," in *The Purposes and Ideals of the Mexican Revolution*, by Luis Cabrera et al. (Philadelphia: American Academy of Political and Social Science, 1917), 24. See also Alberto J. Pani, *Hygiene in Mexico: A Study of Sanitary and Educational Problems* (New York: G. P. Putnam's Sons, 1917).

102 A. Pani, *Hygiene in Mexico*, 178.

103 A. Pani, *Hygiene in Mexico*, 91. Pani put Mexico City's annual death rate at forty-three per thousand. One could dispute his method of including the entire Federal District in his definition of "Mexico City," but the conclusion is nonetheless telling.

104 A. Pani, *Hygiene in Mexico*, 19; italics in the original.

105 Rafael López Rangel, *La planificación de la ciudad de México, 1900–1940* (Mexico City: UAM-Azcapotzalco, 1993), 46–50.

106 Jiménez Muñoz, *Traza del poder*, 155.

107 "Advertisement," *El Demócrata*, March 19, 1922; Erica Berra, "La expansión de la ciudad de México y los conflictos urbanos, 1900–1930" (PhD diss., Centro de Estudios Históricos, Colmex, 1983), 127–128; Jiménez Muñoz, *Traza del poder*, 157.

108 Advertisement in *El Radical*, April 26, 1915.

109 AGN: LCR 418.2/1, "Vecinos de Los Portales a Cárdenas."

110 E. V. Neimeyer, *Revolution at Querétaro: The Mexican Constitutional Convention of 1916–1917* (Austin: University of Texas Press, 1974), 39.

111 For government efforts to sanitize Guadalajara during the revolution, see Rafael Torres Sánchez, *Revolución y vida cotidiana: Guadalajara, 1914–1934* (Sinaloa:

Universidad Autónoma de Sinaloa, 2001), 200–210. For Veracruz, see Andrew Grant Wood, *Revolution in the Street: Women, Workers, and Urban Protest in Veracruz, 1870–1927* (Wilmington, DE: Scholarly Resources, 2001), 22–24.

112 "Constitución Política de los Estados Unidos Mexicanos," *Diario Oficial de la Federación* (February 5, 1917).

113 In 1922 President Obregón nationalized all the waters of the Basin of Mexico, thus following through on the constitutional mandate.

114 Carranza sent Pani to the Paris Peace Conference to convince the international community that Article 27 should be accepted as international law, a task that he unsurprisingly failed to accomplish. See Greg Grandin, "The Liberal Tradition in the Americas: Rights, Sovereignty, and the Origins of Liberal Multilateralism," *American Historical Review* 117, no. 1 (February 2012): 68–91.

115 See Mario Barbosa Cruz for a similar take on the urban elite's simultaneous and contradictory disdain for and adulation of the Mexican popular classes after the revolution. Barbosa Cruz, *El trabajo en las calles: Subsistencia y negociación política en la ciudad de México a comienzos del siglo XX* (Mexico City: Colegio de México, 2008).

116 A good comparison is urbanizing Rio de Janeiro at the beginning of the twentieth century, where an institutional and shared ideological framework for urban rights emerged, if haltingly, under the populist regime of Getulio Vargas in the 1930s. See Jeffrey Needell, "Revolta Contra Vacina of 1904: The Revolt against 'Modernization' in Belle Epoque Rio de Janeiro," *Hispanic American Historical Review* 67, no. 2 (1987): 233–269; Teresa Meade, *"Civilizing" Rio: Reform and Resistance in a Brazilian City, 1889–1930* (University Park, PA: Penn State University Press, 1997); Brodwyn Fischer, *A Poverty of Rights: Citizenship and Inequality in Twentieth-Century Rio de Janeiro* (Stanford, CA: Stanford University Press, 2008). In Buenos Aires, housing and rent laws between 1915 and 1921 established a framework through which to negotiate hygienic and affordable housing, but no parallel framework for environmental struggle emerged in the urban hinterland. See James A. Baer, "Buenos Aires: Housing Reform and the Decline of the Liberal State in Argentina," in *Cities of Hope: People, Protests, and Progress in Urbanizing Latin America, 1870–1930*, ed. Ronn F. Pineo and James Baer (Boulder, CO: Westview, 1998), 129–152.

3. WATER AND HYGIENE IN THE CITY

1 Ariel Rodríguez Kuri, *Historia del desasosiego: La revolución en la ciudad de México, 1911–1922* (Mexico City: Colegio de México, 2010), 207–211.

2 Quoted in Rodríguez Kuri, *Historia del desasosiego*, 210.

3 Quoted in "Las pésimas condiciones higiénicas de la ciudad de México," *El Universal*, May 2, 1922.

4 See, for examples of this kind of perspective in postrevolutionary Mexico, Katherine Bliss, *Compromised Positions: Prostitution, Public Health, and Gender Politics in Revolutionary Mexico City* (University Park, PA: Penn State University Press,

2001); Rafael Torres Sánchez, *Revolución y vida cotidiana: Guadalajara, 1914–1934* (Sinaloa: Universidad Autónoma de Sinaloa, 2001), 200–210; Andrew Grant Wood, *Revolution in the Street: Women, Workers, and Urban Protest in Veracruz, 1870–1927* (Wilmington, DE: S&R Books, 2001); Patrice Olsen, *Artifacts of Revolution: Architecture, Society and Politics in Mexico City, 1920–1940* (Lanham, MD: Rowman and Littlefield, 2008).

5 This estimate derives from the census of 1921, which indicated that within the Federal District only 7 percent of residents owned any sort of property, as well as from salary figures, housing prices, and data from 1950 showing that even then some 80 percent of residents rented. See Dirección General de Estadística, "Tabulados Básicos: Bienes Raices," Censo General de Habitantes, 1921, http://www.beta.inegi.org.mx/proyectos/ccpv/1921/; Alan Gilbert ed, *Housing and Land in Urban Mexico* (La Jolla: Center for U.S.-Mexican Studies, University of California, San Diego, 1989), 20; Mauricio Tenorio-Trillo, *I Speak of the City: Mexico City at the Turn of the Twentieth Century* (Chicago: University of Chicago Press, 2012), 65.

6 Tenorio-Trillo, *I Speak of the City*, chap. 4.

7 Moisés González Navarro, *Población y sociedad, 1900–1970* (Mexico City: UNAM, 1974), 1:178–179.

8 Jorge Durand, "Huelga nacional de inquilinos: Los antecedentes del movimiento urbano popular en México," *Estudios Sociológicos* 7, no. 19 (1989): 67.

9 AHDF: Ayuntamiento, Gobernación, Obras Públicas, Informes: 1240, 261: Romero, Medina, y Cuevas al gobernador, May 30, 1921.

10 See Jorge Jiménez Muñoz, *La traza del poder: Historia de la política y los negocios urbanos en el Distrito Federal, de sus orígenes a la desaparición del Ayuntamiento, 1824–1928* (Mexico City: Codex, 1993), 183; AGN: Obregón/Calles (O/C) 407-1-2, newspaper clipping.

11 Paco Ignacio Taibo II and Rogelio Vizcaíno, *Memoria roja: Luchas sindicales de los años 20* (Mexico City: Ediciones Leega, 1984), 154.

12 Edgar Tavarez López, *Colonia Roma* (Mexico City: Clio, 1996), 39; González Navarro, *Población y sociedad*, 1:148.

13 AHDF: Ayuntamiento, Gobernación, Obras Públicas, Informes, 1240, 261: Romero, Medina, y Cuevas al gobernador, May 30, 1921.

14 Taibo and Vizcaíno, *Memoria roja*, 150–154.

15 Daniela Spenser, *Los primeros tropiezos de la Internacional Comunista en México* (Mexico City: CIESAS, 2009), 101.

16 Spenser, *Primeros tropiezos*, 161; Jaime Tamayo, *El Obregonismo y los movimientos sociales: La conformación del estado moderno en México (1920–1924)* (Guadalajara: Universidad de Guadalajara, 2008), 119.

17 Taibo and Vizcaíno, *Memoria roja*, 155.

18 Spenser, *Primeros tropiezos*, 218.

19 Spenser, *Primeros tropiezos*, 219–220; Barry Carr, *Marxism and Communism in Twentieth-Century Mexico* (Lincoln: University of Nebraska Press, 1992), 40.

20 For a study of the more powerful tenant movement in Veracruz in the spring and summer of 1922, see Wood, *Revolution in the Street*. For Guadalajara, see Tamayo, *Obregonismo*.

21 "El mitín de inquilinos fue disuelto a balazos por la policía," *El Demócrata*, March 18, 1922.

22 Jiménez Muñoz, *Traza del poder*, 184.

23 Taibo and Vizcaíno, *Memoria roja*, 161; Mario Ortega Olivares, *La utopía en el barrio* (Mexico City: UAM-Xochimilco, 1996), 123–124.

24 Taibo and Vizcaíno, *Memoria roja*, 163.

25 Taibo and Vizcaíno, *Memoria roja*, 164; John Lear, *Workers, Neighbors, and Citizens: The Revolution in Mexico City* (Lincoln: University of Nebraska Press, 2001), 357–358.

26 Lear, *Workers, Neighbors, and Citizens*, 357.

27 "No hará la reparación de casas el Sindicato de Inquilinos," *El Demócrata*, May 4, 1922.

28 José C. Valadés, *Memorias de un joven rebelde* 2a parte (Culiacán, Sinaloa: Universidad Autónoma de Sinaloa, 1986), 125; Ortega Olivares, *Utopía*, 126.

29 See "No hará la reparación de casas el Sindicato de Inquilinos," *El Demócrata*, May 4, 1922; various documents in AGN: O/C 47-I-2.

30 "La huelga de inquilinos en el distrito," *El Universal*, May 8, 1922.

31 See Taibo and Vizcaíno, *Memoria roja*, 171; AGN: O/C 47-I-2, "Telegrama de la Liga de Propietarios," June 29, 1922; O/C 407-I-2, "Memorial de la Liga de Propietarios," June 22, 1922.

32 AGN: O/C 47-I-2, "Memorial de la Liga de Defensa de Propietarios de Casas del DF," June 22, 1922.

33 José Guerrero, "La huelga de inquilinos" (Mexico City: Imprenta Correo, n.d.). "Dicen que el rico es ingrato / Por eso se desatina / Y que tienen unos cuartos / Peores que una bartolina / Están toditos chinchentos / Con pulgas y garrapatas / Porque nunca los blanquean / Estas personas ingratas."

34 AGN: O/C 47-I-2, "Carta de Reyna a Obregón," June 1922.

35 See Taibo and Vizcaíno, *Memoria roja*, 175.

36 Spenser, *Primeros tropiezos*, 253.

37 AGN: O/C 731-I-5, "Proyecto de Ley de Inquilinato por el Sindicato de Inquilinos del DF a la Cámara de Diputados," November 1922.

38 AGN: O/C 731-I-5, "Obregón to the Sindicato," December 6, 1922.

39 María Soledad Cruz Rodríguez, *Crecimiento urbano y los procesos sociales en el Distrito Federal (1920–1928)* (Mexico City: UAM-Azcapotzalco, 1994), 125–126.

40 Andrew Grant Wood, "Viva La Revolución Social! Postrevolutionary Tenant Protest and State Housing Reform in Veracruz, Mexico," in *Cities of Hope: People, Protests, and Progress in Urbanizing Latin America, 1870–1930*, ed. Ronn F. Pineo and James Baer (Boulder, CO: Westview, 1998), 113.

41 AGN: O/C 711-C-51-I, various documents.

42 AGN: O/C 711-C-51-I, "Compañía Constructora de Casas de Concreto Armado a Obregón," September 30, 1922.

43 AGN: O/C 711-C-51-I, "Unión de Propietarios a Obregón," September 15, 1922. Their aim was to present the home as a model that builders could use to replace the unhygienic and cramped tenement constructions and permit the "intermingling of poor and rich" for the moral uplift of the masses.

44 AGN: O/C 711-C-51-I, "Jesus Monserrat a Obregón," November 30, 1922.

45 AGN: O/C 711-C-51-I, "Memorandum," October 30, 1922.

46 Archivo Torreblanca-Calles, Fondo Obregón, file 188, inventory 4723, "Proyecto de casa habitación," December 21, 1922.

47 AGN: O/C 711-C-51-I, "Obreros a Obregón," February 16, 1923; "Obreros a Obregón," January 24, 1923.

48 In 1917 Carranza had ceded some land north of the city for tenants to form the colonia Atlampa, perhaps the nation's first colonia proletaria, but this settlement paled in comparison to the rapidity of development in Peralvillo starting in 1923. See Erica Berra, "La expansión de la ciudad de México y los conflictos urbanos, 1900–1930" (PhD diss., Centro de Estudios Históricos, Colegio de México, 1983), 212.

49 The escape from stigma turned out to be temporary. In the self-built peripheral settlements of urbanizing Mexico (and throughout Latin America), a new narrative of opprobrium took root. See Brodwyn Fischer, "A Century in the Present Tense: Crisis, Politics, and the Intellectual History of Brazil's Informal Cities," in *Cities from Scratch: Poverty and Informality in Urban Latin America*, ed. Brodwyn Fischer, Bryan McCann, and Javier Auyero (Durham, NC: Duke University Press, 2014), 9–67. For a fantastic take on the rise of housing rights in urban Chile, see Edward Murphy, *For a Proper Home: Housing Rights in the Margins of Urban Chile* (Pittsburgh: University of Pittsburgh Press, 2015). For the ways housing intersects with questions of family, cultural tastes, social policy, market relations, and state formation, see Edward Murphy, "Introduction: Housing Questions Past, Present, and Future," in *The Housing Question: Tensions, Continuities, and Contingencies in the Modern City*, ed. Edward Murphy and Najib B. Hourani (Farnham, UK: Ashgate, 2013), 1–20.

50 AGN: O/C 711-C-51-I, "Vecinos de Peralvillo a Obregón," October 10, 1924.

51 AGN: O/C 711-C-51-I, "Vecinos a Calles," December 9, 1924.

52 AGN: O/C 711-C-51-IV, "Memorandum por Guillermo Zárraga," June 17, 1927; AGN: O/C 711-C-51-II, "Memorandum," December 30, 1926.

53 Natalia de la Rosa, "Guillermo Zárraga: Un constructor del régimen callista," *Arquitectónica* 7, no. 13 (2008): 41–64; Natalia de la Rosa, "Guillermo Zárraga, planificador: Utopías constructivas y la destrucción de la ciudad" (unpublished manuscript https://www.academia.edu/4828786/Urbanismo_y_Ciencia_Ficci%C3%B3n), 4–11; José Manuel Puig Casauranc, "Por qué y en qué extensión faltan los servicios de urbanización en el Distrito Federal," *Obras Públicas* 1, no. 4 (April 1930): 225–231. Nonetheless, Zárraga became a leading functionalist architect under Calles and went on to teach one of Mexico's most famous functionalist architects, Juan O'Gorman.

54   See James Baer, "Buenos Aires: Housing Reform and the Decline of the Liberal State in Argentina," in Pineo and Baer, *Cities of Hope*, 143–147; Leandro H. Gutiérrez and Juan Suriano, "Workers' Housing and Living Conditions in Buenos Aires, 1880–1930," in *Essays in Argentine Labour History, 1870–1930*, ed. Jeremy Adelman (Basingstoke: Macmillan in association with St. Anthony's College Oxford, 1992), 35–51.

55   James W. Wilkie, *The Mexican Revolution: Federal Expenditure and Social Change since 1910* (Los Angeles: UCLA Press, 1967), 97–104.

56   The limited role of the city council in urban affairs provoked some heated conflicts. One of the more publicized conflicts occurred in 1922 when the mayor, Miguel Alonzo Romero, sought to expand the city's role in public hygiene. His attempts received an acrimonious response from the Superior Health Council and were soundly rejected by Obregón. See Miguel Alonzo Romero, *Un año de sitio en la presidencia municipal: Crónica y comentarios de una labor accidentada* (Mexico City: Editorial Hispano-Mexicana, 1923), 49–55; "Conflicto entre municipio y el Consejo S. de Salubridad," *El Demócrata*, January 19, 1922; Cruz Rodríguez, *Crecimiento urbano*, 101–104. Also see Sergio Miranda Pacheco, *Historia de la desaparición del municipio en el Distrito Federal* (Mexico City: Sábado Distrito Federal, 1998), 146–147.

57   "La ciudad amenazada de quedarse sin agua de un momento a otro," *El Demócrata*, January 8, 1922.

58   See Alonzo Romero, *Un año de sitio*, 41–42.

59   My description of what happened on November 19 is based on Mariano Barragán, "Anexo 1" and "Anexo 1b," in Alonzo Romero, *Un año de sitio*, 394–413; Luis Ruíz, "Anexo 1c," in Alonzo Romero, *Un año de sitio*, 414–419; Ariel Rodríguez Kuri, "Desabasto de agua y violencia política: El motín del 30 de noviembre de 1922 en la ciudad de México; Economía moral y cultura política," in *Formas de descontento y movimientos sociales, siglos XIX y XX*, ed. José Ronzón and Carmen Valdes (Mexico City: UAM-Azcapotzalco, 2000), 171–173.

60   Ruíz, "Anexo 1C," 414.

61   Ruíz, "Anexo 1C," 415–418.

62   AGN: O/C 242-M1-A, "Informe de Barragán a Obregón," December 1, 1922.

63   AGN: O/C 242-M1-A, "Alonzo Romero a Obregón," November 23, 1922.

64   See Barragán, "Anexo 1B," 406.

65   "Un espantoso peligro se cierne sobre la capital," *El Demócrata*, November 23, 1922.

66   "El pueblo está resuelto a deponer el Ayuntamiento de la capital," *El Demócrata*, November 24, 1922.

67   See, for example, "Subsiste la falta de agua, lo que origina efectuar una manifestación," *Excélsior*, November 26, 1922; "La ciudad desesperada por la falta de agua: El público pide que el Ayuntamiento sea disuelto en vista de su ineptitud," *El Universal*, November 22, 1922.

68   See "El pueblo está resuelto a deponer el Ayuntamiento de la capital," *El Demócrata*, November 24, 1922; "El Ayuntamiento está engañando a la ciudad," *El Universal*, November 23, 1922.

69 Ariel Rodríguez Kuri maintains that tap water became a "perceived need" or right once the new system was completed. However, petitions dating back to the 1870s illustrate that many residents adhered to the notion of a right to public water access in the form of fountains, taps, or water carriers much earlier. The difference in the 1920s was that the right to water morphed to mean private access via new technologies, constant service, and a safe supply, further entrenching the links among private family life, the home, and cleanliness. Rodríguez Kuri, "Desabasto de agua."

70 José Lorenzo Cossio, "Las aguas de la ciudad," *Boletín de la Sociedad Mexicana de Geografía y Estadística* 45 (1935–1937): 33–52; José Lorenzo Cossio, *Algunas notas sobre el servicio de agua potable en el Distrito Federal* (Mexico City: E. Rivera, 1933); *Atlas general del Distrito Federal: Geográfico, histórico, comercial, estadístico, agrario* (Mexico City: Taller Gráfico de la Nación, 1930); Jiménez Muñoz, *Traza del poder*, 188.

71 See Juan Ballesteros, *Primer Censo de Edeficios de los Estados Unidos Mexicanos* (Mexico City: Departamento de Estadística Nacional, 1930).

72 See AGN: O/C 242-M1-A2, "Solicitud de la junta de vecinos de la primera delegación," November 28, 1922; Rodríguez Kuri, "Desabasto de agua," 176.

73 I thank Paulina Suárez for this reference. AHDF, Diversiones, "La Semana Teatral (2 a 9 de diciembre)," December 4, 1922.

74 See "Cualidades de agua potable," *Excélsior*, December 11, 1922; "El pueblo, desesperado por la falta de agua, está perforando unos pozos," *Excélsior*, November 26, 1922.

75 "El pueblo está resuelto deponer el Ayuntamiento," *El Demócrata*, November 24, 1922.

76 "La opinión pública se inclina a la suspensión a las elecciones municipales," *Excélsior*, December 2, 1922.

77 Rodríguez Kuri, "Desabasto de agua," 189, 196.

78 See "Motín frente el palacio municipal," *El Universal*, December 1, 1922; AGN: O/C 242-M1-A1, "Resumen del procurador de justicia," December 6, 1922; Rodríguez Kuri, "Desabasto de agua," 189.

79 AGN: O/C 242-M1-A1, "Jefe de la policia judicial al procurador de justicia," December 8, 1922; "Informe del jefe de la gendarmería montada," December 2, 1922.

80 Rodríguez Kuri, "Desabasto de agua," 191–194; AGN: O/C 242-M1-A1, "Informe del jefe de la gendarmeria montada," December 2, 1922; "Jefe de la policía judicial al procurador de justicia," December 8, 1922.

81 AGN: Tribunal Superior de Justicia del Distrito Federal, 307838, December 2, 1922.

82 See Murdo L. MacLeod, "Some Thoughts on the Pax Colonial, Colonial Violence, and Perceptions of Both," in *Native Resistance and the Pax Colonial in New Spain*, ed. Susan Schroeder (Lincoln: University of Nebraska Press, 1998), 134–135. For the riot of 1624, see Chester L. Guthrie, "Riots in Seventeenth-Century Mexico City: A Study of Social and Economic Conditions," in *Greater America: Essays in Honor of Herbert Eugene Bolton*, ed. Adele Ogdon and Engel Sluiter (Berkeley:

University of California Press, 1945), 243–258. For 1692, see Douglas R. Cope, *The Limits of Racial Domination: Plebeian Society in Colonial Mexico City, 1660–1720* (Madison: University of Wisconsin Press, 1994).

83 See various petitions in AGN: O/C 242-M1-A2.

84 AGN: O/C 242-M1-A3, "Grackus a Obregón," December 1, 1922.

85 AGN: O/C 242-M1-A3, "Grupos feministas a Obregón," December 1, 1922. Feminist organizations sought to piggyback on the protest, suggesting feminist sympathizers Carlos Zetina and Salvador Alvarado as potential nominees to run the city.

86 Obregón, quoted in Cruz Rodríguez, *Crecimiento urbano*, 107.

87 For the popular support of expert rule in the Porfiriato, see Anna Rose Alexander, *City on Fire: Technology, Social Change, and the Hazards of Progress in Mexico City, 1860–1910* (Pittsburgh: University of Pittsburgh Press, 2016).

88 Karl Marx, "The Eighteenth Brumaire of Louis Bonaparte," in *The Marx-Engels Reader*, ed. Robert C. Tucker, 2nd ed. (New York: W. W. Norton, 1978), 595.

89 "Apoyo a las Juntas de Vecinos," *Boletín Municipal*, January 21, 1924.

90 "Sincera manifestación de agradecimiento," *Boletín Municipal*, May 7, 1924.

91 "Se fundan otras juntas," *Boletín Municipal*, August 31, 1926.

92 Christina Jiménez traces a similar tradition of vendor organizing in Porfirian Morelos, Michoacán, which strengthened with the revolution and formed the foundation of corporatist politics there. See Jiménez, "From the Lettered City to the Sellers' City: Vendor Politics and Public Space in Urban Mexico, 1880–1926," in *The Spaces of the Modern City*, ed. Gyan Prakash and Kevin M. Kruse (Princeton, NJ: Princeton University Press, 2008), 214–246.

93 Cruz Rodríguez, *Crecimiento urbano*, 94.

94 See Berra, "Expansión de la ciudad," for Cuartelito and other examples; Cruz Rodríguez, *Crecimiento urbano*, 132.

95 Berra, "Expansión de la ciudad," 111; Spiro Kostof, *The City Assembled: The Elements of Urban Form through History* (Boston: Little, Brown, 1992), 60.

96 María del Carmen Collado, "Los sonorenses en la capital," in *Miradas recurentes: La ciudad de México en los siglos XIX y XX*, ed. María del Carmen Collado (Mexico City: Instituto Mora, 2004), 108–109.

97 Jiménez Muñoz, *Traza del poder*, 192–194.

98 AGN: O/C 217-Ch-8, "Postal de Chapultepec Heights Company," 1925; Sergio Miranda Pacheco, *Tacubaya: De suburbia veraniego a ciudad* (Mexico City: UNAM, 2007), 131.

99 Carol McMichael Reese, "The Urban Development of Mexico City," in *Planning Latin American Capital Cities, 1850–1950*, ed. Arturo Almondoz Marte (London: Routledge, 2002), 161–162; on Obregón's original plans for the area, see Miranda Pacheco, *Tacubaya*, 123–124.

100 Peter Hall, *Cities of Tomorrow: An Intellectual History of Urban Planning and Design since 1880*, 4th ed. (West Sussex, UK: Wiley-Blackwell, 2014), 114–115; Alfonso Valenzuela Aguilera, *Urbanistas y visionarios: La planeación de la ciudad de*

México en la primera mitad del siglo XX (Cuernavaca: Universidad Autónoma del Estado de Morelos; Mexico City: Porrúa, 2014), 200.

101 "El debatido asunto del agua potable," *Boletín Municipal*, June 17, 1925.

102 Valenzuela Aguilera, *Urbanistas y visionarios*.

103 The plan was published in its entirety in 1933 but was in the making during the late 1920s. See Carlos Contreras, *El plano regulador del Distrito Federal* (Carlos Contreras, 1933).

104 Asociación para la Planificación de la República, "Editorial sobre el plano regulador de la ciudad de México y sus alrededores," *Planificación* 7 (March 1928): 16–17.

105 See Manuel Perló Cohen, "De como perdió el Ayuntamiento su autonomía sin obtener a cambio una democracia de manzana," *Suplemento Cultural de la Revista Siempre* (July 1980).

106 Diane E. Davis, "El rumbo de la esfera pública: Influencias locales, nacionales e internacionales en la urbanización del centro de la ciudad de México, 1910–1950," in *Actores, espacios y debates en la historia de la esfera pública en la ciudad de México*, ed. Cristina Sacristán and Pablo Piccato (Mexico City: Instituto de Investigaciones Históricas, UNAM, 2005), 258.

107 Vicente Lombardo Toledano, "La supresión del Ayuntamiento libre en el Distrito Federal," *Planificación* 1, no. 9 (May 1928): 24.

108 This administrative change preceded by a few months Calles's centralizing maneuver in founding the National Revolutionary Party (PNR) to unite the nation around the "revolutionary family."

109 AGN: O/C 711-A-45, "Associación de Ingenieros y Arquitectos a Calles," February 3, 1927.

110 See Silvano Palafox, "El reglamento de construcciones de la ciudad de México," *Obras Públicas* 1 (February 1930): 43.

111 Ignacio de la Barra, *Las aguas potables de la ciudad de México: Estudio presentado en la Sociedad Mexicana de Geografía y Estadística* (Mexico City: Claret, 1932).

112 AHDF: Obras Públicas (OP), box 232, folder 2, Alfredo Alvarado, "Fuentes de contaminación del acueducto," August 17, 1929.

113 See "La ciudad sin agua otra vez," *El Universal*, June 14, 1929; "Nuevamente volvió a faltar el agua y la causa no desaparece," *Excélsior*, June 20, 1929.

114 See "Dictador de Aguas Potables que evitará que en la capital sigue faltando el líquido," *Excélsior*, June 20, 1929; "Dictador en materia de aguas," *El Universal*, June 20, 1929.

115 Archivo Histórico de la Secretaría de Salud: Salubridad Pública, Sección Jurídica, caja 15, exp. 2, "Puig Casauranc al secretario del departamento," July 7, 1930.

116 See AHDF: OP, box 138, bundle 1, "Dubois a Puig Casauranc," July 17, 1930; Eugenio Bedollo, "La junta flexible impermeable y su función en el aprovechamiento de agua potable de la ciudad de México," *Revista Mexicana de Ingeniería y Arquitectura* 11, no. 1 (January 1933): 12–13; AHDF: OP, box 138, bundle 1, "Gastos, agusto 1930," and "Dubois a Puig Casauranc," April 12, 1930.

117 AHA: AS, box 33, 418, various documents.

118 AHDF: OP, box 138, bundle 2, "Alvarado a Dubois," March 6, 1930.

119 AHDF: OP, box 7, bundle 3, "Argüelles a Dubois," September 20, 1929; Roberto Gayol, "Perturbaciones producidas en el fondo del valle de México por el drenaje de las aguas del subsuelo," *Revista Mexicana de Ingeniería y Arquitectura* 3, no. 2 (February 1925): 96–132; Gabriel Auvinet Guichard, "El ingeniero Roberto Gayol y Soto y el hundimiento de la ciudad de México," *Geotécnica* 222 (December 2011–February 2012): 8–12.

120 AHDF: OP, box 7, bundle 3, "Petricioli a Dubois," April 7, 1930.

121 AHDF: OP, box 7, bundle 3, "Dubois a Petricioli," April 24, 1930.

122 AHDF: OP, box 7, bundle 3, "Durán a Dubois," April 1930.

123 David LaFrance, "La educación y la salud pública en Puebla, 1920–1940: ¿Avances revolucionarios?," in *Norma y espacio urbano: Ciudad de Puebla, siglos XVI–XX*, ed. Miguel Ángel Cuenya (Puebla: BUAP, 2008), 234.

124 AHDF: OP, box 138, bundle 1, "Beltrán y Puga a Dubois," December 11, 1930. Ignacio de la Barra proposed a similar plan several years later, in which a surge in revenue would be used to expand services to needy neighborhoods. See his *Aguas potables*. For Beltrán y Puga's work on the boundary commission, see Clifton Kroeber, *Man, Land and Water: Mexico's Farmlands Irrigation Policy, 1885–1911* (Berkeley: University of California Press, 1983), 153–155.

125 AHDF: OP, box 138, bundle 1, "Dubois a Beltrán y Puga," December 16, 1930.

126 Roberto Gayol, "Informe sobre varios asuntos relativos a las obras de saneamiento y desagüe de la ciudad de México," *Revista Mexicana de Ingeniería y Arquitectura* 11, no. 3 (March 1933): 76; Pablo de Góngora, "Agua que viene y agua que se va," *El Universal*, June 15, 1929; "Sí hay peligro de inundación," *El Universal*, June 16, 1929; Nicolás Durán, "Política y obras públicas," *Revista Mexicana de Ingeniería y Arquitectura* 11, no. 4 (May 1933): 159.

127 Pablo de Góngora, "Agua que viene y agua que se va," *El Universal*, June 15, 1929.

128 Gayol, "Informe," 76; "Para evitar inundaciones en la ciudad," *El Universal*, August 6, 1931; AGN: O/C 121-C-C-13, "Comisión Auxiliar de Salubridad del DF a Obregón," March 21, 1923.

129 "La ciudad inundada por el chaparrón," *El Universal*, October 15, 1932.

130 "Para evitar inundaciones en la ciudad," *El Universal*, August 6, 1931.

4. THE CITY AND ITS FORESTS

1 AGN: O/C 121-G-S-2, "Solicitud," August 17, 1922; O/C 121-C-C-13, "Comisión Auxiliar de Salubridad a Obregón," March 21, 1923; Fernando Zárraga, "Necesidad de defender la ciudad con un muro de arbolado," *México Forestal* 5, nos. 7–8 (July–August 1927).

2 Miguel Ángel de Quevedo, *Algunas consideraciones sobre nuestro problema agrario* (Mexico City: Victoria, 1916), 108; Miguel Ángel de Quevedo, *Relato de mi vida* (Mexico: n.p., 1943), 55.

3 Quevedo, *Algunas consideraciones*, 105–106.

4   Christopher R. Boyer, "Community, Crony Capitalism and Fortress Conservation in Mexican Forests," in *Dictablanda: Soft Authoritarianism in Mexico*, ed. Paul Gillingham (Durham, NC: Duke University Press, 2014), 226; Miguel Ángel de Quevedo, "El problema de la deforestación en México: Solución práctica del mismo," *México Forestal* 2, no. 7–8 (1924): 64–69.

5   Quevedo, *Algunas consideraciones*, 16.

6   For an incisive portrait of the confusion that beset the early agrarian reform, see Timothy Henderson, *The Worm in the Wheat: Rosalie Evans and Agrarian Struggle in the Puebla-Tlaxcala Valley of Mexico, 1906–1927* (Durham, NC: Duke University Press, 1998).

7   See María Soledad Cruz Rodríguez, *Crecimiento urbano y los procesos sociales en el Distrito Federal (1920–1928)* (Mexico City: UAM, 1994), 160–181.

8   Archivo General Agrario (AGA) 23/949, bundle 1, "Acopilco a Comisión Nacional Agraria," March 1916 and July 11, 1916.

9   AGA 23/911, bundle 2, "Tlaltenango a Comisión Nacional Agraria," February 3, 1916, and February 11, 1916. Country people's condemnation of landowner deforestation during periods of agrarian reform has been a widespread tactic in Latin America. For the case of Chile from 1967 to 1971, see Thomas Miller Klubock, *La Frontera: Forests and Ecological Conflict in Chile's Frontier Territory* (Durham, NC: Duke University Press, 2014), chap. 7.

10   AGA 23/911, bundle 2, "Tornel Olvera al director de Bosques," October 22, 1917.

11   AGA 23/911, bundle 2, "Agrónomo a Comisión Nacional Agraria," July 30, 1920; AGA 23/911, bundle 1, "Informe de topógrafo," October 26, 1920.

12   AGA 23/911, bundle 1, "Luis Vázquez a Comisión Nacional Agraria," August 11, 1921.

13   AGA 23/937, bundle 5, "Nava a Comisión Nacional Agraria," January 15, 1921.

14   AGA 23/937, bundle 17, "Memorandum," May 31, 1922.

15   Emily Wakild has revealed similar examples in Tlaxcala. See Wakild, *Revolutionary Parks: Conservation, Social Justice, and Mexico's National Parks, 1910–1940* (Tucson: University of Arizona Press, 2011), 102.

16   AGA 23/937, bundle 17, "Fernando de Teresa Jr. a Secretaría de Agricultura y Fomento," August 29, 1922; bundle 6, "Susana de Teresa a Comisión Nacional Agraria," January 17, 1923.

17   Jorge Durand, *La ciudad invade al ejido: Proletarización, urbanización y lucha política en el Cerro de Judío, D.F.* (Mexico City: CIESAS, 1983), 47.

18   Nicole Percheron, *Problemas agrarios del Ajusco: Siete comunidades agrarias de la periferia de México, siglos XVI–XX* (Mexico City: Gobierno del Distrito Federal, 2008), 31–33; Carlos Álvarez del Castillo, *La vegetación de la sierra del Ajusco* (Mexico City: INAH, 1987).

19   AGA 23/949, bundle 1, "Censo agrario," October 8, 1925.

20   Information can be found in various AGA files of communities in the area, as well as Forestry Department survey statistics from 1912. See chapter 1.

21   Durand, *La ciudad invade*, 53–55; AGA 23/949, bundle 1, "Resolución Presidencial," April 3, 1924; Martha Schteingart, "Expansión urbana, conflictos sociales y

deterioro ambiental en la ciudad de México," *Estudios Demográficos y Urbanos* 2, no. 3 (1987): 460.

22 AGA 911/23, bundle 1.

23 Elipidio Ordoñez, no title, *Memorias de la Sociedad Científica Antonio Alzate* (1918), 477.

24 Alberto Carreño, "Nubes de polvo," *Boletín de la Sociedad Mexicana de Geografía y Estadística* 8 (1919): 234; Julio Riquelme Inda, "El antiguo lago de Texcoco y las nubes de polvo que invaden la ciudad de México," *Boletín de la Sociedad Mexicana de Geografía y Estadística* 9, no. 2 (1919): 240–244; Miguel Ángel de Quevedo, "La ciudad de México no se hunde por la falta de lagos en sus alrededores," *Memorias de la Sociedad Científica Antonio Alzate* 41 (1922): 51–52; Miguel Ángel de Quevedo, "Las polvaredas de los terrenos tequezquitosos del antiguo lago de Texcoco y los procedimientos de enyerbe para remediarlas," *Memorias de la Sociedad Científica Antonio Alzate* 40 (1922): 533–548; Miguel Ángel de Quevedo, "La necesaria orientación en los trabajos de la desecación del lago de Texcoco y problemas con que ella se ligan," *Memorias de la Sociedad Científica Antonio Alzate* 40 (1922): 265–300.

25 "La amenaza de desolación de nuestro valle," *Excélsior*, June 5, 1923.

26 "Con la destrucción de los bosques la nación se está hundiendo un puñal en el pecho," *El Demócrata*, June 7, 1923. See also "Es inexplicable la morosidad de la cámara de diputados para aprobar la ley forestal," *El Demócrata*, June 2, 1923; "Un desierto como el sahara con sus arenas candentes y sus espejismos, pero sin oasis, se extiende a las puertas de la capital," *El Demócrata*, June 4, 1923.

27 Diana K. Davis, "Desert 'Wastes' of the Maghreb: Desertification Narratives in French Colonial Environmental History of North Africa," *Cultural Geographies* 11 (2004): 359–387. For an examination of this narrative with respect to U.S. forest management, see Karl Jacoby, *Crimes against Nature: Squatters, Poachers, Thieves, and the Hidden History of American Conservation* (Berkeley: University of California Press, 2001).

28 For forest destruction in the colonial era and later recovery, see Daviken Studnicki-Gizbert and David Schecter, "The Environmental Dynamics of a Colonial Fuel-Rush: Silver Mining and Deforestation in New Spain, 1522–1810," *Environmental History* 15 (January 2010): 94–119. For the transition to coal, see Germán Vergara, "Fueling Change: The Valley of Mexico and the Quest for Energy, 1850–1930" (PhD diss., University of California, Berkeley, 2015).

29 See, for example, José García Martínez, "Superficies forestales de la república," *Boletín del Departamento Forestal y de Caza y Pesca* 3, no. 8 (September–November 1937): 125–140.

30 Diana K. Davis, "Desert 'Wastes,'" 371–372; Vasant K. Saberwal, "Science and the Desiccationist Discourse of the 20th Century," *Environment and History* 4, no. 3 (October 1998): 317–320.

31 In 1912 Mariano Barragán had alerted authorities that the Texcoco lakebed was rising in relation to downtown and had underscored sedimentation as the

primary cause. However, drainage and increased aquifer drafting aggravated the problem. See Barragán, *Proyecto de bonificación de las tierras del vaso del lago de Texcoco* (Mexico City: Secretaría de Comunicaciones y Obras Públicas, 1913).

32 This epistemology of forests persists today. See Tim Forsyth and Andrew Walker, *Forest Guardians, Forest Destroyers: The Politics of Environmental Knowledge in Northern Thailand* (Seattle: University of Washington Press, 2008).

33 For the tight relation between state power and forestry, see Peter Vandergeest and Nancy Lee Peluso, "Territorialization and State Power in Thailand," *Theory and Society* 24, no. 3 (June 1995): 385–426.

34 Boyer, *Political Landscapes*, 100.

35 See Roque Martínez, "Cooperativas ejidales: Determinación de zonas forestales y agrícolas; Reglamentación del pastoreo," *México Forestal* 8, no. 4 (April 1930): 67–69; Christopher R. Boyer, "Revolución y paternalismo ecológico: Miguel Ángel de Quevedo y la política forestal en México, 1926–1940," *Historia Mexicana* 57, no. 1 (2007): 105–111.

36 Lane Simonian, *Defending the Land of the Jaguar: A History of Conservation in Mexico* (Austin: University of Texas Press, 1995), 82–83.

37 See Arun Agrawal, *Environmentality: Technologies of Government and the Making of Subjects* (Durham, NC: Duke University Press, 2005).

38 Boyer, *Political Landscapes*.

39 AGN: Secretaría de Agricultura y Recursos Hidráulicos (SARH), Política Forestal, box 265, vol. 2, October 16, 1929.

40 AGN: SARH, Política Forestal, box 265, vol. 2, "Plan de explotación," July 10, 1929; "Los estatutos de la cooperativa forestal de San Nicolás Totolapan," June 12, 1929.

41 Roque Martínez, "Cooperativas ejidales," 68.

42 AGN: SARH, Política Forestal, box 265, vol. 2, "Plan de explotación," June 10, 1929, and June 19, 1929.

43 AGN: SARH, box 1430, vol. 1, "Dictamen Forestal," March 1932; José Luis Calva Tellez, *Economía política de la explotación forestal en México: Bibliografía comentada, 1930–1984* (Mexico City: Universidad Autónoma Chapingo, 1989), 412–413.

44 Boyer, *Political Landscapes*, chaps. 2 and 3.

45 AGN: SARH, Política Forestal, box 265, vol. 4, "Informe del inspector Miguel Ángel Delgado," February 23, 1936.

46 In addition, the procedure to jail an offender in the case of nonpayment of fines was long and tedious, usually resulting in release without punishment.

47 AGN: SARH, Política Forestal, box 265, vol. 2, "Memorandum," July 4, 1929.

48 AGN: SARH, Política Forestal, box 307, vol. 1, "Informe de Luis Macías," December 2, 1930.

49 See, for example, the various petitions by villagers to exploit deadwood in Desierto de los Leones. AGN: LCR 501.2/19.

50 AGN: SARH, Política Forestal, box 307, vol. 1, "Solicitud de Magdalena Contreras," September 21, 1931; September 28, 1931.

51   See AGN, SARH, Política Forestal, box 265, vol. 2, "Informe sobre las condiciones en el pueblo," August 5, 1929; AGN, SARH, Política Forestal, box 265, vol. 2, "Solicitud de trabajadores," July 14, 1929.

52   AGN: SARH, Política Forestal, box 307, vol. 1, "Ávila al servicio forestal," February 28, 1930; AGN: SARH, Política Forestal, box 307, vol. 1, "Cooperativa al servicio forestal," April 23, 1930.

53   AGN: SARH, Política Forestal, box 265, vol. 3, "Informe," October 1932.

54   Wakild, *Revolutionary Parks*, 132.

55   Boyer, *Political Landscapes*, 122.

56   AGA: 23/911, bundle 3, "Memorandum sobre la cooperativa forestal," June 10, 1931.

57   See, for example, the bribery that allowed some villagers to carry out illegal operations in the Ajusco National Park in 1938. AGN: SARH, Política Forestal, box 1430, bundle 2, "Agustín Castro a Quevedo," June 22, 1938.

58   AGA 23/911, bundle 3, "Informe sobre Tlaltenango," February 10, 1934. Such corruption did not prevent a few cooperatives from reinvesting profits into community improvement. San Mateo Tlaltenango, for instance, built water infrastructure for irrigation and domestic use with cooperative funds. See AGA 23/911, bundle 7, "Quevedo a Comisión Nacional Agraria," April 29, 1935.

59   AGN: SARH, Política Forestal, box 265, vol. 3, "Informe," November 7, 1932.

60   Jürgen Buchenau, *Plutarco Elías Calles and the Mexican Revolution* (Lanham, MD: Rowman and Littlefield, 2007), 164–167.

61   Nora Hamilton, *The Limits to State Autonomy: Postrevolutionary Mexico* (Princeton, NJ: Princeton University Press, 1982).

62   Alan Knight, "Cardenismo: Juggernaut or Jalopy?," *Journal of Latin American Studies* 26, no. 1 (February 1994): 73–107; Ben Fallaw, *Cárdenas Compromised: The Failure of Reform in Postrevolutionary Yucatan* (Durham, NC: Duke University Press, 2001); Adrian Bantjes, *As If Jesus Walked on Earth: Cardenismo, Sonora, and the Mexican Revolution* (Wilmington, DE: Scholarly Resources, 1998); Stephen Lewis, *The Ambivalent Revolution: Forging State and Nation in Chiapas, 1910–1945* (Albuquerque: University of New Mexico Press, 2005).

63   AGN: LCR 502/2, "Considerados sobre el Departamento Forestal por Edmundo Bournet," June 6, 1936.

64   Boyer, *Political Landscapes*, 100, 104–105.

65   Christopher R. Boyer and Emily Wakild, "Social Landscaping in the Forests of Mexico: An Environmental Interpretation of Cardenismo, 1934–1940," *Hispanic American Historical Review* 92, no. 1 (February 2012): 100.

66   Boyer and Wakild, "Social Landscaping," 101.

67   "La labor social del Departamento Forestal y de Caza y Pesca, entre la tribu Yaqui," *Boletín del Departamento Forestal y de Caza y Pesca* 1, no. 4 (May–August 1936): 161.

68   "Coordinación entre las labores de los Departamentos Agrario y Forestal y de Caza y Pesca en relación con la dotación y ampliación de ejidos," *Boletín del Departamento Forestal y de Caza y Pesca* 2, no. 2 (February–April 1936): 115.

69 "Informe mensual: Octubre de 1936," *Boletín del Departamento Forestal y de Caza y Pesca* 2, no. 5 (September–December 1936): 107; "Informe sobre los peces procedentes del Japón," *Boletín del Departamento Forestal y de Caza y Pesca* 2, no. 5 (September–December 1936): 163–166.

70 Percheron, *Problemas agrarios*, 184–185.

71 AGA 23/937, bundle 11; 23/937, bundle 18.

72 AGA 23/8761, bundle 1, "Censo Agrario," 1935.

73 Quoted in Wakild, *Revolutionary Parks*, 118.

74 Wakild, *Revolutionary Parks*, 17.

75 Boyer and Wakild, "Social Landscaping," 95; "Coordinación entre las labores," 110.

76 AGA 23/911, bundle 7, "Quevedo a comisión local agraria," April 29, 1935.

77 AGA 23/911, bundle 7, "Quevedo a comisión local agraria," April 29, 1935.

78 AGA 23/911, bundle 7, "Tlaltenango a Cárdenas," September 25, 1935.

79 AGN: LCR 545.3/100, "Memorandum," February 24, 1937; see also AGN: LCR 404.1/1698, "Solicitud de Quevedo," June 11, 1935.

80 Salvador Guerrero, "La conservación forestal y el indígena," *Boletín del Departamento Forestal y de Caza y Pesca* 3, no. 7 (April–August 1937): 133.

81 See, for example, Madhav Gadgil and Ramachandra Guha, *The Fissured Land: An Ecological History of India* (Berkeley: University of California Press, 1993); Roderick P. Neumann, *Imposing Wilderness: Struggles over Livelihood and Nature Preservation in Africa* (Berkeley: University of California Press, 1998); Jacoby, *Crimes against Nature*; Dan Brockington, *Fortress Conservation: The Preservation of the Mkomazi Game Reserve, Tanzania* (Bloomington: Indiana University Press, 2002); Wakild, *Revolutionary Parks*.

82 "Presidential Decree," *Diario Oficial de la Federación*, September 23, 1936.

83 AGN: SARH, Política Forestal, box 1430, bundle 2, "Informe de Gustavo Martínez," October 2, 1942.

84 Boyer and Wakild, "Social Landscaping," 102.

85 "Presidential Decree," *Diario Oficial de la Federación*, June 7, 1937; Wakild, *Revolutionary Parks*, 106.

86 AGA 937, 11, "Decreto Presidencial," April 28, 1937; 937, 18, "Informe," January 26, 1938.

87 AGA 23/928, bundle 6.

88 AGA 23/24040, bundle 1, "Entrambasaguas a Comisión Local Agraria," April 20, 1937.

89 AGA 23/24040, bundle 1, "Departamento Forestal al Departamento Agrario," August 2, 1937.

90 AGA 23/24040, bundle 5, "Resolución Departamento del Distrito Federal," September 20, 1938.

91 AGN: LCR 501.2/19, "Enrique Vergeral a Salvador Guerrero," April 1938.

92 AGN: LCR 151.3/824, "José Guerrero a Cárdenas," April 19, 1939.

93 AGN: SARH, Política Forestal, box 265, vol. 2, "Queja por trabajadores," May 15, 1937.

94 AGN: SARH, Política Forestal, box 307, vol. 1, "Solicitud de Magdalena Contreras." These plans were carried out between 1930 and 1932.

95 Gerardo Murillo (Dr. Atl), the famous Mexican muralist who had served with Pani on Mexico City's Revolutionary Committee for the Relief of the Poor in 1914, came to the defense of hinterland campesinos, a rarity in Mexico's capital. His editorial "Incendio en un bosque" explained that forest fires around the basin were caused not by the rural poor but by careless hikers and campers who left their fires smoldering. See "Incendio en un bosque," *El Universal*, April 26, 1935.

96 AGN: LCR 502/12, "Carta Abierta por la Unión de Trabajadores de Monte," September 1935.

5. DESICCATION, DUST, AND ENGINEERED WATERSCAPES

1 Thomas F. Walsh, *Katherine Anne Porter and Mexico: The Illusion of Eden* (Austin: University of Texas Press, 1992).

2 José Montes de Oca, "Xochimilco y sus chinampas," *Memorias de la Sociedad Científica Antonio Alzate* 45 (1926): 413.

3 Jeffrey Parsons, *The Last Saltmakers of Nexquipayac, Mexico: An Archaeological Ethnography* (Ann Arbor: University of Michigan Museum of Anthropology, 2001), 151.

4 Margarita García Luna, *Nezahualcóyotl: Tierras que surgen de un desequilibrio ecológico; Decretos relativos a los terrenos desecados del lago de Texcoco, 1912–1940* (Toluca, MX: Gobierno del Estado de México, 1990); Matthew Vitz, "'The Lands with Which We Shall Struggle': Land Reclamation, Revolution, and Development in Mexico's Lake Texcoco Basin, 1910–1950," *HAHR* 92, no. 1 (2012): 53.

5 AGN: SCOP 544/251, various petitions, August 1918.

6 AGN: SCOP 544/251, "Informe a Alegre," September 20, 1918.

7 AGN: SCOP 544/251, "Informe a Alegre," September 24, 1918.

8 AGN: SCOP 544/251, "Informe a Alegre," October 2, 1918.

9 García Luna, *Nezahualcóyotl*, 35.

10 AGN: SCOP 544/267, "Informe de Castro," August 1920.

11 AGA 23/2434, bundle 1, "Ejido a la Comisión Nacional Agraria," June 15, 1939.

12 AGN: SCOP 544/224, "Reglamentación de concesiones o permisos para la explotación de diversos aprovechamientos de que son suceptibles, tanto en terrenos como el agua del lago de Texcoco," September 28, 1916. See SCOP 544/228 for the number of four hundred. See also various documents in 544/141, 251, and 256.

13 AGN: SCOP 544/249, "Memorandum," November 4, 1919.

14 The nearby ejidos of San Andrés Mixquic and Tulyehualco also received sizable portions of spring water for irrigation needs during the dry season. See AHA: Aguas Nacionales (AN), 32/408.

15 From the first land grant in the basin, awarded to Iztapalapa in 1915, until 1937, seventeen communities received parts of Hacienda Xico, reducing this symbol of Porfirian rural productivity to a small property.

16 AHA: AS, 289, 6936, "Chinamperos a SAF," October 9, 1930.

17 AHA: AS, 289, 6936, "Feliciano Ramírez a Ortíz Rubio," February 20, 1930; AHA: AS, 289, 6936, "Solicitud," October 7, 1931.

18 AHA: AS, 289, 6936, "Ejidatarios de Tláhuac a SAF," November 27, 1930.

19 AHA: AS, 289, 6936, "Descripción del fallo de la corte."

20 AHA: AS, 289, 6936, various documents.

21 See also Andrew S. Mathews, *Instituting Nature: Authority, Expertise, and Power in Mexican Forests* (Cambridge, MA: MIT Press, 2011).

22 AGA 23/913, bundle 7, "Solicitud de Santiago Atzacoalco," April 14, 1917.

23 AGA 23/913, bundle 7, "Informe de Alejandro Argandar," May 21, 1918.

24 AGA 25/914, bundle 1, "Solicitud de San Juan de Aragón," May 15, 1918.

25 AGA 23/913, bundle 8, "Resolución Presidencial," November 1922.

26 AGA 23/913, bundle 8, "Luis García to Comisión Nacional Agraria," April 28, 1926.

27 AGA 23/914, bundle 3, "Inspección agraria," May 15, 1918.

28 AGA 23/914, bundle 3, "Campesinos a Comisión Nacional Agraria," August 21, 1922.

29 Noriega quoted in AGA 23/914, bundle 3, "Informe por Eduardo Pérez," October 10, 1922.

30 AGA 23/914, bundle 3, "Informe por Edmundo Vázquez," July 29, 1923.

31 Charles Gibson, *The Aztecs under Spanish Rule: A History of the Indians of the Valley of Mexico, 1519–1810* (Stanford, CA: Stanford University Press, 1964): 343; Ola Apenas, "The Pond in Our Backyard," *Mexican Life* 19 (1943): 15–18.

32 AGN: LCR 502.1/1, "Comisariado ejidal a Cárdenas," November 17, 1936.

33 AGA 23/913, bundle 8, "Informe," April 4, 1923; Parsons, *Last Saltmakers*, 149; Teodoro Flores, *El tequesquite del lago de Texcoco* (Mexico City: Anales del Instituto Geológico de Mexico, 1918); Ola Apenas, "The Primitive Salt Production of Lake Texcoco," *Ethnos* 9, no. 1 (1944): 37.

34 Christopher R. Boyer, *Becoming Campesinos: Politics, Identity, and Agrarian Struggle in Postrevolutionary Michoacán, 1920–1935* (Stanford, CA: Stanford University Press, 2003), 76.

35 AGA 23/2171, bundle 7, "Comisariado Ejidal de San Salvador Atenco a Comisión Nacional Agraria," June 26, 1929.

36 Juan Rulfo, *The Burning Plain and Other Stories* (Austin: University of Texas Press, 1971), 12.

37 AHDF: Ayuntamiento, Consejo Superior del Gobierno del Distrito, Saneamiento y Higiene, 645, 8, "Inspector sanitario al Consejo de Gobierno," September 4, 1904.

38 AGA 23/906, bundle 1, "Solicitud dotación," February 18, 1919.

39 AGA 23/906, bundle 5, "Urrutia a la Comisión Agraria," April 24, 1922.

40 AGA 23/939, bundle 1, various documents.

41 AGA 23/939, bundle 6, "Solicitud dotación," February 5, 1922. Also see AGN: O/C 241-C-N-5 for further petitions for bridges and other reimbursement for aqueduct placement.

42 AGA 23/939, bundle 1.

43 Antonio Escobar Ohmstede, "La reforma agraria y los procesos de urbanización de ejidos y comunidades: Los casos de Xochimilco y Santa María Chimalhuacán," in *Estudios campesinos en el Archivo General Agrario,* ed. Antonio Escobar Ohmstede (Mexico City: CIESAS, 2001), 3:23–24.

44 AGA 23/897, bundle 3, "Los ejidatarios de Ciénega Chica a Comisión Local Agraria," January 21, 1928.

45 Martin Reuss, "Seeing like an Engineer: Water Projects and the Mediation of the Incommensurable," *Technology and Culture* 49, no. 3 (July 2008): 531–546; Fernando Coronil, "Smelling like a Market," *American Historical Review* 106, no. 1 (February 2001): 119–129.

46 James C. Scott, *Seeing like a State: How Certain Schemes to Improve the Human Condition Have Failed* (New Haven, CT: Yale University Press, 1998).

47 An excellent analysis of the elite's search for *lo mexicano* during the 1920s can be found in Rick Lopez, *Crafting Mexico: Intellectuals, Artisans, and the State after the Revolution* (Durham, NC: Duke University Press, 2010).

48 This action met the ire of the Xochimilco ejido and the Ministry of Agriculture, which notified the farmers that their drainage work was forbidden because it flooded Xochimilco's ejidal lands. AHA: AS 652/9442, various documents from October 1926.

49 AGN: Abelardo L. Rodríguez (ALR) 552.5/388, "Mariano Moctezuma a las autoridades ejidales," September 26, 1934; Escobar Ohmstede, "Reforma agraria."

50 One newspaper report told of ejido agriculturalists who "look with evil eyes" on those who desired to raise the lake's water level. "Conflictos ribereños," *El Universal,* June 25, 1941.

51 AGN: LCR 418.1/1, "Liga campesina a Cárdenas," February 25, 1935.

52 For one example, see AHA: AS 2084, 31499, "Liga de Comunidades Agrarias a Cárdenas," July 3, 1937.

53 AHA: AS 654, 9481, "Chinamperos a SAF," December 1926.

54 AHA: AS 2234, 32969, "Liga Social Campesina del DF a SAF," August 1933.

55 AGN: Manuel Ávila Camacho (MAC) 404.1/1497; Patricia Romero Lankao and Eike Duffing, "¿Tres procesos contradictorios? Desarrollo urbano, ambiente y políticas en Xochimilco durante el siglo XX," in *A la orilla del agua: Políticas, urbanización y medio ambiente: Historia de Xochimilco en el siglo XX,* ed. María Eugenia Terrones López (Mexico City: Instituto Mora, 2004), 224.

56 AHA: AS 2234, 32969, "Respuesta por SAF," August 1933.

57 AGN: LCR 418/1; Michael Gonzales, "Imagining Mexico in 1921: Visions of the Revolutionary State and Society in the Centennial Celebration in Mexico City," *Mexican Studies/Estudios Mexicanos* 25, no. 2 (summer 2009): 260.

58 AGN: LCR 418.5/11, "Acuerdo," September 12, 1936.

59 AGN: MAC 496/2, "Petición Xochimilco," July 3, 1941.

60 AGN: MAC 496/2, "Petición Xochimilco," July 3, 1941.

61 AGN: MAC 496/2, "Santiago Tepalcatlalpan a Ávila Camacho," May 12, 1941.

62 AGN: MAC 496/2, "Santiago Tepalcatlalpan a Ávila Camacho," May 12, 1941. Of the three, only the Amecameca had a constant flow of water.

63 AGN: MAC 496/2, "Santiago Tepalcatlalpan a Ávila Camacho," May 12, 1941; AGN: LCR 151.3/33, "Campesinos del DF a Cárdenas," December 21, 1934.

64 AGN: LCR 545.3/122, "Mariano Angulo a Cárdenas," August 14, 1940.

65 AGN: LCR 151.3/779, "Isaías Juárez a Cárdenas," January 18, 1938.

66 AGN: LCR 151.3/779, "Liga a Cárdenas," September 2, 1938.

67 "Una espantosa catástrofe," El Universal, June 4, 1935; "400 victimas de una terrible tromba en Xochimilco," Excélsior, June 4, 1935.

68 AGN: LCR 561.3/8; "Una espantosa catástrofe," El Universal, June 4, 1935.

69 "La reconstrucción en la zona devastada," El Universal, June 7, 1935.

70 AGN: MAC 496/2, "Carlos Betancourt al delegado de Milpa Alta, Aarón Camacho López," July 7, 1941; Alfonso Hernández Varela, "Los peligros a que ha estado expuesto el valle de Mexico," Boletín de la Sociedad Mexicana de Geografía y Estadística 57 (September–December 1942): 381.

71 Manuel Marroquín y Rivera, Memoria descriptiva de las obras de provisión de agua potable para la ciudad de México (Mexico City: Müller Hermanos, 1914), 17–19. This argument has been repeated in Alfonso González Martínez, "Sobre el futuro de la bioregión de Xochimilco: La lucha de los chinamperos por sus tierras ejidales," in Pasado, presente y futuro de las chinampas, ed. Teresa Rojas Rabiela (Mexico City: CIESAS-Patronato del Parque Ecológico Xochimilco, 1991), 236–237.

72 Nevin Kresic and Zoran Stevanovic, Groundwater Hydrology of Springs: Engineering, Theory, Management, and Sustainability (Burlington, MA: Butterworth-Heinemann, 2010).

73 Elisabeth Schilling, "Los 'jardines flotantes' de Xochimilco (1938): Una selección," in La agricultura chinampera: Compilación histórica, ed. Teresa Rojas Rabiela (Mexico City: Universidad Autónoma Chapingo, 1983), 93.

74 William T. Sanders, "El lago y el volcán: La chinampa (1957)," in Rojas Rabiela, Agricultura chinampera, 121.

75 AGN: MAC 496/2, "Barrio de Guadalupita a Ávila Camacho," August 14, 1943; "Las chinampas están devorando el lago de Xochimilco," El Universal, April 28, 1935.

76 Archivo Histórico Municipal de Xochimilco, Canales tomo 1, C6, A. P. Baez and R. Belmont, "Algunos aspectos del deterioro del agua en los canales del lago de Xochimilco."

77 This translates literally as "Crazy February, a little more in March."

78 Ernesto Jáuregui, "Dust Storms of Mexico City," International Journal of Climatology 9 (1989): 174.

79 "Una tolvanera ayer invadió la metrópolis," Excélsior, June 1, 1923.

80 Julio Riquelme Inda, "El antiguo lago de Texcoco y las nubes de polvo que invaden a la ciudad de México," Boletín de la Sociedad Mexicana de Geografía y Estadística 9, no. 2 (1919): 242.

81   Miguel Ángel de Quevedo, "La ciudad de México no se hunde por la falta de lagos en sus alrededores," *Memorias de la Sociedad Científica Antonio Alzate* 41 (1922): 51–52.

82   Quevedo, "Ciudad de México," 49.

83   Miguel Ángel de Quevedo, "Las polvaredas de los terrenos tequezquitosos del antiguo lago de Texcoco y los procedimientos de enyerbe para remediarlas," *Memorias de la Sociedad Científica Antonio Alzate* 40 (1922): 534; Miguel Ángel de Quevedo, "La necesaria orientación en los trabajos de la desecación del lago de Texcoco y problemas con que ella se ligan," *Memorias de la Sociedad Científica Antonio Alzate* 40 (1922): 291.

84   AHDF, DDF, OP box 146, bundle 2; Angel Peimbert, A. Petricioli, and L. Mac-Gregor, "Memoria descriptiva del proyecto del Parque Agrícola de la Ciudad de México," *Planificación* 2, no. 5 (October–November 1934): 39; Ismael Molina, "Influencias nocivas a la salubridad pública y la economía nacional: El estado en que se hallan los terrenos del lago de Texcoco," *Planificación* 2, no. 5 (October–November 1934): 38.

85   See, for example, Mark Healey, *The Ruins of the New Argentina: Peronism and the Remaking of San Juan after the 1944 Earthquake* (Durham, NC: Duke University Press, 2011); Mark Carey, *In the Shadow of Melting Glaciers: Climate Change and Andean Society* (Oxford: Oxford University Press, 2010).

86   Carlos Contreras, *El plano regulador del Distrito Federal* (Mexico City: Carlos Contreras, 1933).

87   AGA 23/914, bundle 4.

88   AGN: LCR 545.3/48, "Informe de Felipe Sánchez," March 4, 1934.

89   AGA 23/914, "Memorandum," August 15, 1934.

90   AGA 23/914, "Decreto Presidencial," 1934.

91   See Steen Bo Frandsen, "'The War That We Prefer': The Reclamation of the Pontine Marshes and Fascist Expansion," *Totalitarian Movements and Political Religions* 2, no. 3 (winter 2001): 69–82; David Blackbourn, *The Conquest of Nature: Water, Landscape, and the Making of Modern Germany* (New York: W. W. Norton, 2007); Richard White, *The Organic Machine: The Remaking of the Columbia River* (New York: Hill and Wang, 1995), chap. 3; Paul Josephson, *Industrialized Nature: Brute Force Technology and the Transformation of the Natural World* (New York: Island, 2002).

92   Gilberto Galindo, "Única forma de resolver el problema del lago de Texcoco," *Excélsior*, June 5, 1935; also see Rafael de la Cerda, "Arenitas y tolvaneras," *El Universal*, June 21, 1932.

93   AGN: LCR 545.3/48.

94   AGN: LCR 545.3/48, "Carta a Cárdenas," April 9, 1935.

95   See AGN: LCR 545.3/48, "Quevedo a Cárdenas," May 7, 1936; AGN: LCR 523.7/14; "La reforestación en el vaso de Texcoco," *El Universal*, January 27, 1936; "El Gral: Cárdenas en San Juan de Aragón," *El Universal*, January 31, 1936. Also see "Otra visita a las obras de Texcoco," *El Nacional*, December 3, 1937. This park later

formed what is now the Bosque de Aragón, which houses offices of the National Water Commission.

96 AGA 23/914, bundle 3, "Memorandum de Jorge Rodríguez Moguel," June 4, 1936.

97 AGA 23/914, bundle 4, "Resumen de junta," April 19, 1935.

98 AGA 23/914, bundle 4, "Resumen de junta," April 19, 1935; García Luna, *Nezahualcóyotl*, 62–63.

99 AGA 23/914, bundle 4, "Informe," February 14, 1936.

100 "Magnitud de los trabajos en el vaso del lago de Texcoco," *El Nacional*, May 23, 1937.

101 Jonathan Graham, "A Tale of Two Valleys: An Examination of the Hydrological Union of the Mezquital Valley and the Basin of Mexico," in *Mexico in Focus: Political, Environmental and Social Issues*, ed. José Galindo (New York: Nova Science, 2015), 45–48; AGN: MAC 508.1/177; AHA: AS 2766, 38699.

102 See García Luna, *Nezahualcóyotl*, 62–63.

103 AGN: LCR 889 545.3/48, "Varios ejidos a Cárdenas," February 21, 1939.

104 AGN: LCR 889 545.3/48, "Varios ejidos a Cárdenas," February 21, 1939.

105 AGN: LCR 889 545.3/48, "Peticiones a favor de Favela," March 4, 1939, and March 15, 1939. More than a dozen communities endorsed Favela, including Peñón de los Baños, San Juan de Aragón, Santa Clara, Ixtapam, San Salvador Atenco, and Santiago Atzacoalco.

106 AGN: MAC 523 494/2, "El tesoro de Moctezuma encontrado en el lago de Texcoco," 1942.

107 AGN: MAC 404.1/824, "Frente de Campesinos Ribereños del ex lago de Texcoco a Ávila Camacho," March 4, 1944.

108 See AGN: MAC 404.1/824, chart and map; AHA: Consultivo Técnico (CT), 177, 1424 (see map).

6. THE POLITICAL ECOLOGY OF WORKING-CLASS SETTLEMENTS

1 Miguel Ángel de Quevedo, the prominent planner Carlos Contreras, and Gabriel Oropesa stood out as key urban thinkers advocating public housing, extension of services, and Texcoco reclamation.

2 See the study of Iztapalapa carried out by Hannes Meyer and José Luis Cuevas in Hannes Meyer, "La ciudad de México: Un estudio urbanístico," *Arquitectura* 12 (December 1942): 107.

3 See, for example, Wayne Cornelius, *Politics and the Migrant Poor in Mexico City* (Stanford, CA: Stanford University Press, 1975); Peter Ward and Alan Gilbert, *Housing, the State and the Poor: Policy and Practice in Three Latin American Cities* (Cambridge: Cambridge University Press, 1985); Larissa Lomnitz, *Networks and Marginality: Life in a Mexican Shantytown* (New York: Academic Press, 1977).

4 "Una obra deveras progresista," *Excélsior*, September 22, 1927.

5 AGN: ALR 613/2, "Petición por La Federación de Organizaciones de Colonos," May 1, 1934.

6 For advertisements for Insurgentes Hipódromo and Guadalupe Inn, see *El Universal*, January 2, 1927; "El Hollywood de México," *El Universal*, July 7, 1927.

7   Patrice Olsen, *Artifacts of Revolution: Architecture, Society and Politics in Mexico City, 1920–1940* (Lanham, MD: Rowman and Littlefield, 2008), 202.

8   José Manuel Puig Casauranc, "Por qué y en qué extensión faltan los servicios de urbanización en el Distrito Federal," *Obras Públicas* 1, no. 4 (April 1930): 225–231.

9   Aaron Sáenz, *Informe que rinde el jefe del Departamento del Distrito Federal a la ciudad* (Mexico City: Talleres Gráficos de la Penitenciaría, 1934).

10 "La Liga de Defensa de Propietarios de Casas y la Unión de Propietarios de Casas de la Ciudad de México informan a sus asociados de los principios artículos del reglamento de ing. Sanitaria," *El Universal*, January 31, 1930; Gerardo G. Sánchez Ruíz, *Planificación y urbanismo de la revolución mexicana: Los sustentos de una nueva modernidad en la ciudad de México, 1917–1940* (Mexico City: Universidad Autónoma Metropolitana-Azcapotzalco, 2002), 202.

11 Departamento del Distrito Federal, *El Departamento del Distrito Federal y la habitación para empleados y obreros* (Mexico City: Departamento del Distrito Federal, 1934), 16.

12 Olsen, *Artifacts of Revolution*, 96.

13 On the privatization and control of waste and foul odors in the rise of bourgeois individuality, see Alain Corbin, *The Foul and the Fragrant: Odor and the French Social Imagination* (Cambridge, MA: Harvard University Press, 1986), 61, 143; Dominique Laporte, *History of Shit* (Cambridge, MA: MIT Press, 2000), xii, 28.

14 Georg Leidenberger, "Tres revistas mexicanas de arquitectura: Portavoces de la modernidad, 1923–1950," *Anales del Instituto de Investigaciones Estéticas* 34, no. 101 (November 2012): 109–138; Mauricio Tenorio-Trillo, *I Speak of the City: Mexico City at the Turn of the Twentieth Century* (Chicago: University of Chicago Press, 2012), 64–65.

15 Roderick Ai Camp, *Mexican Political Biographies, 1884–1935* (Austin: University of Texas Press, 1991), 196.

16 See Sáenz, *Informe*, 77–94.

17 See AHDF: OP, box 3, bundle 3, "Vecinos a Puig Casauranc," February 9, 1929. For similar examples from Los Portales and Peralvillo, see box 1, bundle 6, "Andrés Chacón a Puig Casauranc," April 19, 1929; box 232, bundle 1, "Oficina de Cooperación al Departamento de Obras Públicas," December 30, 1931.

18 Carlos Alonso, "La cooperación de particulares para las obras de pavimento y banquetas en la ciudad de México," *Obras Públicas* 2 (February 1930): 107.

19 AHDF: OP, box 232, bundle 1, various documents. For examples of citizen contributions to public works in Porfirian Morelia, see Christina Jiménez, "Popular Organizing for Public Services: Residents Modernize Morelia, Mexico, 1880–1920," *Journal of Urban History* 30, no. 4 (2004): 495–518.

20 See AHDF: OP, box 232, bundle 1, various documents.

21 Property owners would be charged upon completion of the works. See AGN: ALR 6, 011/9, "Ley de Cooperación," 1932.

22 "El mejoramiento de la ciudad de México," *El Universal*, January 28, 1933.

23   AGN: ALR 011/9, "Junta de Iztapalapa a Rodríguez," March 10, 1933; "Junta de Bal-
     buena a Rodríguez," December 6, 1932.

24   AGN: ALR 011/9, "Liga de Defensa de Colonos de la Colonia Obrera a Rodríguez,"
     March 6, 1933; "Vecinos de Nativitas a Rodríguez," March 5, 1933; "Confederación
     de Sindicatos a Rodríguez," March 10, 1933.

25   Gilberto Bosques, The National Revolutionary Party and the Six Year Plan (Mex-
     ico City: Bureau of Foreign Information of the PNR, 1937), 159–160.

26   Oscar Lewis, The Children of Sánchez: Autobiography of a Mexican Family (New
     York: Random House, 1961), 413.

27   John Womack Jr., Zapata and the Mexican Revolution (New York: Vintage, 1968).

28   AGN: LCR 418.2/2, "Vecinos de Paulino Navarro al jefe de policía del D.F.," July 5, 1937.

29   AGN: LCR 418.2/8, "Manifiesto," July 27, 1935.

30   AGN: ALR 616.6/3, "Cargos," July 1, 1933.

31   AGN: LCR 418.2/7, "Ladrón de Guevara a Cárdenas," June 25, 1935; Alex Walker,
     "Historical Influences on the Use of Cement in Mexican Domestic Construction,"
     Construction History 16 (2000): 87–98; Miguel Osorio Marbán, El sector popular
     del PRI (Mexico City: Coordinación Nacional de Estudios Históricos, Políticos y
     Sociales, 1994), 87–88.

32   AGN: LCR 418.2/7, "Margarito Tejeda a Cárdenas," July 16, 1935.

33   AGN: LCR 404.1/303 and LCR 418.2/14.

34   AGN: LCR 418.2/7, "E. Rosales Nuñez a Lázaro Cárdenas," June 1935.

35   "Decreto que declara de utilidad pública la expropiación de una fracción del Ran-
     cho La Vaquita," Diario Oficial de la Federación, June 11, 1935.

36   AGN: LCR 545.2/4, "Bloque a Cárdenas," October 24, 1940.

37   Blanca Estela Suárez Cortez and Diana Birrichaga Gardida, eds., Dos estudios sobre
     usos del agua en México (siglos XIX y XX) (Mexico City: CIESAS, 1997), 120–125.

38   See Bosques, National Revolutionary Party, 180; Luis Aboites Aguilar, "Illusion
     of National Power: Water Infrastructure in Mexican Cities, 1930–1990," in A Land
     Between Waters: Environmental Histories of Modern Mexico, ed. Christopher R.
     Boyer (Tucson: University of Arizona Press, 2012).

39   See Diane E. Davis, Urban Leviathan: Mexico City in the Twentieth Century (Phil-
     adelphia: Temple University Press, 1994).

40   Luis Aboites Aguilar, "Illusion of National Power," 223–225.

41   AGN: LCR 545.3/94, "Julia Acosta a Cárdenas," February 19, 1940. For the notion of
     Cárdenas's rural bias, see Diane E. Davis, Urban Leviathan; Manuel Perló Cohen,
     Estado, vivienda y estructura urbana en el cardenismo (Mexico City: UNAM, 1981).

42   David Harvey, The Urbanization of Capital: Studies in the History and Theory of Cap-
     italist Urbanization (Baltimore: Johns Hopkins University Press, 1985); Claude Bat-
     taillon, La ciudad y el campo en el México Central (Mexico City: Siglo XXI, 1972), 54.

43   See Jorge Jiménez Muñoz, La traza del poder: Historia de la política y los negocios
     urbanos en el Distrito Federal, de sus orígenes a la desaparición del Ayuntamiento
     (Mexico City: Codex, 1993), 212–213; AGN: LCR 418.2/1, "Cirilo Najera a Cárde-
     nas," June 10, 1935.

44 Perló Cohen, *Estado*, 45.

45 "El miedo es el mejor albañil de la ciudad," *Excélsior*, July 18, 1939.

46 Nora Hamilton, *The Limits of State Autonomy: Postrevolutionary Mexico* (Princeton, NJ: Princeton University Press, 1982).

47 Eduardo Hay, "Closing Remarks of Eduardo Hay," *Revista Mexicana de Ingenieria y Arquitectura* 17, no. 6 (June 1939): 341.

48 Departamento del Distrito Federal, *Memorias del Departamento del Distrito Federal (1934–35)* (Mexico City: Departamento del Distrito Federal, 1935), 12–13.

49 See AGN: LCR 545.3/3, "Ley Federal de Expropiación por Causa de Utilidad Pública," n.d.

50 AGN: LCR 545.3/3, "Ley Federal de Expropiación por Causa de Utilidad Pública," n.d.

51 AGN: LCR 545.3/3, "Ley Federal de Expropiación por Causa de Utilidad Pública," n.d.

52 "Texto completo de la Ley de Expropiación que será discutida en las cámaras," *Excélsior*, September 27, 1936.

53 "Un amago a la propiedad privada," *El Universal*, September 30, 1936; "La ley de Expropiación," *Excélsior*, October 29, 1936.

54 "La Ley de Expropiación, en proyecto, restringirá mucho las construcciones urbanas," *Excélsior*, October 25, 1936; "Memorial de la Liga de Defensa de Propietarios de Casas, presentado a la H Cámara de Diputados, sobre el proyecto de Ley de Expropiación," *Excélsior*, October 22, 1936.

55 "Se quiere crear hostilidad a la nueva Ley de Expropiación," *El Nacional*, October 30, 1936.

56 "No existe en México ningún problema por falta de habitación," *Excélsior*, November 28, 1937; Perló Cohen, *Estado*, 45.

57 "Expropiación de tierras urbanas," *Excélsior*, November 23, 1936.

58 "El agrarismo urbano," *Excélsior*, November 20, 1936; "Es problema de capital y no de tierras el reparto de lotes para habitación," *Excélsior*, December 2, 1936.

59 AGN: LCR 545.2/4, "Manuel Duarte a Cárdenas," May 1, 1936.

60 AGN: LCR 545.2/4, "Unión General de Colonos del DF a Cárdenas," March 2, 1938.

61 AGN: LCR 545.2/4, "Proyecto de Ley," September 16, 1936.

62 AGN: LCR 545.3/94, "Liga a Cárdenas," April 25, 1935.

63 AGN: LCR 545.3/94, "Ante proyecto para la creación del Banco Nacional Refaccionario del Hogar," n.d.

64 AGN: LCR 562.11/79, "Confederación Nacional Inquilinaria a Cárdenas," October 18, 1938.

65 *Diario de los debates de la Cámara de Diputados*, no. 16, December 1, 1938.

66 See *Revista Mexicana de Ingeniería y Arquitectura*, various articles from 1938 and 1939.

67 Rafael López Rangel, *La planificación de la ciudad de México, 1900–1940* (Mexico City: UAM-Azcapotzalco, 1993), 8.

68 Unión de Arquitectos Socialistas: *Proyecto de la ciudad obrera en México, DF, doctrina socialista de la arquitectura* (Mexico, 1938).

69 Gabriel M. Oropesa, "Proyecto de Casas de Vecindad para Obreros Pobres: Ponencia dada al Primer Congreso Nacional de Habitaciones Obreras," *Revista Mexicana de Ingeniería y Arquitectura* 8, no. 3 (March 1940): 142.

70 Meyer, "Ciudad de México," 103. Anthropologist Guillermo Bonfil Batalla would glorify communal tenement living in a similar way: as an essential component of the authentic "México profundo" (deep Mexico). See Tenorio-Trillo, *I Speak of the City*, 75.

71 AGN: LCR 135.2/125, "Proyecto de Habitación para el Obrero de Salario Mínimo," January 3, 1935.

72 Juan O'Gorman quoted in Luis Carranza, *Architecture as Revolution: Episodes in the History of Modern Mexico* (Austin: University of Texas Press, 2010), 159.

73 See Olsen, *Artifacts of Revolution*, 224; "Expropiación de terrenos para la colonia de casas destinadas a los maestros," *Excélsior*, December 25, 1937; "Colonia para unos obreros sin trabajo," *Excélsior*, December 18, 1936.

74 Wayne Cornelius, *Politics*, chap. 6.

75 AGN: LCR 562.11/79, "Queja de colonos," August 11, 1938.

76 AGN: LCR 418.2/7, "Alerta, compañeros de la colonia Lázaro Cárdenas!," July 30, 1935.

77 AGN: LCR 418.2/7, various documents.

78 AGN: LCR 418.2/7, "Telegrama," June 17, 1936.

79 AGN: LCR 418.2/7, "Comité Pro-derechos de la Mujer a Cárdenas," January 17, 1937.

80 AGN: LCR 418.2/8, "Manifiesto," July 27, 1935.

81 AGN: LCR 418.2/7, "Telegrama," July 1935.

82 See various documents in AGN: LCR 562.4/38; "Batalla entre falsos colonos," *Excélsior*, March 6, 1939.

83 See AGN: LCR 418.2/101, various documents; 418.2/159, "Vecinos de la antigua Hacienda de los Morales a Cárdenas," December 7, 1938.

84 AGN: LCR 418.2/2, "Hilario García al Bloque Revolucionario," April 26, 1935.

85 AGN: LCR 418.2/170, "Telegrama," March 7, 1939.

86 Cornelius, *Politics*, 327.

87 AGN: LCR 609/168, "Roberto Guerrero Grosso a Cárdenas," March 21, 1939.

88 See "Agua potable en la colonia Peralvillo," *El Universal*, July 13, 1936.

89 See "Queja de los habitantes de la colonia Industrial, contra la Dirección de Aguas del Departamento Central," *El Universal*, January 12, 1939.

90 See AGN: LCR 418.2/93, "Vecinos de Tolteca a Cárdenas," March 10, 1937; LCR 418.2/1, "Eufemia Estrada a Cárdenas," February 8, 1940; Jiménez Muñoz, *Traza del poder*, 242.

91 Pierre Mayol, "The Neighborhood," in *Practice of Everyday Life*, vol. 2, *Living and Cooking*, by Michel de Certeau, Luce Giard, and Pierre Mayol, ed. Timothy J. Tomasik (Minneapolis: University of Minnesota Press, 1998), 10–13.

92 Mayol, "Neighborhood," 11.

93 "Expulsión de unos colonos," *Excélsior*, May 30, 1939; various documents in AGN: LCR 418.2/3.

94 "Benefica labor en favor de los pobres," *El Universal*, January 22, 1939.

95 AGN: LCR 418.2/3, "Saludos a los colonos del Primer Distrito del Distrito Federal," March 20, 1938.

96 AGN: LCR 418.2/16, "Memorandum de Unión Cooperativa de Obreros Libres de la Colonia Alvaro Obregón," February 8, 1935.

97 AGN: LCR 703.4/287, "Vecinos de varias colonias a Cárdenas," June 7, 1938; "Vecinos de Álvaro Obregón a Cárdenas," March 14, 1938; "Paulino Navarro a Cárdenas," June 27, 1938.

98 See Benjamin Smith, *Pistoleros and Popular Movements: The Politics of State Formation in Postrevolutionary Oaxaca* (Lincoln: University of Nebraska Press, 2009); Teresa A. Meade, *"Civilizing" Rio: Reform and Resistance in a Brazilian City, 1889–1930* (University Park, PA: Penn State University Press, 1997). Routinization of protest took hold in Rio at midcentury and again during the 1980s after the fall of the military dictatorship. See Bryan McCann, *Hard Times in the Marvelous City: From Dictatorship to Democracy in the Favelas of Rio de Janeiro* (Durham, NC: Duke University Press, 2013), 195.

99 Emilio Kouri, "Interpreting the Expropriation of Indian Pueblo Lands in Porfirian Mexico: The Unexamined Legacies of Andrés Molina Enríquez," *HAHR* 82, no. 1 (2002): 69–117.

7. INDUSTRIALIZATION AND ENVIRONMENTAL TECHNOCRACY

1 See Martin Reuss, "Seeing like an Engineer: Water Projects and the Mediation of the Incommensurable," *Technology and Culture* 49, no. 3 (July 2008): 531–546; Gregory T. Cushman, *Guano and the Opening of the Pacific World: A Global Ecological History* (New York: Cambridge University Press, 2013); Don Karl Rowney, *Transition to Technocracy: The Structural Origins of the Soviet Administrative State* (Ithaca, NY: Cornell University Press, 1989); Stephen Bocking, "Constructing Urban Expertise: Professional and Political Authority in Toronto, 1940–1970," *Journal of Urban History* 33, no. 1 (November 2006): 51–76.

2 AGN: LCR 502/12, "Ernesto Sánchez P. a Cárdenas," January 31, 1939.

3 AGN: LCR 502/12, "Trabajadores del bosques a Cárdenas," March 14, 1939.

4 AGN: LCR 432/806.

5 "El problema de la carestia del carbón vegetal," *El Nacional*, August 17, 1937; Efraín Jaimes Piñeda, "El problema de la escasez del carbón vegetal y sus posibles substitutos" (master's thesis, Escuela Nacional de Agricultura, Chapingo, 1943), 16.

6 Joachim Radkau, *Wood: A History* (Cambridge: Polity, 2012), 127–129; Antonio Espinosa de los Monteros, *El problema del carbón en el Distrito Federal* (Mexico City: Mundial, 1928), 25.

7 Espinosa de los Monteros, *Problema del carbón*, 25; Rafael H. Martín, "Hornos metálicos para la elaboración moderna y económica del carbón vegetal," *México Forestal* 8 (May 1930): 99–100; Rodrigo Juárez Herrera, "El carbón vegetal en la economía doméstica," *México Forestal* 23 (June 1945): 55–57.

8 Espinosa de los Monteros, *Problema del carbón*, 13. Official statistics registered a sharp decline in the arrival of charcoal at Mexico City's train depots beginning in 1935. In 1933, 160,870 metric tons of charcoal arrived, but in 1935 only 97,505 metric tons. During the late 1930s, the figure hovered around 120,000 metric tons. See Secretaría de Economía, *Anuario Estadístico de los Estados Unidos Mexicanos, 1940* (Mexico City: Dir. General de Estadística, 1942), 619.

9 In the 1930s Mexico City consumed on average about 140,000 metric tons of charcoal per year, the equivalent of about 370 hectares of forest each month in central Mexico. See "Estamos acabando con nuestros hermosos bosques," *El Demócrata*, June 14, 1923; "Entrada de combustibles vegetales a la capital de la república," *Boletín del Departamento Forestal y de Caza y Pesca* 4, no. 3 (June–August 1938): 98–99; "El problema de la carestia del carbón vegetal," *El Nacional*, August 17, 1937.

10 "Un recurso más de preservación forestal," *El Universal*, January 2, 1936; "El Primer Congreso Forestal Mexicano," *México Forestal* 7 (March 1930): 23. While it is probable that forest cover declined over this period, the last official survey of forest cover by state was done in 1911–1913.

11 Official data from the 1920s and 1930s indicate that the Federal District accounted for less than 1 percent of the charcoal brought to the city. While the State of Mexico, which lay partially within the Basin of Mexico, was ranked first on the list of providers, ahead of Michoacán, Puebla, and Morelos, most of the charcoal derived from outside the basin. Espinosa de los Monteros, *Problema del carbón*, 14–15.

12 Jaimes Piñeda, "Problema de la escasez," 16.

13 Lázaro Cárdenas quoted in "Declararse de pública utilidad la venta de combustible vegetal," *Excélsior*, July 20, 1937.

14 Matthew Vitz, "'To Save the Forests': Power, Narrative, and Environment in Mexico City's Cooking Fuel Transition," *Mexican Studies/Estudios Mexicanos* 31, no. 1 (winter 2015): 136–137.

15 "Nuevas estufas Pemex," *El Nacional*, March 6, 1943.

16 AGN: MAC 521/7.

17 AGN: MAC 404.1/487.

18 Mexican stove manufacturers and vendors complained bitterly, through the Mexican Chamber of Commerce, that Pemex had overstepped its boundaries by selling appliances, and at a highly discounted price. AGN: MAC 521/12, various documents; "Nuevas estufas Pemex," *El Nacional*, March 6, 1943; "Petróleo más barato aún: El carbón se irá para siempre," *Excélsior*, January 23, 1942.

19 See "Es urgente substituir el carbón, dijo el ing. Gómez," *El Nacional*, December 22, 1942; "Se están agotando las reservas de carbón en el país," *Novedades*, January 22, 1942; "Urge un nuevo combustible," *El Universal*, December 1, 1941.

20 On the agricultural policies of Gómez after 1940, see Mikael Wolfe, "Mining Water for the Revolution: Marte R. Gómez and the Business of Agrarian Reform in 'La Laguna,' Mexico, 1920s–1960s" (working paper 371, Kellogg Institute, South Bend, IN: University of Notre Dame, July 2010).

21   Enrique Beltrán, *Los recursos naturales de México y su conservación* (Mexico City: Secretaría de Educación Pública, 1946); see "Reportero preguntón," *El Universal*, January 23, 1942; AGN: MAC 521/7, "Organizaciones femeninas a Ávila Camacho," January 12, 1942.

22   Stephen R. Niblo, *Mexico in the 1940s: Modernity, Politics, and Corruption* (Wilmington, DE: Scholarly Resources, 1999).

23   Secretaría de Economía, *Anuario Estadístico de los Estados Unidos Mexicanos, 1951–52* (Mexico City: Dirección General de Estadística, 1954), 756.

24   See AGN: Miguel Alemán Valdés 527/58, "A los señores propietarios de carbonerías," 1943.

25   Oscar Lewis, *The Children of Sánchez: Autobiography of a Mexican Family* (New York: Random House, 1961).

26   AGN: MAC 521/7, "Sindicato de Trabajadores de Bosques a Ávila Camacho," March 30, 1943.

27   AGN: MAC 521/7, various documents.

28   See Angus Wright, "Downslope and North: How Soil Degradation and Synthetic Pesticides Drove the Trajectory of Mexican Agriculture through the Twentieth Century," in *A Land between Waters: Environmental Histories of Modern Mexico*, ed. Christopher R. Boyer (Tucson: University of Arizona Press, 2012), 22–49.

29   Hans Lenz, *Historia del papel en México y cosas relacionadas* (Mexico City: Porrúa, 1990), 553.

30   Héctor Agustín Salvia Spratte, *Los laberintos de Loreto y Peña Pobre* (Mexico City: El Caballito, 1989), 38.

31   AGN: ALR 552.1/818, "Director de San Rafael José de la Macorra a Abelardo Rodríguez," December 21, 1933.

32   H. Lenz, *Historia del papel*, 650.

33   Christopher R. Boyer, "La Segunda Guerra Mundial y la 'crisis de producción en los bosques mexicanos,'" *HALAC* 2, no. 1 (September–February 2012): 7–23; Spratte, *Laberintos*, 72; Boyer, *Political Landscapes*, 130–131.

34   "Decreto por el cual se establece una Unidad Industrial de Explotación Forestal en favor de las fábricas de papel de Loreto y Peña Pobre," *Diario Oficial de la Federación*, January 9, 1947.

35   Presidential decree, October 15, 1947, quoted in Luis Aboites Aguilar, "Amecameca, 1922: Ensayo sobre centralización política y estado nacional en México," *Historia Mexicana* 49, no. 1 (January 1996): 86; Boyer, "Segunda Guerra Mundial."

36   Boyer, *Political Landscapes*, 141–142.

37   AGN: Miguel Alemán Valdés 404.1/3195, "Comité Agrario General a Alemán," October 11, 1949.

38   Boyer, *Political Landscapes*, 131.

39   See Boyer, "Segunda Guerra Mundial"; Enrique Beltrán, *La batalla forestal: Lo hecho, lo no hecho, lo por hacer* (Mexico City: Editorial Cultura, 1964).

40   Bancroft Library Manuscripts: 2011/141, box 1, Dirección General de Aguas y Saneamiento, "Obras de provisión de agua potable para la ciudad de México," 1940.

41 Elisabeth Mansilla Menéndez, "La relación entre la ciudad de México y Xochi-milco," in *Pasado, presente y futuro de las chinampas*, ed. Teresa Rojas Rabiela (Mexico City: CIESAS-Patronato del Parque Ecológico Xochimilco, 1991), 201–204; José Fuentes Zamorate, "El problema agrario en Xochimilco" (professional thesis, UNAM, 1946), 42–43.

42 William T. Sanders, "El lago y el volcán," in *La agricultura chinampera: Compilación histórica*, ed. Teresa Rojas Rabiela (Mexico City: Universidad Autónoma de Chapingo, 1983), 132; Patricia Romero Lankao and Eike. Duffing, "¿Tres procesos contradictorios? Desarrollo urbano, ambiente y políticas en Xochimilco durante el siglo XX," in *A la orilla del agua: Políticas, urbanización y medio ambiente: Historia de Xochimilco en el siglo XX*, ed. María Eugenia Terrones López (Mexico City: Instituto Mora, 2004), 223; Saul Alcántara Onofre, "The Chinampas before and after the Conquest," in *Botanical Progress, Horticultural Innovation, and Cultural Changes*, ed. Michel Conan and W. John Kress (Cambridge: Dumbarton Oaks, 2007), 171.

43 Sanders, "El lago y el volcán," 132.

44 AGN: LCR 545.3/122, "Liga a Cárdenas," 1940.

45 Eucario Pérez, "El drama agrario a un lado de la ciudad de México," *Suceso*, April 9, 1965.

46 AGN: MAC 404.1/1497, "Sinarquistas a Ávila Camacho," January 12, 1944.

47 "La restitución del lago de Xochimilco: Un beneficio para la capital y un atractivo para el turismo," *El Universal*, July 18, 1954; "Xochimilco: Un lago en agonía," *El Nacional*, April 19, 1957.

48 "La restitución del lago de Xochimilco: Un beneficio para la capital y un atractivo para el turismo," *El Universal*, July 18, 1954; see also Eduardo Chávez, "Agua en el valle de México," *México Forestal* 46 (September 1972): 11–12.

49 AHA: Consultivo Técnico 164, 1270, "Memorandum de la Comisión," February 16, 1950.

50 Robert C. West and Pedro Armillas, "Las chinampas de México: Poesía y realidad de los 'jardines flotantes' (1950)," in Rojas Rabiela, *Agricultura chinampera*, 103; Sanders, "El lago y el volcán," 139.

51 Romero Lankao and Duffing, "¿Tres procesos contradictorios?," in Terrones López, *A la orilla*, 226; Ernesto Aréchiga Córdoba, "De la exuberancia al agotamiento: Xochimilco y el agua, 1882–2004," in Terrones López, *A la orilla*, 104.

52 "Mortal epidemia de tifoidea se abate sobre esta metrópoli," *Excélsior*, July 7, 1939.

53 Benito Bucay, "Apuntes de historia de la química industrial en México," *Revista de la Sociedad Química de México* 45, no. 3 (July–September 2001): 136–142.

54 Fernando Vizcaíno, "El lago de Texcoco," *Ingeniería Hidraúlica en México* 3, no. 3 (1949): 17–18.

55 AHA: Consultivo Técnico 177, 1424, Miguel Brambilla, "Lineamientos Generales para el Proyecto de Obras del Vaso del Lago de Texcoco," May 30, 1947.

56 "Intensificación de las obras del Plan Lago de Texcoco," *El Nacional*, December 28, 1972; Francisco Vizcaíno, *La contaminación en México* (Mexico City: Fondo de la

Cultura Económica, 1975): 154; Gerardo Cruickshank, *Proyecto Lago de Texcoco* (Mexico City: Comisión Nacional del Agua, 2005).

57 AGA 23/914, bundle 3, "Comisariado ejidal al Departamento Agrario," October 19, 1949; AGA 23/914, bundle 3, "Ejido al Departamento Agrario," December 11, 1952.

58 "El estudio para fertilizar el vaso Texcoco y los sanos propósitos oficiales," *El Nacional*, April 24, 1935.

59 AGA 23/914, bundle 9.

60 AGA 23/914, bundle 3, "Arías al Departamento Agrario," January 10, 1953; AGA 23/914, bundle 3, "Informe," January 14, 1954.

61 AGA 25/914, bundle 8, "Censo Agrario," 1948. The agrarian census of 1948 put the village's population at 230. In the early 1920s the population had exceeded a thousand people.

62 AGA 23/914, bundle 3, "Informe del Consejo de Vigilancia," January 14, 1955.

63 AGA 23/914, bundle 17, "Petición," April 1955.

64 See AGA 24/939.

65 AGN: LCR 418.2/124, "Memorandum de la Confederación Nacional Campesina," October 8, 1940.

66 Ann Varley, "Urbanization and Agrarian Law: The Case of Mexico City," *Bulletin of Latin American Research* 4, no. 1 (1985): 2; Jorge Durand, *La ciudad invade al ejido: Proletarización, urbanización y lucha política en el Cerro de Judío* (Mexico City: CIESAS, 1983), 71.

67 Norma Angélica Castillo Palma, *Cuando la ciudad llegó a mi puerta: Una perspectiva histórica de los pueblos lacustres, la explosión demográfica y la crisis del agua en Iztapalapa* (Mexico City: UAM-Iztapalapa, 2012), 148; Secretaría de la Economía Nacional, *Sexto Censo de Población, Distrito Federal, 1940* (Mexico City: DDF, 1941), 5; Secretaría de la Economía Nacional, *Séptimo Censo General de Población, Distrito Federal 1950* (Mexico City: DDF, 1950), 23.

68 AGA 272.2/45, bundle 15.

69 Durand, *La ciudad invade*, 73.

70 AGA 272.2/45, bundle 13.

71 AGA 272.2/45, bundle 13.

72 AGA 272.2/45, bundle 13. "Memorandum de Alfonso Tico," April 3, 1948.

73 Durand, *La ciudad invade*, 73–75.

74 AGA 272.2/24, bundles 1–2.

75 AGA 272.2/24, bundles 2 and 13.

76 AGA 272.2/24, bundles 13 and 14.

77 Ejidal expropriations to create population centers were rare until the 1960s, when they became a central component of city land governance. See Ann Varley and Alan Gilbert, "From Renting to Self-Help Ownership? Residential Tenure in Urban Mexico since 1940," in *Housing and Land in Urban Mexico*, ed. Alan Gilbert (La Jolla: Center for U.S.-Mexican Studies, University of California, San Diego, 1989), 13–37; Durand, *La ciudad invade*, 66–69.

78 Varley and Gilbert, "From Renting," 24.

79 Diane E. Davis, *Urban Leviathan: Mexico City in the Twentieth Century* (Philadelphia: Temple University Press, 1994), 105–109.

80 Manuel Perló Cohen, "Política y vivienda en México, 1910–1952," *Revista Mexicana de Sociología* 41, no. 3 (July–September 1979): 803–805.

81 Perló Cohen, "Política y vivienda," 811; Antonio Azuela de la Cueva and María Soledad Cruz Rodríguez, "La institucionalización de las colonias populares y la política urbana en la ciudad de México (1940–1946)," *Sociología* 4, no. 9 (January–April 1989): 118; Miguel Osorio Marbán, *El sector popular del PRI* (Mexico: Coordinación Nacional de Estudios Históricos, Políticos y Sociales, 1994), 88.

82 AGN: LCR 418.2/57, "Unión de la colonia Buenos Aires a Cárdenas," February 2, 1940.

83 "Decreto que declara de utilidad pública la expropiación del terreno de la colonia Buenos Aires," *Diario Oficial de la Federación*, August 8, 1941.

84 "No simpatizan con la higienización," *Excélsior*, September 23, 1941.

85 AGN: MAC 562.11/59, "Carta Abierta a Ávila Camacho del Comité de la Defensa de la Colonia Buenos Aires," 1941.

86 "En contra de las expropiaciones sin causa, en contra de la anarquía," *El Universal*, October 27, 1941.

87 Anahí Ballent, "El arte de saber vivir: Modernización del habitar doméstico y cambio urbano, 1940–1970," in *Cultura y comunicación en la ciudad de México*, ed. Nestor García Canclini et al. (Iztapalapa: UAM-Iztapalapa, 1998), 1:73–77. After these apartment complexes for government employees were inaugurated in the 1940s and early 1950s, Pani set his sights even higher, on the utter destruction and modernist renewal of Tlatelolco, a poor neighborhood north of downtown. This third project replaced a vibrant urban neighborhood—the sort of community activist Jane Jacobs relished—with a series of apartment towers covering over a hundred hectares. See Rubén Gallo, "Tlatelolco: Mexico City's Dystopia," in *Noir Urbanisms: Dystopic Images of the Modern City*, ed. Gyan Prakash (Princeton, NJ: Princeton University Press, 2010), 56–65.

88 "Reglamento de Asociaciones Pro-Mejoramiento de las Colonias del Distrito Federal," in *Legislación sobre fraccionamientos y construcciones urbanas*, edited by Felipe Santibañez (Mexico, 1949), 183–185; "Para mejorar las colonias," *El Nacional*, March 28, 1941; "Forma de mejorar los servicios públicos," *El Universal*, March 19, 1941.

89 This was not to say that all grassroots political activity in urban communities ceased or that the corporatist state was able to impose unilateral authority over local organizations. A recent study of urban populism in post-Vargas São Paulo underscores neighborhood associations' limited "room for maneuver" and "continuous negotiation of autonomy," but more research into the postwar period is needed to throw light on this problematic in Mexico. See Adriano Luiz Duarte, "Neighborhood Associations, Social Movements, and Populism in Brazil, 1945–1953," *Hispanic American Historical Review* 89, no. 1 (February 2009): 137.

90 Varley, "Urbanization and Agrarian Law," 9.

91 Mario Pani, "La Ciudad Satélite de México," *Nivel* 5 (May 1959): 1–6.

CONCLUSION

1   José Emilio Pacheco, *Battles in the Desert and Other Stories*, trans. Katherine Silver (New York: New Directions, 1987), 82.

2   Alfonso Reyes, "Visión de Anáhuac" in Alfonso Reyes, *Visión de Anahuac y otros ensayos* (Mexico City: Fondo de Cultura Económica, 1995), 11.

3   Gilberto Galindo, "Única forma de resolver el problema del lago de Texcoco," *Excélsior*, June 5, 1935; Rafael de la Cerda, "Arenitas y tolvaneras," *El Universal*, June 21, 1932.

4   Paul B. Sears, "Dust in the Eyes of Science," *The Land* 3 (1948): 341.

5   Alfonso Reyes, "Palinodia del polvo," in Reyes, *Visión de Anahuac*, 211.

6   AHA: AS 118, 939, Fernando Madrid Mendizábal, "Breve reseña histórica de los principales problemas hidráulicos y sus derivados que han tenido que resolverse para hacer habitable la ciudad de México," 1946.

7   Gregory T. Cushman, *Guano and the Opening of the Pacific World: A Global Ecological History* (New York: Cambridge University Press, 2013), 140.

8   For texts representative of this harmonious and progressive view of Mexico's capital, see Baltasar Dromundo, *La metrópoli mexicana* (Mexico City: Colección Nezahualcóyotl, 1957), 150–151; Ubaldo Vargas Martínez, *La ciudad de México, 1325–1960* (Mexico City: DDF, 1961), 155–156.

9   By 1950 the aquifer was being exploited at a faster rate than rainwater could recharge it. See Gian Carlo Delgado-Ramos, "Water and the Political Ecology of Urban Metabolism: The Case of Mexico City," *Journal of Political Ecology* 22 (2015): 104.

10   "La ciudad inundada," *El Universal*, July 15, 1951.

11   Cushman, *Guano*, 190–195.

12   William Vogt, *Road to Survival* (New York: W. Sloane Associates, 1948); William Vogt, *El hombre y la tierra* (Mexico City: Secretaría de Educación Pública, 1944).

13   Juan de Díos Bojórquez, "Cuestiones vitales para el valle de México," *México Forestal* 28 (April 1950): 32. See also Paul B. Sears, *Deserts on the March* (Norman: University of Oklahoma Press, 1935).

14   Díos Bojórquez, "Cuestiones," 28.

15   Enrique Beltrán, El hombre y su ambiente: Ensayo sobre el valle de México (Mexico City: Fondo de Cultura Económica, 1958); Tom Gill, *Land Hunger in Mexico* (Washington, DC: Charles Lathrop Pack Forestry Foundation, 1951).

16   See Gonzalo Blanco Macías, "The Water Supply in Mexico City: Its Relation to Renewable Natural Resources," in *Proceedings of the Interamerican Conference on Conservation of Renewable Natural Resources, Denver, CO, September 7–20, 1948* (Washington, DC: Department of State, 1949), 363–369; Enrique Beltrán, *Los recursos naturales de México y su conservación* (Mexico City: SEP, 1946); Beltrán, *El hombre y su ambiente*.

17   Blanco Macías, "Water Supply," 364.

18   Blanco Macías, "Water Supply," 366. Blanco Macías trumpeted his proposals for the Basin of Mexico widely. See his "La reconquista ecológica del valle de México,"

El Universal, November 29, 1951; "Las tolvaneras o tormentas de polvo en el valle de México: Sus causas y sus remedios" (paper presented at the Primer Congreso Interamericano de Campesinos y Agrónomos, Mexico City, September 23, 1949, available in AHA: AS 2766, 38699).

19 Miguel Rebolledo, *Hundimiento e inundaciones en la ciudad de México* (Mexico City: B. de Silva, 1952), 40.

20 Guillermo Zárraga, *La tragedia del valle de México* (Mexico: Stylo, 1958), 29. On postwar Malthusianism, see Thomas Robertson, *The Malthusian Moment: Global Population Growth and the Birth of American Environmentalism* (New Brunswick, NJ: Rutgers University Press, 2012).

21 Diego Cañedo, *El gran planificador* (Mexico City: Casas, 1971).

22 Alberto T. Arai, *El hundimiento de la ciudad de México y su posible solución urbanística: VIII Congreso Panamericano de Arquitectos* (Mexico City: Impresión Económica, 1952), 10.

23 The commission consisted of the president, a high official of the Ministry of Hydraulic Resources, a representative from each state that composed the Basin of Mexico (the Federal District, the State of Mexico, and Hidalgo), a representative from the Association of Architects and Engineers, and a chief engineer. See Manuel Perló Cohen, *Historia de las obras, planes y problemas hidráulicos en el Distrito Federal* (Mexico: UNAM, 1989).

24 Secretaría de Recursos Hidráulicos y la Comisión Hidrológica de la Cuenca del Valle de México, "Breve descripción de la cuenca del valle de México, sus problemas hidráulicos y modos de resolverlos," *Ingeniería Hidráulica* 13 (July–September 1959): 1–17; Comisión Hidrológica de la Cuenca del Valle de México, "Boletín hidrológico de la cuenca del valle de México," *Ingeniería Hidráulica* 7 (1953): 78–105; Adolfo Orive Alba, "Los problemas del valle de México," *Ingeniería Hidráulica* 6 (April–June 1952): 5–16; Eduardo Chávez, "Obras contra inundaciones en la ciudad de México," *Ingeniería Hidráulica* 10 (January–March 1956): 11–23.

25 Comisión Hidrológica de la Cuenca del Valle de México, "Informe de los trabajos de estudio," *Revista Mexicana de Ingeniería y Arquitectura* 30, no. 1 (January–March 1952): 9.

26 Mauricio Gómez Mayorga, *La ciudad y la gente* (Mexico City: Jus, 1979), 242.

27 The settlements helped justify the need for expert control over the Texcoco bed. Commission members viewed the lower classes through the lens of social control in the name of environmental management. They regularly complained of "invasions" of lands set aside for infrastructure or floodplains, and they built barriers around Lake Texcoco to keep urban squatters out. Archivo del Palacio de Minería: Comisión Hidrológica de la Cuenca del Valle de México, *Actas correspondientes a las sesiones núms. 71 a 99 efectuadas el año de 1953*, Actas 73, 78.

28 Gustavo Díaz Ordaz and Alfonso Corona de Rosal, *La gran ciudad, 1966–1969* (Mexico City: Departamento del Distrito Federal, 1970), 23. This massive infrastructure project, ongoing today, was joined by the equally massive Cutzamala water-supply project in the early 1980s.

29 Eduardo Chávez, "Agua en el valle de México," *México Forestal* 46 (September 1972): 11–12.

30 Nabor Carrillo, "Influence of Artesian Wells in the Sinking of Mexico City" (1947), in *Volumen Nabor Carrillo, Comisión Impulsora y Coordinadora de la Investigación Científica*, Anuario 47 (Mexico City: Secretaría de Hacienda y Credito Público, 1969), 7–14; Donald Helm, "Field-Based Computational Techniques for Predicting Subsidence Due to Fluid Withdrawal," in *Man-Induced Land Subsidence*, ed. Thomas L. Holzer (Boulder, CO: Geological Society of America, 1984), 11.

31 Fernando Hiriart and Raúl J. Marsal, "Proyecto Texcoco," in *El hundimiento de la ciudad de México y Proyecto Texcoco*, ed. Comité Técnico de Proyecto Texcoco (Mexico City: Secretaría de Hacienda y Crédito Público 1969), 149–165.

32 Gerardo Aldana Martínez, "Degradación y recuperación de suelos en el pie de Monte Alto Texcocano," in *Mundo rural, ciudades y población del Estado de México* (Toluca, Mexico: Universidad IberoAmericana, 1990), 318–319.

33 For descriptions of the public works, see Secretaría de Recursos Hidráulicos, *Plan Lago de Texcoco* (Mexico City: SRH, 1975); Gerardo Cruickshank, *Proyecto Lago de Texcoco* (Mexico City: Comisión Nacional del Agua, 2005). The city used part of the federal property as its chief garbage dump until 2012, a scourge to the nearby residents of Ciudad Nezahualcóyotl.

34 Gobierno del Distrito Federal, *Vuelta a la ciudad lacustre: Memorias del congreso* (Mexico City: Gobierno del Distrito Federal, 1998).

35 During the 1970s and 1980s, the state created Ecoplans of the Federal District and of the Valley of Mexico and the Federal District Urban and Ecological Reorganization Program, among others. Yet in the early 1980s engineers embarked on another project of engineering grandiosity: the Cutzamala water-supply system. It did not immediately receive the same rebuke that deep drainage did, in part because its effects were felt by marginalized Mazahua indigenes far from Mexico City and because it was seen as the only means by which to alleviate land subsidence within the basin.

36 Beatriz Canabal Cristiani, *Xochimilco: Una identidad recreada* (Coyoacán: Universidad Autónoma Metropolitana-Xochimilco, 1997), 229; Matthew Klingle, *Emerald City: An Environmental History of Seattle* (New Haven, CT: Yale University Press, 2007).

37 My description of the Xochimilco recuperation project is based on Araceli Peralta Flores and Jorge Rojas Ramírez, *Xochimilco y sus monumentos históricos* (Mexico City: INAH, 1992); Jorge Legorreta, "Xochimilco: El rescate de una histórica tradición lacustre," in *Ensayos sobre la ciudad de México: Reencuentro con nuestro patrimonio cultural*, ed. Magdalena Mas and Isabel Tovar Arrecherderra (Mexico City: Universidad IberoAmericana, 1994), 6:15–58; Jorge Legorreta, "Transformación y restauración lacustre de la ciudad de México," in *Ciudad de México: A Debate*, ed. Jorge Legorreta (Mexico City: UAM-Azcapotzalco, 2008); Canabal Cristiani, *Xochimilco*; Ernesto Aréchiga Cordoba, "De la exuberancia al

agotamiento: Xochimilco y el agua, 1882–2004," in *A la orilla del agua: Políticas, urbanización y medio ambiente en el siglo XX*, ed. María Eugenia Terrones López (Mexico City: Instituto Mora, 2004), 97–149.

38   See Keith Pezzoli, *Human Settlements and Planning for Ecological Sustainability: The Case of Mexico City* (Cambridge, MA: MIT Press, 1998).

39   See, for example, Hong Kal, "Flowing Back to the Future: The Cheongye Stream Restoration and the Remaking of Seoul," *Asia-Pacific Journal* 9, no. 27 (July 2011): 1–17; Colin McFarlane, "Governing the Contaminated City: Infrastructure and Sanitation in Colonial and Post-colonial Bombay," *International Journal of Urban and Regional Research* 32, no. 2 (June 2008): 415–435; René Véron, "Remaking Urban Environments: The Political Ecology of Air Pollution in Delhi," *Environment and Planning A* 38 (2006): 2093–2109.

40   See Adam Rome, *The Bulldozer in the Countryside: Suburban Sprawl and the Rise of American Environmentalism* (Cambridge: Cambridge University Press, 2001); Christopher Sellers, *Crabgrass Crucible: Suburban Nature and the Rise of Environmentalism in Twentieth-Century America* (Chapel Hill: University of North Carolina Press, 2012).

41   Mike Davis and Daniel Bertrand Monk, *Evil Paradises: Dreamworlds of Neoliberalism* (New York: Verso, 2007).

42   David Harvey, *Justice, Nature, and the Geography of Difference* (Cambridge, MA: Blackwell, 1996), 417.

43   The work of organizations such as Taller 13 and Isla Urbana stands out.

44   One promising campaign is "Agua para todos" (Water for All), led by Elena Burns and Pedro Moctezuma Barragán.

45   Harvey, *Justice*, 417.

BIBLIOGRAPHY

ARCHIVES

Archivo del Palacio de Minería
Archivo General Agrario (AGA)
Archivo General de la Nación (AGN)
    Fondo Emiliano Zapata
    Ramo Presidentes
        Abelardo L. Rodríguez (ALR)
        Emilio Portes Gil
        Lázaro Cárdenas del Río (LCR)
        Manuel Ávila Camacho (MAC)
        Miguel Alemán Valdés (MAV)
        Obregón/Calles (O/C)
    Secretaría de Agricultura y Fomento (SAF)
    Secretaría de Agricultura y Recursos Hidráulicos (SARH)
    Secretaría de Comunicaciones y Obras Públicas (SCOP)
    Tribunal Superior de Justicia del Distrito Federal
Archivo Histórico del Agua (AHA)
    Aguas Nacionales (AN)
    Aguas Superficiales (AS)
    Consultivo Técnico
Archivo Histórico de la Secretaría de Salud
    Salubridad Pública
Archivo Histórico del Distrito Federal (AHDF)
    Ayuntamiento
    Consejo Superior del Gobierno del Distrito Federal
    Departamento del Distrito Federal (DDF)
    Diversiones

Gobierno del Distrito Federal (GDF)
Obras Públicas (OP)
Archivo Histórico Municipal de Xochimilco
Archivo Torreblanca-Calles
Fondo Obregón
Bancroft Library Manuscripts

PERIODICALS

Boletín de la Sociedad Mexicana de Geografía y Estadística
Boletín del Consejo de Salubridad
Boletín Municipal
El Demócrata
El Diario del Hogar
Diario de los Debates de la Cámara de Diputados
Diario Oficial de la Federación
Excélsior
El Hijo del Ahuizote
El Imparcial
El Nacional
Novedades
La Nueva Era
El País
El Radical
El Sol
Suceso
El Universal

BOOKS, CHAPTERS, ARTICLES, AND ONLINE SOURCES

Aboites Aguilar, Luis. *El agua de la nación: Una historia política de México (1888–1946)*. Mexico City: Centro de Investigaciones y Estudios Superiores en Antropología Social, 1998.
———. "Amecameca, 1922: Ensayo sobre centralización política y estado nacional en México." *Historia Mexicana* 49, no. 1 (January 1996): 55–93.
———. "Illusion of National Power: Water Infrastructure in Mexican Cities, 1930–1990." In *A Land between Waters: Environmental Histories of Modern Mexico*, edited by Christopher R. Boyer, 218–244. Tucson: University of Arizona Press, 2012.
Abrams, Philip. "Notes on the Difficulty of Studying the State." *Journal of Historical Sociology* 1, no. 1 (March 1988): 58–89.
Agostoni, Claudia. *Monuments of Progress: Modernization and Public Health in Mexico City, 1876–1910*. Calgary: University of Calgary Press, 2003.
Agrawal, Arun. *Environmentality: Technologies of Government and the Making of Subjects*. Durham, NC: Duke University Press, 2005.

Alberti, Marina. *Advances in Urban Ecology: Integrating Humans and Ecological Processes*. Boston: Springer Science, 2008.

Alcántara Onofre, Saúl. "The Chinampas before and after the Conquest." In *Botanical Progress, Horticultural Innovation, and Cultural Changes*, edited by Michel Conan and W. John Kress, 159–175. Washington, DC: Dumbarton Oaks Research Library and Collection, 2007.

Alcázar, Ramón I. *Poesias de Ramón I. Alcázar*. Mexico City: Imprenta de I. Cuplido, 1860.

Aldana Martínez, Gerardo. "Degradación y recuperación de suelos en el pie de Monte Alto Texcocano." In *Mundo rural, ciudades y población del Estado de México*, edited by Manuel Miño Grijalva, 313–322. Toluca, Mexico: Colegio Mexiquense, 1990.

Alexander, Anna Rose. *City on Fire: Technology, Social Change, and the Hazards of Progress in Mexico City, 1860–1910*. Pittsburgh: University of Pittsburgh Press, 2016.

Alonso, Carlos. "La cooperación de particulares para las obras de pavimento y banquetas en la ciudad de México." *Obras Públicas* 2 (February 1930).

Alonzo Romero, Miguel. *Un año de sitio en la presidencia municipal: Crónica y comentarios de una labor accidentada*. Mexico City: Editorial Hispano-Mexicana, 1923.

Altamirano, Fernando. "Estudios relativos a la evaporación del lago de Texcoco." In *Estudios referentes a la desecación del lago de Texcoco, año de 1895*, edited by Instituto Médico Nacional, 11–40. Mexico City: Secretaría de Fomento, 1895.

Álvarez Amezquita, José, Miguel E. Bustamante, Francisco Fernández del Castillo, and Antonio López Picasos. *Historia de la salubridad y de la asistencia en México*. Mexico City: Secretaría de Salubridad y Asistencia, 1960.

Álvarez del Castillo, Carlos. *La vegetación de la sierra del Ajusco*. Mexico City: Instituto Nacional de Antropología e Historia, 1987.

Alzate y Ramírez, José Antonio de. *Periodismo científico en el siglo XVIII*. Mexico City: Universidad Autónoma Metropolitana-Xochimilco, 2001.

———. *Proyecto de desecar la laguna de Tescuco y las de Chalco y San Cristóbal* (Mexico City: Gobierno de la Ciudad de México, 1998).

Anaya Pérez, Marco Antonio. *Rebelión y revolución en Chalco-Amecameca, Estado de México, 1821–1921*. Vol. 2. Mexico City: Instituto Nacional de Estudios Históricos de Las Revoluciones de México, 1997.

Angelo, Hillary, and David Wachsmuth. "Urbanizing Urban Political Ecology: A Critique of Methodological Cityism." In *Implosions/Explosions: Towards a Study of Planetary Urbanization*, edited by Neil Brenner, 372–385. Berlin: Jovis, 2014.

Apenas, Ola. "The Pond in Our Backyard." *Mexican Life* 19 (1943): 15–18.

———. "The Primitive Salt Production of Lake Texcoco." *Ethnos* 9, no. 1 (1944): 35–40.

Appuhn, Karl. "Friend or Flood?: The Dilemmas of Water Management in Early Modern Venice." In *The Nature of Cities: Culture, Landscape, and Urban Space*, edited by Andrew C. Isenberg, 79–102. Rochester, NY: University of Rochester Press, 2006.

————. "Inventing Nature: Forests, Forestry, and State Power in Renaissance Venice." *Journal of Modern History* 72, no. 4 (2000): 861–889.

Aragón, Agustín. "Palabras dichas en el entierro del Ing. Manuel Marroquín y Rivera." *Revista Mexicana de Ingeniería y Arquitectura* 5 (1927): 224–226.

Arai, Alberto T. *El hundimiento de la ciudad de México y su posible solución urbanística: VIII Congreso Panamericano de Arquitectos.* Mexico City: Impresión Económica, 1952.

Archivo General de la Nación, *Documentos inéditos sobre Emiliano Zapata y el cuartel general: Seleccionados del Archivo de Genovevo de la O, que conserva el Archivo General de la Nación.* Mexico City: Archivo General de la Nación, 1979.

Aréchiga Córdoba, Ernesto. "De la exuberancia al agotamiento: Xochimilco y el agua, 1882–2004." In *A la orilla del agua: Políticas, urbanización y medio ambiente en el siglo XX*, edited by María Eugenia Terrones López, 97–149. Mexico City: Instituto Mora, 2004.

Arrom, Silvia, and Servando Ortol, eds. *Riots in the Cities: Popular Politics and the Urban Poor in Latin America, 1765–1910.* Wilmington, DE: Scholarly Resources, 1996.

Asociación para la Planificación de la República. "Editorial sobre el plano regulador de la ciudad de México y sus alrededores." *Planificación* 1, no. 7 (March 1928): 16–19.

Atlas general del Distrito Federal: Geográfico, histórico, comercial, estadístico, agrario. Mexico City: Taller Gráfico de la Nación, 1930.

Auvinet Guichard, Gabriel. "El ingeniero Roberto Gayol y Soto y el hundimiento de la ciudad de México." *Geotécnica* 222 (December 2011–February 2012): 8–12.

Ávila Espinosa, Felipe. *Los orígenes del zapatismo.* Mexico City: Colegio de México, 2001.

Azuela de la Cueva, Antonio, and María Soledad Cruz Rodríguez. "La institucionalización de las colonias populares y la política urbana en la ciudad de México (1940–1946)." *Sociología* 4, no. 9 (January–April 1989): 111–133.

Baer, James. "Buenos Aires: Housing Reform and the Decline of the Liberal State in Argentina." In *Cities of Hope: People, Protests, and Progress in Urbanizing Latin America, 1870–1930*, edited by Ronn F. Pineo and James Baer, 89–129. Boulder, CO: Westview, 1998.

Balbontín, Manuel. "El lago de Texcoco." *Boletín de la Sociedad Mexicana de Geografía y Estadística* 1 (1873): 372–377.

Ballent, Anahí. "El arte de saber vivir: Modernización del habitar doméstico y cambio urbano, 1940–1970." In *Cultura y comunicación en la ciudad de México*, edited by Nestor García Canclini, Anahí Ballent, María Teresa Ejea, Ángela Giglia, Raúl Nieto, Eduardo Nivón, Patricia Ramírez Kuri, Ana Rosa Mantecón, and Patricia Safa Barraza, 1: 65–131. Mexico City: Universidad Autónoma Metropolitana-Iztapalapa, 1998.

Ballesteros, Juan. *Primer Censo de Edificios de los Estados Unidos Mexicanos.* Mexico City: Departamento de la Estadística Nacional, 1930.

Bannister, Jeffrey M., and Stacie G. Widdifield. "The Debut of Modern Water in Early 20th-Century Mexico City: The Xochimilco Potable Waterworks." *Journal of Historical Geography* 46 (2014): 36–52.

Bantjes, Adrian. *As if Jesus Walked on Earth: Cardenismo, Sonora, and the Mexican Revolution.* Wilmington, DE: Scholarly Resources, 1998.

Barbosa Cruz, Mario. *El trabajo en las calles: Subsistencia y negociación política en la ciudad de México a comienzos del siglo XX.* Mexico City: Colegio de México, 2008.

Barra, Ignacio de la. *Las aguas potables de la ciudad de Mexico: Estudio presentado en la Sociedad Mexicana de Geografía y Estadística.* Mexico City: Claret, 1932.

Barragán, Mariano. "Anexo 1." In Miguel Alonzo Romero, *Un año de sitio en la presidencia municipal: Crónica y comentarios de una labor accidentada,* 394–400. Mexico City: Editorial Hispano-Mexicana, 1923.

———. "Anexo 1B." In Miguel Alonzo Romero, *Un año de sitio en la presidencia municipal: Crónica y comentarios de una labor accidentada,* 401–413. Mexico City: Editorial Hispano-Mexicana, 1923.

———. "Memoria del saneamiento y cultivo del lago de Texcoco" (1910). In Carlos Contreras Servín, "El crecimiento urbano de la ciudad de México y la desecación del lago de Texcoco." *Relaciones* 76 (1998): 118–153.

———. *Proyecto de bonificación de las tierras del vaso del lago de Texcoco.* Mexico City: Secretaría de Comunicaciones y Obras Públicas, 1913.

Basurto, Jorge. "La conciencia tranquila: Entrevista con Ignacio Torres Vda. de Álvarez." In *Vivencias femeninas de la Revolución,* edited by Jorge Basurto, 15–48. Mexico City: Instituto Nacional de Estudios Históricos de Las Revoluciones de México, 1993.

Battaillon, Claude. *La ciudad y el campo en el México Central.* Mexico City: Siglo XXI, 1972.

Beatty, Edward. *Technology and the Search for Progress in Modern Mexico.* Berkeley: University of California Press, 2015.

Becher, Carl Christian. *Cartas sobre México: La República Mexicana durante los años decisivos de 1832-3.* Mexico City: UNAM, 1959.

Bedollo, Eugenio. "La junta flexible impermeable y su función en el aprovechamiento de agua potable de la ciudad de México." *Revista Mexicana de Ingeniería y Arquitectura* 11, no. 1 (January 1933): 1–15.

Beer, Gabriella de. *Luis Cabrera: Un intelectual en la revolución mexicana.* Translated by Ismael Pizarro and Mercedes Pizarro. Mexico City: Fondo de Cultura Económica, 1984.

Belina, Ladislao de. "Influencia de la altura sobre la vida y salud del habitante de Anáhuac, por el socio Dr. de Belina." *Boletín de la Sociedad Mexicana de Geografía y Estadística* 4 (1878): 298–303.

Beltrán, Enrique. *La batalla forestal: Lo hecho, lo no hecho, lo por hacer.* Mexico City: Editorial Cultura, 1964.

———. *El hombre y su ambiente.* Mexico City: Fondo de Cultura Económica, 1958.

———. *Los recursos naturales de México y su conservación.* Mexico City: Secretaría de Educación Pública, 1946.

Bennett, Jane. *Vibrant Matter: A Political Ecology of Things.* Durham, NC: Duke University Press, 2010.

Berra, Erica. "La expansión de la ciudad de México y los conflictos urbanos, 1900–1930." PhD diss., Mexico City: Centro de Estudios Históricos, Colegio de México, 1983.

Blackbourn, David. *The Conquest of Nature: Water, Landscape and the Making of Modern Germany.* New York: W. W. Norton, 2007.

Blanco Macías, Gonzalo. "The Water Supply in Mexico City: Its Relation to Renewable Natural Resources." In *Proceedings of the Interamerican Conference on Conservation of Renewable Natural Resources, Denver, CO, September 7–20, 1948*, 363–369. Washington, DC: Department of State, 1949.

Bliss, Katherine. *Compromised Positions: Prostitution, Public Health, and Gender Politics in Revolutionary Mexico City.* University Park, PA: Penn State University Press, 2001.

Bocking, Stephen. "Constructing Urban Expertise: Professional and Political Authority in Toronto, 1940–1970." *Journal of Urban History* 33, no. 1 (November 2006): 51–76.

Bosques, Gilberto. *The National Revolutionary Party and the Six Year Plan.* Mexico City: Bureau of Foreign Information of the Partido Nacional Revolucionario, 1937.

Boyer, Christopher R. *Becoming Campesinos: Politics, Identity, and Agrarian Struggle in Postrevolutionary Michoacán, 1920–1935.* Stanford, CA: Stanford University Press, 2003.

———. "Community, Crony Capitalism and Fortress Conservation in Mexican Forests." In *Dictablanda: Soft Authoritarianism in Mexico*, edited by Paul Gillingham, 217–235. Durham, NC: Duke University Press, 2014.

———. "La Segunda Guerra Mundial y la 'crisis de producción en los bosques mexicanos.'" *Historia Ambiental Latinoamericana y Caribeña* 2, no. 1 (September–February 2012): 7–23.

———. *Political Landscapes: Forests, Conservation, and Community in Mexico.* Durham, NC: Duke University Press, 2014.

———. "Revolución y paternalismo ecológico: Miguel Ángel de Quevedo y la política forestal en México, 1926–1940." *Historia Mexicana* 57, no. 1 (2007): 91–138.

Boyer, Christopher R., and Emily Wakild. "Social Landscaping in the Forests of Mexico: An Environmental Interpretation of Cardenismo, 1934–1940." *Hispanic American Historical Review* 92, no. 1 (February 2012): 73–106.

Brockington, Dan. *Fortress Conservation: The Preservation of the Mkomazi Game Reserve, Tanzania.* Bloomington: Indiana University Press, 2002.

Bucay, Benito. "Apuntes de historia de la química industrial en México." *Revista de la Sociedad Química de México* 45, no. 3 (July–September 2001): 136–142.

Buchenau, Jürgen. *Plutarco Elías Calles and the Mexican Revolution.* Lanham, MD: Rowman and Littlefield, 2007.

Cabrera, Luis. "Carta abierta a Presidente Francisco Madero April 27, 1911." In *Obras políticas*, edited by Eugenia Meyer, 1: 200–213. Mexico City: Instituto Nacional de Estudios Históricos de Las Revoluciones de México, 1985.

———. "La reconstitución de los ejidos de los pueblos como medio de suprimir la esclavitud del jornalero mexicano." In *Revolución e historia en la obra de Luis Cabrera*, edited by Eugenia Meyer (Mexico City: Fondo de Cultura Económica, 1994): 124–152.

———. "The Restoration of the Ejido." In *The Mexico Reader*, edited by Gilbert M. Joseph and Timothy J. Henderson, 344–350. Durham, NC: Duke University Press, 2002.

———. "La Revolución es la Revolución." In *La revolución es la revolución: documentos*, edited by Luis Cabrera and Humberto Hiriart Urdanivia, 137–145. Guanajuato: Gobierno del Estado de Guanajuato, 1977.

Calderón de la Barca, Francis. *La vida en México.* Mexico City: Porrúa, 1979.

Calva Tellez, José Luis. *Economía política de la explotación forestal en México: Bibliografía comentada, 1930–1984.* Mexico City: Universidad Autónoma Chapingo, 1989.

Camacho de la Rosa, Gerardo. *Raíz y razón de Totolapan: El drama de la Guerra Zapatista.* Mexico City: Gobierno del Distrito Federal, 2007.

Camp, Roderick Ai. *Mexican Political Biographies, 1884–1935.* Austin: University of Texas Press, 1991.

Campanella, Thomas J. *The Concrete Dragon: China's Urban Revolution and What It Means for the World.* New York: Princeton Architectural Press, 2008.

Canabal Cristiani, Beatriz. *Xochimilco: Una identidad recreada.* Coyoacán: Universidad Autónoma Metropolitana-Xochimilco, 1997.

Candiani, Vera. *Dreaming of Dry Land: Environmental Transformation in Colonial Mexico City.* Stanford, CA: Stanford University Press, 2014.

Cañedo, Diego. *El gran planificador.* Mexico City: Casas, 1971.

Cañizares-Esguerra, Jorge. "How Derivative Was Humboldt?: Microcosmic Narratives in Early Modern Spanish America and the (Other) Origins of Humboldt's Ecological Sensibilities." In *Nature, Empire, and Nation: Explorations of the History of Science in the Iberian World*, edited by Jorge Cañizares-Esguerra, 112–128. Stanford, CA: Stanford University Press, 2006.

———. "Landscapes and Identities: Mexico, 1850–1900." In *Nature, Empire, and Nation: Explorations of the History of Science in the Iberian World*, edited by Jorge Cañizares-Esguerra, 129–168. Stanford, CA: Stanford University Press, 2006.

Capello, Ernesto. *City at the Center of the World: Space, History, and Modernity in Quito.* Pittsburgh: University of Pittsburgh Press, 2011.

Carey, Mark. *In the Shadow of Melting Glaciers: Climate Change and Andean Society.* Oxford: Oxford University Press, 2010.

Carr, Barry. *Marxism and Communism in Twentieth-Century Mexico.* Lincoln: University of Nebraska Press, 1992.

Carranza, Luis. *Architecture as Revolution: Episodes in the History of Modern Mexico.* Austin: University of Texas Press, 2010.

Carreño, Alberto. "Nubes de polvo." *Boletín de la Sociedad Mexicana de Geografía y Estadística* 8 (1919): 233–236.

Carrillo, Nabor. "Influence of Artesian Wells in the Sinking of Mexico City" (1947). In *Volumen Nabor Carrillo, Comisión Impulsora y Coordinadora de la Investigación Científica*, 7–14. Yearbook 47. Mexico City: Secretaría de Hacienda y Crédito Público, 1969.

Castillo Palma, Norma Angélica. *Cuando la ciudad llegó a mi puerta. Una perspectiva histórica de los pueblos lacustres, la explosión demográfica y la crisis del agua en Iztapalapa.* Mexico City: Universidad Autónoma Metropolitana-Iztapalapa, 2012.

Castonguay, Stéphane, and Michèle Dagenais. Introduction to *Metropolitan Natures: Environmental Histories of Montreal*, edited by Stéphane Castonguay and Michèle Dagenais, 1–16. Pittsburgh: University of Pittsburgh Press, 2011.

———, eds. *Metropolitan Natures: Environmental Histories of Montreal*. Pittsburgh: University of Pittsburgh Press, 2011.

Chapa, Sostenes N. *San Gregorio Atlapulco, Xochimilco, D.F.* Mexico City: 1959.

Chávez, Eduardo. "Agua en el valle de México." *México Forestal* 46 (September 1972): 11–12.

———. "Obras contra inundaciones en la ciudad de México." *Ingeniería Hidráulica* 10 (January–March 1956): 11–23.

Chazkel, Amy. *Laws of Chance: Brazil's Clandestine Lottery and the Making of Urban Public Life.* Durham, NC: Duke University Press, 2011.

Coatsworth, John. *Growth against Development: The Economic Impact of Railroads in Porfirian Mexico.* DeKalb: Northern Illinois University Press, 1981.

Collado, María del Carmen. "Los sonorenses en la capital." In *Miradas recurrentes: La ciudad de México en los siglos XIX y XX*, edited by María del Carmen Collado, 102–131. Mexico City: Instituto Mora, 2004.

Comisión Especial para Estudio de Abastecimiento de Aguas de la Ciudad de México. *Informe sobre el proyecto del Ing. Marroquín y Rivera, Estudio sobre las proposciones del Sr. Mackenzie.* Mexico City: Secretaría de Fomento, 1902.

Comisión Hidrológica de la Cuenca del Valle de México. "Boletín hidrológico de la cuenca del valle de México." *Ingeniería Hidráulica* 7 (1953): 78–105.

———. "Informe de los trabajos de estudio." *Revista Mexicana de Ingeniería y Arquitectura* 30, no. 1 (January–March 1952): 1–17.

Connolly, Priscilla. *El contratista de don Porfirio: Obras públicas, deuda y desarrollo desigual.* Mexico City: Fondo de Cultura Económica, 1997.

Consejo Superior de Salubridad. *Informes rendidos por los inspectores sanitarios de Cuartel.* Mexico City: Imprenta del Gobierno, 1898.

"Constitución Política de los Estados Unidos Mexicanos." *Diario Oficial de la Federación* (February 5, 1917).

Contreras, Carlos. *El plano regulador del Distrito Federal.* Mexico City: Carlos Contreras, 1933.

Contreras Servín, Carlos. "La desecación del lago de Texcoco." *Relaciones* 76 (fall 1998): 132–153.

Contreras Tirado, Bonifacio. *El doctor Aureliano Urrutia: Ciencia y política durante el Porfiriato y el Huertismo*. Mexico City: Centro de Estudios Históricos sobre el Porfiriato, 2003.

Conway, Richard. "Lakes, Canoes, and the Aquatic Communities of Xochimilco and Chalco, New Spain." *Ethnohistory* 59, no. 3 (summer 2012): 541–568.

"Coordinación entre las labores de los Departamentos Agrario y Forestal y de Caza y Pesca en relación con la dotación y ampliación de ejidos." *Boletín del Departamento Forestal y de Caza y Pesca* 2, no. 2 (February–April 1936).

Cope, Douglas R. *The Limits of Racial Domination: Plebeian Society in Colonial Mexico City, 1660–1720*. Madison: University of Wisconsin Press, 1994.

Corbin, Alain. *The Foul and the Fragrant: Odor and the French Social Imagination*. Cambridge, MA: Harvard University Press, 1986.

Cornelius, Wayne. *Politics and the Migrant Poor in Mexico City*. Stanford, CA: Stanford University Press, 1975.

Coronil, Fernando. "Smelling like a Market." *American Historical Review* 106, no. 1 (February 2001): 119–129.

Craib, Raymond. *Cartographic Mexico: A History of State Fixations and Fugitive Landscapes*. Durham, NC: Duke University Press, 2004.

Crónicas y debates de las sesiones de la Soberana Convención Revolucionaria. Vol. 2. Mexico City: Biblioteca del Instituto Nacional de Estudios Históricos de la Revolución Mexicana, 1965.

Cronon, William. *Nature's Metropolis: Chicago and the Great West*. New York: W. W. Norton, 1991.

Cruickshank, Gerardo. *Proyecto Lago de Texcoco*. Mexico City: Comisión Nacional del Agua, 2005.

Cruz Rodríguez, María Soledad. *Crecimiento urbano y los procesos sociales en el Distrito Federal (1920–1928)*. Mexico City: Universidad Autónoma Metropolitana-Azcapotzalco, 1994.

Cushman, Gregory T. *Guano and the Opening of the Pacific World: A Global Ecological History*. New York: Cambridge University Press, 2013.

Dávalos, Marcela. *Basura e ilustración: La limpieza de la ciudad de México a finales del siglo XVIII*. Mexico City: INAH, 1997.

Davis, Diana K. "Desert 'Wastes' of the Maghreb: Desertification Narratives in French Colonial Environmental History of North Africa." *Cultural Geographies* 11 (2004): 359–387.

———. *Resurrecting the Granary of Rome: Environmental History and French Colonial Expansion in North Africa*. Athens: Ohio University Press, 2007.

Davis, Diane E. "El rumbo de la esfera pública: Influencias locales, nacionales e internacionales en la urbanización del centro de la ciudad de México, 1910–1950." In *Actores, espacios y debates en la historia de la esfera pública en la ciudad de México*, edited by Cristina Sacristán and Pablo Piccato, 233–271. Mexico City: Instituto de Investigaciones Históricas, UNAM, 2005.

———. *Urban Leviathan: Mexico City in the Twentieth Century.* Philadelphia: Temple University Press, 1994.

Davis, Mike, and Daniel Bertrand Monk. *Evil Paradises: Dreamworlds of Neoliberalism.* New York: Verso, 2007.

Delgado-Ramos, Gian Carlo. "Water and the Political Ecology of Urban Metabolism: The Case of Mexico City." *Journal of Political Ecology* 22 (2015): 98–114.

Denevan, William. "The Pristine Myth: The Landscape of the Americas in 1492." *Annals of the Association of American Geographers* 82, no. 3 (September 1992): 369–386.

Departamento del Distrito Federal. *El Departamento del Distrito Federal y la habitación para empleados y obreros.* Mexico City: Departamento del Distrito Federal, 1934.

Departamento del Distrito Federal. *Memorias del Departamento del Distrito Federal (1934–35).* Mexico City: Gobierno del Distrito Federal, 1935.

Departamento del Distrito Federal. *Memorias del Departamento del Distrito Federal 1939–1940.* Mexico City: Departamento del Distrito Federal, 1940.

Desagüe del valle de México: Documentos relativos al proyecto de ejucación. Mexico City: Secretaría de Fomento, 1888.

Deverell, William Francis, and Greg Hise, eds. *Land of Sunshine: An Environmental History of Metropolitan Los Angeles.* Pittsburgh: University of Pittsburgh Press, 2005.

Díaz Ordaz, Gustavo, and Alfonso Corona de Rosal. *La gran ciudad, 1966–1969.* Mexico City: Departamento del Distrito Federal, 1970.

Díos Bojórquez, Juan de. "Cuestiones vitales para el valle de México." *México Forestal* 28 (April 1950): 27–36.

Dirección General de Estadística. "Tabulados Básicos: Bienes Raices." Censo General de Habitantes, 1921. http://www.beta.inegi.org.mx/proyectos/ccpv/1921/.

Dolores Morales, María. "La expansión de la ciudad de México en el siglo XIX: El caso de los fraccionamientos." In *Ciudad de México: Ensayo de construcción de una historia,* edited by Alejandra Moreno Toscano and Carlos Aguirre, 189–200. Mexico City: Secretaría de Educación Pública, 1978.

Domínguez, Norberto. "Discurso pronunciado en honor de Manuel Marroquín y Rivera." *Revista Mexicana de Ingeniería y Arquitectura* 5 (1927): 265–267.

Dromundo, Baltasar. *La metrópoli mexicana.* Mexico City: Colección Nezahualcóyotl, 1957.

Duarte, Adriano Luiz. "Neighborhood Associations, Social Movements, and Populism in Brazil, 1945–1953." *Hispanic American Historical Review* 89, no. 1 (February 2009): 111–139.

Durán, Nicolás. "Política y obras públicas." *Revista Mexicana de Ingeniería y Arquitectura* 11, no. 5 (May 1933): 153–160.

Durand, Jorge. *La ciudad invade al ejido: Proletarización, urbanización y lucha política en el Cerro de Judío, D.F.* Mexico City: Centro de Investigación y Estudios Superiores en Antropología Social, 1983.

———. "Huelga nacional de inquilinos: Los antecedentes del movimiento urbano popular en México." *Estudios Sociológicos* 7, no. 19 (1989): 61–78.

Eiss, Paul. *In the Name of El Pueblo: Place, Community, and the Politics of Community in Yucatán*. Durham, NC: Duke University Press, 2010.

"El Primer Congreso Forestal Mexicano." *México Forestal* 7 (March 1930): 23–24.

"Entrada de combustibles vegetales a la capital de la república." *Boletín del Departamento Forestal y de Caza y Pesca* 4, no. 3 (August 1938): 98–99.

Escobar Ohmstede, Antonio. "La reforma agraria y los procesos de urbanización de ejidos y comunidades: Los casos de Xochimilco y Santa María Chimalhuacán." In *Estudios campesinos en el Archivo General Agrario*, edited by Antonio Escobar Ohmstede, 3:13–116. Mexico City: CIESAS, 2001.

Espinosa, Luis and Isidro Díaz Lombardo, "Reseña técnica de la ejecución del Gran Canal y de las obras de arte, 1886–1900." In *Memoria histórica, técnica y administrativa de las obras del desagüe del valle de México, 1449–1900*, edited by Luis González Obregón, Vol. 1: 433–508. Mexico City: Oficina Impresora de Estampillas, 1902.

Espinosa, Mariola. "Globalizing the History of Medicine, Disease, and Public Health in Latin America." *Isis* 104, no. 4 (December 2013): 798–806.

Espinosa de los Monteros, Antonio. *El problema del carbón en el Distrito Federal*. Mexico City: Mundial, 1928.

Fallaw, Ben. *Cárdenas Compromised: The Failure of Reform in Postrevolutionary Yucatan*. Durham, NC: Duke University Press, 2001.

Fischer, Brodwyn. "A Century in the Present Tense: Crisis, Politics, and the Intellectual History of Brazil's Informal Cities." In *Cities from Scratch: Poverty and Informality in Urban Latin America*, edited by Brodwyn Fischer, Bryan McCann, and Javier Auyero, 9–67. Durham, NC: Duke University Press, 2014.

———. *A Poverty of Rights: Citizenship and Inequality in Twentieth-Century Rio de Janeiro*. Stanford, CA: Stanford University Press, 2008.

Flores, Teodoro. *El tequesquite del lago de Texcoco*. Mexico City: Anales del Instituto Geológico de México, 1918.

Forsyth, Tim, and Andrew Walker. *Forest Guardians, Forest Destroyers: The Politics of Environmental Knowledge in Northern Thailand*. Seattle: University of Washington Press, 2008.

Frandsen, Steen Bo. "'The War That We Prefer': The Reclamation of the Pontine Marshes and Fascist Expansion." *Totalitarian Movements and Political Religions* 2, no. 3 (winter 2001): 69–82.

Friedrich, Paul. *Agrarian Revolt in a Mexican Village*. Chicago: University of Chicago Press, 1977.

Fuentes Zamorate, José. "El problema agrario en Xochimilco." Professional thesis, UNAM, 1946.

Gadgil, Madhav, and Ramachandra Guha. *The Fissured Land: An Ecological History of India*. Berkeley: University of California Press, 1993.

Galindo y Villa, Jesús. *Historia sumaria de la ciudad de México*. Mexico City: Editorial Cultura, 1925.

———. *Reseña histórica-descriptiva de la ciudad de México.* Mexico City: Díaz de Leon, 1901.

Gallo, Rubén. *Mexican Modernity: The Avant Garde and the Technological Revolution.* Cambridge, MA: MIT Press, 2005.

———. "Tlatelolco: Mexico City's Dystopia." In *Noir Urbanisms: Dystopic Images of the Modern City,* edited by Gyan Prakash, 53–72. Princeton, NJ: Princeton University Press, 2010.

Gamboa, Federico. *Santa: A Novel of Mexico City.* Translated by John Charles Chasteen. Chapel Hill: University of North Carolina Press, 2010.

Gandy, Matthew. *Concrete and Clay: Reworking Nature in New York City.* Cambridge, MA: MIT Press, 2002.

Garay, Adrián de. *Juicio sobre las obras del desagüe del valle de México: Triunfo de las ideas del ingeniero Francisco de Garay.* Mexico City, 1930.

García Acosta, Virginia, and Gerardo Suárez Reynosa. *Los sismos en la historia de México.* Mexico City: Universidad Nacional Autónoma de México, 2001.

García Cubas, Antonio. *Cuadro geográfico, estadístico, descriptivo e histórico de los Estados Unidos Mexicanos.* Mexico City: Secretaría de Fomento, 1885.

———. *Geografía e historia del Distrito Federal.* Mexico City: Murguía, 1892.

García Luna, Margarita. *Nezahualcóyotl: Tierras que surgen de un desequilibrio ecológico; Decretos relativos a los terrenos desecados del lago de Texcoco, 1912–1940.* Toluca, MX: Gobierno del Estado de México, 1990.

García Martínez, José. "Superficies forestales de la república." *Boletín del Departamento Forestal y de Caza y Pesca* 3, no. 8 (September–November 1937): 125–140.

Garner, Paul. *British Lions and Mexican Eagles: Business, Politics, and Empire in the Career of Weetman Pearson in Mexico, 1889–1919.* Stanford, CA: Stanford University Press, 2011.

Gayol, Roberto. *Dos problemas de vital importancia para México: La colonización y el desarrollo de la irrigación.* Mexico City: Montes de Oca, 1906.

———. "The Drainage of Mexico City." *Public Health Papers and Reports* 17 (1891). http://www.ncbi.nlm.nih.gov/pmc/articles/PMC2266410/?page=1.

———. "Informe sobre varios asuntos relativos a las obras de saneamiento y desagüe de la ciudad de México." *Revista Mexicana de Ingeniería y Arquitectura* 11, NO. 3 (March 1933): 69–93.

———. "Perturbaciones producidas en el fondo del valle de México por el drenaje de las aguas del subsuelo." *Revista Mexicana de Ingeniería y Arquitectura* 3, no. 2 (February 1925): 96–132.

———. *Proyecto de desagüe y saneamiento para la ciudad de México.* Mexico City: Secretaría de Fomento, 1892.

Gibson, Charles. *The Aztecs under Spanish Rule: A History of the Indians of the Valley of Mexico, 1519–1810.* Stanford, CA: Stanford University Press, 1964.

Gilbert, Alan ed. *Housing and Land in Urban Mexico.* La Jolla: Center for U.S.-Mexican Studies, University of California, San Diego, 1989.

Gill, Tom. *Land Hunger in Mexico*. Washington, DC: Charles Lathrop Pack Forestry Foundation, 1951.

Gilly, Adolfo. *La revolución interrumpida*. Mexico City: ERA, 1994.

Gobierno del Distrito Federal. *Vuelta a la ciudad lacustre: Memorias del congreso.* Mexico City: Gobierno del Distrito Federal, 1998.

Gomezcésar, Iván. *Pueblos arrasados: El zapatismo en Milpa Alta*. Mexico City: Gobierno del Distrito Federal, 2009.

Gómez Mayorga, Mauricio. *La ciudad y la gente*. Mexico City: Jus, 1979.

Gonzales, Michael. "Imagining Mexico in 1921: Visions of the Revolutionary State and Society in the Centennial Celebration in Mexico City." *Mexican Studies/Estudios Mexicanos* 25, no. 2 (summer 2009): 247–270.

González Hernández, Gonzalo. "El problema agrícola en los terrenos del antiguo vaso del lago de Texcoco." *México Forestal* 11 (July 1933): 133–142.

González Martínez, Alfonso. "Sobre el futuro de la bioregión de Xochimilco: La lucha de los chinamperos por sus tierras ejidales." In *Pasado, presente y futuro de las chinampas*, edited by Teresa Rojas Rabiela, 229–245. Mexico City: Centro de Investigación y Estudios Superiores en Antropología Social-Patronato del Parque Ecológico Xochimilco, 1991.

González Navarro, Moisés. "México en una laguna." *Historia Mexicana* 4 (1955): 506–522.

———. *Población y sociedad, 1900–1970*. Vol. 1. Mexico City: Universidad Nacional Autónoma de México, 1974.

González Obregón, Luis. *Memoria histórica, técnica y administrativa de las obras del desagüe del valle de México, 1449–1900*. Mexico City: Oficina Impresora de Estampillas, 1902.

Graham, Jonathan. "A Tale of Two Valleys: An Examination of the Hydrological Union of the Mezquital Valley and the Basin of Mexico." In *Mexico in Focus: Political, Environmental and Social Issues*, edited by José Galindo, 31–80. New York: Nova Science, 2015.

Graham, Stephen, and Simon Marvin. *Splintering Urbanism: Networked Infrastructure, Technological Mobilities, and the Urban Condition*. London: Routledge, 2001.

Grandin, Greg. "The Liberal Tradition in the Americas: Rights, Sovereignty, and the Origins of Liberal Multilateralism." *American Historical Review* 117, no. 1 (February 2012): 68–91.

Grove, Richard. *Green Imperialism: Colonial Expansion, Tropical Island Edens and the Origins of Environmentalism, 1600–1860*. Cambridge: Cambridge University Press, 1995.

Guerrero, José. "La huelga de inquilinos." Mexico City: Imprenta Correo Mayor, n.d.

Guerrero, Julio. *La genesis del crimen en México: Estudio de psiquiatría social*. Paris: Bouret, 1901.

Guerrero, Salvador, "La conservación forestal y el indígena." *Boletín del Departamento Forestal y de Caza y Pesca* 3, no. 7 (April–August 1937): 130–137.

Guthrie, Chester L. "Riots in Seventeenth-Century Mexico City: A Study of Social and Economic Conditions." In *Greater America: Essays in Honor of Herbert Eugene Bolton*, edited by Adele Ogdon and Engel Sluiter, 243–258. Berkeley: University of California Press, 1945.

Gutiérrez, Leandro H., and Juan Suriano. "Workers' Housing and Living Conditions in Buenos Aires, 1880–1930." In *Essays in Argentine Labour History, 1870–1930*, edited by Jeremy Adelman, 35–51. Basingstoke: Macmillan in association with St. Anthony's College Oxford, 1992.

Gutiérrez de McGregor, María Teresa, and Jorge González Sánchez. *Geohistoria de la ciudad de México (siglos XIV a XIX)*. Mexico City: Universidad Nacional Autónoma de México, 2002.

Hale, Charles. *Transformation of Liberalism in Late Nineteenth-Century Mexico*. Princeton, NJ: Princeton University Press, 1989.

Hall, Peter. *Cities of Tomorrow: An Intellectual History of Urban Planning and Design since 1880*. 4th ed. Chichester, West Sussex, UK: Wiley-Blackwell, 2014.

Hamilton, Nora. *The Limits to State Autonomy: Postrevolutionary Mexico*. Princeton, NJ: Princeton University Press, 1982.

Hard, Mikael, and Andrew Jamison. *Hubris and Hybrids: A Cultural History of Technology and Science*. New York: Routledge, 2005.

Harvey, David. *Justice, Nature, and the Geography of Difference*. Cambridge, MA: Blackwell, 1996.

———. *The Urbanization of Capital: Studies in the History and Theory of Capitalist Urbanization*. Baltimore: Johns Hopkins University Press, 1985.

Hay, Eduardo. "Discurso de clausura por el Sr. ing. Eduardo Hay." *Revista Mexicana de Ingeniería y Arquitectura* 17, no. 6 (June 1939): 341–343.

Healey, Mark. *The Ruins of the New Argentina: Peronism and the Remaking of San Juan after the 1944 Earthquake*. Durham, NC: Duke University Press, 2011.

Helm, Donald. "Field-Based Computational Techniques for Predicting Subsidence due to Fluid Withdrawal." In *Man-Induced Land Subsidence*, edited by Thomas L. Holzer, 1–22. Boulder, CO: Geological Society of America, 1984.

Henderson, Timothy. *The Worm in the Wheat: Rosalie Evans and Agrarian Struggle in the Puebla-Tlaxcala Valley of Mexico, 1906–1927*. Durham, NC: Duke University Press, 1998.

Hernández Varela, Alfonso. "Los peligros a que ha estado expuesto el valle de México." *Boletín de la Sociedad Mexicana de Geografía y Estadística* 57 (September–December 1942): 363–388.

Herrera, Alfonso L. "Fauna del lago de Texcoco." In *Estudios referentes a la desecación del lago de Texcoco, año de 1895*, edited by the Instituto Médico Nacional, 41–62. Mexico City: Secretaría de Fomento, 1895.

Heynen, Nik, Maria Kaika, and Erik Swyngedouw, eds. *In the Nature of Cities: Urban Political Ecology and the Politics of Urban Metabolism*. London: Routledge, 2006.

Hiriart, Fernando, and Raúl J. Marsal. "Proyecto Texcoco." In *Nabor Carrillo: El hundimiento de la ciudad de México y Proyecto Texcoco*, edited by Comité Técnico de Proyecto Texcoco, 149–165. Mexico City: Secretaría de Hacienda y Crédito Público, 1969.

Horta Duarte, Regina. "Between the National and the Universal: Natural History Networks in Latin America in the Nineteenth and Twentieth Centuries." *Isis* 104, no. 4 (December 2013): 777–787.

Humboldt, Alexander von. *Ensayo político sobre el Reino de la Nueva España*. Mexico City: Porrúa, 1984.

———. *Political Essay on the Kingdom of New Spain*. London: Longman, 1811.

Ibargüengoitia, Jorge. "Call the Doctor." In *The Mexico City Reader*, edited by Ruben Gallo and Lorna Scott Fox, 195–197. Madison: University of Wisconsin Press, 2004.

"Informe mensual: Octubre de 1936." *Boletín del Departamento Forestal y de Caza y Pesca* 2, no. 5 (September–December 1936): 103–112.

"Informe sobre los peces procedentes del Japón." *Boletín del Departamento Forestal y de Caza y Pesca* 2, no. 5 (September–December 1936): 163–166.

Isenberg, Andrew C. "Banking on Sacramento: Urban Development, Flood Control and Political Legitimization, 1848–1862." In *The Nature of Cities: Culture, Landscape, and Urban Space*, edited by Andrew C. Isenberg, 103–121. Rochester, NY: University of Rochester Press, 2006.

———. "New Directions in Urban Environmental History." In *The Nature of Cities: Culture, Landscape, and Urban Space*, edited by Andrew C. Isenberg, xi–xvii. Rochester, NY: University of Rochester Press, 2006.

Jacoby, Karl. *Crimes against Nature: Squatters, Poachers, Thieves, and the Hidden History of American Conservation*. Berkeley: University of California Press, 2001.

Jáuregui, Ernesto. "Dust Storms of Mexico City." *International Journal of Climatology* 9 (1989): 169–180.

Jiménez, Christina. "From the Lettered City to the Sellers' City: Vendor Politics and Public Space in Urban Mexico, 1880–1926." In *The Spaces of the Modern City*, edited by Gyan Prakash and Kevin M. Kruse, 214–246. Princeton, NJ: Princeton University Press, 2008.

———. "Popular Organizing for Public Services: Residents Modernize Morelia, Mexico, 1880–1920." *Journal of Urban History* 30, no. 4 (2004): 495–518.

Jiménez Muñoz, Jorge. *La traza del poder: Historia de la política y los negocios urbanos en el Distrito Federal, de sus orígenes a la desaparición del Ayuntamiento*. Mexico City: Codex, 1993.

Johns, Michael. *The City of Mexico in the Age of Díaz*. Austin: University of Texas Press, 1997.

Joseph, Gilbert M., and Daniel Nugent, eds. *Everyday Forms of State Formation: Revolution and the Negotiation of Rule in Modern Mexico*. Durham, NC: Duke University Press, 1994.

Joseph, Gilbert M., and Alan Wells. "Modernizing Visions, 'Chilango' Blueprints, and Provincial Growing Pains: Mérida at the Turn of the Century." *Mexican Studies/Estudios Mexicanos* 8, no. 2 (summer 1992): 167–215.

Josephson, Paul. *Industrialized Nature: Brute Force Technology and the Transformation of the Natural World*. New York: Island, 2002.

Juárez Flores, José Juan. "Besieged Forests at Century's End: Industry, Speculation, and Dispossession in Tlaxcala's La Malintzin Woodlands, 1860–1910." In *A Land between Waters: Environmental Histories of Modern Mexico*, edited by Christopher R. Boyer, 100–123. Tucson: University of Arizona Press, 2012.

Juárez Herrera, Rodrigo. "El carbón vegetal en la economía doméstica." *México Forestal* 23 (June 1945): 55–57.

Junta Directiva de Desagüe y Saneamiento. *Report on the Valley Drainage Works and the Sanitation Works of Mexico City, November 1, 1896*. Mexico City: Tipografía Artística Ramón F. Riveroll, 1896.

Kal, Hong. "Flowing Back to the Future: The Cheongye Stream Restoration and the Remaking of Seoul." *Asia-Pacific Journal* 9, no. 27 (July 2011): 1–17.

Katz, Frederick. "Violence and Terror in the Russian and Mexican Revolutions." In *A Century of Revolution: Insurgent and Counterinsurgent Violence during Latin America's Long Cold War*, edited by Greg Grandin, 45–61. Durham, NC: Duke University Press, 2010.

Kelman, Ari. "Boundary Issues: Clarifying New Orleans's Murky Edges." In *Cities and Nature in the American West*, edited by Char Miller, 195–204. Reno: University of Nevada Press, 2010.

Klingle, Matthew. *Emerald City: An Environmental History of Seattle*. New Haven, CT: Yale University Press, 2007.

Klubock, Thomas Miller. *La Frontera: Forests and Ecological Conflict in Chile's Frontier Territory*. Durham, NC: Duke University Press, 2014.

Knight, Alan. "Cardenismo: Juggernaut or Jalopy?" *Journal of Latin American Studies* 26, no. 1 (February 1994): 73–107.

———. *The Mexican Revolution*. 2 vols. Cambridge: Cambridge University Press, 1986.

Kostof, Spiro. *The City Assembled: The Elements of Urban Form through History*. Boston: Little, Brown, 1992.

Kouri, Emilio. "Interpreting the Expropriation of Indian Pueblo Lands in Porfirian Mexico: The Unexamined Legacies of Andrés Molina Enríquez." *Hispanic American Historical Review* 82, no. 1 (2002): 69–117.

Kreiger, Peter, ed. *Transformaciones del paisaje urbano en México: Representación y registro visual*. Mexico City: Museo Nacional de Arte, 2012.

Kresic, Nevin, and Zoran Stevanovic. *Groundwater Hydrology of Springs: Engineering, Theory, Management, and Sustainability*. Burlington, MA: Butterworth-Heinemann, 2010.

Kroeber, Clifton. *Man, Land and Water: Mexico's Farmlands Irrigation Policy, 1885–1911*. Berkeley: University of California Press, 1983.

"La labor social del Departamento Forestal y de Caza y Pesca, entre la tribu Yaqui." *Boletín del Departamento Forestal y de Caza y Pesca* 1, no. 4 (May–August 1936): 160–161.

LaFrance, David. "La educación y la salud pública en Puebla, 1920–1940: ¿Avances revolucionarios?" In *Norma y espacio urbano: Ciudad de Puebla, siglos XVI–XX*, edited by Lilián Illades Aguiar, 199–243. Puebla: Benemérita Universidad Autónoma de Puebla, 2008.

Laporte, Dominique. *History of Shit.* Cambridge, MA: MIT Press, 2000.

Latour, Bruno. *We Have Never Been Modern.* Cambridge, MA: Harvard University Press, 1993.

Lear, John. *Workers, Neighbors, and Citizens: The Revolution in Mexico City.* Lincoln: University of Nebraska Press, 2001.

Lefebvre, Henri. *The Urban Revolution.* Translated by Robert Bononno. Minneapolis: University of Minnesota Press, 2003.

Legorreta, Jorge. "Transformación y restauración lacustre de la ciudad de México." In *Ciudad de México: A Debate,* edited by Jorge Legorreta, 207–223. Mexico City: Universidad Autónoma Metropolitana-Azcapotzalco, 2008.

———. "Xochimilco: El rescate de una histórica tradición lacustre." In *Ensayos sobre la ciudad de México: Reencuentro con nuestro patrimonio cultural,* edited by Magdalena Mas and Ísabel Tovar Arrechederra, 6:15–58. Mexico City: Universidad IberoAmericana, 1994.

Leidenberger, Georg. "Tres revistas mexicanas de arquitectura: Portavoces de la modernidad, 1923–1950." *Anales del Instituto de Investigaciones Estéticas* 34, no. 101 (November 2012): 109–138.

Leitner, Ulrike. "Humboldt's Work on Mexico." *Quipu* 13, no. 1 (2000): 7–23.

Leman-Stefanovic, Ingrid, and Stephen B. Scharper, eds. *The Natural City: Re-envisioning the Built Environment.* Toronto: University of Toronto Press, 2012.

Lenz, Hans. *Historia del papel en México y cosas relacionadas.* Mexico City: Porrúa, 1990.

Lewis, Oscar. *The Children of Sánchez: Autobiography of a Mexican Family.* New York: Random House, 1961.

Lewis, Stephen. *The Ambivalent Revolution: Forging State and Nation in Chiapas, 1910–1945.* Albuquerque: University of New Mexico Press, 2005.

Lombardo Toledano, Vicente. "La supresión del Ayuntamiento libre en el Distrito Federal." *Planificación* 1, no. 9 (May 1928): 17–24.

Lomnitz, Larissa. *Networks and Marginality: Life in a Mexican Shantytown.* New York: Academic Press, 1977.

Lopez, Rick. *Crafting Mexico: Intellectuals, Artisans, and the State after the Revolution.* Durham, NC: Duke University Press, 2010.

López Rangel, Rafael. *La planificación de la ciudad de México, 1900–1940.* Mexico City: Universidad Autónoma Metropolitana-Azcapotzalco, 1993.

López Rosado, Diego. *Historia del abasto de productos alimenticios a la ciudad de México.* Mexico City: Fondo de Cultura Económica, 1988.

Lorenzo Cossio, José. "Las aguas de la ciudad." *Boletín de la Sociedad Mexicana de Geografía y Estadística* 45 (1935–1937): 33–52.

———. *Algunas notas sobre el servicio de agua potable en el Distrito Federal.* Mexico City: E. Rivera, 1933.

———. *Guía retrospectiva de la ciudad de México.* 2nd ed. Mexico City: Segumex, 1990.

Lorenzo Río, María Dolores. *El estado como benefactor: Los pobres y la asistencia pública en la ciudad de México, 1877–1905.* Mexico City: Colegio de México, 2011.

Lyon, G. F. *Residencia en México, 1826: Diario de una gira con estancia en la República de México.* Mexico City: Fondo de Cultura Económica, 1984.

MacLeod, Murdo L. "Some Thoughts on the Pax Colonial, Colonial Violence, and Perceptions of Both." In *Native Resistance and the Pax Colonial in New Spain*, edited by Susan Schroeder, 129–142. Lincoln: University of Nebraska Press, 1998.

Mansilla Menéndez, Elizabeth. "La relación entre la ciudad de México y Xochimilco." In *Pasado, presente y futuro de las chinampas*, edited by Teresa Rojas Rabiela, 201–204. Mexico City: Centro de Investigaciones y Estudios Superiores en Antropología Social-Patronato del Parque Ecológico Xochimilco, 1991.

Marroquín y Rivera, Manuel. *Memoria descriptiva de las obras de provisión de agua potable para la ciudad de México.* Mexico City: Müller Hermanos, 1914.

———. *Proyecto de abastecimiento y distribución de aguas potables para la ciudad de México.* Mexico City: Secretaría de Fomento, 1901.

Martín, Rafael H. "Hornos metálicos para la elaboración moderna y económica del carbón vegetal." *México Forestal* 8 (May 1930): 99–100.

Martínez, Ignacio R. *La raíz de zacatón y su explotación.* Mexico City: Secretaría de Industria y Comercio, 1914.

Martínez, Roque. "Cooperativas ejidales: Determinación de zonas forestales y agrícolas; Reglamentación del pastoreo." *México Forestal* 8, no. 4 (April 1930): 67–69.

Martínez Baca, Roberto. *La raíz de zacatón: Su explotación y comercio exterior.* Mexico City: Secretaría de Relaciones Exteriores, 1938.

Marx, Karl. "The Eighteenth Brumaire of Louis Bonaparte." In *The Marx-Engels Reader*, edited by Robert C. Tucker, 594–617. 2nd ed. New York: W. W. Norton, 1978.

Mathews, Andrew S. *Instituting Nature: Authority, Expertise, and Power in Mexican Forests.* Cambridge, MA: MIT Press, 2011.

Matteson, Kieko. *Forests in Revolutionary France: Conservation, Community and Conflict, 1669–1848.* New York: Cambridge University Press, 2015.

Mayer, Brantz. *México: lo que fue y lo que es.* Translated by Francisco Delpiane. Mexico City: Fondo de Cultura Económica, 1953.

Mayol, Pierre. "The Neighborhood." In *Practice of Everyday Life*, vol. 2, *Living and Cooking*, by Michel de Certeau, Luce Giard, and Pierre Mayol, translated by Timothy J. Tomasik, 7–14. University of Minnesota Press, 1998.

McCann, Bryan. *Hard Times in the Marvelous City: From Dictatorship to Democracy in the Favelas of Rio de Janeiro.* Durham, NC: Duke University Press, 2013.

McFarlane, Colin. "Governing the Contaminated City: Infrastructure and Sanitation in Colonial and Post-colonial Bombay." *International Journal of Urban and Regional Research* 32, no. 2 (June 2008): 415–435.

Meade, Teresa A. *"Civilizing" Rio: Reform and Resistance in a Brazilian City, 1889–1930.* University Park, PA: Penn State University Press, 1997.

———. "Living Worse and Costing More: Resistance and Riot in Rio de Janeiro, 1890–1917." *Journal of Latin American Studies* 21 (1989): 241–266.

Medina, Carlos A. *Exposición que hace el ingeniero a todos los habitantes de la ciudad de México.* Mexico City: Dublán y cía, 1884.

Mejia Pavony, Germán. *Los años del cambio: Historia urbana de Bogotá, 1820–1910.* Bogotá: Universidad Javeriana, 2000.

Melosi, Martin M. *The Sanitary City: Urban Infrastructure in America from the Colony to the Present.* Baltimore: Johns Hopkins University Press, 2000.

Meyer, Hannes. "La ciudad de México: Un estudio urbanístico." *Arquitectura* 12 (December 1942): 96–109.

Meyer, Michael. *Huerta: A Political Portrait.* Lincoln: University of Nebraska Press, 1973.

Miller, Shawn William. *An Environmental History of Latin America.* Cambridge: Cambridge University Press, 2007.

Miranda Pacheco, Sergio. *Historia de la desaparición del municipio en el Distrito Federal.* Mexico City: Sábado Distrito Federal, 1998.

———. *Tacubaya: De suburbia veraniego a ciudad.* Mexico City: Universidad Nacional Autónoma de México, 2007.

Molina, Ismael. "Influencias nocivas a la salubridad pública y la economía nacional: El estado en que se hallan los terrenos del lago de Texcoco." *Planificación* 2, no. 5 (October–November 1934): 38.

Molina Enríquez, Andrés. *Los grandes problemas nacionales (1909) y otros textos.* Mexico City: ERA, 1979.

Monsiváis, Carlos. *Apocalipstick.* Mexico City: Debate, 2009.

———. "Identity Hour." In *The Mexico Reader: History, Culture, Politics,* edited by Gilbert M. Joseph and Timothy J. Henderson, 613–618. Durham, NC: Duke University Press, 2002.

Montes de Oca, José. "Xochimilco y sus chinampas." *Memorias de la Sociedad Científica Antonio Alzate* 45 (1926): 413–428.

Morgan, Tony. "Proletarians, Políticos, and Patriarchs: The Use and Abuse of Cultural Customs in the Early Industrialization of Mexico City, 1880–1910." In *Rituals of Rule, Rituals of Resistance: Public Celebrations and Popular Culture in Mexico,* edited by William H. Beezley, Cheryl English Martin, and William E. French, 151–172. Wilmington, DE: Scholarly Resources, 1994.

Murphy, Edward. *For a Proper Home: Housing Rights in the Margins of Urban Chile.* Pittsburgh: University of Pittsburgh Press, 2015.

———. "Introduction: Housing Questions Past, Present, and Future." In *The Housing Question: Tensions, Continuities, and Contingencies in the Modern City,* edited by Edward Murphy and Najib B. Hourani, 1–20. Farnham, UK: Ashgate, 2013.

Musset, Alain. *El agua en el valle de México, siglos XVI–XVIII.* Mexico City: Pórtico de la Ciudad de México, 1992.

Nash, Linda. *Inescapable Ecologies: A History of Environment, Disease, and Knowledge.* Berkeley: University of California Press, 2007.

Needell, Jeffrey. "Revolta Contra Vacina of 1904: The Revolt against 'Modernization' in Belle Epoque Rio de Janeiro." *Hispanic American Historical Review* 67, no. 2 (1987): 233–269.

Needham, Andrew. *Power Lines: Phoenix and the Making of the Modern Southwest.* Princeton, NJ: Princeton University Press, 2014.

Needham, Andrew, and Allen Dieterich-Ward. "Beyond the Metropolis: Metropolitan Growth and Regional Transformation in Postwar America." *Journal of Urban History* 35, no. 7 (2009): 944–969.

Neimeyer, E. V. *Revolution at Querétaro: The Mexican Constitutional Convention of 1916–1917.* Austin: University of Texas Press, 1974.

Neumann, Roderick P. *Imposing Wilderness: Struggles over Livelihood and Nature Preservation in Africa.* Berkeley: University of California Press, 1998.

Niblo, Stephen R. *Mexico in the 1940s: Modernity, Politics, and Corruption.* Wilmington, DE: Scholarly Resources, 1999.

Offen, Karl. "The Geographical Imagination, Resource Economies, and Nicaraguan Incorporation of the Mosquitia, 1838–1908." In *Territories, Knowledges, and Commodities: Latin American Environmental History in the Nineteenth and Twentieth Centuries,* edited by Christian Brannstrom, 50–89. London: Institute of Latin American Studies, 2004.

Olsen, Patrice. *Artifacts of Revolution: Architecture, Society and Politics in Mexico City, 1920–1940.* Lanham, MD: Rowman and Littlefield, 2008.

Oñate Villareal, Abdiel. "Banca y agricultura en México: La Caja de Préstamos para Obras de Irrigación y Fomento de la Agricultura, 1908–1926." PhD diss., Mexico City: Colegio de México, 1984.

Ordoñez, Elipidio. Untitled article. *Memorias de la Sociedad Científica Antonio Alzate* 39 (1918): 477–478.

Orive Alba, Adolfo. "Los problemas del valle de México." *Ingeniería Hidráulica* 6 (April–June 1952): 5–16.

Oropesa, Gabriel M. "Proyecto de casas de vecindad para obreros pobres: Ponencia dada al Primer Congreso Nacional de Habitaciones Obreras." *Revista Mexicana de Ingeniería y Arquitectura* 8, no. 3 (March 1940): 135–142.

Orozco y Berra, Manuel ed.. *Memoria para la carta hidrográfica pare el valle de México.* Mexico City: A. Boix, 1864.

Orsi, Jared. *Hazardous Metropolis: Flooding and Urban Ecology in Los Angeles.* Berkeley: University of California Press, 2004.

Ortega Olivares, Mario. *La utopía en el barrio.* Mexico City: Universidad Autónoma Metropolitana-Xochimilco, 1996.

Orvañanos, Domingo. "Geografía y climatología del lago de Texcoco." In *Estudios referentes a la desecación del lago de Texcoco, año de 1895,* edited by Instituto Médico Nacional, 83–96. Mexico City: Secretaria de Fomento, 1895.

Osorio Marbán, Miguel. *El sector popular del PRI*. Mexico City: Coordinación Nacional de Estudios Históricos, Políticos y Sociales, 1994.

Otter, Chris. "Locating Matter: The Place of Materiality in Urban History." In *Material Powers: Cultural Studies, History and the Material Turn*, edited by Tony Bennet and Patrick Joyce, 38–59. New York: Routledge, 2010.

Pacheco, José Emilio. *Battles in the Desert and Other Stories*. Translated by Katherine Silver. New York: New Directions, 1987.

Palacio Castañeda, Germán, ed. *Historia ambiental de Bogotá y la Sábana, 1850–2005*. Bogotá: Universidad Nacional de Colombia, 2008.

Palafox, Silvano. "El reglamento de construcciones de la ciudad de México." *Obras Públicas* 1 (February 1930): 42–44.

Palerm, Ángel. *Obras hidráulicas prehispánicas en el sistema lacustre del valle de México*. Mexico City: Instituto Nacional de Antropologia y Historia, 1973.

Pani, Alberto J. *Apuntes autobiográficos*. Mexico City: Instituto Nacional de Estudios Históricos de las Revoluciones de México, 2003.

———. *Hygiene in Mexico: A Study of Sanitary and Educational Problems*. New York: G. P. Putnam's Sons, 1917.

———. "The Sanitary and Educational Problems of Mexico." In *The Purposes and Ideals of the Mexican Revolution*, edited by Luis Cabrera, Ygnacio Bonilla, Alberto J. Pani, Juan E. Rojo, and Leo Stanton Rowe, 22–26. Philadelphia: American Academy of Political and Social Science, 1917.

Pani, Mario. "La Ciudad Satélite de México." *Nivel* 5 (May 1959): 1–6.

Parsons, Jeffrey. *The Last Saltmakers of Nexquipayac, Mexico: An Archaeological Ethnography*. Ann Arbor: University of Michigan Museum of Anthropology, 2001.

Payno, Manuel. "Bosques y arboledos." *Boletín de la Sociedad Mexicana de Geografía y Estadística* 2 (1870): 77–94.

Paz, Octavio. "Return to the Labyrinth of Solitude." In *The Labyrinth of Solitude*, translated by Lysander Kemp, 327–354. New York: Grove, 1985.

Peimbert, Ángel, A. Petricioli, and L. MacGregor. "Memoria descriptiva del proyecto del Parque Agrícola de la Ciudad de México." *Planificación* 2, no. 5 (October–November 1934): 39.

Peñafiel, Antonio. *Memoria sobre las aguas potables de la capital de México*. Mexico City: Secretaría de Fomento, 1884.

Peralta Flores, Araceli, and Jorge Rojas Ramírez. *Xochimilco y sus monumentos históricos*. Mexico City: Instituto Nacional de Antropología y Historia, 1992.

Percheron, Nicole. *Problemas agrarios del Ajusco: Siete comunidades agrarias de la periferia de México, siglos XVI–XX*. Mexico City: Gobierno del Distrito Federal, 2008.

Pérez Gavilán, Ana Isabel. "Chávez Morado, destructor de mitos: Silencios y aniquilaciones de la ciudad (1949)." *Anales del Instituto de Investigaciones Estéticas* 87 (2005): 65–116.

Perló Cohen, Manuel. "De como perdió el Ayuntamiento su autonomía sin obtener a cambio una democracia de manzana." *Suplemento Cultural de la Revista Siempre* (July 1980).

————. *Estado, vivienda y estructura urbana en el cardenismo.* Mexico City: Universidad Nacional Autónoma de México, 1981.

————. *Historia de las obras, planes y problemas hidráulicos en el Distrito Federal.* Mexico City: Universidad Nacional Autónoma de México, 1989.

————. *El paradigma porfiriano: Historia del desagüe del valle de México.* Mexico City: Porrúa, 1999.

————. "Política y vivienda en México, 1910–1952." *Revista Mexicana de Sociología* 41, no. 3 (July–September 1979): 769–835.

Pezzoli, Keith. *Human Settlements and Planning for Ecological Sustainability: The Case of Mexico City.* Cambridge, MA: MIT Press, 1998.

Piccato, Pablo. *City of Suspects: Crime in Mexico City, 1900–1931.* Durham, NC: Duke University Press, 2001.

Pilcher, Jeffrey. *The Sausage Rebellion: Public Health, Private Enterprise, and Meat in Mexico City, 1890–1917.* Albuquerque: University of New Mexico Press, 2006.

Piñeda, Efraín Jaimes. "El problema de la escasez del carbón vegetal y sus posibles substitutos." Master's thesis, Escuela Nacional de Agricultura, Chapingo, 1943.

Pineda Gómez, Francisco. *La revolución del sur, 1912–1914.* Mexico City: ERA, 2005.

Platt, Howard. *Shock Cities: The Environmental Transformation and Reform of Manchester and Chicago.* Chicago: University of Chicago Press, 2005.

Poumarede, J. A. *Desagüe del valle de México.* Mexico City: Imprenta de I. Cumplido, 1860.

Pozo, Ignacio. *Informe sobre el ramo de aguas presentado al Ayuntamiento de 1887.* Mexico City: Ireneo Paz, 1888.

Puig Casauranc, José Manuel. "Colonias o fraccionamientos sin servicios o con servicios muy deficientes." *Obras Públicas* 1, no. 4 (April 1930): 215–221.

————. "Por qué y en qué extensión faltan los servicios de urbanización en el Distrito Federal." *Obras Públicas* 1, no. 4 (April 1930): 225–231.

Quevedo, Miguel Ángel de. *Algunas consideraciones sobre nuestro problema agrario.* Mexico City: Victoria, 1916.

————. "El problema de la deforestación en México: Solución práctica del mismo." *México Forestal* 2, nos. 7–8 (July–August 1924): 64–69.

————. *Espacios libres y reservas forestales de las ciudades: Su adaptación a jardines, parques y lugares de juego; Aplicación a la ciudad de México.* Mexico City: Gomar y Busson, 1911.

————. "La ciudad de México no se hunde por la falta de lagos en sus alrededores." *Memorias de la Sociedad Científica Antonio Alzate* 41 (1922): 49–61.

————. *La cuestión forestal.* Mexico City: Secretaría de Fomento, 1908.

————. "La necesaria orientación en los trabajos de la desecación del lago de Texcoco y problemas con que ella se ligan." *Memorias de la Sociedad Científica Antonio Alzate* 40 (1922): 265–300.

————. "Las polvaredas de los terrenos tequezquitosos del antiguo lago de Texcoco y los procedimientos de enyerbe para remediarlas." *Memorias de la Sociedad Científica Antonio Alzate* 40 (1922): 533–548.

————. *Relato de mi vida.* Mexico City: n.p., 1943.

Radkau, Joachim. *Nature and Power: A Global History of the Environment.* Oxford: Oxford University Press, 2008.

————. *Wood: A History.* Cambridge, UK: Polity, 2012.

Ramírez Plancarte, Francisco. *La ciudad de México durante la revolución constitucionalista.* Mexico City: Botas, 1941.

Rebolledo, Miguel. *Hundimiento e inundaciones en la ciudad de México.* Mexico City: B. de Silva, 1952.

Reese, Carol McMichael. "Nacionalismo, progreso y modernidad en la cultura arquitectónica de la ciudad de México." In *Hacía otra historia del arte en México: La amplitud del modernismo y la modernidad,* edited by Stacie G. Widdifield, 175–219. Mexico City: Conaculta, 2004.

————. "The Urban Development of Mexico City." In *Planning Latin American Capital Cities, 1850–1950,* edited by Arturo Almondoz Marte, 139–169. London: Routledge, 2002.

"Reglamento de Asociaciones Pro-Mejoramiento de las Colonias del Distrito Federal." In *Legislación sobre fraccionamientos y construcciones urbanas,* edited by Felipe Santibañez, 183–186. Mexico City, 1949.

Reuss, Martin. "Seeing like an Engineer: Water Projects and the Mediation of the Incommensurable." *Technology and Culture* 49, no. 3 (July 2008): 531–546.

Reyes, Alfonso. "Palinodia del polvo." In Alfonso Reyes, *Visión de Anahuac y otros ensayos,* 211–215. Mexico City: Fondo de Cultura Económica, 1995.

————. "Visión de Anáhuac." In Alfonso Reyes, *Visión de Anahuac y otros ensayos,* 7–30. Mexico City: Fondo de Cultura Económica, 1995.

Richmond, Douglas W. *Venustiano Carranza's Nationalist Struggle, 1893–1920.* Lincoln: University of Nebraska Press, 1983.

Río de la Loza, Leopoldo. "Un vistazo al lago de Tetzcoco: Su influencia en la salubridad de México." In *Memoria para la carta hidrográfica del valle de México,* edited by Manuel Orozco y Berra, 174–184. Mexico City: A. Boix, 1864.

Riquelme Inda, Julio. "El antiguo lago de Texcoco y las nubes de polvo que invaden la ciudad de México." *Boletín de la Sociedad Mexicana de Geografía y Estadística* 9, no. 2 (1919): 240–244.

Robertson, Thomas. *The Malthusian Moment: Global Population Growth and the Birth of American Environmentalism.* New Brunswick, NJ: Rutgers University Press, 2012.

Rodgers, Daniel. *Atlantic Crossings: Social Politics in the Progressive Era.* Cambridge, MA: Belknap, 1998.

Rodríguez Kuri, Ariel. "Desabasto de agua y violencia política: El motín del 30 de noviembre de 1922 en la ciudad de México; Economía moral y cultura política." In *Formas de descontento y movimientos sociales, siglos XIX y XX,* edited by José

Ronzón and Carmen Valdés, 167–201. Mexico City: Universidad Autónoma Metropolitana-Azcapotzalco, 2000.

———. *La experiencia olvidada: El Ayuntamiento de México; Política y gobierno, 1876–1912.* Mexico City: Colegio de México, 1996.

———. "Gobierno local y empresas de servicios: La experiencia de la ciudad de México durante el Porfiriato." In *Ferrocarriles y obras públicas,* edited by Priscilla Connolly and Sandra Kuntz Ficker, 165–190. Mexico City: Instituto Mora, 1999.

———. *Historia del desasosiego: La revolución en la ciudad de México, 1911–1922.* Mexico City: Colegio de México, 2010.

Rome, Adam. *The Bulldozer in the Countryside: Suburban Sprawl and the Rise of American Environmentalism.* Cambridge: Cambridge University Press, 2001.

Romero, José. *Guía de la ciudad de México y demás municipalidades del Distrito Federal con los datos más recientes de su régimen político como asiento de los supremos poderes de la Federación.* Mexico City: Librería de Porrúa Hermanos, 1910.

Romero Lankao, Patricia and Eike Duffing. "¿Tres procesos contradictorios? Desarrollo urbano, ambiente y políticas en Xochimilco durante el siglo XX." In *A la orilla del agua: Políticas, urbanización y medio ambiente: Historia de Xochimilco en el siglo XX,* edited by María Eugenia Terrones López, 211–252. Mexico City: Instituto Mora, 2004.

Rosa, Natalia de la. "Guillermo Zárraga, planificador: Utopías constructivas y la destrucción de la ciudad." Unpublished manuscript on academia.edu. https://www.academia.edu/4828786/Urbanismo_y_Ciencia_Ficci%C3%B3n.

———. "Guillermo Zárraga: Un constructor del régimen callista." *Arquitectónica* 7, no. 13 (2008): 41–64.

Roseberry, William. "Hegemony and the Language of Contention." In *Everyday Forms of State Formation: Revolution and the Negotiation of Rule in Modern Mexico,* edited by Gilbert M. Joseph and Daniel Nugent, 355–366. Durham, NC: Duke University Press, 1994.

Ross, Paul. "From Sanitary Police to Sanitary Dictatorship: Mexico's Nineteenth Century Public Health Movement." PhD diss., University of Chicago, 2005.

———. "Mexico's Superior Health Council and the American Public Health Association: The Transnational Archive of Porfirian Public Health, 1887–1910." *Hispanic American Historical Review* 89, no. 4 (2009): 573–602.

Ross, Stanley. *Francisco I. Madero: The Apostle of Democracy.* New York: Columbia, 1955.

Rowney, Don Karl. *Transition to Technocracy: The Structural Origins of the Soviet Administrative State.* Ithaca, NY: Cornell University Press, 1989.

Ruíz, Luis. "Anexo 1C." In Miguel Alonzo Romero, *Un año de sitio en la presidencia municipal: Crónica y comentarios de una labor accidentada,* 414–419. Mexico City: Editorial Hispano-Mexicana, 1923.

Rulfo, Juan. *The Burning Plain and Other Stories.* Austin: University of Texas Press, 1971.

Saberwal, Vasant K. "Science and the Desiccationist Discourse of the 20th Century." *Environment and History* 4, no. 3 (October 1998): 309–343.

Sachs, Aaron. *The Humboldt Current: Nineteenth-Century Exploration and the Roots of American Environmentalism*. New York: Viking, 2006.

Sáenz, Aaron. *Informe que rinde el jefe del Departamento del Distrito Federal a la ciudad*. Mexico City: Talleres Gráficos de la Penitenciaría, 1934.

Salazar, Luis. "On the Distribution of Water in the City of Mexico." Translated by Alfred Sears. *Transactions of the American Society of Civil Engineers* 3, no. 1 (1892): 336–349.

Salvia Spratte, Héctor Agustín. *Los laberintos de Loreto y Peña Pobre*. Mexico City: El Caballito, 1989.

Sánchez Ruíz, Gerardo G. "Epidemias, obras de saneamiento y precursores del urbanismo: La ciudad de México rumbo al primer centenario." *Secuencia* 78 (September–December 2010): 123–147.

———. *Planificación y urbanismo de la revolución mexicana: Los sustentos de una nueva modernidad en la ciudad de México, 1917–1940*. Mexico City: Universidad Autónoma Metropolitana-Azcapotzalco, 2002.

Sánchez Vargas, Eduardo. "La ciudad de México de 1900 a 1920." In *Mi pueblo durante la revolución*, edited by Alicia Olivera Sedano, 1:151–190. Mexico City: Museo Nacional de Culturas Populares, 1985.

Sanders, William T. "El lago y el volcán: La chinampa (1957)." In *La agricultura chinampera: Compilación histórica*, edited by Teresa Rojas Rabiela, 115–157. Mexico City: Universidad Autónoma de Chapingo, 1983.

Sanders, William T., Jeffrey R. Parsons, and Robert S. Santley. *The Basin of Mexico: Ecological Processes in the Evolution of a Civilization*. New York: Academic Press, 1979.

Santamaría, Miguel. *Las chinampas del Distrito Federal: Informe rendido al director de agricultura*. Mexico City: Secretaría de Fomento, 1912.

Santiago, Myrna. *The Ecology of Oil: Environment, Labor, and the Mexican Revolution, 1900–1938*. Cambridge: Cambridge University Press, 2006.

Schama, Simon. *Landscape and Memory*. New York: A. A. Knopf, 1995.

Schilling, Elisabeth. "Los 'jardines flotantes' de Xochimilco (1938): Una selección." In *La agricultura chinampera: Compilación histórica*, edited by Teresa Rojas Rabiela, 71–98. Mexico City: Universidad Autónoma Chapingo, 1983.

Schteingart, Martha. "Expansión urbana, conflictos sociales y deterioro ambiental en la ciudad de México." *Estudios Demográficos y Urbanos* 2, no. 3 (1987): 449–477.

Schwartz, Manuel. "La desecación del lago de Texcoco." *Boletín Oficial del Consejo Superior del Gobierno del Distrito Federal* 27, no. 2 (1913): 417–420.

Scott, James C. *Domination and the Arts of Resistance: Hidden Transcripts*. New Haven, CT: Yale University Press, 1990.

———. Foreword to *Everyday Forms of State Formation: Revolution and the Negotiation of Rule in Modern Mexico*, edited by Gilbert M. Joseph and Daniel Nugent, vii–xii. Durham, NC: Duke University Press, 1994.

———. *Seeing like a State: How Certain Schemes to Improve the Human Condition Have Failed*. New Haven, CT: Yale University Press, 1998.

Sears, Paul B. *Deserts on the March*. Norman: University of Oklahoma Press, 1935.

———. "Dust in the Eyes of Science." *The Land* 3 (1948): 341–346.

Secretaría de Economía. *Anuario Estadístico de los Estados Unidos Mexicanos, 1940.* Mexico City: Dirección General de Estadística, 1942.

———. *Anuario Estadístico de los Estados Unidos Mexicanos, 1951–52.* Mexico City: Dirección General de Estadística, 1954.

Secretaría de la Economía Nacional. *Séptimo Censo General de Población, Distrito Federal 1950.* Mexico City: Departamento del Distrito Federal, 1950.

———. *Sexto Censo de Población, Distrito Federal, 1940.* Mexico City: Departamento del Distrito Federal, 1941.

Secretaría de Fomento. *Memoria de la Secretaría de Fomento, años de 1911–1912.* Mexico City: Secretaría de Fomento, 1913.

Secretaría de Recursos Hidráulicos. *Plan Lago de Texcoco.* Mexico City: Secretaría de Recursos Hidráulicos, 1975.

Secretaría de Recursos Hidráulicos and la Comisión Hidrológica de la Cuenca del Valle de México. "Breve descripción de la cuenca del valle de México, sus problemas hidráulicos y modos de resolverlos." *Ingeniería Hidráulica* 13 (July–September 1959): 1–17.

Sedrez, Lise. "The Bay of All Beauties: State and Environment in Guanabara Bay, Rio de Janeiro, Brazil, 1875–1975." PhD diss., Stanford University, 2004.

Sellers, Christopher. *Crabgrass Crucible: Suburban Nature and the Rise of Environmentalism in Twentieth-Century America.* Chapel Hill: University of North Carolina Press, 2012.

Simonian, Lane. *Defending the Land of the Jaguar: A History of Conservation in Mexico.* Austin: University of Texas Press, 1995.

Smith, Benjamin. *Pistoleros and Popular Movements: The Politics of State Formation in Postrevolutionary Oaxaca.* Lincoln: University of Nebraska Press, 2009.

Snodgrass, Michael. *Deference and Defiance in Monterrey: Workers, Paternalism and Revolution in Mexico, 1890–1950.* Cambridge: Cambridge University Press, 2003.

Sotomayor, Arturo. *La metrópoli mexicana y su agonía.* Mexico City: Universidad Nacional Autónoma de México, 1973.

Spenser, Daniela. *Los primeros tropiezos de la Internacional Comunista en México.* Mexico City: Centro de Investigación y Estudios Superiores en la Antropología Social, 2009.

Steinberg, Ted. "Down to Earth: Nature, Agency and Power in History." *American Historical Review* 107, no. 3 (2002): 798–820.

Stroud, Ellen. "Does Nature Always Matter? Following Dirt through History." *History and Theory* 42, no. 4 (2003): 75–81.

———. *Nature Next Door: Cities and Trees in the American Northeast.* Seattle: University of Washington Press, 2012.

Studnicki-Gizbert, Daviken, and David Schecter. "The Environmental Dynamics of a Colonial Fuel-Rush: Silver Mining and Deforestation in New Spain, 1522–1810." *Environmental History* 15 (January 2010): 94–119.

Suárez Cortez, Blanca Estela, and Diana Birrichaga Gardida, eds. *Dos estudios sobre usos del agua en México (siglos XIX y XX)*. Mexico City: Centro de Investigación y Estudios Superiores en la Antropología Social, 1997.

Sundberg, Juanita. "Placing Race in Environmental Justice Research in Latin America." *Society and Natural Resources* 21, no. 7 (2008): 569–582.

Szuchman, Mark D. "The City as Vision: The Development of Urban Cultures in Latin America." In *I Saw a City Invincible: Urban Portraits of Latin America*, edited by Gilbert M. Joseph and Mark D. Szuchman, 1–32. Wilmington, DE: Scholarly Resources, 1996.

Taibo, Paco Ignacio, II, and Rogelio Vizcaíno. *Memoria roja: Luchas sindicales de los años 20*. Mexico City: Ediciones Leega, 1984.

Tamayo, Jaime. *El Obregonismo y los movimientos sociales: La conformación del estado moderno en México (1920–1924)*. Guadalajara: Universidad de Guadalajara, 2008.

Tavares López, Edgar. *Colonia Roma*. Mexico City: Clio, 1996.

Tenorio-Trillo, Mauricio. *I Speak of the City: Mexico City at the Turn of the Twentieth Century*. Chicago: University of Chicago Press, 2012.

———. *Mexico at the World's Fairs: Crafting a Modern Nation*. Berkeley: University of California Press, 1996.

Terres, José. "Influencia del desagüe del valle de México en la higiene de la capital." In *Estudios referentes a la desecación del lago de Texcoco: año de 1895*, edited by Instituto Médico Nacional, 63–81. Mexico City: Secretaría de Fomento, 1895.

Terrones López, María Eugenia. "La ciudad de México y su hinterland: El círculo virtuoso." In *Problemas de la urbanización en el valle de México, 1810–1910*, edited by Mario Barbosa and Salomon González, 91–125. Mexico City: Universidad Autónoma Metropolitana-Cuajimalpa, 2009.

Terry, T. Philip. *Terry's Guide to Mexico*. New York: Houghton Mifflin, 1911.

Therborn, Göran. *The Ideology of Power and the Power of Ideology*. London: Verso, 1999.

Torentini, Francisco. *El florecimiento de México*. Ill. ed. Mexico City: Bouligny and Schmidt, 1906.

Torres Sánchez, Rafael. *Revolución y vida cotidiana: Guadalajara, 1914–1934*. Sinaloa: Universidad Autónoma de Sinaloa, 2001.

Tortolero Villaseñor, Alejandro. "The Drainage of Central Mexican Waterscapes: Lake Drainage and Its Consequences during the Porfiriato." In *Territories, Commodities, and Knowledges: Latin American Environmental Histories in the Nineteenth and Twentieth Centuries*, edited by Christian Brannstrom, 121–147. London: Institute for the Study of the Americas, 2001.

———. "Los usos del agua en el valle de Chalco: Del Antiguo Régimen a la gran hidráulica." In *Tierra, agua, y bosques: La historia medioambiental en el México Central*, edited by Alejandro Tortolero Villaseñor, 219–251. Mexico City: Instituto Mora, 1996.

———. "Water and Revolution in Morelos, 1850–1915." In *A Land between Waters: Environmental Histories of Modern Mexico*, edited by Christopher R. Boyer, 124–149. Tucson: University of Arizona Press, 2012.

Trujillo Bolio, Mario. *Operarios fabriles en el Valle de México (1864–1884): Espacio, trabajo, protesta y cultura obrera*. Mexico City: Colmex, 1997.

Tutino, John. "The Revolutionary Capacity of Rural Communities: Ecological Autonomy and Its Demise." In *Cycles of Conflict, Centuries of Change: Crisis, Reform, and Revolution in Mexico*, edited by Elisa Servin, Leticia Reina, and John Tutino, 211–268. Durham, NC: Duke University Press, 2007.

Unión de Arquitectos Socialistas. *Proyecto de la ciudad obrera en México, DF: Doctrina socialista de la arquitectura*. Mexico, 1938.

Urquiza García, Humberto, and Luz Emilia Aguilar Zinser. "El tlacuache, el coco y el eucalipto." *Nexos en línea*, June 17, 2013. http://registropersonal.nexos.com.mx/?p=3826.

Valadés, José C. *Memorias de un joven rebelde*. Part II. Culiacan, Sinaloa: Universidad Autónoma de Sinaloa, 1986.

Valenzuela Aguilera, Alfonso. *Urbanistas y visionarios: La planeación de la Ciudad de México en la primera mitad del siglo XX*. Cuernavaca: Universidad Autónoma del Estado de Morelos: Mexico City: Porrúa, 2014.

Vandergeest, Peter, and Nancy Lee Peluso. "Territorialization and State Power in Thailand." *Theory and Society* 24, no. 3 (June 1995): 385–426.

Vargas Martínez, Ubaldo. *La ciudad de México, 1325–1960*. Mexico City: Departamento del Distrito Federal, 1961.

Varley, Ann. "Urbanization and Agrarian Law: The Case of Mexico City." *Bulletin of Latin American Research* 4, no. 1 (1985): 1–16.

Varley, Ann, and Alan Gilbert. "From Renting to Self-Help Ownership? Residential Tenure in Urban Mexico since 1940." In *Housing and Land in Urban Mexico*, edited by Alan Gilbert, 13–37. La Jolla: Center for U.S.-Mexican Studies, University of California, San Diego, 1989.

Vergara, Germán. "Fueling Change: The Valley of Mexico and the Quest for Energy, 1850–1930." PhD diss., University of California, Berkeley, 2015.

Véron, René. "Remaking Urban Environments: The Political Ecology of Air Pollution in Delhi." *Environment and Planning A* 38 (2006): 2093–2109.

Villicaña, Ernesto Lemoine. *El desagüe del valle de México durante la época independiente*. Mexico City: Universidad Nacional Autónoma de México, 1978.

Vitz, Matthew. "'The Lands with Which We Shall Struggle': Land Reclamation, Revolution, and Development in Mexico's Lake Texcoco Basin, 1910–1950." *Hispanic American Historical Review* 92, no. 1 (2012): 41–71.

———. "'To Save the Forests': Power, Narrative, and Environment in Mexico City's Cooking Fuel Transition." *Mexican Studies/Estudios Mexicanos* 31, no. 1 (winter 2015): 125–155.

Vizcaíno, Fernando. "El lago de Texcoco." *Ingeniería Hidráulica en México* 3, no. 3 (1949): 17–20.

Vizcaíno, Francisco. *La contaminación en México.* Mexico City: Fondo de la Cultura Económica, 1975.

Vogt, William. *El hombre y la tierra.* Mexico City: Secretaría de Educación Pública, 1944.

————. *Road to Survival.* New York: W. Sloane Associates, 1948.

Wakild, Emily. *Revolutionary Parks: Conservation, Social Justice, and Mexico's National Parks, 1910–1940.* Tucson: University of Arizona Press, 2011.

Walker, Alex. "Historical Influences on the Use of Cement in Mexican Domestic Construction." *Construction History* 16 (2000): 87–98.

Walsh, Thomas F. *Katherine Anne Porter and Mexico: The Illusion of Eden.* Austin: University of Texas Press, 1992.

Ward, Peter, and Alan Gilbert. *Housing, the State and the Poor: Policy and Practice in Three Latin American Cities.* Cambridge: Cambridge University Press, 1985.

West, Robert C., and Pedro Armillas. "Las chinampas de México: Poesía y realidad de los 'jardines flotantes' (1950)." In *La agricultura chinampera: Compilación histórica,* edited by Teresa Rojas Rabiela, 99–114 . Mexico City: Universidad Autónoma de Chapingo, 1983.

White, Richard. "From Wilderness to Hybrid Landscapes: The Cultural Turn in Environmental History." *Historian* 66, no. 3 (2004): 557–564.

————. *The Organic Machine: The Remaking of the Columbia River.* New York: Hill and Wang, 1995.

Wilkie, James W. *The Mexican Revolution: Federal Expenditure and Social Change since 1910.* Los Angeles: University of California Press, 1967.

Wolfe, Mikael. "Mining Water for the Revolution: Marte R. Gómez and the Business of Agrarian Reform in La Laguna, México, 1920s–1960s." Working paper 371, Kellogg Institute, July 2010, University of Notre Dame, South Bend, IN.

————. *Watering the Revolution: An Environmental and Technological History of Agrarian Reform in Mexico.* Durham, NC: Duke University Press, 2017.

Womack, John, Jr. *Zapata and the Mexican Revolution.* New York: Vintage, 1968.

Wood, Andrew Grant. *Revolution in the Street: Women, Workers, and Urban Protest in Veracruz, 1870–1927.* Wilmington, DE: Scholarly Resources, 2001.

————. "Viva La Revolución Social! Postrevolutionary Tenant Protest and State Housing Reform in Veracruz, Mexico." In *Cities of Hope: People, Protests, and Progress in Urbanizing Latin America, 1870–1930,* edited by Ronn F. Pineo and James Baer, 88–128. Boulder, CO: Westview, 1998.

Woolley, Christopher. "Conservation against Justice: Environment, Monarchy, and New Spain's Council on Forests." Paper presented at the annual meeting of the Rocky Mountain Council for Latin American Studies, Tucson, AZ, April 11, 2015.

Wright, Angus. *The Death of Ramón González: The Modern Agricultural Dilemma.* Austin: University of Texas Press, 2005.

————. "Downslope and North: How Soil Degradation and Synthetic Pesticides Drove the Trajectory of Mexican Agriculture through the Twentieth Century."

In *A Land between Waters: Environmental Histories of Modern Mexico*, edited by
Christopher R. Boyer, 22–49. Tucson: University of Arizona Press, 2012.

Zamudio Varela, Graciela. "La imagen de la naturaleza en la obra de José Antonio
Alzate." In *José Antonio Alzate y la ciencia mexicana*, edited by Teresa Rojas
Rabiela, 79–90. Morelia, Michoacán: Universidad Michoacana, 2000.

Zárraga, Fernando. "Necesidad de defender la ciudad con un muro de arbolado."
México Forestal 5, nos. 7–8 (July–August 1927): 68–70.

Zárraga, Guillermo. *La tragedia del valle de México*. Mexico City: Stylo, 1958.

Zavala, Adriana. "Mexico City in Juan O'Gorman's Imagination." *Hispanic Research
Journal* 8, no. 5 (December 2007): 491–506.

Zayas Enríquez, Rafael de. *Los estados unidos mexicanos: Sus condiciones naturales y
sus elementos de prosperidad*. Mexico City: Secretaría de Fomento, 1893.

Zea, Leopoldo. *Positivism in Mexico*. Austin: University of Texas Press, 1974.

Zimmer, Anna. "Urban Political Ecology: Theoretical Concepts, Challenges, and
Suggested Future Directions." *Erdkunde* 64, no. 4 (October–December 2010):
343–354.

Zolov, Eric. "Notas sobre la capital en su contribución hegemónica." In *Los úl-
timos cien años, los próximos cien . . .*, edited by Ariel Rodríguez Kuri and
Sergio Tamayo Flores Alatorre, 111–126. Mexico City: Universidad Autónoma
Metropolitana-Azcapotzalco, 2004.

INDEX

———

Note: Page numbers followed by *f* indicate a figure. Those followed by *t* indicate a table.

of, 110, 125–35, 195–99; housing policies of, 211; industrialization under,
193–200; lakeshore land reclamation
policies of, 158–63, 210; nationalization of oil by, 59, 199; national park
creation of, 130–34; Party of the
Mexican Revolution and, 134, 182,
184, 190; six-year plan (sexenio) of,
126–27, 159, 165, 171, 194; working-
class political mobilization under,
165, 171–77, 179–80, 191–92, 280n98
Careaga, Luis, 155–56, 162, 223
Carranza, Venustiano, 65; Constitutionalist forces of, 69, 72–74; Constitutionalist governance under, 74–78,
81, 111; election loss of 1920, 85; labor
repression by, 76; lakeside ejido land
and water policies of, 137–46; land reform law of, 74–78, 111–17, 120, 137–38,
256nn113–14; military spending by,
93; Pani's sanitation leadership under,
75–78, 110; political goals of, 70, 77
Carreño, Alberto, 118, 155
Carrillo, Nabor, 230–32
Casa del Obrero Mundial, 72–73
Castro, Agustín, 124
Centro Médico, 215
chahuixtle fungus, 204–5
Chao, Manuel, 72
Chapultepec Heights, 101–2
Chapultepec Morales colonia, 185
charcoal economy, 196–200,
201f, 281nn8–11. See also forest
conservation
Chávez, Eduardo, 223–24, 230
Chazkel, Amy, 72
chinampería. See agriculture
La Ciudad de México por allí de 1970
(Tejeda), 2
Ciudad Nezahualcóyotl, 208–9, 219f,
229, 288n33
Ciudad Satélite, 216–17
civitas, 11

colonial era: drainage infrastructure of,
4, 8–9, 22–23; drinking water systems
of, 31; mining of, 118
colonos proletarios. See working-class
subdivisions
common lands, 109; agrarian reform
and ejido grants of, 74–78, 111–17, 120,
137–46, 176, 193–95, 204–5, 207–10,
256nn113–14, 270nn14–15; Cabrera's
redistribution proposal for, 60–62,
111; customary rights to, 15, 61, 66–68;
federal enclosure of, 58–59, 66, 114,
138–39; housing development on,
210–17, 284n61, 284n77, 285n87; private
appropriation of, 60–61, 114–15; social
forestry and, 117–35; timber concessions
on, 43–44, 111, 202–3; usufruct rights to,
66, 140–42. See also agriculture
Comte, Auguste, 23
Constitutionalist governance, 65, 69,
72–78, 111; centralized environmental
governance of, 81–82, 104–5; environmental planning under, 77–78, 256n115;
environmental rights movements and,
81–108; housing rights under, 15, 81–93;
Labor Department of, 85; Laborist
hegemony of, 100–103, 104, 262n92;
labor repression by, 76; land reform
and nationalization under, 74–78,
111–17, 256nn113–14; military spending
by, 93; neighborhood associations of,
100–102; Pani's sanitation leadership
in, 75–78, 110, 255n103; Querétaro
Constitutional Convention of, 77–78,
81, 111; real estate speculation under,
76–77, 101–2; strike-prone political
culture of, 94; suburban development
under, 101–3; technocratic urban
planning of, 99–106; water rights and,
15, 81, 94–100; water system repairs and
expansion under, 105–8, 264n124. See
also Carranza, Venustiano; Obregón,
Álvaro; postrevolutionary era

Constitution of 1857, 52
Constitution of 1917, 53, 77–78, 193, 219;
    housing mandates of (Article 123),
    77, 83, 86, 168; municipal governance
    mandates of (Article 115), 104; water
    and forest conservation mandates of
    (Article 27), 77–78, 112, 117, 179–80,
    256nn113–14
Contreras, Carlos, 103–4, 157, 180, 275n1
Contribution Law for Public Works
    of the Federal District, 170–71, 186,
    189–90
Convention of Aguascalientes govern-
    ment, 69–74; disruption of Mexico
    City under, 70–74; local sovereignty
    under, 69–70, 253n78
cooperative forestry, 117–35, 195–96,
    268n58. See also forest conservation
Cornelius, Wayne, 182
Corral, Luis, 67
Council on Forests, 28
critical geography, 12–14, 239n43
Cronon, William, 239n44
Cuajimalpa, 10
Cuevas, José Luis, 101–2, 180
customary land rights. See common
    lands
Cutzamala water-supply project,
    287n28, 288n35

Davis, Mike, 233
Defense Committee of Buenos Aires,
    215
deforestation, 28–29, 34–35, 43; charcoal
    production and, 196–98, 281n20; deg-
    radation narrative of, 118–20; by local
    haciendas, 114–15, 265n9; paper mills
    and, 198, 200, 202–3; soil erosion and,
    28–29, 34, 39, 54, 118–19, 219; timber
    concessions and, 43–44, 111, 202–3.
    See also forest conservation
de la Barra, Ignacio, 264n124
de la Cerda, Rafael, 159

de la Lama, José G., 101, 185
de la O, Genovevo, 252n42
de la Vega, Ricardo, 112–14, 155
del Valle colonia, 167
Department of the Federal District
    (DDF), 104–6, 157–58, 167, 170–71,
    190–91. See also Federal District
Desagüe Commission, 35–36
Desagüe General del Valle de México,
    20–22, 75
Deserts on the March (Sears), 225–27
desiccation theory, 28–29
Desierto de los Leones National Park,
    9, 122, 130
Díaz, Felix, 64
Díaz, Porfirio, 11, 19, 23, 75, 111. See also
    the Porfiriato
Díaz Ordaz, Gustavo, 230
Díos Bojórquez, Juan de, 77, 227
Doheny, Edward, 24–25
Domínguez, Belisario, 65
drainage (desagüe) systems, 35–39, 54,
    222–23, 246n83; colonial era infra-
    structure of, 4, 8–9, 22–23; desicca-
    tion paradigm of, 15–16, 29, 32–33, 39,
    54, 137–40, 142–43, 147–56, 223–30,
    287n27; flooding and, 38, 108, 139,
    148–51, 186–87, 219, 225, 226f; Gayol's
    sewer design and, 20, 24, 29, 33, 36,
    37–38; impact on indigenous agricul-
    ture of, 39–42, 49, 247n107; of Lake
    Chalco, 24, 32–34, 39–40, 245n65; of
    Lake Texcoco, 15–16, 29, 32–33, 36,
    39–40, 137–40; of Lake Xochimilco,
    15–16, 32–33, 37, 39–40, 149–50; land
    subsidence and, 36–39; privatization
    debates over, 33, 245n65; updating
    and expansion of, 229–30, 287n28.
    See also sewage systems
drinking water systems, 222–23; colonial
    systems of, 31; commercial bottled
    water and, 106; Constitutionalist
    improvements of, 105–8, 264n124;

environmental technocracy, 15–16, 20–24, 29–35, 220–21; under Constitutionalist governance, 77–78, 99–106, 256n115; in forest management, 123; industrialization and, 193–217; in the modern ecological city, 224–34, 288n35, 289nn43–44; Porfirian positivism and, 23–29, 41, 60, 99, 108, 247n103

Escandón, Pablo, 37

Espinosa, Luis, 20, 23–24, 42; drainage design plan of, 33, 36, 38–39; water conservation policies of, 29

Excursionist Club, 133

Ex Hipódromo de Peralvillo, 90–92, 101–2, 108, 166, 172, 259n48

Expropriation Law, 177–82, 191–93

expropriation of land: housing development and, 177–82, 191–93, 210–11; industrial development and, 213–15

Favela, José, 162, 275n105

Federal District, 30; car-centered development in, 101–2; Carranza's environmental governance of, 81–82; centralized governance of, 104–5, 108, 157–58, 167, 170, 190–91, 262n108; Convention government of, 70–74; death rates in, 255n103; environmental rights movements in, 81–108; investment in infrastructure of, 169–71; local access to forest products in, 68; Mexican Revolution in, 53–54; municipal governments of, 46–47, 71, 75, 81–82, 94, 100–102, 104–5, 260n56; municipalities of, 24, 241n18; Pani's sanitation leadership in, 75–78, 110, 255n103

Federal District Urban and Ecological Reorganization Program, 288n35

Federation of Forest Cooperatives, 121–25

Federation of the Colonias Proletarias of the Eastern District, 189–90

Felipe Ángeles colonia, 185, 189

fertilization projects, 54–55, 138–39, 144–45, 207. See also agriculture

forest conservation, 11, 15–16, 28, 108–35, 220; bureaucratic administration of, 195–96; Calles's policies on, 120–26; Cárdenas's agrarian reforms and, 110, 125–35; Carranza's land reform law and, 111–17; charcoal and wood economies and, 4, 26–27, 44, 68, 71–72, 114, 117, 195–200, 201f, 281nn8–11; constitutional mandates on, 77–78, 112, 117, 179–80, 256nn113–14; customary use policies and, 43–45, 61–63, 67–69, 110–17, 253n64; by ejido-based forest cooperatives, 117–35, 195–200, 268n58; enforcement of, 45, 62–63, 66–67, 122–23, 193, 252n47, 267n46; hacienda-based deforestation and, 114–15, 265n9; Huerta's policies on, 66–69, 110, 117; hydrologic logic of, 34, 55, 155, 245n68; industrialized economy and, 200–205; local village support of, 68–69, 123, 124; Madero's policies on, 61–64, 117; Mexican Forestry Society promotion of, 119–20; in national parks, 122, 130–34, 196; Porfiriato policies on, 21, 34–35, 43–45, 111; post-revolutionary policies on, 69, 109–35; Quevedo's views on, 29, 34–35, 42–45, 63, 78, 100, 109–11, 117–20, 252n47; railroad and manufacturing demands for wood and, 25–27, 109, 118–19, 195, 242n26; social and racial inequalities and, 39, 43–45, 61; special plan for Mexico City in, 128–30; technocratic management of, 123; timber concessions and, 43–44, 111, 202–3; urban logic of, 133–35, 270n95; zacatán root extraction and, 44–45, 62–63, 67–69, 128, 248n123, 253n64; Zapatista response to, 61–69, 112–14, 120, 252n42. See also common lands; deforestation

base of, 216; neoliberal policies of, 231–33; technocratic approach of, 224

Insurgente Miguel Hidalgo National Park, 130

Isla Urbana, 289nn43–44

Iztacalco, 210–13

Iztaccíhuatl-Popocatépetl National Park, 130

Iztapalapa, 163, 210–13, 270n15

Iztapalapa Neighborhood Improvement Committee, 170

Jacobs, Jane, 285n87

Jaimes Piñeda, Efraín, 198

Jardines del Pedregal, 216–17

Jiménez, Christina, 262n92

Jiménez Moral, Jorge, 212–13

Joseph, Gilbert M., 239n45

Juárez, Benito, 19

Junta de Mejoras Materiales, 91–92

Kalach, Alberto, 233

Katayama, Sen, 85

King, Rosa, 37

Knight, Alan, 64–65

Laborist Party, 87, 97, 99–104, 262n92

Ladrón de Guevara, Ángel, 174, 183–84, 189

Lake Chalco, 3; abundant wildlife of, 10; agricultural economy of, 9–10, 39–40; diminished surface area of, 138; ejido land and water rights at, 151; map of, 5f; Noriega's drainage project for, 24, 32–34, 40, 245n65

Lake Nabor Carrillo, 230–31

Lake Texcoco, 3, 136–63; abundant wildlife of, 10, 39, 42; agricultural economy of, 9–10, 15–16, 39–40, 207–10; airport construction in, 234; Carrillo's re-creation project for, 230–32, 288n33; Ciudad Neza-hualcóyotl at, 208–9; diminished

surface area of, 5f, 138; draft-and-drain paradigm and desiccation of, 15–16, 29, 32–33, 39, 40, 54, 137–43, 154–56, 223–30, 287n27; dust storms and pollution from, 2, 9, 15, 33, 39, 54, 74, 109–10, 118, 137, 139, 154–56, 207; ejido land and water rights at, 66, 141–45, 157–58, 160–63, 193, 195, 207–10; engineering practices at, 147–48, 154–63; federal lands at, 58–59, 66, 138–42, 208–9; flooding of, 16, 38, 108, 119, 137, 139, 164–65; Gran Canal de Desagüe of, 20–21, 22f, 33, 36, 139–40; as health threat, 9, 22–23, 27–28, 31–33, 137, 139, 154–56; housing development at, 16, 25, 164, 180, 213–16, 287n27; industrialized salt production from, 207–10, 221, 284n61; land reclamation projects at, 54–61, 65–66, 144–46, 155–63, 207–8, 222, 230–31, 250nn13–14, 250n17, 274n95; map of changing levels of, 5f; map of reclamation of, 57f; salinity of, 65–66, 138–39, 144, 155, 157–58, 195, 207; sedimentation in lakebed of, 9, 36, 54, 66, 108–9, 138, 266n31; as wastewater destination, 8–9

Lake Xochimilco, 3, 136–63; agricultural economy of, 9–10, 15–16, 39–40, 147; aquifer recharge rates of, 152–53; chinampería practices at, 138, 141, 145–54, 206, 232; Churubusco River diversion into, 205–6; Condesa pump accident at, 94–97, 105, 260n59; desiccation and pollution of, 138, 195, 204–6, 220–21; draft-and-drain paradigm at, 15–16, 32–33, 39–40, 138, 149–50, 223–30, 272n48; ecological rescue plan for, 231–32; ejido land and water rights at, 137–38, 141–46, 149, 151, 193, 195, 204–5, 232, 270nn14–15, 272n48; engineering practices at, 147–54, 163; flooding from, 148–49,

mestizaje, 40–41
Mexican Communist Party (PCM), 85–87, 89
Mexican Eagle Petroleum Company, 24–25
Mexican Forestry Society, 119–20, 197, 202
Mexican Institute of Renewable Natural Resources, 227
Mexican Revolution, 11–12, 14–16, 48–54, 69–70, 220, 240n48; Carranza's Constitutionalist forces of, 69–70, 72–74, 112; Carranza's Constitutionalist governance in, 74–78; Convention of Aguascalientes government and, 69–74; environmental rights demands of, 15–16, 52–53, 78, 220, 256n115; foreshadowing of, 48–52; Huerta's opposition to, 64–69; Madero era of, 38, 51–64; refugees from, 45–46, 84; Ten Tragic Days of, 64, 73; Villa's Northern Division in, 65, 69–71; Zapatista rebellion of, 53–55, 59, 61–74, 112–14, 120. *See also* postrevolutionary era
Mexican Society for Geography and Statistics, 23, 155
Mexican Workers Confederation, 175, 194, 214
Mexico City. *See* Basin of Mexico; Federal District
Mexico City Agricultural Park, 156–63
"Mexico City as Interpreted by Its Painters" competition and show, 1–2
México Forestal journal, 120
Meyer, Hannes, 180–81, 215, 224
Meyer, Michael, 64–65
Meza, Guillermo, 2
Ministry of Agriculture and Development, 195–96
Ministry of Development, 43
Ministry of Hydraulic Resources, 207, 222–23

Ministry of Public Works and Communications (SCOP), 90, 92, 96, 149, 151
Miranda, Joaquín, 62, 76
Moderna colonia, 176, 212
modernist architecture, 168–69
modernization, 4–6; Porfiriato goals of, 11–12, 14, 15, 23, 32, 237n35; postwar capitalist project of, 1–2, 6, 218–19. *See also* urbanization of Mexico City
Modotti, Tina, 83
Molina Enríquez, Andrés, 60, 77, 111, 191
Molino de Flores de Nezahualcóyotl National Park, 130
Monk, Daniel, 233
Monserrat, Jesus, 90
Monsiváis, Carlos, 3
Montes de Oca, José, 137
Mora, José María Luis, 22–23
Morones, Luis, 85, 87, 96, 104
Moya, Rodrigo, 226f
Múgica, Francisco, 83, 127, 177–78, 194, 214
Mulholland, William, 42
Mumford, Lewis, 7
Muñoz Cota, Jorge, 189–90
Murillo, Gerardo, 270n95
Mussolini, Benito, 158

Napoleon III, Emperor of France, 19
Nápoles colonia, 167, 186–87
National Agrarian Commission, 55, 111–12
National Agrarian Credit Bank, 157
National Autonomous University of Mexico, 213, 216
National Campesino Confederation, 194, 210–11, 214
National Confederation of Popular Organizations, 194, 214, 216
National Engineering School, 23
National Irrigation Commission, 208
National Medical Institute, 23
national parks, 122, 130–34, 196

National Preparatory School, 23
National Revolutionary Party (PNR), 172, 262n103
National Tenant Confederation, 180
National Urban Mortgage and Public Works Bank, 170, 180
Nava, Francisco, 116
Nava, Jésus, 125
Nava, Meletino, 59–60
Navarro, Macario, 91, 172–75, 183
Neighborhood Improvement Committees, 100–101
Nieto, Ramón, 198
Noriega, Iñigo, 24–25, 59, 61; irrigation project of, 24, 32–34, 40, 245n65; land appropriation by, 61; profit-seeking motives of, 33
Noriega, Remigio, 32–33, 41, 47, 59, 212; lakeshore haciendas of, 141–42, 144, 172–174, 250n13; land appropriation by, 61, 91
Nugent, Daniel, 239n45

Obregón, Álvaro, 69, 70, 72–74, 78; assassination of, 104; election of 1920 of, 85; housing policies of, 89–93, 166, 172–74; lakeshore ejido policies of, 138–39, 146; land reform policies of, 112, 141, 144; military spending by, 93; proposal on municipalities of, 104; tenant strikes of 1922 and, 87–89; water riots of 1922 and, 94–100, 260n56. *See also* Constitutionalist governance
Obrera colonia, 167, 170–71
Offen, Karl, 240n3
O'Gorman, Juan, xii, 1–2, 168, 181, 259n53
oil production, 195; Cárdenas's nationalization of, 59, 199; urban fuel demands and, 199–202
oppression. *See* sociospatial scope of urbanization

Orive Alba, Adolfo, 229
Oropesa, Gabriel, 181, 224, 275n1
Orozco, Pascual, 54
Orozco y Berra, Manuel, 8, 19
Ortíz Rubio, Pascual, 156–57, 169
Owens Valley project (California), 42

Pacheco, José Emilio, 218
Padilla, Ezequiel, 184
Paisaje de la Ciudad de México (O'Gorman), xii, 1–2
Palafox, Silvano, 105
Pani, Alberto: architectural work of, 37; in Carranza's government, 73, 75–78, 110, 255n103, 256n114, 270n95; Hotel Reforma of, 170; tenement investments of, 169–71
Pani, Mario, 170, 215–17, 285n87
paper mills, 70, 108, 195; coal-based energy and, 108; deforestation and, 25–26, 43–44, 198, 200, 202–3; hydroelectric power and, 133
Party of the Mexican Revolution (PRM), 134; conversion to the PRI of, 194; neighborhood improvement associations and, 216; privatization policies of, 214; tripartite corporatism of, 194, 220; urban poor and, 182, 184, 190
Paseo de la Reforma, 25
Pasteur, Louis, 27
Patiño, Alonzo, 155
Patria Nueva colonia, 189
Paulino Navarro colonia, 172
Payno, Manuel, 26–29
Paz, Octavio, 3
Pearson, Weetman, 20, 36
Peimbert, Angel, 156–56
Pemex, 195, 199–200, 281n18
Peñafiel, Antonio, 9, 27, 34, 39
Peñón de los Baños, 5f, 139–40, 143–44, 157, 160, 163
Peralvillo colonia, 186–87
Pérez Granja, Saul, 97–98

sociospatial scope of urbanization, 7–9,
13–16, 219–20; class-based environmental hierarchies in, 11, 15–16, 24,
39–52, 69, 219–20, 249n132; earthquake risks and, 52; environmental
rights demands and, 15–16, 52–53,
78, 81–108, 256n115; foreshadowing
of revolution and, 48–52; land rights
and, 66–68; peripheral working-class
subdivisions and, 16, 25, 164–94;
racism towards indigenous practices
and, 39–47; tenant strikes and water
riots, 16, 81–100, 165, 257n5, 261n69;
territorial struggles between urban
and hinterland populations in, 13–15,
45–47, 89, 133–35, 239n44, 240n48,
270n95. *See also* common lands;
environmental rights
sodium carbonate and sodium chloride,
10
Sosa, Antonio, 129
Sosa Texcoco, 207
Sotomayor, Arturo, 2–3, 6
Soviet Union, 85
Stampa, Manuel, 90
Steinberg, Ted, 53
Suárez, Pino, 56, 64
Superior Health Council, 82, 260n56
Swyngedouw, Erik, 239n43

Taller 13, 289nn43–44
technocracy. *See* environmental
technocracy
Tejeda, Carlos, 2
Tejeda, Margarito, 183, 189
Tenant Defense League, 180, 184
Tenant League of the Federal District,
83–84
tenant strike of 1922, 15, 82–89, 165,
257n5; defeat of, 89; demands of,
86, 89; government response to, 87;
landowner responses to, 88; May Day
rallies of, 86–87; Mexican Commu-

nist Party and, 85–87, 89; participants
in, 87, 88f
Tenant Union of the Federal District, 86
Tennesee Valley Authority, 159
Tepeyac-Insurgentes colonia, 187
Tepeyac National Park, 130
Tepito vecindad, 166f
Tequixquiac tunnel, 36
Teresa family (Hacienda Eslava), 116
Texcoco Improvement Works, 139
textile factories, 108; hydroelectric
power in, 133; wood power of, 25–26,
43–44
Tláhuac, 5f, 10, 142–45, 204–6
Tolsa, Manuel, 29
La Tolvanera (Meza), 2
Torquemada, Juan de, 28, 54, 223
Treaty of Guadalupe Hidalgo, 19

Union of Socialist Architects, 181, 228
United States interventions, 19
urban caciques, 182–90
urban environmental imaginary, 20,
29–35, 116, 240n3
urbanization of Mexico City, 6–14,
218–34; automobile-based policies
of, 101–2, 217; building and sanitary
codes in, 46–47, 84, 164, 167, 168,
190–91; centralized governance in,
104–5, 108, 157–58, 167, 170, 190–91,
262n108; class-based environmental hierarchies in, 11, 15–16, 24,
39–52, 69, 219–20, 233, 249n132;
Constitutionalist-era suburban
development, 101–3; demographic
and spatial expansion in, 13, 24–25,
38–39, 41, 45–47, 84, 165, 171, 195,
231; the ecological city and, 223–34,
288n35, 289nn43–44; environmental
technocracy in, 15, 20–24, 29–35, 54,
77–78, 99–106, 118, 180–81, 224–34,
256n115, 288n35, 289nn43–44; green
space in, 90, 100–102; industrial-

ization in, 193–220; mestazije and, 40–41; migration from the countryside and, 195; peripheral working-class subdivisions in, 16, 25, 164–94; political ecology framework of, 8–13; Porfirian era approaches to, 11–12, 14, 15, 19–50, 237n35; postrevolutionary era of, 11–16, 51–78, 239n45; sociospatial scope of, 7–9, 11, 13–16, 24, 39–47, 239n44, 240n48; speculative growth in, 76–78, 101–2, 204, 211, 215, 219–20; unauthorized subdivisions in, 45–47, 76–77, 171–75; urban logic of conservation in, 84, 133–35. *See also* drainage (desagüe) systems; drinking water systems; forest conservation; housing; public health; sewage systems

urban political ecology. *See* political ecology of urbanization

urban populism, 285n89

Urquidi, Manuel, 54–55, 56, 111

Urrutia, Aureliano, 42, 60–61, 70, 145

Valadés, José, 84–86, 89

Valencia, Enrique, 123

Valley of Mexico, 3, 235n7. *See also* Basin of Mexico

Vargas, Getulio, 256n116

Vázquez brothers (Hacienda Buenavista), 114–15

20 de Noviembre colonia, 186

Veracruz tenant strikes, 85, 87–89, 92

Vidales, Jesús, 184

Villa, Pancho, 65, 69–74; Carranza's government and, 74; Convention of Aguascalientes government and, 69–74; Northern Division of, 69, 71; Obrégon's war against, 74; political goals of, 70

Villa, Rafael de, 189

Villa Cortés, 211

Villareal, Filiberto, 83

Vogt, William, 225–27

wastewater. *See* sewage systems

water conservation, 29

water riot of 1922, 15, 82, 94–100, 105; government response to, 98–99; popular demands of, 99–100, 261n69; protest actions of, 97–99

water systems. *See* drainage (desagüe) systems; drinking water systems; forest conservation; sewage systems

waterways. *See* Lake Chalco; Lake Texcoco; Lake Xochimilco; Lerma River

White, Richard, 239n43

Womack, John, Jr., 172

worker-settlers, 171–77

working-class subdivisions, 16, 25, 164–94, 220; caciquismo and power in, 182–90; community identification in, 188; funding of infrastructure in, 169–71, 186, 189–90; land expropriation policies and, 177–82, 191–93, 210–11, 213–15; political mobilization of, 165, 167, 171–77, 179–80, 191, 280n98; public housing projects in, 90–93, 101–2, 108, 166, 168–70, 172, 179n70, 180–81, 215–16, 221–22, 259n43, 259n48; sanitation initiatives of, 168–71, 186–87; unauthorized construction of, 171–75; unsanitary conditions of, 165–67, 186–87. *See also* housing

World War II, 202–3

Xochimilco, 5f, 42–43, 62, 67, 70, 143t, 145–50, 204–6, 232. *See also* Lake Xochimilco

Yañez, Enrique, 181

Yucatán, 83

zacatán (broom) root: local access to, 44–45, 62–63, 67–69, 128, 248n123; private monopolies of, 44, 63, 67–68, 128, 253n64

Zalce, Alfredo, 2

Zamora, Adolfo, 180–81

Zapata, Emiliano, 53–54, 64, 65; Plan of Ayala of, 54, 55, 75; political goals of, 70

Zapatista rebellion, 53–55, 59, 61–74, 112–14, 120; Carranza's government and, 74; Convention of Aguascalientes government and, 69–74, 254n78; government forest management policies and, 61–69, 112–14, 120, 252n42;

Huerta's war against, 66–67; land reform policies of, 112–14; threats to Mexico City by, 59–63, 68, 70–74, 112–14

Zárraga, Fernando, 92, 109, 155, 223

Zárraga, Guillermo, 92, 108, 109, 155, 168, 228, 259n53

Zayas Enríquez, Rafael de, 39

Zetina, Carlos, 262n85

Zuiderzee land reclamation (Netherlands), 58